Engendering Archaeology

Social Archaeology

General Editor
Ian Hodder, University of Cambridge

Advisory Editors
Margaret Conkey, University of California at Berkeley
Mark Leone, University of Maryland
Alain Schnapp, U.E.R. d'Art et d'Archéologie, Paris
Stephen Shennan, University of Southampton
Bruce Trigger, McGill University, Montreal

Published

In preparation

Engendering Archaeology

Women and Prehistory

*Edited by Joan M. Gero
and Margaret W. Conkey*

Basil Blackwell

Copyright © Basil Blackwell Ltd 1991

First published 1991

Basil Blackwell Ltd
108 Cowley Road, Oxford, OX4 1JF, UK

Basil Blackwell Inc.
3 Cambridge Center
Cambridge, Massachusetts 02142, USA

British Library Cataloguing in Publication Data

A CIP catalogue record for this book is available from the British Library

Library of Congress Cataloging in Publication Data

Engendering archaeology: women and prehistory/edited by
Joan M. Gero and Margaret W. Conkey
p. cm. — (Social archaeology)
ISBN 0–631–16505–3 — ISBN 0–631–17501–6 (pbk.)
1. Women, Prehistoric. 2. Feminism. 3. Archaeology – Philosophy.
4. Sexual division of labor – History – Philosophy. I. Gero, Joan M.
II. Conkey, Margaret Wright, 1944– . III. Series.
GN799.W66E54 1991
305.4'09'01—dc20 90–35335
CIP

Typeset in 10.5 on 12pt Stemple Garamond
by Hope Services (Abingdon) Ltd.
Printed In Great Britain by
T. J. Press Ltd, Padstow, Cornwall

Contents

List of Contributors

Elizabeth M. Brumfiel, Department of Anthropology & Sociology, Albion College, Albion, MI 49224, USA.

Cheryl P. Claassen, Department of Anthropology, Appalachian State University, Boone, NC 28608, USA.

Margaret W. Conkey, Department of Anthropology, University of California, Berkeley, CA 94720, USA.

Joan M. Gero, Department of Anthropology, University of South Carolina, Columbia, SC 29208, USA.

Russell G. Handsman, American Indian Archaeological Institute, Box 260, Washington, CT 06793, USA.

Christine A. Hastorf, Department of Anthropology, University of Minnesota, Minneapolis, MN 55455, USA.

Thomas L. Jackson, 740 East Bel Mar Drive, La Salva Beach, CA 95076, USA.

Henrietta L. Moore, Department of Social Anthropology, London School of Economics, Houghton Street, London WC2, UK.

Susan Pollock, Department of Anthropology, S.U.N.Y. Binghamton, Binghamton, NY 13901, USA.

Janet D. Spector, Department of Anthropology, University of Minnesota, Minneapolis, MN 55455, USA.

Ruth E. Tringham, Department of Anthropology, University of California, Berkeley, CA 94720, USA.

Patty Jo Watson and Mary C. Kennedy, Department of Anthropology, Washington University, St Louis, MO 63130, USA.

Rita P. Wright, Department of Anthropology, New York University, New York, NY 10003, USA.

Alison Wylie, Department of Philosophy, University of Western Ontario, London Ontario, N6A 3K7, Canada.

"I would like to know what life was like ten thousand years ago," Pepe was saying. "I think of it often. Nature would have been the same. The same trees, the same earth, the same clouds, the same snow falling in the same way on the grass and thawing in the spring. People exaggerate the changes in nature so as to make nature seem lighter." He was talking to a neighbour's son who was on leave from the army. "Nature resists change. If something changes, nature waits to see whether the change can continue, and, if it can't, it crushes it with all its weight! Ten thousand years ago the trout in the stream would have been exactly the same as today."

"The pigs wouldn't have been!"

"That's why I would like to go back! To see how things we know today were first learnt. Take a *chevreton*. It's simple. Milk the goat, heat the milk, separate it and press the curds. Well, we saw it all being done before we could walk. But how did they once discover that the best way of separating the milk was to take a kid's stomach, blow it up like a balloon, dry it, soak it in acid, powder it and drop a few grains of this powder into the heated milk? I would like to know how the women discovered that!"

John Berger, *Pig Earth* (1979)

Preface

A volume using explicitly feminist social theory in archaeological research is long overdue. By the mid 1980s it was no secret that archaeology was lagging far behind our sister disciplines in getting even exploratory research about women onto our analytical and interpretive stages, where women are explicitly sought as sociocultural subjects. Conkey and Spector's call for an archaeology of gender ("Archaeology and the Study of Gender"), a call that had been circulating in manuscript form for some years prior to publication in volume 7 of *Advances in Archaeological Method and Theory* (1984), was recognized both as compelling and timely, and it seemed certain, after so forceful an agenda had been set, that articles, chapters, and books would begin pouring out to introduce gender as a fundamental social construct. Surely archaeologists would now begin to inspect gender dynamics in different socio-historical contexts, to recognize androcentric concepts and their role in keeping women out of prehistory, and to populate the past with engendered women and men. We were amazed that these vacuums still existed three years later when the editors of Basil Blackwell's "Social Archaeology" series approached us to work on such a piece.

In fact, the enormity of the task of compiling the first such volume was immediately obvious. There was simply no archaeological literature to cite as contributions, nor was there any defined circle of experts to fall back upon. The same troublesome assumptions that incited Conkey and Spector's critique were still being used unquestioningly in the formulation and interpretation of archaeological hypotheses. A tiny smattering of literature identified the *existence* of women in prehistory, or determined whether (all?) women's status was "high" or "low" in different societies, at the same time that the popular but essentially unsubstantiated idea of powerful neolithic goddesses was gaining popularity outside the canon of professional archaeological research. Women's roles in biosocial, evolutionary change during hominization received some attention (though not from archaeologists), but by and large prehistory was still a largely unchallenged male territory, inhabited by "populations" who, when sexed, continued to play out contemporary gender roles (women quietly fulfilling domestic obligations; men visibly taking on the rest of what people did in prehistory). The situation clearly called for help. If an archaeology of gender were to emerge, it would necessitate learning how to make women (and by implication, engendered social life) an object of archaeological study, as well as familiarizing ourselves with the theoretical and epistemological resources available to this endeavor.

We recognized the need for a collective effort to take on these challenges, and in 1986 began organizing a research conference, inviting researchers who had a solid and demonstrated working knowledge either of specific classes of archaeological data (e.g. ceramics, botanical remains, shellfish) and/or of particular perspectives in prehistory (e.g. complex hunter-gatherers, early agricultural societies). Participants all agreed to become involved in restructuring their own data, or data with which they had long familiarity, or in reformulating familiar research questions along radically new lines (although many confessed they hadn't a clue as to how to begin). The emphasis was deliberately placed on *prehistoric* analyses rather than on ethnoarchaeological, historic, or ethnohistoric studies since prehistoric contexts presented the greatest methodological challenges to our androcentric thinking, and all researchers were charged with producing tightly focused case studies in which gender was an explicit analytic category.

We have much gratitude to express for the success of the "Women and Production in Prehistory" conference, held at the Wedge Plantation in Georgetown, in the South Carolina low country, in April 1988. Both the Wenner-Gren Foundation for Anthropological Research and the National Science Foundation supported the costs of travel and of our five days together; Basil Blackwell publishers contributed additional support to make our stay nicer. Our discussants, Henrietta Moore (Cambridge University), Irene Silverblatt (University of Connecticut), and Peter White (University of Sydney) were superb teachers and critics, generously introducing us to new literatures and perspectives, gently reminding us when we slid back to old ways of thinking.

Our gratitude also goes to the University of South Carolina for allowing us to use the Wedge facilities, to the helpful staff at the Wedge, and to Robin Burke and Kimberly Grimes who made enormous contributions to arranging the travel and the hospitality at the Wedge. Pat Watson deserves special praise and hallelujahs for her salvation address. Our days of intense exchange, isolated in the sultry spring of the

South, proved intoxicating and invigorating beyond expectation: we left with our heads ringing and our imaginations stretched.

The fact that many chapters in this volume are substantially different from the drafts read at the Wedge suggests how much we learned in the course of this endeavor. There are also two papers read at the Wedge that we are sorry not to be able to include here: Doug Price's contribution on gender differences in bone chemistry as a result of diet was the only paper that proceeded directly and entirely from empirical sex differences in skeletal materials; the time conflicts that prevented its inclusion here are regrettable although related material is partially covered in Hastorf's chapter on food. Likewise, we are sorry not to include Prudence Rice's chapter on pottery, and applaud Rita Wright's willingness to attempt her pottery chapter without benefit of the Wedge conference and discussion.

Many of us read updated versions of our "Wedge papers" in a 1989 symposium at the 54th Annual Meeting of the Society for American Archaeology in Atlanta and felt the profound changes in the year that had passed: now we could see an audience for our ideas, and we could recognize how far our theoretical, epistemological, and methodological thinking had evolved in our reworkings of our papers. The comments of SAA discussants Tom Patterson and Linda Cordell were another source of inspiration for the final versions of these papers.

We hope that some of our excitement can be felt in these pages which could not have come about without yet another support team. Dorothy O'Dell and Deannie Stevens in the Department of Anthropology at the University of South Carolina helped with numerous administrative details, both for the conference and the volume, and Kathy Bolen worked tirelessly on the details of getting the volume into shape and especially hard on the index, which we greatly appreciate.

Finally, thanks are due to Stephen Loring and Les Rowntree for their active and tacit engagement with this project and their contributions to household production and management; even without typing the manuscript for us, their support was palpable.

Joan M. Gero
Margaret W. Conkey

Part I

Considerations for an
Archaeology of Gender

1

Tensions, Pluralities, and Engendering Archaeology: An Introduction to Women and Prehistory

Margaret W. Conkey and Joan M. Gero

> The open future rests on a new past.
> Donna Haraway, *Signs: Journal of Women in Culture and Society* (1978)

The title of this volume is *Engendering Archaeology: Women and Prehistory*; the chapters are intended to contribute to the study of gender systems in both prehistory and the practice of archaeology. Although both men and women have gender, we have chosen to focus on women as a means to engender the past because we believe that to take one – and one previously neglected – sex/gender as an entry point into the study of past human societies is particularly effective, challenging, and supported by a now substantial interdisciplinary literature.

In the past two decades, feminist thinking has profoundly transformed the study of sociocultural subjects in virtually every field it has touched, even where researchers have not all embraced a feminist perspective. The development of critical traditions and scholarship has impacted both the content and method of social and historical knowledge, grappling with what has been recognized (Westkott 1979: 424–5) as an appalling absence of concepts that tap women's experience, a limited and limiting view of women as an unchanging essence, and a deeply permeated narrowness to the concept of the human being reflected in limited ways of understanding human behavior.

The transformation of the social and historical sciences because of feminist-inspired critiques and scholarship (cf. Farnham 1987) has proceeded rapidly, and encompasses a multiplicity of approaches and studies. In anthropology alone there are studies that recognize and detail androcentrism and male bias (e.g. Ardener 1975; Scheper-Hughes 1985);

studies that reclaim women not merely as objects but as subjects (e.g. in Reiter 1975); and critical reworkings of the category "woman" and a reorientation of research towards the study of gender and difference (e.g. Lamphere 1987; Moore 1988). Within anthropology, sociocultural anthropologists have successfully employed gender as an analytical concept throughout these 20 years (e.g. Abu-Lughod 1986; Ardener 1977; Collier and Yanagisako 1987; Dwyer 1978; Friedl 1975; Gailey 1987b; Goodale 1971; Kessler and MacKenna 1978; LaFontaine 1978; Lutz 1988; MacCormack and Strathern 1980; Ong 1988; Ortner and Whitehead 1981; Reiter 1975; Rogers 1975; Rosaldo and Lamphere 1974; Sacks 1979; Sanday 1981; Silverblatt 1988; Strathern 1972; Weiner 1976; Yanagisako 1979).

Archaeology is now in a position to benefit greatly from these developments. All along, inquiries into prehistoric human social life (e.g. Slocum 1975; Tanner 1981; Tanner and Zihlman 1976; Zihlman 1978); and into archaeological subjects and contexts (e.g. Barstow 1978; Rorhlich-Leavitt 1977) have figured prominently in the framing and elaboration of feminist critiques, even without the involvement of practicing archaeologists. Questions about "origins" (of sexual divisions of labor, of gender asymmetries), about historical trajectories (women and the rise of states), about transformations of gender relations (e.g. with colonization) have figured prominently in the literature, even if archaeologists themselves were not addressing (or even framing) such questions (e.g. Cucchiari 1981; Etienne and Leacock 1980; Gailey 1987a, b; Leacock 1981, 1983; Rapp 1977; Silverblatt 1987). Between the literature of popular culture (e.g. Davis 1971; Eisler 1987; Morgan 1972), which quickly stepped in to do what archaeologists themselves were not doing (after diLeonardo forthcoming), and the implicitly gendered (and gender-biased) archaeologies (see Conkey and Spector 1984; Conkey with Williams, forthcoming) that have been put forth, there is a diverse but problematic corpus of views on women and men in prehistory and on what constitutes an archaeological perspective on gender.

But archaeology can now take up the challenge of engendering the past in explicit and theoretically informed ways, given, for example, a developing body of theory that addresses such questions as the centrality of gender to class formation (e.g. Ryan 1981), to the workings of political power (e.g. Scott (1988), to the organization of production and units of production (e.g. Hartsock 1983), or to the uses of space (e.g. Ardener 1981; Moore 1986) and the development of technological systems (e.g. McGaw 1982, 1989). As Wylie (this volume) so cogently argues, the general theoretical resources exist to make women and gender explicit foci of archaeological study, and, as well, we are in a position to draw from and contribute to emergent theoretical developments within archaeology, particularly in the "post-processualist" directions that take social and symbolic theories as central.

Although theoretical resources now exist for archaeology, we can learn much from these two decades of emerging gender scholarship, particularly in the social and historical sciences. It became clear very quickly and very early that gender biases are not rectified simply: the structuring biases do not change merely by the addition of "new data" and of "case studies" about women. Rather, the profound critique of traditional research practices that emerged – and continues to emerge – has led not only to feminist critiques of methodologies and of the category "woman" and "women's experience", but also to the development of conceptual categories useful, if not absolutely necessary, to understanding the significance of gender groups, gender relations, and gender meanings (e.g. Scott 1986). A fundamental goal of feminist theory has become the analysis of gender relations that includes – "but is *not limited to* – what are often considered the feminist issues: the situation of women and the analysis of domination" (Flax 1987: 622–3, emphasis added).

Although the issues raised by feminist inquiries embody a difficult challenge to archaeology, we feel that the challenge is one that archaeologists can no longer afford *not* to take; not to inquire into gender processes as they play out in historical and prehistorical contexts is to undermine the possibilities both for richer prehistories and for richer, more nuanced understandings – being sought and called for by many social scientists and others – of gender as historical process.

This project then, is simultaneously about women in prehistoric societies – as subjects of archaeological inquiry and also a source of previously undervalued and untapped experience – and about the development of the conceptual and analytical category of gender in archaeological research and interpretation. We have three aims in the volume: first, to continue to expose gender bias in all phases of archaeological inquiry, from assumptions and concepts, to models, to the nature of acceptable evidence, to received knowledge; then, to "find" women in archaeological contexts and to identify their participation in gender relations, gender ideologies, and gender roles; and finally, to problematize underlying assumptions about gender and difference. We believe that the studies presented here, as approaches that have been more or less informed by the "results" of two decades of evolution in feminist theory, successfully focus on women in various prehistoric contexts while *simultaneously* addressing assumptions about gender relations, about the enterprise of prehistoric research, and about the relation of the past to the present.

It should not be surprising, then, to see here – as has happened in so many other disciplines – that in seeking to reinstate women as agents and subjects, some authors have come to question the very canons of the field. By "reclaiming for women that which has historically been denied to them" (Keller 1987: 237), archaeology has much to gain from the task of a feminist theoretic in science, which is, as outlined by Keller, to "distinguish that which is parochial from that which is universal in the scientific impulse" (1987: 237–8). The feminist approaches to the interpretation of archaeological data in this volume illustrate only some of the ways in which our previously unexamined assumptions about "mankind" and "man's past" are fundamentally restructured by a deliberate focus on women in past productive systems and human societies.

The tailoring of gender and feminist theories and insights to prehistory has the potential to radically alter extant notions about prehistoric humans and human evolution, notions that underlie *all* of anthropology. But the extant and emergent body of theory on gender and body of gender analyses are not merely a resource for this radical alteration, nor are they merely an isomorphic or parallel disciplinary "source" from which to borrow (after Strathern 1987: 277). Rather, the theorizing and analyses constitute a double challenge for archaeology: a challenge to "analyze gender", but also a challenge to reframe *how to think about gender* (or any other social) *relations*. We are not simply in a situation where new theoretical and methodological resources exist and can be easily borrowed and applied. We must agree with Wylie's caveat (this volume) about the richness of the "now available" research and theorizing about gender; namely, that archaeologists should not merely hold out for a fully developed gender theory nor consider the gender theory that is now available to be a static "source" from which we can easily borrow after a "quick study".

Rather, we need to consider explicitly *how* these ways of thinking can help us in our own (archaeological) discourses, analyses, interpretations (after Flax 1987: 623). How are we to develop our *own* conceptual frameworks, even though these will surely be inspired, enriched, and given highly specific content and direction by the wider theorizing and research that is, itself, rapidly evolving and changing.

In many ways, this process of developing new conceptual frameworks should not be new to archaeologists who have had to develop ways to think about cultural systems, cultural ecology, or any number of conceptual perspectives that have infused our archaeologies. We have long gone about our archaeological interpretations employing concepts that are no less complex nor more concrete than "gender" and "gender relations"; our researches of the past decades, for example, are full of references to such concepts as "population pressure", "resource stress", or "sociotechnic subsystems" that have been taken to be very "real" and determining processes. It is unlikely that any archaeologist has ever "seen" a "subsistence-settlement system", whereas we *know* there were men and women in prehistoric societies.

Given the relations of archaeology to gender theorizing and feminist research, it is not surprising that this volume is, in many ways, transitional, both in terms of the discipline of archaeology and in terms of our own thinking. To an extent, the inquiries here have followed out of traditional concerns and have been formulated around the traditional obstacles to an engendered past. Feminist scholarship in archaeology, demanding fundamental alterations in basic assumptions, first requires a painstaking retooling of definitions, data sets, textual sources, and functional assignments. In many cases, concepts and problems have had to be redefined and reframed before our engendered narratives and conceptual categories can be taken on and deepened. Some of us envision a more radically feminist archaeology (Conkey and Gero 1988), only glimmerings of which may be visible in these chapters.

Thus, we feel certain tensions within this volume, as we do archaeologies of gender and as we take feminist perspectives to our archaeological work. At the most inclusive level, tensions may stem from the fact that many contributors are caught between a rapidly evolving literature in feminist theory and feminist anthropology on the one hand,[1] and, on the other hand, the practice of archaeology that has barely engaged in social theory, much less in feminist theory, and that has been demonstrably androcentric in its sociopolitics (cf. Gero 1983, 1985, 1988; Kramer and Stark 1988), and in its discourse and interpretive results (Conkey and Spector 1984).

On another level, there are also the tensions of the directions of the project: to what extent must we provide answers to the conceptual or ideational "red flags" that regularly confront feminists: the role of biology, for instance, or the so-called invisibility of relevant data? Such issues have been raised both within and outside of archaeology, and contributors to this volume clearly have had to decide the degree to which they feel it necessary to respond to the voiced and unvoiced critiques of feminism. Some obviously have felt a need for and have structured a more direct route to alternative agendas.

Finally, in some of the essays that are collected here, there is the emergent phenomenon that the researchers themselves have been substantially changed by their analyses; there is, for some, an underlying tension between describing (the data, the interpretation, the past) and transforming these through a feminist lens. This tension, sustained in both the researchers and in the objects of knowledge, often yields an archaeology that is not merely an archaeology about women and men, but an archaeology *for* them as well (cf. Westkott 1979). What's been hard about writing these papers is not so much the lack of model studies to follow or the absence of "suitable" data that are identified and classified by sex, but rather that we are all still writing – or trying to write – with a voice that is not yet familiar to us, a voice(s) that we don't yet have. To inquire into how these voices might take shape, however, we can work from the theoretical resources now at hand to see how we might engage with the past through the lenses of "sex/gender systems".

On the Concept of Gender

The literature on gender as an analytical concept and category and as historical process is rich, growing, and extends far beyond the discipline of anthropology (e.g. Abel and Abel 1983; Collier and Yanagisako 1987; Flax 1987; Hess and Ferree 1987). From this richness, we can consider only a few salient aspects of current conceptualizations of gender, emphasizing those that impinge most directly upon our endeavor in this volume. Most importantly, we want to show how gender theory allows for entries into archaeological analysis independent from the empiricist and positivist epistemologies and procedures that have had such a problematic (and limiting) effect on archaeological interpretation (see e.g. Shanks and Tilley 1987a, 1987b, 1989; Watson 1986; Wylie 1981 and this volume).

Underlying the framework for engendering archaeology is a rejection of the biological determinism that is implicit in many models of sex role differentiation. Indeed, were we to accept that females stand at a static and predictable distance from males, and that it is this distance that fundamentally determines gender roles and meanings, then gender studies in prehistory would consist of nothing more than an exposition of endless variations on the unchanging theme of fixed gender inequality (Scott 1986). In contrast to that view are the conceptualizations of gender as culturally and socially constructed, as historically and culturally contingent, recognizing that gender roles and relations are constituted and given meaning in historically and culturally specific ways. Gender, then, is a constitutive element of human social relations, based on culturally perceived and culturally inscribed differences and similarities between and among males and females.

Gender is taken to be an issue of history, which is something that archaeologists have tended to ignore or drawn upon only selectively. In fact, one might paraphrase J. Shapiro's recent suggestion about anthroplogists to note that archaeologists "have not yet come to terms with gender as a social act" (Shapiro 1983: 112). As an issue of history, gender is always "in production", emergent in the process of human existence. Thus, epistemologically, gender is not a bounded and static phenomenon, "out there" to be "found" and circumscribed; it is not a "thing" nor an "it".

Taking gender as a process that is constructed as a relationship or set of relationships, necessarily embedded within other cultural and historical social institutions and ideologies such as status, class, ethnicity, and race, means that gender cannot be understood simply in terms of female and male activities. It also means that there are no cross-cultural "discoveries" of what constitutes either men's or women's experience (Rosaldo 1980). Masculinities and femininities, as aspects of gender, are simply different human possibilities that have emerged historically, even situationally (Westkott 1979: 424).

> Gender relations enter into and are constituent elements in every aspect of human experience. In turn, the experience of gender relations for any person and the structure of gender as a social category are shaped by the interactions of gender relations and other social relations such as class and race. Gender relations thus have no fixed essence; they vary both within and over time. (Flax 1987: 622–3)

For archaeologists, as we discuss below, this means that the study of gender cannot be reduced to nor is it dependent upon traditional epistemologies and methods for making gender activities "visible" in the archaeological record, nor are there any universals or generalizations to be invoked or assumed in our inquiries. That gender is conceptualized as a process means that we archaeologists must be cautious about any simple equations of male, of female, of gender with any tool, feature, activity, role, or ideology.

To many researchers, gender is not only relational, social process, and a dynamic of human social and cultural life, but in fact is a primary structuring principle (e.g. Delphy 1984), in the sense that gender beliefs, roles, etc. set certain foundational parameters and establish certain guiding "rules" for the enactment of daily life. The idea of gender as a structuring principle immediately leads to a radical realignment of traditional archaeological categories that typically trivialize, minimize, degrade, and/or ignore what are thought to be women's contributions and roles in production and cultural construction; this is clearly shown by many of the chapters in this volume.

Yet even as a structuring principle, gender is so multi-dimensional and structures social relations in such different ways that we have to be more impressed by the variability than the homogeneity implied by the idea of a (single) "structuring principle". Given the tremendous changes in the meaning of sexual difference visible to us in historic time for Anglo-American cultures (e.g. Merchant 1980, 1989), and among non-western cultures as documented by anthropology, we must not foreclose on the potential variability in gender roles, relations, and ideologies in prehistory. If men and women are defined relative to one another with such definitions changing over time, *the changes in the significance of gender groups in the past* (Davis 1975–6: 90, emphasis added) become a relevant, viable, and compelling arena for investigations and interpretation.

Gender, as Scott (1986) has argued, is indeed a "useful category of (pre) historical analysis". Gender illustrates ways in which particular roles and relationships are socially constructed, especially – for archaeologists – in relation to the productive and material world. Where the production and manipulation of the material realm *can* be associated – conceptually or otherwise – with women (or men), we may then most easily (given present methodologies) be able to observe the productive roles and contributions of women, make inferences about the division of labor, observe how the material objects participate in constituting social identities and social meanings, and explore how the social category of, for example, "female" may have been constructed and played out in past social systems.

The expression of gender, then, is not expected to be consistent, unchanging, everywhere, or merely localized. The expression of gender is expectedly variable, and it may not always take material form. The conceptualizations of gender do give us, as archaeologists, some "clues" as to where and how to inquire into gender, its dynamics and expressions: what are the locations and contexts within which gender is most likely brought into play? What are the likely spatial contexts in any given prehistorical context of gender relations, of gender tensions, gender dynamics? What is the structure of "work", of time, of scheduling, of "household cycles", of symbolic life? How might these be the contexts within which gender might be "at work"? How and in what ways do people make and use material culture in establishing, producing, changing, or challenging gender relations, gender ideologies, gender roles? What kinds of "marked" and/or "bounded" contexts might obtain and how might these provide clues to the heightening/ebbing dynamics of gender?

If gender relations, conflicts, statuses, and roles are historical forces, then how do we investigate the specific historical conditions under which gender concepts and categories are brought into existence and how they structure and constitute specific historical circumstances? How do we begin then, to frame an archaeology of gender, to reclaim women and men in non-sexist ways in prehistory? How are we inspired by, and do we respond to, the feminist critiques of archaeology and of the wider domain of science (cf. Harding 1986; Keller 1985; Wylie et al. 1989)?

The Issue of Gender Attribution

Given the prevailing theoretical posture of most contemporary archaeology, engendering archaeology almost immediately becomes a question of *method*. For many researchers, the greatest conceptual and analytical barrier to engendering archaeology is the problem of gender attribution, which, in turn, is conceived of in terms of having the "right" methods or data to link specific features of the "archaeological record" such as tools, hearths, ceramics, etc. with males and/or females. These gender links usually, and problematically, depend upon assumptions about what males/females do (or, on what they did in prehistory). There are a number of important problems with this kind of thinking that explains why engendering archaeology has taken so long and that reveals the complexity and richness of what engendering archaeology is all about.

Before discussing the specific issues that are thrown into relief by the area of "gender attribution" in archaeology, we want to be quite clear about our perspectives on this issue: we do not see that a feminist approach to archaeology is dependent upon some sort of methodological breakthrough that will suddenly render women (and even men) "archaeologically visible". Being able to "assign" certain activities or material culture to males and/or females is not *the* goal; it is not an end nor is it *the* means. We will try to show why gender attribution is not even a necessary stage in the process whereby we engender the past, although it *is* certainly and inextricably part of the inquiry. While it would be extremely helpful to attribute specific features to a specific gender, and while gender associations are integral to research that takes gender as a subject, we refuse to feel limited by the notion that we *must* provide gender attributions and must do so with a certain "fixity".

If gender attribution were all there were to archaeologies of gender, and if that, in turn, were merely dependent upon some new method or data that provides the link between "the record" and gender, we could expect an immediate but very circumscribed archaeology of gender. Indeed it *is* consistent with the traditional intellectual program of archaeology to appeal to some sort of empirical breakthrough – a new method, a new technique – as the central task to accomplish if we are to locate women and men in prehistory, and from there to take on more inclusive considerations such as gender relations. All too often an appeal to methodological breakthroughs (and notions of what is considered to *be* a methodological breakthrough) is merely a search for a methodological "band-aid" and obscures the more fundamental and problematic assumptions about men and women, about gender and gender relations, that need to be made explicit, if not questioned.

The so-called "archaeological invisibility of women" illustrates some of the issues exposed by a dependence on gender attribution and/or the hoped-for breakthroughs in method to "reveal" gender. There has long been the claim that if only we could find pollen in early hominid sites to counteract the overwhelming visibility of the more durable bone residues left by the scavenging (formerly, hunting) males (Isaac 1978), *then* we would have women in the Plio-Pleistocene; there would be women in "early man" studies. This is, of course, not the point at all. Such purported "invisibles" (e.g. gathered plant remains equated with women's productive labors) are diversions, in the guise of methods and epistemological issues, away from more substantive and foundational issues of gender inquiry. Why is there a "need" to "find" females and not the same "need" to "find" males who are, by implication, already present, active, and the primary contributors to the archaeological record and the human past?

Larger questions that should lie at the heart of evolutionary studies are neglected by focusing on methdological "visibility": has there always been a sexual division of labor? has there always been gender? what alternative forms of labor division might exist? how might such divisions of tasks, in fact, "create" gender? (after Hartmann 1981; Rubin 1975). Even if some version of *a* sexual division of labor *is* one of the entry points through which we can engender our narratives about the past, this division of labor – as an object of knowledge – should not go unquestioned or unchallenged.

By taking so many alternative approaches to women and prehistory, the contributions to this volume are good examples that expose how limited and limiting the gender attribution "band-aid" approach would be. Most of the studies here show how one can engender the past and our narratives of prehistory without relying upon gender attributions or new methods. Most of them illustrate how much more there is to understanding gender in prehistory – and our interpretations thereof – than the attribution of particular activities and materials to men and/or women.

If only because gender is much more than male and female activities, involving gender ideologies, gender roles, gender relations, and all of the ways in which gender intersects with and is influenced by other aspects of social life, there can be no archaeology of gender that is limited to and defined by gender attributions. Archaeologists committed to archaeologies of gender need not be "professional magicians" who can render visible the "invisible" women of the past (after Schmidt and Schmidt 1976). In archaeology, we can "use" gender to "do" more and to "say" more; gender can illustrate the ways in which particular roles and relationships in societies are constructed.

A second set of issues is also implicated by the concern for gender attribution. Gender attribution, as a method, is embedded in and leads to questions about basic epistemological issues of archaeology: how do we "traverse the distance between hypothesis and evidence?" (after Longino and Doell 1983). At one level, it has long been the case that archaeologists have drawn upon ethnographic and/or ethnohistoric accounts for our models, analogies, and plausibility arguments. These have been crucial (e.g. Wylie 1985) – and highly debatable (e.g. Freeman 1968; Gould and Watson 1982; Wobst 1978) – in the task of traversing these distances. It has, however, been amply shown not only *that* ethnography and ethnohistory must be questioned in terms of andro-centric (and ethnocentric) biases, but also *how* those biases enter into the practice and construction of ethnography (e.g. Ardener 1975; Kessler and MacKenna 1978; Moore 1988, especially 1–4).

The problems for archaeology are immediate: how do we scrutinize our ethnographic/ethnohistoric sources for biases? As many of the chapters in this volume show, this is a central part of our task in engendering prehistory and archaeology at this point in the evolution of gender thinking. There are many illuminating critiques upon which to draw; there are critiques of fundamental constructs or analytical categories: of "kinship" (e.g. Collier and Yanagisako 1987); of "the family" (e.g. Glenn 1987; Liebowitz 1978); of "the domestic" as domain (e.g. Rosaldo 1980); of "the household" (e.g. Hartmann 1981); of the "naturalness" of competition and scarcity (e.g. Gross and Averill 1979); of "nature", of "culture" (e.g. MacCormack and Strathern 1980); of alliance theory (e.g. Rubin 1975); of "the state" (e.g. Gailey 1985; McGuire 1985; Silverblatt 1988). There are also rewritings of traditional ethnographies (e.g. Weiner 1976) and of evolutionary scenarios (e.g. Tanner 1981) that reveal the questionable assumptions of previous research, and there are even critiques (e.g. Fedigan 1986; Harding 1986, especially 92–110; Longino and Doell 1983)[2] of the provocative gynecentric responses (such as "Woman-the-Gatherer") to the prevailing androcentric (such as "Man-the-Hunter") narratives and interpretations.

At another level of epistemic concern, the appeal to methodological "gaps" and thus to methodological "needs" and "breakthroughs" perpetuates a favored and limiting mode of archaeological research – namely, the more positivist/empiricist side of archaeology (see Gibbon 1989; Wylie 1981 and this volume) – by ignoring or dismissing an archaeology of gender (or any social theory) because it does not appear to be "testable". Yet, archaeologists regularly disaggregate materials or assemblages by space, by time, by period, and even by such social notions as status: why has this not been done by sex, by gender? To take apart the archaeological record along the lines of sex, age, and gender would be relatively novel; it has not often been done explicitly or consistently, much less as informed by theory. Analyzing gender could build upon fairly standard archaeological reasoning involving associational linkages or conceptual connections that have, after all, been accepted as archaeological logic for other phenomena, such as resource stress, population increases or even for social phenomena such as status. Archaeologists have regularly depended upon long "strings" of inferential assumptions to move from some purported measures of similarities or differences, for example, in archaeological materials, to interpretations about such relatively abstract concepts as "style", "ethnicity", "exchange systems", "social competition", "decision-making hierarchies" and so forth. Indeed, linkages and associational arguments between artifacts, socioeconomic contexts, and other (than gender) social constructs and processes such as "status" have featured prominently in archaeological inquiry (e.g. Renfrew and Shennan 1982). Those who resist the inquiry into gender on the grounds that it is somehow "less testable" or "too abstract" should scrutinize the means by which we have engaged – and sometimes productively – with equally "abstract" concepts and the chains of logic required in our inquiries.

The study of gender, like all of what we do, is a knowledge-making enterprise. Our "tests" are not against an absolute truth; we are "testing" alternatives and evaluating plausibility arguments, and all of these have confirmational implications. Our questions and approaches are complex and varied but this is due less to vacillations about how to proceed and due more, perhaps, to the very fluidity and yet pervasiveness of both gender relations and the challenges of new theorizings (after Flax 1987: 638).

An archaeology that takes gender as a valid, central, and important concept parallels an archaeology that foregrounds the individual as an active social agent (e.g. Shanks and Tilley 1987a, 1987b, 1989). That is, we need to adopt a model of gender-as-agency to understand changes in prehistory even if, because of the nature of the archaeological materials, the specific activities of specific genders is often inaccessible to us (after Shennan 1986: 334). Engendering the past becomes much more than "finding" men and women. It is trying to understand how gender "works" in all of its dimensions: as gender ideology, gender roles, gender relations, as well as a significant source of cultural meanings related to the construction of social lives. Before gender attribution is a methodological or procedural issue, it is a conceptual issue, and we must conceptualize "it" and think about "it" in ways that make "it" archaeologically useful.

What Happens When We Engender the Past?

By adopting gender as an analytical concept, we believe we can – and in this volume have begun to – radically redefine both prehistory and archaeological reasoning. By placing women and gender issues at the center of our interpretations of prehistory and by inquiring into what cultural meanings might have been bound up with engendered activities, and by inquiring further how these meanings contributed to the construction of social life, a fundamentally new prehistory ensues. An engendered past addresses many longstanding concerns of archaeology: the formation of states, trade and exchange, site settlement systems and activity areas, the processes of agriculture, lithic production, food production, pottery, architecture, ancient art – but throws them into new relief. An engendered past replaces the focus on the remains of prehistory with a focus on the people of prehistory; it rejects a reified concept of society or culture as an object of study, does away with the earliest, biggest, the best examples of prehistoric forms, and concentrates instead on the continuities and dialectics of life, the interpersonal and intimate aspects of social settings that bind prehistoric lives into social patterns.

The chapters of this volume illustrate an important first step in engendering a supposedly gender-neutral, but in fact androcentric, past. The transformations introduced to the subject of archaeology are seen clearly in these pages despite the deliberate attempt to represent a broad cross-section of rather traditional archaeological topics, chosen to cross-cut the discipline both by socio-historic periods and by classes of material culture (e.g. lithics, ceramics). Notably, the focus on gender has shaped the scope and texture of the volume. These chapters, for instance, make virtually no mention of abstracted paleoenvironments, nor of the landmark sites or artifacts that are regularly paraded out by archaeologists to "stand for" entire cultural periods or ways of life. The usual archaeological narratives that showcase the finest material expressions (intertwined with lessons of control over resources or labor), the dazzling displays of "man's" ability as mounted in enormous piles of mammoth bones or towering adobe walls, as palaces and pyramids, are eschewed.

Most forcefully, these chapters place issues of interpersonal relations at the forefront, substituting these for the more conventional concepts of power politics, governance, and authority. The inquiry here is into the social dynamics of the everyday activities of prehistoric life, activities that comprise most of the hours of prehistoric time for most of the people, and that account for the greatest accumulations of material in the archaeological record: ceramic and lithic production in residential contexts (women modifying pot designs or attaching handles to ceramic vessels in new fashions, or flaking river cobbles for implements of everyday use); gardening (women selecting plant strains for the next year's harvest); procuring, producing, and distributing food (women shellfishing, pounding acorn, preparing and cooking seed crops); producing everyday items from common raw materials (women making cord and weaving fibres of cotton, wool, maguey, preparing and sewing hides and leather clothing); women burying their dead, constructing, modifying, and burning their domiciles. If the rulers and decision-makers are mostly out of sight in these scenarios, another cast of people and another realm of action is revealed that has remained hidden in our purportedly gender-neutral analyses.

Of course, the scenarios in these papers can, and are here shown to, accumulate to a larger scale of structure and change, one that we are more accustomed to tracking in our studies of the past – it is the women opting to weave instead of garden that provides the dynamics for Aztec exchange networks and market systems, or women selecting and accumulating shell mounds in which to bury their dead that can account for the Archaic shell mounds, or women using bedrock mortars rather than mobile milling stones that "fix" settlements among Archaic foragers in California. Wars are carried out and states built from revolutions in cooking technology and from the creation of new strains of corn with new growing tolerances. The seeds of such radical revisions in prehistory are traced here, through gender, to their roots in daily activities and interpersonal patterns.

Were this dramatic revision in the scale and scope of archaeology the essence of what an archaeology of gender could be expected to deliver, we might expect the evolution of a newly distinct – engendered – archaeology that would coexist with traditional subjects of archaeological inquiry. Some investigators would undertake "male" areas of study, concentrating on large-scale, political and technical developments, while others did "female", engendered studies of the past, with attention to personal interactions and interpersonal relations. At best, the two areas might complement one another; more probably, even if two areas of study did emerge and coexist, the political economy of archaeology (Conkey with Williams forthcoming; Gero 1985; Wobst and Keene 1983) would marginalize the engendered perspective as irrelevant to the "real" (gender-neutral/androcentric) past.

But in fact, as these chapters make clear, engendered and "gender-neutral" versions of how the past is told cannot coexist as parallel and alternative foci. Gender is inextricably connected with other variables and dynamics of social and cultural life, many of which are longstanding archaeological concerns – trade, craft specialization, state formation, status, alliances, households, divisions of labor, architecture, imagery, ritual. An account of state formation without consideration of gender, or an account of gender relations in states without consideration of class, are partial and ideologically loaded accounts. Thus, gender cannot be separated out from other archaeological concerns and, by extension, be marginalized as a separate "speciality".

Gender *does* matter, and the lessons that spill over from an engendered past directly challenge the dominant paradigm at the level of the most fundamental assumptions and most basic classificatory categories. Such lessons are amply illustrated in these pages where again and again profound questions are raised about the way in which society is constituted and whether it should be endowed with goals and an "elan vital" of its own (Kus 1984; see also Mann 1986); about the relationship of individual social actors, with their subjective experiences, to "societies" that produce surpluses, process information, or manifest control hierarchies (Kus 1984); about the importance of meaning and meaningful activity in social relationships and in the theoretical models we employ to understand these relationships; about the field methods we adopt to sample selectively "the" archaeological record; about the criteria we use to subdivide prehistoric time; about the "proper" way to write archaeology.

These chapters show how engendering the past is much more inclusive and extensive than finding ingenious ways to attribute gender to material lifeways. Perhaps the very first lesson we take from these chapters is that gender can be studied in archaeology, even deep in prehistory and even without the "smoking gun" (i.e. indirect gendered evidence) of skeletal remains. Authors here illustrate various "routes" to women and to gender, at the same time examining and questioning modern gender ideology as (in)appropriate for prehistoric models, careful of the ready traps of translating modern gender roles into past prehistoric contexts. Several authors do build on longstanding assumptions and gender stereotypes of women's roles, accepting some activities such as cooking (Hastorf), gardening (Watson and Kennedy), shellfishing (Claassen), or potting (Wright) as perhaps associated with women far back into time. These authors then go on to examine, clarify, and draw implications from these associations, once they have made them explicit.

In contrast, other chapters challenge the exclusion of women from specific activities like flintknapping (Gero), insisting that there is no logical, empirical or ethnographic basis for extrapolating gender roles for prehistoric tool production from modern experimental knappers. One chapter (Pollock) relies on a careful reading of iconographic representations to raise questions about "images of women" (Pollock

1977) and takes us to the brink of the theoretical terrain of ideology and representation that archaeologists can no longer avoid.

Several authors "find" women by exploring the spatial implications of gender (Tringham, Conkey, Hastorf, Jackson), using the spatial context to frame the marking of gender expression, as well as its more localized associations with specific activities, or recognizing that architecture (in its wider sense, to include bedrock outcrops, rock shelters, as well as "houses") provides a vehicle for the mediation as well as the negotiation of tensions between the sexes.

Almost all routes to gender in prehistory depend to a lesser or greater extent, and more or less explicitly, on ethnographic or ethnohistoric data for analogical comparisons, or for direct historical continuities, of women's associations with particular activities or materials. The dangers of this tricky path are obvious; by uncritically accepting women and gender roles from – or as reported for – modern or recent societies as models for women and gender in past societies, do we not risk collapsing and homogenizing the very variability that we find so compelling in gender studies? As an aid to studying prehistoric gender, most of these chapters use analogical reasoning and ethnographic/historic comparison guardedly and as links more than fulcrums in their chains of reasoning.

But even more than ethnographic insights, gender is revealed in prehistory by the body of feminist theory that in this volume informs almost every piece. Lessons from the most general outlines to the very specific points of feminism are reflected in every chapter, starting perhaps from the overarching fact that archaeology is consistently told to us from a male perspective that adopts "male" as the norm and proceeds from the male experience. In the received view, art is male, with females sometimes as subjects/objects; males take over agriculture where scheduling conflicts arise because agriculture is the more critical activity. Tools, their production and use, are male concerns and are intimately involved with the evolution of "man". Empires are made by men, and the underlying labor and energy directly attributable to women lies hidden. Optimal foraging models are operationalized by using male foraging models and ignoring well-documented female patterns of, for instance, shellfishing. When female labor is considered in optimal foraging models (e.g. in Hawkes et al.'s discussion (1988) of "hard-working Hadza grandmothers"), it is viewed more in terms of how societies "use" otherwise useless (i.e. in reproductive terms) post-menopausal females rather than in terms of women's personal productive labors or skills as scavengers/hunters.

Authors in this volume repeatedly expose the subtle and not-so-subtle means by which female labor is devalued: Hastorf suggests that the entire field of paleoethnobotany has been neglected in archaeological practice and interpretation because seed recovery, related to food preparation and the "domestic" sphere, is identified with women's work. Tringham notes that although – or because – households, regardless of the specific constitution of the resident group, surely include women, they are considered marginal to the "great events" of prehistory. Even when women in households are considered, this has been almost exclusively in terms of "activity areas" rather than in terms of productive labor, or the negotiation of gender relations, or the organization and carrying out of fundamental economic and social processes. In fact, many of the studies in this volume do center around the economy, management and production of households which, as Brumfiel argues, are critical to the ability of a population to sustain population growth as well as to develop large-scale, labor-intensive works that a state requires.

The devaluing of women's work comes to archaeology in part through an equally androcentric filter of ethnography where shellfishing is consistently characterized as a low-ranked foodstuff at least in part because of its association with female collectors (Claassen); pottery-making is assigned to males although it is more often than not carried out in association with teams that include females (Wright); flake tools are virtually disregarded in the glossaries and taxonomies of "man-made" tools, surely in part because they are not exclusively identified with male producers and users (Gero). Higher value is placed on European trade goods such as metal tips for awls over the Indian-produced bone awl handles, since men would have traded the tips and women would have made the handles (Spector).

But the study of gender ramifies through the practice of archaeology in other ways as well. For instance, attention to gender forces us to reassess the production sequences that are undertaken in ancient technologies and to consider the social implications of dividing labor into different combinations and arrangements of tasks, and by different social groupings. By trying to pair one gender with the production of a particular item of material culture, we are forced to question whether the notion of "craft specialization" can accommodate the more nuanced ideas of technical or task specialization. Together with a new focus on interdependent social relations of production, more adequate explanations of production processes are achieved while at the same time challenging the western (male) notions of radical individualism that typically underlie ideas of production in archaeology.

Similarly, introduced changes in material culture forms, whether as changes in ceramic forms and designs (Wright), in plant morphology (Watson and Kennedy), or in the appearance of new art forms (Handsman), when inspected through an engendered prehistory, emerge as the result of conscious and deliberate actions with intended outcomes.

In these chapters, authors note the dull, passive vocabulary that is characteristically used to discuss change in material forms, especially for commonly used items and especially where production is assumed to be in the hands of women; new styles simply "appear" and then "change", designs are just "added/dropped", and new techniques are somehow "discovered" – automatically, without apparent reason, and seemingly without human interference! In the same way, agriculture "is adopted", perhaps by women but seemingly without thought (Watson and Kennedy). The explicit attention to gender calls for a replacement of this implied unconsciousness with a vocabulary that recognizes intent and control over cultural material.

Or again, the infusion of gender in prehistoric studies raises a serious challenge to simple functionalist notions of objects, activities, aggregations, institutions; all of these are now seen to go beyond fulfilling immediate material needs because they are undertaken and carried out in specific ways that facilitate, inhibit, reinforce, or undermine patterns of interpersonal life. With the recognition of the centrality of social life, including gender dynamics, in all human groups, we have to confront humans as symbolists as much as materialists (Conkey). Thus, while it is commonplace to recognize the function of food as providing sustenance, by applying gender concepts to food systems a much wider socio-political arena is demonstrated to be involved with food collection, food processing, food distribution, and food consumption (Hastorf). As gender is recognized as structuring archaeological materials at all levels, from single events to general systems, then what things "are for" is necessarily redefined.

These chapters show us that adopting a feminist perspective gives us another, a different, a female perspective on what things "are for", how social change proceeds, and how archaeological myths are built. Prehistory actually looks different. Neolithic "art" is not merely in the realm of aesthetics but is about the appropriation of female labor (Handsman); projectile points are not necessarily the dominant material culture of stone age, nor is hunting the only (significant) activity (Conkey). The phenomenal growth of the Aztec empire resulted not only from the astute statesMANship of its politicians but also from the product of women's labor (Brumfiel). The concept of "tool" isn't congruent with "projectile point" or even with retouched bifaces but consists predominantly of unretouched flakes (Gero).

At an even more fundamental level, the use of gender as an analytical category challenges the central epistemological issues of modern archaeology: the hypothetico-deductive program for testing propositions. An engendered archaeology refuses to be limited to exploring only those aspects of the past that have been deemed "testable" and insists, moreover, that other programs have in fact proceeded from a strongly developed theoretical position (e.g. systems theory) that itself was assumed and never subjected to a testing cycle. In this regard, gender inspections are perhaps on firmer ground than most theoretical paradigms, including systems theory, since the "seeing" of either systems or gender in the archaeological record is a non-empirical vision. At least there is empirical evidence for women while arguments about whether or not "systems" are meaningful analytic units are less easily settled.

Thus we "find" women because we know they are there, and we study gender in the past because we know something about how it "works". This clear alternative to and refutation of positivism, coupled with an insistence on the centrality of social theory as relevant to archaeology, emerges from almost all these chapters. Testability of the positivist sort can no longer be the foremost criterion by which we choose what to know about the past, and the very notion of using the past to "test" knowledge is called into question by these papers. This rejection of "testability", especially of the sort called for by "narrow empiricists" or "artifact physicists" (after Watson 1986), is not, however, a call for raising our tolerance levels for speculation (cf. Wylie 1989). To reject empiricism as a means of knowing is not the same as abandoning "empirical depth". Rather, in recognizing that archaeology is more interpretive than positivist, and more committed to the development of social theory that will be able to pay "close historical attention to the complex processes and details of social change" (Stacy and Thorne 1985: 310, referring to Thompson 1979), means that our knowledge of the past must still be "close to the ground and honed by the case at hand" (ibid.: 310).

By placing gender at the center of our studies, we problematize the most fundamental categories by which we know the world, including – in archaeology – such commonplace units as the "chronological" divisions (actually often technological or progressive evolutionary criteria) used to subdivide prehistoric time. If items of material culture – technological features whose adoption is seized upon to characterize prehistoric periods – are not items used by or made by women, are they acceptable or even useful for defining and bounding human experience into distinguishable segments? On the other hand, were we to separate prehistoric time into chunks of similarly experienced lifeways for women, would these boundaries be recognizable to prehistorians? Is the Solutrean–Magdalenian "boundary" gender-neutral? To the extent that – and in those contexts where – male and female experiences in prehistory are non-overlapping, any form of periodization may be no more than an awkward and biasing obfuscation that homogenizes as pan-human what is essentially male – or, less often, female – in prehistoric change. Like all classification systems, periodizations depend upon the questions being asked; we can expect multiple schemes.

The very ways we write archaeology are challenged by feminists' notions of discourse, by rejection of an object/subject polarity, and by resistance to the authoritative and hierarchical texts that situate authors in unassailable positions of authority over readers. Several of the authors in this volume are clearly mistrustful of the objectification embodied in most archaeological accounts, including their cults of authority: the authority of statistics, of the passive voice, the exaggeratedly objective eye, the single line of evidence, the single cause, the only perspective. Feminist reasoning insists on the relevance and importance of multiple perspectives (Tringham), on personal experience (Spector), on narration as an explanatory route and a source of understanding, essential to the act of interpretation (Handsman). The reformulation of text may be essential to rewriting prehistory, highlighting the active voice not only of prehistoric peoples, but of the authors of texts as well.

Finally, the study of gender in archaeology contributes to changing the more inclusive anthropological frameworks that we put around the experiences of humans, since a revised archaeology stands to play a significant role in restructuring the inquiry of anthropology and related social and historical disciplines. There are convincing arguments that anthropology, particularly because of information provided by archaeology, retains an inherent evolutionism (of a transformational, progressive sort, cf. Dunnell 1980), and is essentially comparative in its practice (Marcus and Clifford 1985). Consequently, the covert and unquestioned assumptions about the social lives of prehistoric hunter-gatherers and how these have changed with the "progression" towards more complex societies through the "rise" of "the" state, underlie the ways in which ethnographers approach their subject.

As archaeologists have pointed to (or even only suggested) the origin of the nuclear family and of pair-bonding ("read" monogamy), these categories legitimated the analytical units and unquestioned features of human social life. But now, revisions in archaeology of these categories and features of early human life provide the necessary restructuring of concepts called for in anthropology by feminist research, including the progressive evolutionism within which most of the field is embedded. In fact, it is arguable whether the larger transformations in how human experience is conceptualized and understood can proceed without a (feminist) archaeology.

We believe that the papers in this volume probe the epistemological contours of archaeological knowledge, and in more diverse ways than we at first could have imagined or anticipated. For some, to think more broadly about understanding gender is not necessarily to criticize fundamental epistemologies. For others, inquiry into gender-as-process is simultaneously a scrutiny of assumptions and epistemologies, and simultaneously a questioning of our objects of knowledge, if not also of our structuring paradigms. This volume is about these processes, which are emergent and transitional for archaeology: about conceptualizing gender, about the roles and kinds of critiques involved, about how to engender our practice as well as our prehistories.

There is a difference in the prehistories that consider gender, and there are differences in doing archaeology about and/or by women. Because how we represent others and how we represent "difference" is important, we are not seeking any single cross-cultural discovery of what constitutes men's or women's lives. Our task is to intervene in those archaeological processes that portray prehistoric women, men, or their relations as interchangeable and identical.

By adopting gender as an explicit conceptual and analytical category, by applying gender concepts and categories to familiar and original sets of archaeological data, women are brought into view as active producers, innovators and contextualizers of the very material world by which we know the past. Women may, in fact, be shown as responsible for generating and distributing an extraordinarily large proportion of materials in the archaeological record, for controlling the production of a large number of classes of archaeological materials, for structuring the spatial organization of classic tracts of the archaeological record, and for early and innovative manipulations of technology, resulting in major technological and sociocultural changes.

But a volume that inquires explicitly into women in prehistory is not justified merely on the grounds of a past exclusion of women in our archaeologies, and that we are now providing additional information and new "facts". The social knowledge that we hope to engender, and the difference that archaeologies of gender can make, is an "open, contingent and humanly-compelling" social knowledge that is in explicit contrast to the more traditional social knowledge that is "closed, categorical, and human-controlling" (after Westkott 1979: 430). Gender *is* an issue of archaeology and of prehistory.

NOTES

1   One could take as an additional tension, as does Strathern (1987), the idea noted above concerning feminist scholarship as a "resource". She discusses the "awkward relationship" of anthropology (and, by implication, of any discipline, including archaeology) that is immediately entailed by feminist scholarship. The relationship (that is more like a paradox) is rooted in the fact

that, on the one hand, feminist scholarship works (and we want it to work) *across* disciplines, "which means that it cannot be parallel with them" (ibid.: 276). Yet for feminist scholarship to register an impact on mainstream theorizing in any field, it must, on the other hand, "be construed as an isomorphic sister 'discipline' from which ideas and concepts could be borrowed" (ibid.: 277).

Even further, she notes the tension experienced by those who practice feminist anthropology and how they are "caught between [cultural] structures: the scholar is faced with two different ways of relating to his or her subject matter. The tension must be kept going; there can be no relief in substituting one for the other" (ibid.: 286; see also Ong 1988).

2   These critiques of biology and evolutionary concepts are integral not only to human evolutionary narratives but to the prevailing progressive (cf. Dunnell 1980) and adaptationist modes of thinking in archaeology.

3   Or, as Moore (1988: 6) has succinctly put it, "Attempts to assign subdisciplinary status to feminist anthropology have more to do with processes of political containment than with serious intellectual considerations."

REFERENCES

Abel, Elizabeth and Emily K. Abel (1983). *The Signs Reader: Women, Gender, and Scholarship.* Chicago: University of Chicago Press.
Abu-Lughod, Lila (1986). *Veiled Sentiments: Honor and Poetry in a Bedouin Society.* Berkeley: University of California Press.
Ardener, Edwin (1975). "Belief and the Problem of Women: The Problem Revisited." In *Perceiving Women,* S. Ardener, ed. New York: John Wiley, 1–28.
Ardener, Shirley (1977). *Perceiving Women.* New York: John Wiley.
——— (1981). *Women and Space: Ground Rules and Social Maps.* London: Croom Helm.
Barstow, Ann (1978). "The Uses of Archaeology for Women's History: James Mellaart's Work on the Neolithic Goddess of Catal Hüyük." *Feminist Studies* 4(3): 7–18.
Collier, Jane and Sylvia Yanagisako (1987). *Gender and Kinship: Essays Toward a Unified Analysis.* Stanford: Stanford University Press.
Conkey, Margaret and Joan Gero (1988). "Towards Building a Feminist Archaeology." Paper presented at 53rd annual meeting, Society for American Archaeology, Phoenix, AZ.
Conkey, M. and J. Spector (1984). "Archaeology and the Study of Gender." In *Advances in Archaeological Method and Theory,* vol. 7, M. Schiffer, ed. New York: Academic Press, 1–38.
Conkey, M. with Sarah H. Williams (forthcoming). "Original Narratives: The Political Economy of Gender in Archaeology." In *Gender at the Crossroads of Knowledge: Feminist Anthropology in the Post-Modern Era.* Micaela diLeonardo, ed. Berkeley: University of California Press.

Cucchiari, Salvatore (1981). "The Gender Revolution and the Transition from Bisexual Horde to Patrilocal Band: The Origins of Gender Hierarchy." In *Sexual Meanings*, S. Ortner and H. Whitehead, eds. Cambridge: Cambridge University Press, 31–79.

Davis, Elizabeth Gould (1971). *The First Sex*. New York: Putnam.

Davis, Natalie Z. (1975–6). "Women's History in Transition: The European Case." *Feminist Studies* 3: 90.

Delphy, Christine (1984). *Close to Home: A Materialist Analysis of Women's Oppression*. Diana Leonard, ed. London: Hutchinson (in assoc. with the Explorations in Feminism Collective).

diLeonardo, Micaela (forthcoming). "Gender, Culture and Political Economy: Feminist Anthropology in Historical Perspective." In *Gender at the Crossroads of Knowledge: Feminist Anthropology in the Post-Modern Era*. Micaela diLeonardo, ed. Berkeley: University of California Press.

Dunnell, Robert (1980). "Evolutionary Theory and Archaeology." In *Advances in Archaeological Method and Theory*, vol. 3, M. Schiffer, ed. New York: Academic Press, 35–99.

Dwyer, Daisy (1978). *Images and Self-Images: Male and Female in Morocco*. New York: Columbia University Press.

Eisler, Riane (1987). *The Chalice and the Blade: Our History, Our Future*. San Francisco: Harper & Row.

Etienne, Mona and Eleanor Leacock, eds (1980). *Women and Colonization: Anthropological Perspectives*. New York: Praeger.

Farnham, Christine, ed. (1987). *The Impact of Feminist Research in the Academy*. Bloomington: Indiana University Press.

Fedigan, Linda Marie (1986). "The Changing Role of Women in Models of Human Evolution." *Annual Review of Anthropology* 15: 25–66.

Flax, Jane (1987). "Postmodernism and Gender Relations in Feminist Theory." *Signs: Journal of Women in Culture and Society* 12(4): 621–43.

Freeman, L. G. (1968). "A Theoretical Framework for Interpreting Archaeological Materials." In *Man the Hunter*, R. B. Lee and I. Devore, eds. Chicago: Aldine, 262–7.

Friedl, Ernestine (1975). *Women and Men*. New York: Holt, Rinehart & Winston.

Gailey, Christine (1985). "The State of the State in Anthropology." *Dialectical Anthropology* 9(1–4): 65–91.

—— (1987a). "Evolutionary Perspectives on Gender Hierarchy." In *Analyzing Gender*, Beth B. Hess and Myra Marx Ferree, eds. Beverley Hills: Sage Press, 32–67.

—— (1987b). *From Kinship to Kingship: Gender Hierarchy and State Formation in the Tongan Islands*. Austin: University of Texas Press.

Gero, Joan (1983). "Gender Bias in Archaeology: A Cross-Cultural Perspective." In *The Socio-Politics of Archaeology*, J. M. Gero, D. Lacy, and M. L. Blakey, eds. Amherst: University of Massachusetts, Department of Anthropology Research Report No. 23, 51–7.

—— (1985). "Socio-politics of Archaeology and the Woman-at-Home Ideology." *American Antiquity* 50: 342–50.

—— (1988). "Gender Bias in Archaeology: Here, Then, and Now." In *Feminism Within the Science and Health-Care Professions: Overcoming Resistance*, Sue Rosser, ed. Oxford: Pergamon Press, 33–43.

Gibbon, Guy (1989). *Explanation in Archaeology.* Oxford: Basil Blackwell.

Glenn, Evelyn Nakano (1987). "Gender and the Family." In *Analyzing Gender*, Beth B. Hess and Myra Marx Ferree, eds. Newbury Park: Sage Publications, 348–80.

Goodale, Jane (1971). *Tiwi Wives: A Study of the Women of Melville Island, North Australia.* Seattle: University of Washington Press.

Gould, Richard, and Patty Jo Watson (1982). "A Dialogue on the Meaning and Use of Analogy in Ethnoarchaeological Reasoning." *Journal of Anthropological Archaeology* 1: 355–81.

Gross, M. and M. B. Averill (1983), "Evolution and Patriarchal Myths of Scarcity and Competition." In *Discovering Reality: Feminist Perspectives on Epistemology, Metaphysics, Methodology and Philosophy of Science*, Sandra Harding and Merrill Hintikka, eds. Dordrecht, Holland: D. Reidel, 71–95.

Haraway, Donna (1978). "Animal Sociology and a Natural Economy of the Body Politic. Part II. The Past Is the Contested Zone: Human Nature and Theories of Production and Reproduction in Primate Behavior Studies." *Signs: Journal of Women in Culture and Society* 4: 37–60.

Harding, Sandra (1986). *The Science Question in Feminism.* Ithaca: Cornell University Press.

Hartmann, Heidi (1981). "The Family as Locus of Gender, Class and Political Struggle: The Example of Housework." *Signs: Journal of Women in Culture and Society* 6(3): 366–94.

Hartsock, Nancy (1983). "The Feminist Standpoint: Developing the Ground for a Specifically Feminist Historical Materialism." In *Discovering Reality: Feminist Perspectives on Epistemology, Metaphysics, Methodology and Philosophy of Science*, Sandra Harding and Merrill Hintikka, eds. Dordrecht, Holland: D. Reidel, 283–310.

Hawkes, K., J. F. O'Connell, and N. G. Blurton Jones (1988). "Hard-working Hadza Grandmothers." In *Comparative Socioecology: The Behavioral Ecology of Humans and Other Mammals*, V. Standen and R. Foley, eds. Oxford: Blackwell Scientific Publications, 341–65.

Hess, Beth B. and Myra Max Feree (1987). *Analyzing Gender.* Newbury Park: Sage Publications.

Isaac, Glynn Ll. (1978). "The Food-sharing Behavior of Protohuman Hominids." *Scientific American* 238(4): 90–108.

Keller, Evelyn Fox (1985). *Reflections on Gender and Science.* New Haven: Yale University Press.

—— (1987). "Feminism and Science." In *Sex and Scientific Inquiry*, Sandra Harding and Jean F. O'Barr, eds. Chicago: University of Chicago Press. (Originally 1982, *Signs: Journal of Women in Culture and Society* 7(3): 589–602).

Kessler, Suzanne, J. and Wendy McKenna (1978). *Gender: An Ethnomethodological Approach.* New York: John Wiley & Sons.

Kramer, Carol and Miriam Stark (1988). "The Status of Women in Archaeology." *Anthropology Newsletter (American Anthropological Association)* 29(9): 1, 11–12.

Kus, Susan (1984). "The Spirit and Its Burden: Archaeology and Symbolic Activity." In *Marxist Perspectives in Archaeology*, M. Spriggs, ed. Cambridge: Cambridge University Press, 101–7.

LaFontaine, J. S., ed. (1978). *Sex and Age as Principles of Social Differentiation.* New York: Academic Press.

Lamphere, Louise (1987). "Feminism and Anthropology: The Struggle to Reshape Our Thinking about Gender." In *The Impact of Feminist Research in the Academy*, Christine Farnham, ed. Bloomington: Indiana University Press, 11–33.

Leacock, Eleanor (1981). "History, Development, and the Division of Labor by Sex: Implications for Organization." *Signs: Journal of Women in Culture and Society* 7(2): 474–91.

—— (1983). "Interpreting the Origins of Gender Inequality: Conceptual and Historical Problems." *Dialectical Anthropology* 7: 263–83.

Liebowitz, Lila (1978). *Males, Females, Families.* North Scituate, MA: Duxbury Press.

Longino, Helen and Ruth Doell (1983). "Body, Bias, and Behavior: A Comparative Analysis of Reasoning in Two Areas of Biological Science." *Signs: Journal of Women in Culture and Society* 9(2): 206–27.

Lutz, Catherine (1988). *Unnatural Emotions: Everyday Sentiments on a Micronesian Atoll and Their Challenge to Western Theory.* Chicago: University of Chicago Press.

Mann, M. (1986). *A History of Power from the Beginning to AD 1760.* Cambridge: Cambridge University Press.

Marcus, George and James Clifford (1985). "The Making of Ethnographic Texts: A Preliminary Report." *Current Anthropology* 26(2): 267–71.

MacCormack, Carol and Marilyn Strathern, eds. (1980). *Nature, Culture and Gender.* Cambridge: Cambridge University Press.

McGaw, Judith (1982). "Women and the History of American Technology." *Signs: Journal of Women in Culture and Society* 7(4): 798–828.

—— (1989). "No Passive Victims, No Separate Spheres." In *Context, History and History of Technology*, Stephen H. Cutliffe and Robert C. Post, eds. Bethlehem, PA: Lehigh University Press, 172–91.

McGuire, Randall (1985). "Conceptualizing the State in a Post-processual Archaeology." Paper presented at annual meetings, American Anthropological Association, Washington, DC.

Merchant, Carolyn (1980). *The Death of Nature: Women, Ecology and the Scientific Revolution.* New York: Harper & Row.

—— (1989). *Ecological Revolutions: Nature, Gender, and Science in New England.* Chapel Hill: University of North Carolina Press.

Moore, Henrietta (1986). *Space, Text and Gender: An Anthropological Study of the Marakwet of Kenya.* Cambridge: Cambridge University Press.

—— (1988). *Feminism and Anthropology.* Cambridge: Polity Press.

Morgan, Elaine (1972). *The Descent of Woman.* New York: Stein & Day.

Ong, Aihwa (1988). "Colonialism and Modernity: Feminist Re-presentations of Women in Non-western Societies." *Inscriptions* 3/4: 79–93.

Ortner, Sherry B. and Harriet Whitehead, eds. (1981). *Sexual Meanings: The Cultural Construction of Gender and Sexuality.* Cambridge: Cambridge University Press.

Pollock, Griselda (1977). "What's Wrong with Images of Women." *Screen Education* 24 (Autumn). (Reprinted 1987 in *Looking On: Images of Women in the Visual Arts and Media*, Rosemary Betterton, ed. New York: Pandora.)

Rapp, Rayna (1977). "Ge ider and Class: An Archaeology of Knowledge Concerning the Origin of the State." *Dialectical Anthropology* 2(4): 309–16.

Reiter, Rayna (Rapp) (1975). *Toward an Anthropology of Women.* New York: Monthly Review Press.

Renfrew, Colin and Stephen Shennan, eds. (1982). *Ranking, Resources, and Exchange.* Cambridge: Cambridge University Press.

Rogers, Susan (1975). "Female Forms of Power and the Myth of Male Dominance: A Model of Female/Male Interaction in Peasant Society." *American Ethnologist* 2: 727–57.

Rohrlich-Leavitt, Ruby (1977). "Women in Transition: Crete and Sumer." In *Becoming Visible: Women in European History*, R. Bridenthal and C. Koonz, eds. Boston: Houghton Mifflin, 36–59.

Rosaldo, Michelle Zimbalist (1980). "The Use and Abuse of Anthropology: Reflections on Feminism and Cross-cultural Understanding." *Signs: Journal of Women in Culture and Society* 5(3): 389–417.

Rosaldo, Michelle Zimbalist and Louise Lamphere, eds (1974). *Woman, Culture, and Society.* Stanford: Stanford University Press.

Rubin, Gayle (1975). "The Traffic in Women: Notes on the 'Political Economy' of Sex." In *Toward an Anthropology of Women*, Rayna Rapp Reiter, ed. New York: Monthly Review Press, 157–210.

Ryan, Mary (1981). *Cradle of the Middle Class: The Family in Oneida County, New York.* Cambridge: Cambridge University Press.

Sacks, Karen (1979). *Sisters and Wives: The Past and Future of Sexual Equality.* Westport: Greenwood Press.

Sanday, Peggy Reeves (1981). *Female Power and Male Dominance: On the Origins of Sexual Inequality.* Cambridge: Cambridge University Press.

Scheper-Hughes, Nancy (1983). "The Problem of Bias in Androcentric and Feminist Anthropology." *Women's Studies* 10: 109–16.

Schmidt, Delores Barrancano and Earl Robert Schmidt (1976). "The Invisible Woman: The Historian as Professional Magician." In *Liberating Women's History: Theoretical and Critical Essays*, Berenice A. Carroll, ed. Urbana: University of Illinois Press, 42–54.

Scott, Joan Wallach (1986). "Gender: A Useful Category of Historical Analysis." *American Historical Review* 81: 1053–75.

—— (1988). *Gender and the Politics of History.* New York: Columbia University Press.

Shanks, M. and C. Tilley (1987a). *Re-constructing Archaeology.* Cambridge: Cambridge University Press.

—— (1987b). *Social Theory and Archaeology.* Albuquerque: University of New Mexico Press.

—— (1989). "Archaeology into the 1990s" *Norwegian Archaeological Review* 22(1): 1–54.

Shapiro, Judith (1983). "Anthropology and the Study of Gender." In *A Feminist Perspective on the Academy.* E. Langland and W. Gove, eds. Chicago: University of Chicago Press, 110–29.

Shennan, Stephen (1986). "Towards a Critical Archaeology?" *Proceedings of the Prehistoric Society* 52: 327–56.

Silverblatt, Irene (1987). *Moon, Sun and Witches: Gender Ideologies and Class in Inca and Colonial Peru.* Princeton: Princeton University Press.

—— (1988). "Women in States." *Annual Review of Anthropology* 17: 427–60.

Slocum, Sally (1975). "Woman the Gatherer: Male Bias in Anthropology." In *Toward an Anthropology of Women*, Rayna Rapp Reiter, ed. New York: Monthly Review Press, 36–50. (Originally presented at 1970 AAA meetings, San Diego, California, by Sally Linton.)

Stacey, Judith and Barrie Thorne (1985). "The Missing Feminist Revolution in Sociology." *Social Problems* 32(4): 301–16.

Strathern, Marilyn (1972). *Women in Between: Female Roles in a Male World: Mount Hagen, New Guinea.* London: Seminar Press.

—— (1987). "An Awkward Relationship: The Case of Feminism and Anthropology." *Signs: Journal of Women in Culture and Society* 12(2): 276–92.

Tanner, Nancy (1981). *On Becoming Human.* Cambridge: Cambridge University Press.

Tanner, Nancy and Adrienne Zihlman (1976). "Women in Evolution. Part I. Innovation and Selection in Human Origins." *Signs: Journal of Women in Culture and Society* 1(3): 104–19.

Thompson, E. P. (1979). *The Poverty of Theory and Other Essays.* New York: Monthly Review Press.

Watson, Patty Jo (1986). "Archaeological Interpretation, 1985." In *American Archaeology, Past and Future.* D. Meltzer, J. Sabloff, and D. Fowler, eds. Washington: Smithsonian Institution Press, 439–57.

Weiner, Annette (1976). *Women of Value, Men of Renown.* Austin: University of Texas Press.

Westkott, Marcia (1979). "Feminist Criticism of the Social Sciences." *Harvard Educational Review* 49: 422–30.

Wobst, H. Martin (1978). "The Archaeo-ethnology of Hunter-gatherers, or the Tyranny of the Ethnographic Record in Archaeology." *American Antiquity* 43: 303–9.

Wobst, H. Martin and Arthur Keene (1983). "Archaeological Explanation as Political Economy." In *The Socio-politics of Archaeology.* J. Gero, D. Lacy, and M. Blakey, eds. Amherst: University of Massachusetts, Department of Anthropology Research Report No. 23, 79–90.

Wylie, Alison (1981). "Positivism and the New Archaeology." Ph.D. dissertation, Department of Philosophy, State University of New York, Binghamton.

—— (1985). "The Reaction Against Analogy." In *Advances in Archaeological*

Method and Theory, vol. 8, M. Schiffer, ed. New York: Academic Press, 63–111.

—— (1989) "Feminist Analyses of Social Power. Substantive and Epistemological Issues." Paper prepared for Wenner-Gren Foundation Conference, Critical Approaches in Archaeology, Material, Life, Meaning, and Power, Cascai, Portugal.

Wylie, Alison, Kathleen Okruhlik, Sandra Morton, and Leslie Thielen-Wilson (1989). "Feminist Critiques of Science: The Epistemological and Methodological Literature." *Women's Studies International Forum* 12: 379–88.

Yanagisako, Sylvia (1979). "Family and Household: The Analysis of Domestic Groups." *Annual Review of Anthropology* 8: 161–205.

Zihlman, Adrienne (1978). "Women in Evolution, Part II: Subsistence and Social Organization in Early Hominids." *Signs: Journal of Women in Culture and Society* 4(1): 4–20.

2

Gender Theory and the Archaeological Record: Why Is There No Archaeology of Gender?

Alison Wylie

I have long been puzzled by two questions about archaeology which derive from my feminist commitments. First, why is there no counterpart in archaeology to the vibrant traditions of research on women and gender now well established in most other social scientific fields? And, second, what are the prospects, at this juncture, for the development of an archaeology of gender? This discussion is, of necessity, a preliminary exploration of these questions; my aim is to focus them and consider some possible answers suggested by parallels with the development of analyses in other fields.

Why Is There No Archaeology of Gender?

One commonplace and, I will argue, unsatisfactory explanation for the lack of gender research in archaeology is that women and gender are inaccessible in archaeological contexts; archaeology is too limited methodologically to sustain such research. Unlike other social sciences where the tangible presence of women poses a direct challenge to androcentric theorizing, in archaeology the very identification of women subjects and women's activities is inherently problematic; they must be reconstructed from highly enigmatic data. On this account, archaeology could not be expected to pursue questions about gender until a body of theory is developed in other fields that do have direct access to women and gender capable of making them visible in the archaeological record.

It is perhaps relevant to this methodological account that contemporary gender theory is often represented as developing through three stages, to be discussed more fully below: critiques of androcentrism in science; "remedial" research that focuses on women; and finally, broader reconceptualizations of existing subject fields which produce integrative

31

theories concerning "sex/gender systems" (Harding 1983, originally Rubin 1975) and which document their diversity and interaction with other structuring factors, including (crucially, for archaeology) the material conditions and dimensions of cultural life. On the methodological account, it is only now, as this third stage in the development of feminist inquiry unfolds, that a sufficiently sophisticated understanding of gender is becoming available to make women and gender a possible object of archaeological study.

Although, as I will argue later, the methodological constraints are by no means trivial, there are at least two difficulties with this account. First, it is not clear that the necessary theoretical resources are only now becoming available. The three phases of development are not so sharply separable as to be exclusive of one another. "Remedial" research was very often undertaken as a means of exposing the androcentrism of existing research – it was essential to the preceding, critical phase – and many of those engaged in it raised self-critical (third-stage) questions about their own framework assumptions almost immediately (see, for example, the contributions in Rosaldo and Lamphere 1974, and the discussions of Schlegel 1974 and Tilly 1978). In fact, feminist researchers in fields with strong traditions of gender research continue to work in all three areas. What this pattern of development indicates is, then, that the crucial condition for the initial development of feminist critiques in fields like anthropology and history is not that women are directly accessible as subjects, but rather that the researcher is prepared to see them *as* subjects. And what researchers need in order to see women as subjects (or to bring them into view as subjects) is not a fully developed gender theory – such was clearly not available when feminist researchers first began their inquiry – but a conceptual framework that raises the relevant questions, directing attention to gender and providing the impetus to study women's activities and experiences. The women who were entering the social sciences in increasing numbers in the early 1960s and were the main force behind the development of research on women and gender drew on the popular ("second wave") women's movement of the period for these conceptual resources; they were typically feminists whose sensitivity to gender issues in research was a function of their political commitments. By the early 1980s, when the first paper arguing explicitly for gender studies in archaeology appeared (Conkey and Spector 1984), the critical insights of this original contingent of feminist researchers had crystallized into an extremely rich conceptual framework, one which was, as Conkey and Spector demonstrated, more than sufficiently rich to sustain a critical analysis of the androcentrism inherent in archaeology and to initiate a program of archaeological research into gender.

A second difficulty with the methodological account is that it is globally self-defeating for archaeology if taken seriously. It assumes that archaeologists can (or must) wait for *external* development of the background knowledge necessary to open up a new area like gender research. In order to use their data effectively as evidence of such socio-cultural phenomena, they do certainly require a body of linking principles, often built up in "actualistic" contexts, but these are not normally provided by anyone but an archaeologist who undertakes such research with the specific aim of establishing them. If it were true that gender research in archaeology could not develop until external fields provided these necessary theoretical tools, archaeologists could happily sidestep any concern with gender indefinitely. If these conditions were generalized, however, it would follow that archaeology could move very little beyond description of the archaeological record to consider any of the questions about socio-cultural dynamics that have become central to the field in recent years.

It is clear, then, that the failure to develop an archaeology of gender cannot be considered wholly or exclusively a matter of methodological constraint unique to archaeology. Such external conditions as are necessary to initiate the archaeological study of women and gender have long been in place; the sex/gender has been "discovered" (Harding 1983), and it is now widely understood that social scientific research must take gender and women into account if it is to be academically credible. In addition, archaeologists routinely take the initiative in expanding the bases for archaeological interpretation in the areas necessary to make relatively intangible (i.e. socio-political, economic, ideational) dimensions of past cultures accessible, when they have determined that these are relevant for understanding the archaeological record and its cultural antecedents. The real question is, then, why archaeologists have not taken steps to overcome the methodological limitations with which they inevitably deal, *in this particular problem area.*

Why have archaeological resources for gender analysis not been developed?

It is unlikely that any one factor will prove responsible for the pervasive lack of interest in gender issues in archaeology; although the effect is monolithic, the experience of other fields suggests that it is multiply determined.

In many cases, despite ignoring gender and women as direct objects of inquiry, archaeologists do make explicit claims (or assumptions) about the status of women and the nature of gender structures in prehistoric societies. In this, gender structures that are common in the West (or in a select range of ethnographic contexts) are unreflectively projected onto archaeological subjects as stable, uncontroversial features of the cultural environment in the context of reconstructive and explanatory arguments about the cultural past. The result is a tendency, which is quite explicit in some areas, to assume that women and gender structures are simply irrelevant to the explanatory understanding of cultural dynamics; being stable, they can never account for changes or development in cultural systems. Alternatively, it seems to be assumed that there is, in effect, nothing to learn about gender; if "biology is destiny" where gender is concerned, then biological males and females can be assumed always to have occupied the range of sharply differentiated and hierarchical roles that are represented as "naturally" theirs in familiar contemporary societies. Although feminist critiques have demonstrated unequivocally that such "essentialist" assumptions about gender – hallmarks of contemporary sex role ideology – are unsustainable empirically, often on the very evidence collected by those most intent on affirming them, they continue to influence even those social and life sciences in which feminist critiques have a strong presence (e.g. anthropology; Strathern 1987). The centrality of essentialist assumptions to archaeological theorizing is clearly one reason why archaeologists have not taken any strong initiative in developing the resources necessary for studying gender.[1]

In other cases, however, the role of gender ideology is much more subtle. Attention may be systematically directed away from gender and women, not because of any explicit beliefs about their status or (ir)relevance, sexist or otherwise, but as a secondary consequence of commitment to theories which focus on other classes of variables as the primary determinants of cultural behavior. Conkey and Spector (1984) suggest, for example, that gender research has not gotten off the ground because the dominant research programs in archaeology – systems analysis and processual archaeology generally – endorse a preoccupation with large-scale (system-level) processes of development at the expense of any consideration of internal, local structuring principles like gender (1984: 22–3). In effect, feminists in archaeology would *first* have to challenge the broad, field-defining framework assumptions (e.g. about the causal efficacy of variables other than gender and, implicitly, about the inefficacy of gender) that underlie long-established traditions of research, before they could initiate research on gender and women. They could not begin by simply "adding women" in a relatively less threatening stage of "remedial" research and *then* broaden the scope of their critique, leaving the most challenging analyses to a later, third stage of research.

Although this is an intuitively plausible explanation for the lack of interest in gender, it is important to recognize that nothing in the nature of systemic approaches or a concern with large-scale culture process, as such, precludes a concern with internal variables such as gender.[2]

In fact, many feminists argue that sex/gender categories and dynamics are fundamental, system-wide structuring principles in all societies (despite wide diversity in the form they take) and conclude on this basis that any adequate model of system-level processes must take gender structures into account. But even if this were not accepted, it surely remains an empirical question whether the behaviour of a given system (cultural or otherwise) is, under specific circumstances, primarily determined by external rather than internal variables, or whether a variable like gender is relevant for explaining particular events and patterns of system development; it cannot be determined a priori that gender lies outside the scope of systemic analysis (even if the scale of analysis is fixed).

When specific "systemic" approaches are considered, however, it is clear that one which has been influential in archaeology, that associated with the eco-system model defended originally by New Archaeologists, does tend to exclude the analysis of gender. Although earlier versions considered socio-political variables of all sorts crucial to the understanding of cultural systems, the recent formulations due to Binford explicitly rule out any consideration of what he refers to as internal "ethnographic" variables, which would seem, on some construals at least, to include gender.

Unintended consequences: the eco-system paradigm

Binford advances two sets of reasons for rejecting "ethnographic" variables as a proper object of archaeological inquiry. The first is substantive; he believes they have no relevance for an archaeological understanding of cultural systems. And the second is methodological; he holds that any concern with such variables undermines the possibility of realizing the kind of scientific rigor he considers appropriate for archaeological inquiry (Binford 1983, 1986a, 1986b). According to the first line of argument, archaeologists should focus on large-scale structures and long-term "dynamics", not just because these promise a unique understanding of cultural systems, but because, on Binford's view, they determine the form of the internal, micro-variables that comprise the ethnographic lifeworld (e.g. the beliefs and intentions of participants). Ethnographic phenomena are, in effect, dependent variables; "institutions and cultural forms must be thought of as having a life independent of their participants, inasmuch as they are the conditioners of the participants' behaviour" (1983: 221). Any adequate explanation of cultural systems therefore requires an understanding of system-level mechanisms, specifically those that mediate adaptive responses to the material environment. Significantly, recent feminist analyses of gender run directly counter to this thesis about the dependent status of "ethnographic" variables. It is a fundamental tenet of most feminist theorizing that gender (including sex/gender institutions as well as gender identities, gender roles, and gender ideology) is a highly variable *social* construct which incorporates irreducibly symbolic and ideational components; this is the reason why sex/gender systems are so highly variable and why materialist analyses of all kinds have such difficulty comprehending them (Sargent 1981). Understood in these terms, gender is in important respects a paradigm of the historically and contextually sensitive variables repudiated by Binford as "ethnographic".

In addition to rejecting these "soft" variables on theoretical grounds – as irrelevant to explanatory understanding – Binford argues that it is self-defeating to take them as the object of archaeological analysis because they are notoriously difficult to reconstruct with any reliability on the basis of archaeological data. Here a variant of the methodological argument reemerges. He insists that, "we will not grow, nor will we gain a realistic sense of problem, until we adopt a systemic paradigm" (1983: 392); those who argue, contra this "paradigm", for investigation of the symbolic, ideational dimensions of human action, are said to foreclose the possibility of developing a "responsible" scientific archaeology (1986b: 403). They engage a "participant perspective" – an insider's view – which is utterly unattainable for archaeology. Because the archaeologist "is outside history in the participant sense", Binford argues it is crucial to explore the possibility of understanding "from a different perspective – the perspective of the macroforces that condition and modify lifeways in contexts unappreciated by the participants within complex thermodynamic systems" (1986a: 474). To do otherwise is to "posture", to engage in irresponsible "moralizing" rather than serious scientific inquiry.

What is at stake here is the credibility of the objectivist ideal to which Binford subscribes, and with this the locus of resistance to feminist initiatives (among others) shifts from the theoretical to the epistemological realm. The methodological arguments against "ethnographic" concerns are routinely coupled with attacks on any who suggest that, because archaeological understanding is inevitably context-relative, such ideals may be in principle unattainable. Binford insists that if archaeologists just make a commitment to "work responsibly" in evaluating archaeological claims against "the world of experience" – the "external world [that] exists in its own right" (1986b: 403) – they will be in a position to eliminate socio-political biases. He seems to believe, in fact, that non-cognitive considerations (such as might undermine objectivity) only play a role in theory formation and evaluation if researchers allow them to, and suggests two reasons for this weakness of scientific resolve. Sometimes he characterizes his opponents as (mere) theorists who have failed (or refused) to see the power of properly scientific methods of hypothesis evaluation. More often he impugns their stance as deliberately obstructionist and attributes it to a kind of intellectual hubris, a need to believe that human understanding (among other forms of human activity) is distinguished by its autonomy from the constraints of an external, human independent reality; they are preoccupied with notions of "free will" (1986a: 466 and 1986b: 402) which they feel they must vindicate at all costs. Just this sort of "value judgement" (1986b: 400), Binford maintains, can and should be eliminated from contexts of theory evaluation, including, by implication, the feminist theorizing about gender that embodies such an orientation.[3]

There are, then, at least two ways in which the content of dominant archaeological theories can obscure women and gender as subjects: directly, by incorporating assumptions about women and gender that explicitly deny their relevance for understanding the subject domain, and indirectly, by selectively directing attention to certain categories of variable or dimensions of the subject domain (e.g. as causally efficacious) that exclude women or gender on the assumption that they are irrelevant to its understanding. If the research enterprise is also dominated by ideals of objectivity that suggest that its aim must be to establish a single, coherent, and comprehensive ('true') understanding of the subject, it will be insulated against critiques that endorse a plurality of perspectives (e.g. ones that, by contrast with Bindford's late eco-determinist approach, direct attention to constructed or idiosyncratic aspects of the subject domain like gender), or which point reflexively to inherent socio-political (e.g. androcentric) bias in what is otherwise "good science".

In addition, it will be obvious that however detailed an analysis is developed of these two kinds of cognitive factors, the question still remains: *why* has a body of beliefs and practices emerged (and persisted) in archaeology that tends to obscure gender as a subject of inquiry? Although this question may be partly answered by appeal to antecedent intellectual developments, it will inevitably require a consideration of non-cognitive factors: the socio-political and economic conditions under which archaeologists work that are responsible for their acceptance of particular assumptions about sex roles as unquestionable truisms and, more generally, for their predisposition to endorse certain broad modes of practice and theoretical orientations that direct attention away from variables like gender. Despite their profound importance, I am not in a position to elaborate an account of these factors, although I note that important work has begun in the area (e.g. Gero 1983; Kelley and Hanen

1988: 129–36) which offers some clues as to the mechanisms that produce and reproduce the gender structures of the discipline.[4]

In what follows I will, however, consider the course of development of feminist critiques and research in the other fields, filling in some of the details of the three-stage model outlined above as a basis for addressing my second introductory question concerning the prospects for the development of an archaeology of gender.

Androcentric Research: "Bad Science" or "Science as Usual"?

Initial critiques and "remedial" research

Feminist critics typically began with analyses that were designed to expose pervasive patterns of androcentric exclusion and misrepresentation in science; they detailed cases where researchers had ignored women as a subject and gender as a variable, or had illegitimately generalized the attributes of one gender to the society as a whole, treating male activities and experiences as a societal norm in the construction of explanatory theory. A classic example is Gilligan's (1982) critique of Kohlberg's influential model of the development of moral reasoning in children which she found to be based on entirely male samples. Her point of departure was puzzlement about the fact that female children prove systematically slower to develop then males of the same age when measured against the criteria of Kohlberg's stages, and her analysis showed that, by taking male development as a standard, his model simply reads out a range of divergent patterns of development, the "different voice(s)" that became the subject of her own research. Equally blatant bias in domain definition has long been evident in anthropology and in the life sciences. Consider Lévi-Strauss's famous observation: "the entire village left the next day in about 30 canoes, leaving us alone with the women and children in the abandoned houses" (cited by Eichler and Lapointe 1985: 11).

In most cases these critical analyses were not understood, at the outset at least, to pose any serious challenge to the efficacy of scientific method or to the fundamental theoretical assumptions about social and psychological subject matters informing established modes of inquiry; feminist critics saw themselves as having exposed instances of "bad" science. They did not object to scientific method per se, but rather to the fact that it had not been rigorously or widely enough applied, and in this spirit they argued that, for the sake of comprehensiveness and accuracy, the method should be extended to a new dimension of the subject domain – to women, women's spheres of interest and activity, and gender – and, in its critical mode, to those specific presuppositions about the subject domain that had precluded the study of women and gender. With this they initiated "remedial" research which made women and their activities – "women worthies", "women victims", and "women's contributions" (see, for example, Harding 1986) – the primary focus of investigation.

It soon emerged, however, that the process of "adding women" would entail much more profound reassessment of orienting theoretical and epistemological presuppositions than had been anticipated. For one thing, it frequently proved impossible to maintain traditional models of encompassing social systems when women's roles and activities were taken into account. Slocum's (1975) ground-breaking work with "hunter-gatherers" not only transformed our understanding of the groups she studied – far from being confined to a home base, dependent on males for their survival, women gatherers proved to contribute the majority of the dietary intake in such societies and to be at least as mobile and self-sufficient as the men – but it also forced comprehensive reassessment of a whole network of assumptions about the constraints operating on early human populations that figure centrally in theories about human and cultural evolution. Similar examples are to be found in virtually all the social sciences and also, Haraway and others argue, in animal behavior studies where the gender roles of contemporary Western societies are projected onto animal populations, the results then being used to argue that these roles are inevitable – "natural" (Haraway 1978).

In addition to challenging dominant theories in existing fields, "remedial" research also proved limited in its own right. Women worthies and women's contributions were often judged against criteria that had been developed in consideraton of male-associated activities (or, activities that male scholars thought worthy of investigation). The women writers, artists, and political figures who were rediscovered were those whose work approximated that of great men, and the distinctive qualities of their lives and expression as women (indeed, women's contributions that deviated from these androcentric models) were ignored. Intent on documenting common patterns in the victimization of women, feminist researchers frequently overlooked diversity in the experiences of women (due, for example, to class and race differences, and historical, cultural diversity) and, in resisting the erasure of women, they emphasized gender difference, often presuming the existence of a dichotomous opposition between men and women and an association of each with distinct and exclusive spheres of activity (domestic vs. public, productive vs. reproductive). In short, early feminist research tended to incorporate framework assumptions that reproduced or inverted the androcentric assumptions underlying the patently sexist research it was meant to challenge.

These inherent difficulties were quickly recognized. As soon as the first wave of feminist anthropology was published (e.g. Ardener 1975; Rosaldo and Lamphere 1974), critical reviews appeared in which it was argued that, for example, in many contexts "kinship and family" cannot be separated from "politics and economy" nearly as sharply as in our own societies and that even in them, the "dichotomous conceptualization" taken over by Ortner, Rosaldo, and others may not capture the reality of interaction between spheres and between genders (Tilly 1978: 168; see also Schlegel 1974). Critics of Gilligan's remedial work in developmental psychology likewise objected that she "does not transcend the·limitation inherent in the developmental perspective itself' (Auerbach et al. 1985: 151) inasmuch as she takes over the "naturalistic conception of development" central to Kohlberg's scheme and postulates a structurally comparable set of distinct and static stages, each leading inexorably to the next (ibid. 152).[5] The general point made in these critiques is that the early analyses incorporate a "stereotyped characterization of women's roles in terms of the cliché of male dominance" (Leacock 1977: 17); their treatment of women is incomplete – it simply mirrors the incompleteness of androcentric research – and it depends on analytic categories that preserve the very tendency to treat women as a homogeneous "natural" (biologically determined) class typical of androcentric research.[6] Broadening the field of inquiry to consider women without directly challenging this essentialism simply moves the reproduction of sexist theory to a new level; the results were often androcentric (and ethnocentric) theories about women, or about a domain newly recognized to include female subjects.

Many feminist researchers have subsequently reassessed their early work in light of these critiques. For example, Rosaldo (1980) ultimately rejected the assumption, central to her initial studies of gender, that "public" and "domestic" spheres can be sharply distinguished, concluding that gender is not "a unitary fact determined everywhere by the same sorts of concerns but, instead, the complex product of a variety of social forces" which may generate a wide range of different sex/gender structures.[7] More generally, feminist researchers have reoriented their work around the principle that "what had been taken as 'natural' was in fact man-made, both as a social order and as description of that order as natural and physically determined" (Kelly-Gadol 1987: 19, originally 1976); they insist that gender relations and gender must be treated as contextually and historically specific constructs (e.g. Scott 1986: 1074),[8] at the same time as they produce compelling evidence that gender is, in its various forms, a fundamental structuring principle which cannot be ignored or reduced to other (more tractable) factors. The hallmark of these new initiatives is a commitment to "disrupt the notion of fixity" (Scott 1986: 1075). They are informed by a general mistrust of explanations that appeal to fundamental processes, static and unitary origins, or centralized and coherent power structures (1986: 1067), and they focus, by contrast, on the localized strategies by which social categories and structures are constructed. It is these features of feminist theorizing that, as indicated above, directly counter Binford's tendencies to privilege systemic variables and levels of analysis.

Feminist empiricism and standpoint theory

Feminist critiques have proven to be radicalizing not just theoretically, but also epistemologically. Having exposed successive levels of andro-centric bias in the content of extant theories, and even in their own counter-theories, feminist critics began to question the efficacy of scientific method. If science is self-corrective and objective, then the question arises of why androcentric bias persisted, undiscovered, for so long in so many fields and, even more challenging, why it has so often remained to researchers with explicit political (i.e. feminist) commitments to expose this bias. Some began to suspect that perhaps scientific methods are part of the problem, not the solution, to androcentrism; perhaps feminist critiques should be seen as indicting not just instances of "bad science", but science as such, "good science", "science as usual" (see Harding 1986).

In a recent survey of psychologial and human physiological research, Fausto-Sterling (1985) confronts this difficulty directly. She describes case after case in which sex-difference researchers ignored negative results, failed to use appropriate control groups and generalized from inappropriately small samples, misapplied techniques of statistical analysis, manipulated variables to produce essentially tautological results, and sometimes even falsified their data. Most of the popularized claims about sex-differences in intelligence, levels of aggression, cognitive abilities, and so on, prove to be based on seriously flawed (empirically and methodologically discredited) research. Nevertheless, the "paradox" remains that much of this excedingly bad research was done by "intelligent, serious men and women . . . they are good scientists", who frequently built prestigious careers on this work (Fausto-Sterling 1985: 9). Her critique thus calls into question what is, on the face of it, "science as usual".

In the end, however, Fausto-Sterling reverts to what might be described as a "feminist empiricist" position (following Harding 1986). She rejects the option of "denouncing the entire scientific enterprise as corrupt" or inherently androcentric (1985: 9), at least in part because she is concerned to guard against the possibility that feminist research might itself be dismissed as "merely political", or marginalized as an alternative view that has credibility only for feminists if an uncompromising standpoint theory were accepted. Feminist critiques and counter-theories are to be recommended, she insists, as, in the main, the results of good (indeed, better) science, and in this she remains committed to the view that there are context and standpoint-transcendent (objective) standards against which the quality of a science and the credibility of its results can be judged. Her final assessment is that "myths of gender" were produced by otherwise "good" scientists because the dominant ideology about sex differences was so widely accepted that they simply did not see the need for very high standards of proof and were not alert to ways in which their research design and results might be questioned. The scepticism with which feminists regard this ideology demands higher standards and brings an "angle of vision" to bear that allows the discovery of mistakes and possibilities that had been overlooked. Their *standpoint* as feminists determines that they will use the tools of scientific method conscientiously and effectively in investigating the subject domain, judged against the (quasi-empiricist) standards of scientific rationality that they share with the authors of the sexist research they criticize. In this, Fausto-Sterling circumscribes the role of socio-political factors; they may determine when and by whom specific discoveries will be made, but they do not determine the nature of these discoveries or the content of the scientific understanding to which they contribute.

Others who consider such cases embrace more radical "standpoint" theories. Smith (1974, 1979), for example, draws the conclusion that the subject reality is itself a construct, a negotiated product of scientific practice considered as a social process. One's socio-political standpoint determines not just whether you will be in a position to recognize that a crucial variable, like gender, has been overlooked, but also the content of your own understanding of gender. Nevertheless, Smith insists that the deliverances of different standpoints do not have equal claim on us. On her view, the insights of feminists are to be preferred; they have greater breadth and accuracy because, as members of an oppressed and disenfranchised group who recognize their situation, feminists will be painfully aware of institutions and standing conditions (implicit social conventions and power structures) that put them at a disadvantage, while the beneficiaries of this disadvantage typically ignore or deny the existence of any such constraints. While this suggests that, as on Fausto-Sterling's account, socio-political factors simply establish an "angle of vision" that allows some to see more clearly than others, the measures of adequacy being those that are standard for all scientific theories (empirical adequacy and explanatory power), she also sometimes suggests that a feminist standpoint is, in itself, a ground for epistemic privilege. In this she draws on the model of marxist standpoint theory which privileges the science of the proletariat because of the political consciousness it embodies.

Postmodern critiques

Standpoint theories are inherently unstable, in part because they impute to women researchers (as remedial research did to women subjects) a uniformity of perspective – a "standpoint" – that cannot be sustained when the diversity of their circumstances and experiences are examined in any detail (see Harding 1986, chapter 7). Those who take such cricitisms seriously tend to move in either of two directions: towards a renewed commitment to feminist empiricism with its denial that socio-political factors play any very major role in theory evaluation – as in the case of Fausto-Sterling, where scientific criteria of adequacy are presumed to exist that transcend all particular standpoints and allow independent assessment of standpoint specific claims – or, alternatively, in the direction of much more radical, "postmodern", critiques of science which abandon the presumption of epistmic privilege that standpoint theorists and empiricists alike seek to justify. This latter option arises when feminist critics consider the possibility that, given its manifest failure to expose and correct sexist presuppositions, perhaps scientific method is itself androcentric; perhaps extant forms of practice do not merely allow androcentric bias to enter and persist but actually generate this bias.[9] On this basis, postmodern critics challenge all appeals to foundational, transcontextually valid standards, including feminist empiricist appeals to standard canons of scientific rationality. They insist that no knowledge claims, nor any methods or criteria for establishing them, can be formulated independent of any particular (socio-political) standpoints, but they conclude, contra standpoint theory, that women's experiences and perspectives are just one among many standpoints that have been obscured by the "totalizing" theories of the Enlightenment tradition. When diversity is taken seriously, and these deviant standpoints are seen to be deeply divided among themselves as well as from the dominant (white, male, Western) world view, Flax (1986) and sometimes Harding (1986) conclude that any search for a commensurating framework which will encompass and unify all frameworks – the central aim of Enlightenment science – must be abandoned. Such a framework is not only unattainable, on their view, but the quest for it is pernicious; "Only to the extent that one person or group can dominate the whole can 'reality' appear to be governed by one set of rules or constituted by one privileged set of relationships" (Harding 1986: 193, from Flax 1986). The worry about such conclusions, often considered good reason to dismiss them out of hand, is that once they are accepted, there seem to be no grounds (beyond arbitrary personal preference) for choosing among alternative accounts; each is as good as any other, considered in its appropriate context. And, in fact, even feminists who strongly endorse the pluralism of postmodernism resist these relativist implications; they, like Fausto-Sterling, are unwilling to give up the claim that the deliverances of sexist science are false, not just from a feminist standpoint but, in some sense, from any standpoint ("objectively"). One response, advocated by Harding, is "ambivalence". She recommends that we give up the compulsive search for "master theories" and embrace post-modernism as an indispensable source of inspiration concerning possibilities that lie beyond existing modes of inquiry and understanding. Yet, at the same time, she insists that we should not abandon the "successor science" projects of feminist empiricism and standpoint theory; these are indispensable "epistemological tools" in a context where "neither feminist theory nor feminist politics stands in a relationship of reciprocity to patriarchal theories and politics" (Harding 1986: 195). We should just "learn to live with" the inconsistencies and tensions created by the juxtaposition of these divergent approaches. Whether or not this ambivalence is very widely acceptable (I have serious doubts about it in its present formulation; Wylie 1987), it is based on a close reading of the debates generated by feminist critiques of science which makes it clear that we cannot easily dismiss any of the positions represented; even though inconsistency results from any attempt to embrace them all, each does capture an essential feature of our epistemic situation.

The Prospects for an Archaeology of Gender

Counterparts in archaeology

Contentious though the more radical genres of feminist critique may seem, they bear a striking resemblance to non-feminist (post- and anti-positivist) critiques of science that have emerged in recent years, including ones that have had considerable influence on, or have developed independently in, archaeology. For example, contextualist analyses due to Kuhn (1970) and to Hanson (1958), which have played a prominent role in recent archaeological debates (since Hill and Evans 1972 and, e.g., Binford and Sabloff 1982), are a frequent point of departure for feminist critiques of science (e.g. Harding 1987a: 5 and

1987b; Keller 1985: 4–6; Keller 1987; Wylie and Okruhlik 1987). Feminists and non-feminists alike conclude that where theory inevitably overreaches evidence, and evidence is in any case theory-ladened, appeals to "the facts" cannot settle questions of theory choice on their own. The conclusion drawn by feminist critics of science and by critical archaeologists is that the slack is inevitably taken up by socio-political factors that determine the framework assumptions of the scientific community and of individual theorists.

In developing this last point, feminist critics (Harding 1986: 50, 198) have also been influenced by sociologists of science who argue that scientists construct not only scientific theory but also scientific facts through an ongoing (irreducibly social and political) process of negotiation among the various participants in the research (e.g. Latour and Woolgar 1986; Garfinkel 1967). As indicated earlier, Dorothy Smith (also, e.g., Hartsock 1983) adds the insights of marxist and neo-marxist "standpoint" theory, which render this analysis in terms of the class-specific interests and location of researchers. Although archaeologists have been more directly influenced by Critical Theorists like Habermas, and marxist-structuralists like Althusser, than by sociologists of science, there has been an enormous growth of interest in socio-political analysis in recent years which has generated a series of internal case studies strikingly like those undertaken by sociologists of science. They establish that the choice of archaeological problem, the range of models considered in interpreting the record, the methods and standards of adequacy invoked in assessing these models, and the conclusions that get entrenched as received knowledge, are all directly influenced by political, institutional factors (e.g. Gero et al. 1983; Leone 1982; contributions to Pinsky and Wylie, 1989, among many others).

Finally, it is most striking that the epistemic considerations which generate Harding's ambivalence have become pivotal in current debates between those who resist the emerging insights of contextualist critics, chiefly Binford, and those who embrace them, whom he vilifies as obscurantists and socio-political "moralizers" (1986b: 400). Binford, of course, remains a stalwart advocate of "scientific" (objectivist) procedures and standards. The recognition that archaeological data stand as evidence only under interpretation (i.e. it is theory-laden) simply means, on his account, that the requisite interpretive theory must be independently established (Binford and Sabloff 1982). He evidently does not consider that contextualist arguments about theory-ladenness and underdetermination affect theories developed in actualistic contexts, even though it was precisely these contexts that were the subject of Kuhn's original analysis (see Watson 1986: 447). And he rejects any alternatives to his eco-system model of the cultural subject out of hand, reaffirming his conviction that a systematic study of actualistic contexts will produce the "Rosetta stone" linking principles necessary to secure reconstructive hypotheses about all explanatorily relevant aspects of past cultures. It is given this that he insists the arguments of "posturers" pose no serious threat to the ideals of objectivity and empirical proof, or to the ambition of making archaeology a science that embodies these ideals; the systematic confrontation of ideas with "experience" (in actualistic and archaeological contexts) can settle evaluative questions without any intrusion of socio-political factors.

It is a significant irony that nowhere, in these programmatic disputes, does Binford develop an argument supporting his claims about the scope of contextualist arguments, or defend the credibility of the eco-system model of culture on empirical grounds. By contrast, Hodder, among others, *has* advanced a number of compelling empirical reasons for seriously questioning Binford's assumptions about the causal primacy of system-level processes (see Hodder 1982) which, it should now be obvious, closely parallel the arguments used by feminist researchers to show that gender cannot be ignored, and that it is a socio-cultural (symbolic, "normative") construct. In fact, the construction and maintenance of gender ideology, and its tangible expression in material culture, is the focus of many of Hodder's ethnographic analyses. Binford likewise takes no account of the historical and methodological consid-erations that have forced critical archaeologists, along with most historians and philosophers of science, to reconsider the positivist/empiricist self-image of science which he still embraces (e.g. evidence of the multi-stability of empirical perception, and of the historical instability of even the best established scientific theories). His final argument is always programmatic/pragmatic: commitment to a systemic model of culture and to scientific method is a necessary condition for productive archaeological research, where objectivist ideals set the standard against which archaeological success is measured. I find it hard to avoid the conclusion that Binford's own position is at least as much a "paradigmatic posture" as those he opposes; in the end he is unable to defend his commitment to objectivism on any but ideological and pragmatic grounds.

The interesting question is, then, why Binford should ignore the inconsistencies in his arguments, and prove so intransigent in foreclosing discussions that raise questions about framework assumptions which, by his own objectivist principles, he should be prepared to address.[10] There is no doubt that the "post-processual" counter-arguments he resists yield some uncomfortable conclusions about the scope and security of archaeological inquiry. If the "inside", ideational dimensions of cultural systems are crucial (i.e. causally efficacious in shaping the system as a whole) and are not related in any determinate way to the sorts of material preserved in the archaeological record (or to reconstructable, material conditions of life), then archaeological understanding of past cultural systems may be irrevocably limited in some areas. And if linking principals are as underdetermined by the evidence that supports them as archaeological interpretation itself, there may be very few "anchors" capable of establishing reconstructive hypotheses with the security Binford demands. Perhaps Binford's motivation in resisting these arguments is rather like that which leads Harding to endorse ambivalence and, in this spirit, to insist that we cannot afford to give "successor science" projects (the analog to Binford's research program) despite the implausibility of their foundationalism. In more positive terms, Binford seems concerned not to lose sight of the extent to which, despite underdetermination and interpretative instability, "experience" does impose quite sharp constraints on what we can claim about past or present conditions. As feminists often point out, *contra* radical relativism and much postmodernism, it is as much a part of our daily and scientific experience that we can encounter evidence we did not expect, evidence that forces revision of even our most secure assumptions, as that we find the evidence malleable.[11]

The difference between Binford and Harding is that Binford does not acknowledge his own dependence on a non-cognitive justification for his program which directly counters his insistence that such justifications are unnecessary "moralizing". The danger in this of particular relevance here is that, in denying the viability of any alternative to the analysis of "macroforces" operating on cultural systems (with the attendant emphasis on scientific testing procedures), Binford rules out consideration of precisely the "ethnographic", meaning-constituted, history and context-specific "insides" of cultural systems that an archaeology of gender would take as its central object of analysis.

My suspicion is that if the current debate were not so profoundly rhetorical on both sides – if it were possible to consider more systematically what the aims of archaeological research are and what they require – it would become clear that Binford need not feel so compelled to choose (or to force a choice) between dichotomous options. No doubt macroscale analysis of cultural systems – their broad evolutionary and adaptive patterns – will yield important explanatory insights that an "ethnographic" perspective could never provide. Nevertheless, I suspect that there will always come a point where it must be acknowledged that much interesting and explanatorily relevant detail is lost to such an approach; internal variables, some of which are "ethnographic", will be found to play a role in shaping system dynamics that cannot be accounted for in the functional, adaptive terms Binford requires. And even when system-level models do prove to be explanatorily self-sufficient, there will always be a great deal to be learned by filling in such detail, the value or import of which cannot be determined in advance. The research on gender in innumerable fields attests to this.

Most important, it would seem to be an empirical question, not a question that can be settled in advance by pragmatic arguments, what success can be expected of the divergent research programs envisioned by Binford and by his contextualist critics. The fact that the latter may well engage methodologies and epistemic standards which are non-standard in scientific contexts[12] while the former are self-consciously scientific, seems no reason to insist on exclusive loyalty in either direction. We do know that each approach is inherently limited, therefore, the sensible strategy would be to encourage a diversity of options.[13] Harding's deliberate amibivalence begins to seem quite attractive when considered in face of the sharply adversarial conflict that presently divides archaeology, particularly given that an archaeology of gender will inevitably engage the issues central to the debate. I conclude that some degree of tolerance of methodological and theoretical pluralism will be essential if an archaeology of gender is to get off the ground, and that this need not entail an abandonment of the commit-ment to methodological or theoretical rigor in inquiry.

Prospects

I take the prospects for development of an archaeology of gender to be very good in the early 1990s for two reasons. In the first place, archaeologists now have 20 years of experience with gender analysis in closely aligned fields – 20 years of theoretical and methodological development – on which to draw. Even though this work lacks archaeological reference points, it has significantly refined "gender" as an analytic category and it does delineate the questions that are appropriate to ask in relation to it; it sets a clear agenda for work in the area. For one thing, aligned critiques of androcentrism should alert archaeologists to the sorts of preconceptions about women and gender implicit in established models that may be a source of both direct and indirect androcentric bias. For another, the comprehensive reassessment of accepted socio-cultural theories forced by the new research raises a number of specific questions that only archaeology can begin to answer: questions about the long term evolution and diversity of sex/gender systems. In taking up the first, critical task, archaeologists will be entering a counterpart to the first stage of gender research, and in addressing these latter questions they move into a constructive (second and third) stage of inquiry in which they have the potential of making very significant contributions both to archaeology and to the new gender-sensitive theoretical initiatives currently transforming the social sciences.

Inasmuch as the existing research on gender has established that it is a socio-cultural construct whose structure and evolution cannot be presumed to follow a predetermined, "natural" pattern, archaeological inquiry will have to focus on the particularities of gender constructs, especially their symbolic and ideational dimensions, in specific contexts. The agenda of an archaeology of gender thus converges on at least some of the initiatives associated with critical archaeology and with symbolic and structural approaches in archaeology. Given this, the second reason why gender research has a good chance of getting off the ground in archaeology now is because debates internal to archaeology, conceived quite independently of any concern with gender, are beginning to loosen the grip of the sorts of methodological and theoretical commitments that mitigate against taking gender seriously. It is most important, at this juncture, that we move beyond the rhetorical, confrontational terms of the present debate and determine independently, with reference to established traditions of gender research in other contexts, what elements of these arguments are plausible, and what their implications are for gender research within archaeology.

NOTES

1   This point is made in some detail by other contributions to the present volume (see, in particular, Watson and Kennedy). An example which drew independent critique on ethnographic grounds is the assumption, central to the original Hill/Longacre studies of pueblo social structure, that ceramic production was due to women in the proto- and prehistoric Southwest; Conkey and Spector consider this example, among others (1984: 12). Critics quickly pointed out that the association of ceramic production with women is by no means a universal pattern. Such assumptions are so pervasive they are the norm, rather than the exception.

2   I am indebted to Elizabeth Brumfiel and to ongoing discussion with participants in the conference, "Women and Production in Prehistory", for clarifying this point.

3   For an articulation of feminist intuitions that move in exactly the opposite direction, see Longino's recent critique of determinism in biological theory (1987: 59).

4   A priority of any archaeology of gender must be to come to grips with gender reflexively, as one socio-political factor among others that shapes not just the opportunities of individuals but, through this, the selection of problem areas, test hypotheses, and categories of analysis, the design of

research strategies and, ultimately, the content of those knowledge claims that come to be accepted as plausible or credible within the discipline.

5   Auerbach et al. argue more specifically in this treatment that Gilligan tends to "idealize the moral development of women" ignoring, in particular, the circumstances of "class, race, and religion" which are crucial in shaping transitions between stages (1985: 157). This tendency to idealize female-associated characteristics that have been denigrated or ignored, and to generalize them to women as a class (what Auerbach et al. identify as a tendency to essentialism), is especially an issue for "remedial" studies of the victimization of women. In a reflective criticism of her own work with female holocaust survivors, Joan Ringelheim (1985) asks whether, in seeking evidence of greater resilience and resourcefulness among women in prison camps, she might not have obscured, or at least minimized, some persistently dysfunctional aspects of their gender-associated social relations and attitudes.

6   See also Soble's (1983) summary of this difficulty and Rowbotham's more popular discussion (1979). Soble characterizes the limitations of early research on women as a "reifying mistake" (1983: 299). The first step in correcting the sexism of social science was to counter the lack of attention that had been paid to women as subjects; the approach was to "treat women as a sociological group and systematically study the properties of women as women, as members of this class" (1983: 299). But, he continues, "this trend has had the effect of overemphasizing the properties of women as women"; it perpetuates an "enforced homogenization": "To overcome the invisibility of women, women were studied. But studying women as a group has produced an understanding of women which ignores the influence of race, class, politics, geography, religion, etc." (1983: 299).
On Rowbotham's account, the starting point for "an emerging feminist anthropology" was an interest in the question why "the world has always belonged to the men", and why men's activities are so widely valued above women's. This translated into analyses which sought to delineate the forms that male dominance take cross-culturally. "But these anthropological approaches contain a certain political awkwardness. Feminists who rejected women's biological inferiority were elaborately documenting apparently universal social secondariness to men" (Rowbotham 1979: 11). This involves not only political awkwardness but also straightforward incoherence inasmuch as feminist researchers were, at the same time, producing good empirical and theoretical reasons – judged against the standards embraced by those whose androcentric research they criticize – for rejecting naturalistic assumptions about women's status (see Fausto-Sterling 1985).

7   She also argues in this context that the ideological, symbolic dimension of gender is of primary importance: "women's place in human social life is not in any direct sense a product of the things she does (or even less a function of what, biologically, she is) but of the meaning her activities acquire through concrete social interactions" (Rosaldo 1980: 400). This is a theme that emerges in historical contexts as well. For example, Scott (1986) argues that any understanding of gender must focus on the *meaning* of women's

roles and activities, as the hallmark of genuinely historical inquiry and in resistance to falsely universality (causal) approaches. It diverges sharply from the analyses given by feminist researchers who seek a material basis of women's oppression, for example, Rubin's (1975) and Hartman's (1981) analyses of the material dimension of reproductive and domestic labor.

8 Kelly-Gadol, for example, focuses on the implications of taking gender seriously as an analytic category for historical periodizations (1987: 16–17, originally 1976); they will have to be reassessed in terms of divergent gender standpoints. She suggests, in this connection, that a profound reorientation will follow from seeing women and family structures as "a productive and social force". Slocum likewise argues that a parallel reorientation in anthropology would result if cultural development were approached in terms of inventions relating to reproductive and domestic labor (as described by Rowbotham 1979: 11). I take it that Spector's proposals for a task-differentiation framework of analysis in ethnoarchaeology represents one strategy for affecting such a reorientation (Spector 1983).

9 This sort of argument is developed when feminist critics point to ways in which specific research methods – chiefly quantitative methods – reinforce the tendency to ignore dimensions of experience relevant for understanding the role of gender and the status of women. See for example Armstrong and Armstrong (1987).

10 As a key proponent of the New Archaeology, Binford was after all a strong champion of reflexive criticism. Certainly he insisted that just such questions be addressed when they arose in connection with traditional research, and he has recently reaffirmed the value of exploring alternatives to entrenched forms of practice (Binford and Sabloff 1982: 152–3).

11 I note that, in fact, the primary exponents of the "posture" Binford opposes are similarly ambivalent about these conclusions, despite systematically endorsing critical arguments which would seem to entail them as unavoidable consequences. For example, Hodder insists that "although the evidence does not exist with any objectivity, it does nevertheless exist in the real world – it is tangible and it is there, like it or not", moreover, "whatever our perceptions or world view, we are constrained by the evidence, and brought up against its concreteness" (1986: 95).

12 For example, they may favor various models of textual analysis which produce very different sorts of understanding and presuppose criteria of adequacy quite distinct from those of standard scientific practice.

13 The same might be said of the methodological implications of (or rationale for) focusing on macro-processes and structures. It may well prove that in some cases, so-called "ethnographic" variables are more reliably accessible than systemic variables. It may be generally the case that, given the technology and background knowledge presently available, archaeologists can expect greater success and security of results focusing on the latter, but this surely should not be taken as a measure of all future possibility. Indeed, Binford's own abhorrence of "traditional" stances which assumed research to be inherently limited in particular areas counsels caution about any a priori pronouncement on questions about accessibility.

REFERENCES

Ardener, Shirley, ed. (1975). *Perceiving Women*. London: J. M. Dent.
Armstrong, Pat and Hugh Armstrong (1987). "Beyond Numbers: Problems with Quantitative Data." In *Women and Men: Interdisciplinary Readings on Gender*, Greta Hofmann Nemiroff, ed. Montreal: Fitzhenry & Whiteside, 54–79.
Auerbach, Judy, Linda Blum, Vicki Smith, and Christine Williams (1985). "On Gilligan's *In a Different Voice*." *Feminist Studies* 11: 149–61.
Binford, Lewis R. (1983). *Working at Archaeology*. New York: Academic Press.
—— (1986a). "In Pursuit of the Future." In *American Archaeology Past and Future*, David J. Meltzer, Don D. Fowler, and Jeremy A. Sabloff, eds. Washington: Smithsonian Institution Press, 459–79.
—— (1986b). "Data, Relativism and Archaeological Science." *Man* 22: 391–404.
Binford, Lewis R. and Jeremy A. Sabloff (1982). "Paradigms, Systematics, and Archaeology." *Journal of Anthropological Research* 38: 137–53.
Conkey, Margaret W. and Janet D. Spector (1984). "Archaeology and the Study of Gender." In *Advances in Archaeological Method and Theory*, vol. 7, Michael B. Schiffer, ed. New York: Academic Press, 1–38.
Eichler, Margrit and Jeanne Lapointe (1985). *On the Treatment of the Sexes in Research*. Ottawa: Social Sciences and Humanities Research Council of Canada.
Fausto-Sterling, Anne (1985). *Myths of Gender: Biological Theories About Women and Men*. New York: Basic Books.
Flax, Jane (1986). "Gender as a Social Problem: In and for Feminist Theory." *American Studies/Amerika Studien* (as cited by Harding, 1986: 264).
Garfinkel, H. (1967). *Studies in Ethnomethodology*. New Jersey: Prentice-Hall.
Gero, Joan M. (1983). "Gender Bias in Archaeology: A Cross-Cultural Perspective." In *The Socio-Politics of Archaeology*, Joan M. Gero, David M. Lacy, and Michael L. Blakey, eds. Amherst: University of Massachusetts, Department of Anthropology, Research Report No. 23, 51–7.
Gero, Joan M., David M. Lacy, and Michael L. Blakey, eds (1983) *The Socio-politics of Archaeology*. Amherst: University of Massachusetts, Department of Anthropology, Research Report No. 23.
Gilligan, Carol (1982). *In a Different Voice: Psychological Theory and Women's Development*. Cambridge, MA: Harvard University Press.
Hanson, Norwood Russell (1958). *Patterns of Discovery*. Cambridge: Cambridge University Press.
Haraway, Donna (1978). "Animal Sociology and a Natural Economy of the Body Politic, Part I: A Political Physiology of Dominance, and Part II: The Past is the Contested Zone." *Signs* 4: 21–60.
Harding, Sandra (1983). "Why has the Sex/Gender System Become Visible Only Now?" In *Discovering Reality: Feminist Perspectives on Epistemology, Metaphysics, Methodology, and Philosophy of Science*, Sandra Harding and Merrill B. Hintikka, eds. Boston: Reidel, 311–24.

—— (1986) *The Science Question in Feminism*. Ithaca, New York: Cornell University Press.

—— (1987a). "Introduction: Is there a Feminist Method?" In *Feminism and Methodology: Social Science Issues*, Sandra Harding, ed. Bloomington: Indiana University Press, 1–14.

—— (1987b). "The Method Question." *Hypatia* 2: 19–36.

Hartmann, Heidi (1981). "The Family as the Locus of Gender, Class, and Political Struggle: The Example of Housework." *Signs* 6(3): 366–94.

Hartsock, Nancy C. M. (1983). "The Feminist Standpoint: Developing the Ground for a Specifically Feminist Historical Materialism." In *Discovering Reality: Feminist Perspectives on Epistemology, Metaphysics, Methodology, and Philosophy of Science*, Sandra Harding and Merrill B. Hintikka, eds. Dordrecht, Holland: Reidel, 283–310.

Hill, James and R. K. Evans (1972). "A Model for Classification and Typology." in *Models in Archaeology*, David L. Clarke, ed. London: Methuen, 231–72.

Hodder, Ian (1982). *Symbols in Action*. Cambridge: Cambridge University Press.

—— (1986). *Reading the Past: Current Approaches to Interpretation in Archaeology*. Cambridge: Cambridge University Press.

Keller, Evelyn Fox (1985). *Reflections on Gender and Science*. New Haven: Yale University Press.

—— (1987). "The Gender/Science System: or Is Sex to Gender as Nature is to Science?" *Hypatia* 2: 37–51.

Kelley, Jane and Marsha P. Hanen (1988). *Archaeology and the Methodology of Science*. Albuquerque: University of New Mexico Press.

Kelly-Gadol, Joan (1987). "The Social Relations of The Sexes: Methodological Implications of Women's History." In *Feminism and Methodology: Social Science Issues*, Sandra Harding, ed. Bloomington: Indiana University Press, 14–28. (Originally published in 1976.)

Kuhn, Thomas S. (1970). *The Structure of Scientific Revolutions*. Chicago: Chicago University Press, 2nd edn.

Latour, Bruno and Steve Woolgar (1986). *Laboratory Life: The Construction of Scientific Facts*. Princeton: Princeton University Press, 2nd edn.

Leacock, Eleanor B. (1977). "Women in Egalitarian Societies." In *Becoming Visible. Women in European History*, Renate Bridenthal and Claudia Koontz, eds. Boston: Houghton Mifflin, 11–35.

Leone, Mark P. (1982). "Some Opinions about Recovering Mind." *American Antiquity* 47(4): 742–60.

Longino, Helen E. (1987). "Can There Be a Feminist Science?" *Hypatia* 2: 51–65.

Pinsky, Valerie and Alison Wylie, eds (1989). *Critical Traditions in Archaeology: Essays in the Philosophy, History, and Socio-politics of Archaeology*. Cambridge: Cambridge University Press.

Ringelheim, Joan (1985). "A Reconsideration of Research." *Signs* 10: 741–91.

Rosaldo, Michelle Z. (1980). "The Use and Abuse of Anthropology: Reflections on Feminism and Cross-Cultural Understanding." *Signs* 5(3): 389–417.

Rosaldo, Michelle Z. and Louise Lamphere, eds (1974). *Women, Culture and Society*. Stanford: Stanford University Press.

Rowbotham, Sheila (1976). "When Adam Delved and Eve Span . . ." *New Society* 47: 10–12.

Rubin, Gayle (1975). "The Traffic in Women: Notes on the 'Political Economy' of Sex." In *Toward an Anthropology of Women*, Rayna Reiter, ed. New York: Monthly Review Press, 157–210.

Sargent, Lydia, ed. (1981). *Women and Revolution: A Discussion of the Unhappy Marriage of Marxism and Feminism*. Boston: South End Press.

Schlegel, Alice (1974). "Women Anthropologists Look at Women." *Reviews in Anthropology* (November): 553–9.

Scott, Joan W. (1986). "Gender: A Useful Category of Historical Analysis." *American Historical Review* 91(5): 1053–1075.

Slocum, Sally (1975). "Woman the Gatherer: Male Bias in Anthropology." In *Toward an Anthropology of Women*, Rayna Reiter, ed. New York: Monthly Review Press, 36–50. (Originally presented at 1970 AAA meetings, San Diego.)

Smith, Dorothy E. (1974). "The Social Construction of Documentary Reality." *Sociological Reality* 44: 258–67.

—— (1979). "A Sociology for Women." In *The Prism of Sex: Essays in the Sociology of Knowledge*, J. Sherman and E. T. Beck, eds. Madison: University of Wisconsin Press, 135–82.

Soble, Alan (1983). "Feminist Epistemology and Women Scientists." *Metaphilosophy* 14(3–4): 291–307.

Spector, Janet (1983). "Male/Female Task Differentiation Among the Hidatza: Toward the Development of an Archaeological Approach to the Study of Gender." In *The Hidden Half: Studies of Native Plains Women*, Patricia Albers and Beatrice Medicine, eds. Washington: University Press of America, 77–100.

Strathern, Marilyn (1987). "An Awkward Relationship: The Case of Feminism and Anthropology." *Signs* 12(2): 276–92.

Tilly, Louise (1978). "The Social and the Study of Women: A Review Article." *Comparative Studies in Society and History* 20: 163–73.

Watson, Patty Jo (1986). "Archaeological Interpretation, 1985." In *American Archaeology Past and Future*, Don D. Fowler and Jeremy A. Sabloff, eds. Washington: Smithsonian Institution Press, 439–58.

Wylie, Alison (1987). "The Philosophy of Ambivalence: Sandra Harding on *The Science Question in Feminism*." *Canadian Journal of Philosophy*, supplementary volume 13, 59–73.

Wylie, Alison and Kathleen Okruhlik (1987). "Philosophical Feminism: Challenges to Science." *Resources for Feminist Research* 16(3): 12–16.

Part II

Space and Gender Relations

3

Contexts of Action, Contexts for Power: Material Culture and Gender in the Magdalenian

Margaret W. Conkey

We are learning that the writing of women into (pre)history necessarily involves redefining and enlarging traditional notions of (pre)historical significance, to encompass personal subjective experience, as well as public and political activities. It is not too much to suggest that however hesitant the actual beginnings, such a methodology implies not only a new (pre)history of women, but also a new (pre)history.
Paraphrased from Gordon, Buhle, and Dye "The Problem of Women's History" (1976), as cited by Scott (1986: 1054)

Introduction

This chapter is about the conceptual reorientations that will be necessary if we are to engender the archaeology of the European Upper Paleolithic. The purpose is not to "reveal" Magdalenian women (or men); rather, it is to propose a model for those *contexts* of Magdalenian life where gender roles and engendered meanings are most likely to have been "at work". I will primarily try to show *why* these may be relevant contexts for an archaeology of gender relations in the Magdalenian, and then how – procedurally – this kind of an approach might be carried out, given certain analytical concepts and categories of data.

In a first attempt at this topic, I engaged in a great deal of theoretical preambling both about our assumptions about gender and about how we have conceptualized the European Upper Paleolithic (encompassing the Magdalenian), and I thought that this was merely an excuse to avoid coming to grips with what I was increasingly unable to do: "find" – with a certain fixity – women in Magdalenian archaeological sites. But I also

57

realized that they were not too much harder to "find" – with fixity – than men. The real problem, it seemed to me, was that there are very few people, especially as active agents, in most Paleolithic discussions. Our conceptualizations so far of the (Ice Age) times, of the "adaptations", and of their evolutionary positioning, and our consequent archaeologies have muted the possibilities for an archaeology of Magdalenian social lives, including gender.

As archaeologists we usually take archaeological evidence to be *a record of* social life, of social institutions (e.g. of band society). Usually we explain the nature of the contemporary archaeological record by reference to such social phenomena. For example, some of my past work has been an attempt to explain certain features of the Magdalenian archaeological record, e.g. diversity in assemblages of engraved bones (Conkey 1980, 1989), by reference to such social phenomena as hunter-gatherer aggregations. But here I will instead advocate using archaeological evidence not as a record of some given predetermined social form but to elucidate strategies of social action, of social formation, of social production and reproduction. And it will be, I suggest, in those contexts of action and contexts for power that gender relations (role conflicts, statuses), *as historical forces*, can not only be inferred but also shown to be part of the processes by which the social categories and structures – the ones we usually take as given – are, in fact, constructed.

Magdalenian Hunter-gatherers and Possibilities for Engendered Contexts

As a brief summary of background information, we can make the following empirical generalizations about Magdalenian hunter-gatherers, based primarily on archaeological data and interpretation from south-western France and northwestern Spain. "The Magdalenian" is the most recent of a series of named industries of the "classic" Upper Paleolithic sequence of southwestern Europe, being defined primarily on the basis of materials from sites in southwestern France. "The Magdalenian" is a chrono-cultural classification, a "period" (ca.17,000–10,000 years ago), and a grand finale to a Eurocentric Stone Age/Ice Age. There are Magdalenian manifestations in Belgium, Germany, Switzerland, Moravia, Italy, Spain, and centered on France.

Although at least 6 subdivisions of the Magdalenian have long been recognized (Breuil 1912), the integrity and applicability (especially to occurrences outside of the Périgord of France) of these six stages are questionable. The peoples who made the distinctive assemblages of stone tools (raclettes, burins), and especially the distinctive bone and antler materials that define the Magdalenian, appear to have been successful hunters who are most well known to us for their taking of reindeer. Certainly many other resources have been found in the archaeological remains, such as bovids, other cervids, and ibex. There is also evidence for salmon and for taking other marine resources, ranging from shellfish to a few seals. There appears to be some variety in the kinds of sites they created although most of what we know is disproportionately based on cave and rockshelter excavations. (The open-air sites of the Isle valley (Gaussen 1980) and especially of the Paris Basin (e.g. Audouze 1987, Leroi-Gourhan and Brezillon 1983; Pigeot 1987) are notable exceptions.) Good cases have been made (e.g. White 1985) that some Magdalenians selected strategically significant locales, such as at river fords or other "passages obligés", where animals must cross and where spawning fish would be readily accessible.

Above all, the Magdalenian period appears to have yielded a wealth of material objects; this is the time to which most cave wall-painting is attributed, and the engraving and "decorative" carving of bone and antler has left thousands of items (most of them fragmented or broken) in archaeological deposits. There are awls, spearpoints, harpoons, needles, chisels, compound tools to be hafted, engraved ribs, carved "sceptres", spear-throwers, perforated pieces of all sizes and shapes, and discs (figure 3.1 a–d). There are also thousands of plaquettes of stone, many with multitudinous and fine line engravings, but these seem to derive from only several sites (e.g. La Marche, Limeuil, Enlène) that have yielded *hundreds* of plaquettes per site.

Magdalenian burials – a primary archaeological source of potential attribution of sex – are few and generally without "grave goods". But in the "art" of the Magdalenian there is a range of depictions that have been considered to be human: from a few female statuettes (most of the more famous, i.e. "Venus", ones are attributable to earlier periods, cf. Delporte (1979) or Gamble (1982)) to the many "caricatures" engraved on plaquettes from La Marche, to the supposed schematic female outlines on some cave walls (Lalinde) or blocs (Gönnersdorf) (figure 3.2 a–d). None of the cave wall art explicitly illustrates humans in activities of any sort (save the famous man-with-disembowelled-bison and bird-on-stick from the "Well" at Lascaux, for which there are as many interpretations as there are interpreters). Thus, we have almost no direct linkages between humans (either skeletal or in "art") and activities, tools, or obvious symbolic referrents.

These are peoples who smoked meat (fish?), developed complex processing techniques for pigments, moved shells from both the Atlantic and Mediterranean all around the southwest of Europe, who could at least make three-strand rope, and certainly developed quite a sewing

Figure 3.1 Four of the dozens of engraved and/or sculpted bone/antler artifacts from the site of La Vache (Ariège), France. All were excavated from the "Salle Monique" area of the cave, and are attributed to the "second period of the Pyrenean Magdalenian" (Simmonet 1987). All are curated at the Musée des Antiquités National (M.A.N.), St-Germain-en-Laye, France.

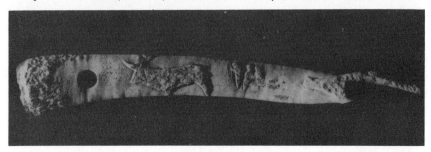

3.1a Deer antler, 30.7 cm long, engraved in typical "champlevé" style with what has been interpreted to be the "hunt of an aurochs" (wild cow). Note the three anthropomorphic forms, presumably with spears held by one, to the right of the aurochs figure. (Photo by M. Assemat (M.A.N. 83.364).)

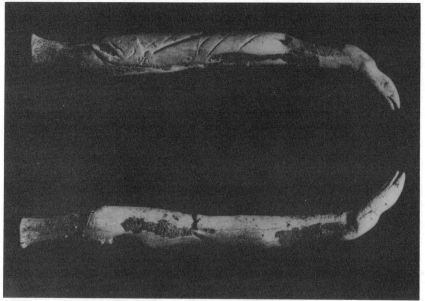

3.1b The so-called "sceptre" made on reindeer antler bearing five different images done by the "champlevé" (raised) technique: a salmonid, a cervid, a horse, a feline, and a bird. One structuralist reading of this would attribute the images to (our) different classifactory domains: water (salmonid), land (both herbivores: horse and cervid, and carnivore: felid), and air (bird). (Photo by M. Assemat (M.A.N. 83.346).)

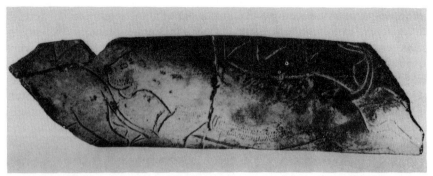

3.1c Three felines (presumably cave lions) in a row, engraved on a now fragmented bone (rib) that is 13 cm long in its current refitted state. The fine engraving and the detailed treatment of the lions' coat are exceptionally done. (Photo by M. Assemat (M.A.N. 38.347).)

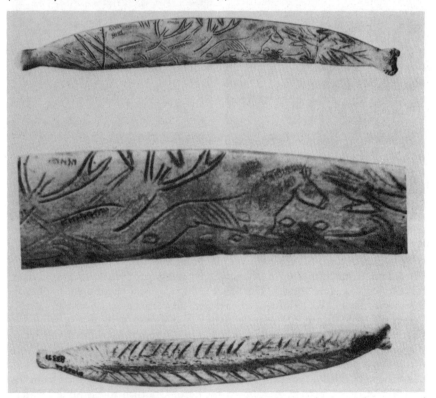

3.1d A bone, 16.3 cm, called the "pendant with the leaping horse". The engraved horse is considered simple in depiction but realistically in a jumping position, surrounded by schematic imagery of antler racks and geometrics. (Photo by M. Assemat (M.A.N. 83.351).)

technology, as evidenced by the hundreds of bone eyed-needles found distinctively in Magdalenian sites. People processed hides, set up stone pavements as surfaces on which to camp, made lamps to light the way into caves, and even intentionally broke some material objects. Caches of long lithic blades have been found, and somehow people circulated lithic raw materials throughout certain regions. Stylistic similarities in art and in other material culture have been cited, suggesting long-distance interactions of some sort (though not necessarily direct contacts) (figure 3.3).

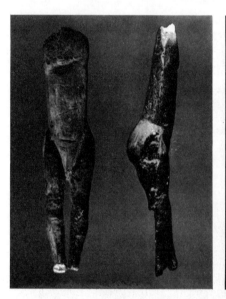 

Figure 3.2 A variety of images said to be of females and attributed to the Magdalenian period. All are from sites in France.
3.2a A female statuette, 7.6 cm tall, carved from mammoth tusk, excavated from the site of Laugerie Basse (Dordogne), France, and attributed to Leroi-Gourhan's Style IV, although its precise provenance is uncertain. Leroi-Gourhan (1965: figure 53) reports that it was found with works from the Magdalenian III, IV, and V, and in lacking a head appears related to a number of Magdalenian figures (statuettes, engravings, and low reliefs). (Photo by Jean Vertut (with permission) from Leroi-Gourhan (1965: 428).)
3.2b Schematic figure, "probably woman", incised on a limestone bloc from the Abri Murat (Lot), France. Attributed by Leroi-Gourhan to his Style IV (late Upper Paleolithic, i.e. Magdalenian), this would be grouped by many analysts with other imagery taken to be side-profile incised schematic images of females, such as at Lalinde, Gönnersdorf, or Les Combarelles (see figure 3.2d). (Photo by Jean Vertut (with permission) from Leroi-Gourhan (1965: 428).)

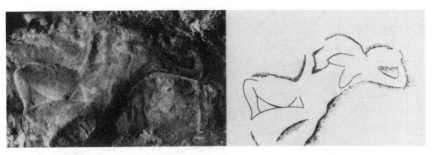

3.2c So-called "reclining woman" in relief on the wall (left side of site) at Le Magdeleine (Tarn), France, which is a small cave with four still decipherable low-relief figures: two females and two animals (a horse and a bison). All are considered to be of the same date, with the horse and bison as "typically Magdalenian in style" (Sieveking 1979: 90). This particular female relief is probably more than 50 cm long, and, although done on the wall of a cave, all the relief figures are only about six meters from the present entrance and thus are lit by daylight. The comment on these two female figures made by the priest and Paleolithic art specialist, Abbé Henri Breuil, says much about the projection of contemporary views on female-as-object onto Paleolithic "men": these images were engraved there "to give Paleolithic man pleasure during his meals" (Breuil 1954, cited by Ucko and Rosenfeld 1967: 119). (Photo by Jean Vertut (with permission) and drawing from Leroi-Gourhan (1965: 438).)

3.2d So-called "female figures in profile" from the engraved cave art site of Les Combarelles (Dordogne), France. (Photo by Jean Vertut (with permission) and drawing from Leroi-Gourhan (1965: 440).)

The known sites occupied by Magdalenians are clearly not representative, since they have been explored since the mid to late 1800s; survey, whether systematic or not, is not part of most regional archaeology (Conkey 1987). But there are some sites that seem particularly "rich" in archaeological materials; other sites do seem to have been locales of limited occupation in either time and/or function. The seasonal nature of

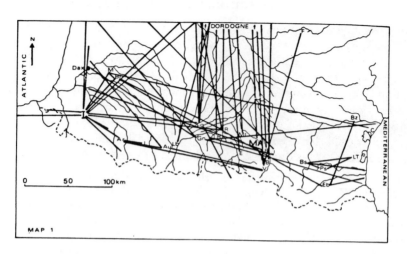

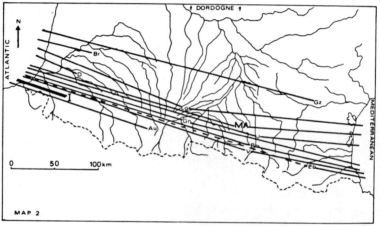

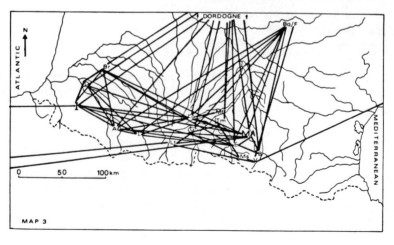

most occupations (there is little, if any, evidence for year-round occupations), the rather striking existence of "super-sites" (Bahn 1982), and the suggestive ethnographic accounts from both Eskimos (Mauss and Beuchat 1904) and the !Kung San (e.g. Lee 1980) have promoted the notion that a plausible subsistence/settlement pattern for the Magdalenian would be one involving seasonal aggregations of otherwise dispersed hunter-gatherers. As we have usually told the story, Magdalenian peoples would have come together to take advantage of seasonally-clustered or dense resources and (presumably) to carry out (unspecified) social/cultural activities as well.

If we are interested in not just "peopling" this Magdalenian period but in pursuing an approach that takes gender as an analytical concept, how would we "do" an archaeology of gender for the materials and locales we have gathered together under the label "Magdalenian"? If we take gender relations (conflicts, statuses, roles, etc.) as historical forces (see chapter 1), then we might turn our attention to those forces and those histories. One question might be: *what are the specific historical conditions under which gender "categories" are brought into being?*

Thus, one pathway into the archaeology of gender could be through understanding certain *contexts* – certain kinds of sites or of living situations – in terms of the social formations that "produced" the contexts. These may be some of the specific historical conditions under which gender concepts and relations were brought into play in prehistoric lives. We could, therefore, and for a variety of possible reasons, first look at Magdalenian sites that *may* have been locales where larger than usual numbers of people came together.

In the archaeological literature on hunter-gatherers – where "types" of sites are so important – these are often referred to as "aggregation" sites. Although this is one of the few – if not the only – "types" of hunter-gatherer sites that has a label suggesting social (rather than techno-environmental, as in hunting stand, lithic workshop, kill site) activities, most aggregation sites are usually accounted for primarily in ecological terms (resource abundance; locational criteria).

But there are many problems with this as a "type" and even more so with our abilities to identify aggregation sites, archaeologically, with

Figure 3.3 Maps showing, at a very gross scale, the extent and direction of "connections" or inter-regional links among Magdalenian sites, as viewed from the Pyrenees. Map 1 shows the links between sites as evidenced by lithic materials and fossils; Map 2 shows the distribution of shells from the Atlantic and from the Mediterranean to varying sites; Map 3 shows the links between sites as indicated by what have been judged to be similarities in "art" styles and forms. (Maps from Bahn (1982), by kind permission.)

security, especially for the Upper Paleolithic (cf. Conkey 1980, including *CA* comments; also Conkey forthcoming). These serious methodological problems do not, however, negate the position being taken here that on the one hand, there *do* exist sites and archaeological records for which we have to invoke something like a larger than usual grouping. And, on the other hand, these are contexts within which gender roles and relations certainly were brought into play and can furthermore be potentially inferred. In the next two sections of this chapter, I will first explore why the archaeological materials from some of the so-called aggregation sites have the most potential to elucidate historical forces of gender relations; and second, I will discuss how we might use conceptual connections and archaeological materials to bring gender-related strategies of social action into our Paleovisions.

Contexts of Action, Contexts for Power

There are at least three contexts of action that can be related to these so-called aggregation sites; contexts and actions that are obscured by the usual homogenizing and functional terms given to such sites, such as "base camp". These three contexts are not mutually exclusive domains, and each one allows a different perspective or "frame" onto the production of gender relations. We can think of these frames in terms of the phrases "beyond-the-households", "sequential hierarchies", and "being connected" that I will discuss below. Each one suggests varying social interactions and social orders in which partitionings of people would have come into play, partitionings that almost certainly would have sorted out along the axes of sex, age, and gender.

Based on local archaeological data, we can propose a *model for* (not a "model of") some southwest European Magdalenian locales to have been places where either synchronically and/or diachronically, many activities went on and/or are represented, where large group sizes could have been accommodated (due to topography and terrain), and that tend to have a (composite) archaeological record that is both *different* from that of other sites in a region and is often (in some general ways) *similar* to that of other such locales (e.g. abundant and diverse material culture; differentially rich accumulations of such things as "portable art"; evidence for processing and manufacture of lithic and bone/antler materials), and located at what appear to us to have been "strategic" sites for taking of certain resources (e.g. reindeer or other aggregated cervids; fish; shellfish).

The contemporary archaeological record from these sites is usually accounted for by reference to a socioecological phenomenon, hunter-gatherer aggregations. These are taken to be otherwise dispersed hunter-gatherers who "need" to aggregate to take advantage of clumped, seasonally dense resources and who "need" to reaffirm social ties, exchange mates, carry out rituals, and trade. But what kind of insights into both social processes and gender relations might be gained from taking another approach to these sites and their evidence?

There is widespread acceptance among anthropologists that differentiation by sex and age is fairly widespread and fundamental in human societies, and these may be the first axes along which differentiation will emerge. We may never know why or the many different ways in which such differentiation came into being, but if we are interested in understanding the manifestations and contexts of sex and age differentiation, we might be able to reason as follows.

LaFontaine summarizes the different case studies in her edited volume by noting that "the *effect* of sex and age differentiation is to create a social order beyond the household" (1978: 17, emphasis added). Now, there are no simple answers to the questions that inquiries into sex differentiation raise: does sex differentiation always carry meanings that structure social action? how does this sex differentiation transform into gender? And, as well, there are many problems with a narrow reading of the term, "household", that locates this social order as "beyond the household" (see in Moore 1988). But I think the idea that LaFontaine raises is that there exist minimal, small, and/or fundamental productive and/or residential units – which for mobile hunter-gatherers are likely to be some varieties of extended family units – and that there are situational groupings beyond this fundamental residential/productive unit (i.e. the "beyond-the-households"). Although differentiations of some sort are likely to exist *within* the "fundamental units" (and, most likely, age and sex would be primary axes of differentiation here), could we, however, suggest that sex and/or age differentiations are most likely to have come into existence and to have generated certain features of social order when there *are* occasions that are "beyond the households"? That is, if we want to locate contexts within which sex and age differentiation may have been noticeably "at work", and perhaps based more on notions of social order than when in the smaller, more face-to-face dynamics of the "households", should we not try to identify and understand these occasions "beyond-the-households"?

If some Magdalenian hunter-gatherers were, in fact, coming together in groups "beyond-the-households", as can be inferred from archaeological data, these aggregations-as-social-process may well be the best *contexts* for elucidating how sex and age differentiation may have been not only "at work" but also constitutive processes in the "aggregation". The sphere of social action created by groups and individuals coming together is a sphere that, more specifically, may have been *created by* the sexual and/or age-based divisions of labor *and* by the divisions of time and space associated with this division (LaFontaine 1978: 17).

There is always a whereness to meaning-making and experience, and to power – a spatial frame. The spatial dimension could be one frame through which we might view historical production and reproduction of social formations. Thus, we could direct our attention to the Magdalenian "aggregation" locales, where spheres "beyond the households" would be created, where differentiation by sex and age are most probable, and where that differentiation carries meanings that structure social action.

I once tried to argue (Conkey 1985) – but not taking gender into account at all! – for social aggregations to be contexts in which some renegotiation of social relations must take place and that material culture of a redundant symbolic sort may have been part of the processes whereby these new or "other" social relations were constituted. This argument drew, in part, on the ideas of Johnson (1982), who suggested that there had to be some adjustments made in social regulating mechanisms when a new scale of "group" came into being. These adjustments, he suggests, were often in the form of "sometimes" (or sequential) hierarchies.

Although there are some serious problems with the functional/adaptive tenets of his model (and therefore, of my adoption of it as well) that invoke stress ("scalar stress") as the generating factor for socio-cultural reorganizations, I think it is reasonable to expect that when contexts of "beyond-the-households" come into existence that there will be some sorts of rearrangement and renegotiation of social relationships. Obviously, the formations that might develop could be variable. For example, in analyzing the situation of Inupiat Eskimo groups, who came together seasonally for communal whale hunts, ethnographers differ as to the degree and form of extra-familial social integration that came into existence at these "villages" (cf. Burch 1980 vs. Spencer 1959, as cited by Cassell n.d.): from minimal, involving only exchange of goods, to extensive, involving development of an ideology of kinship to promote extra-familial integration and cooperation. Riches (1982) would also challenge the idea that a "new" social formation *must* result when otherwise dispersed social units come together at a particular locale that is strategically situated to take certain resources. He cites instances of what he calls "hunter crowding", which involves only minimal negotiation of social relations and no apparent ritual, exchange, ceremonials, or even contact among most of the congregating individuals.[1]

The point here is to consider the idea that, if we do have locales where situations "beyond the households" take place – where differentiations based on sex and age are most likely, where there had to have been divisions of labor if only because the record suggests that no one person is doing everything that is represented by the site's contents and not every one is doing it all (e.g. evidence for "craft" specializations), and which occur at any one time (an occupation "season") – social rearrangements, social partitionings, or even negotiations of some form would have have been likely.

To pursue this archaeologically, we perhaps need to address several difficult questions. If we know that divisions of labor exist and that differentiations along the lines of sex and age are most likely, how do we know that a *sexual* division of labor existed? What archaeological data would indicate this? Must we try to differentiate between a well-defined distrbution of labor tasks based on sex and more flexible arrangements that may divide labor, since no one does everything, but do not carry gender-laden meanings? To address these questions, it seems as if we need to understand a relatively "synchronic" context, as the context into which gender relations would likely intervene.

Unfortunately, this "synchronic" context will be difficult to come to understand using the particular archaeological record we have so far for the Magdalenian of southwestern Europe, if only because of the requisite for some occupational integrity to the excavation units. With most of the relevant sites having been excavated about a century ago, the kind of stratigraphic resolution and especially intra-site provenance that could help us sort out the "synchronic" frame is very tenuous (for example, see comments on Conkey 1980). Yet, as I discuss below there are alternative ways of viewing the data from some of these sites – even if it is more of a composite record than one of a discrete occupational "event" – that begin to show how we might infer gender in the Upper Paleolithic; we need not wait for methodological improvements or a Paleolithic Pompeii.

It is widely assumed there were social relations or connections among the peoples of southwestern Europe during Magdalenian times (e.g. Bahn 1982; Otte forthcoming); it is likely that these social ties would have been of variable commitment and duration (Gamble 1986). The widespread movements of people and materials that is attested to by the Magdalenian archaeological record (see figure 3.3), can be taken as evidence for what we might call, loosely, the non-local practice of power, and as evidence that the distance(s) over which power is enacted and practiced can be considerable. An ethnographic instance for one hunter-gatherer system, in which both men and women were full and differential participants, would be the *hxaro* (long-distance, individual-to-individual, indirect) exchange system documented for the !Kung San by Wiessner (1977, 1984).

There is plenty of opportunity for and high probability that gender

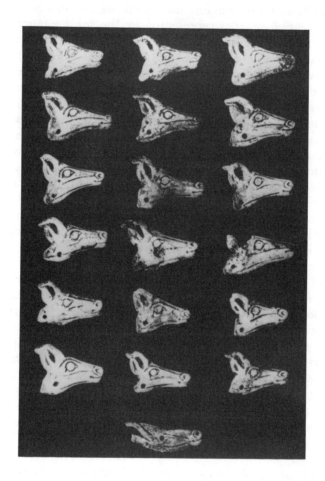

Figure 3.4 A group of nineteen "contours découpées", all depicting ibex heads or, more likely, heads of the Pyrenean ibex (isard) except for the one bison head at the center bottom. Each head is about 5.5 cm, and the imagery is the same on both sides of the "contours découpées". All were cut from the hyoid (throat) bone of horse. These are presumed to have formed the elements of a necklace. All were found together at the site of Labastide (Hautes-Pyrénées), France, from the excavations of G., L., and R. Simmonet, and are attributed to the "first period of the Pyrenean Magdalenian" (Simmonet 1987: 12). (Photo by R. Simmonet with kind permission.)

relations will be involved in enacting the power of "connectedness". It appears that much of the material culture that was being made and is found at the "aggregation" locales is material culture that has distinctive and strikingly differential spatio-temporal distributions throughout "Magdalenian space". For example, there are very distinctive so-called "decoupées" (figure 3.4) – bone cut-outs of animal heads – from a limited number of sites concentrated within a fairly constrained chrono-cultural period (Magdalenian IV) centered on the Pyrenees region. I think we can move toward the peopling of the Magdalenian through such materials; the interpretive challenge is, of course, to elucidate how engendered social action might have been one of the social forces at work. To begin this, let's think about the possible social relations of production.

Material Culture, Social Relations of Production, and Engendered Contexts of Social Action

In addition to an increased attention to the archaeology of gender, there have been other interesting and relevant theoretical directions in archaeology that are important contributors to the archaeological study of gender and to a feminist archaeology, especially the changing theoretical views on human material culture (e.g. Miller 1983; Shanks and Tilley 1987: 79–117).

Many archaeologists have come to the view that human material culture is more than a passive reflection of (what have been taken to be) more important (than material culture) aspects of human life, such as a reflection of social structure, a reflection or expression of cosmology or attitudes towards death. Rather, they take the idea that material culture is an active, constitutive feature of human life, that humans are symbolists and materialists simultaneously, that the production of human culture and the production of meaning is actively effected with material culture – material culture that both constructs and is constructed by cultural and social action.

Thus, a feminist archaeology (cf. Conkey and Gero 1988) that takes gender as a primary structuring principle and as a process of relations *and* that takes material culture as active and constitutive of social life, including gender relations and forces, is thus methodologically empowered to look at how material culture is part of the processes of gender relations: how and in what ways do people make and use material culture in establishing, producing, changing, and challenging gender relations?

The materials found in most of these so-called aggregation sites represent a wide range of productive processes, although many of the processes/actions (such as hurling, presumably in hunting, with an elaborately carved spear-thrower) most likely did not take place *at* (or, in the case of cave sites, *in*) the site itself. In fact, there is so much *material* culture attributable to the Magdalenian, so much 'marking', that it is ever so likely that at least some of it has to do with gender.[2] Furthermore, the variability in this particular record is such both in range and in content that it cannot fully or even mostly be accounted for by the preferred archaeological account of ecological theory (not even from the "new" cultural ecology). Social and/or symbolic accounts must be entertained.[3]

If we assume that both men and women (and children) were at these Magdalenian "beyond-the-households" locales, and that gender as process had come into human existence,[4] we can also assume gendered behaviors, attitudes, activities, and uses of materials. In trying out an explicitly engendered approach to the Magdalenian, I see several possible ways of proceeding; only one will be considered here. I thought it might be revealing to inspect a particular site, its materials, its contexts; a site that has possibilities of having been a "beyond-the-households"/"larger-group-than-usual" locale. I chose these data so as to follow up the previous discussion as to why it may be in these contexts – out of all our Magdalenian data and materials – that we are likely to elucidate social forces and processes, including gender.

Cueto de la Mina: a Late Magdalenian "beyond-the-households" locale?

Cueto de la Mina is a long, narrow rockshelter and a small cave at the southern end of a narrow ridge that parallels the coast of Cantabrian Spain, and that today is only 1.8 km from the Cantabrian Sea (Bay of Biscay). The site was discovered and excavated beginning in 1914 by the Conde de la Vega del Sella, an active and rather professional archaeologist for his time. "Considering the early date of these excavations, they were exceptionally meticulous", reports Straus (1975: 123). All of the excavated earth was screened, which "permitted finding the smallest flakes and fragments of needles" (Vega del Sella 1916: 13, as cited by Straus 1975: 124). The Conde excavated in three sectors and from them combined a sequence of Paleolithic occupation from the Aurignacian through three Magdalenian levels to an Asturian. "This sunny alcove, with abundant fresh water, was clearly a favorite dwelling place for men [sic] throughout the entire Upper Paleolithic and early post-Paleolithic periods" (Straus 1975: 121).

Thus, Cueto de la Mina is described, as are most other sites of Paleolithic hunter-gatherers, primarily with reference to ecological setting and resources, as if these were the primary (only?) structuring factors for hunter-gatherer settlement (but cf. Wiessner 1982).[5] Cueto de la Mina is "eminently well sheltered", with a "panoramic view" from the top of the ridge in which it is located. The cave and shelter face onto a relatively flat, almost semicircular "front yard", and there are several other caves and shelters suitable – and used – for occupation by Paleolithic peoples (e.g. La Riera and La Bricia, both of which have yielded Magdalenian materials) which can be seen from and are within earshot of the overhang at Cueto de la Mina. These sites are in a geographical and ecological setting of "regularly patterned topographic variations" of at least four somewhat parallel zones from the coastal plain to the high peaks of the Picos de Europa.

Certainly in terms of the "ecostrategic" criteria usually invoked for an "aggregation" locale, Cueto de la Mina would meet the requirements: adequate space at the cave/shelter and in front to accommodate a larger-than-usual group size (at least 30–50 people), and even to segregate activities spatially; at a strategic locale to take a variety of seasonally dense or otherwise abundant and diverse resources. As we will see, the faunal list from the Magdalenian levels attests to the taking of the requisite range of resources.

In reading about the site, however, one does not get much sense of the *people* who occupied it, their activities while there, or any of the social dynamics. The Conde de la Vega del Sella was interested in what the site yielded that would contribute to the regional paleoclimatic model he was proposing (1916). He gives a basic "list" of the "finds": the lithics, the fauna, the bone and antler artifacts. More recent considerations of the site's materials have focused on such things as how the engraved bones and antlers fit into various hypotheses about the regional Magdalenian engraving styles and design structure (Conkey 1978, 1980, 1981), on how the lithics found there fit into a reevaluation of Magdalenian lithic typologies (e.g. Utrilla 1981), or on how the fauna found there fit into regional models for resource exploitation throughout the Paleolithic (e.g. Clark and Straus 1983; Freeman 1973, 1981).

Cueto de la Mina has not really been considered among the Magdalenian "super-sites" (e.g. El Pendo or Altamira in Cantabrian Spain; Isturitz or Mas d'Azil in the Pyrenees), but there were both the above-cited (traditional) physical/ecological attributes and a somewhat diverse inventory of archaeological materials that lead us to look at the site from another angle: a group(s) of people had engaged in diverse productive activities and among them socially meaningful differentiation along the lines of sex and age is likely.

I have chosen Cueto de la Mina for consideration here, rather than one of the more usually acknowledged "super-sites", for several reasons. First, the super-sites have indeed yielded diverse and complex material culture inventories, they involve complex and/or problematic stratigraphies, and have varied and long excavation histories that, taken together, make for a lengthy and challenging beginning project. Second, I hope to show that, *even* with a site of more limited an inventory, it is possible to elucidate the social, to read more from the record, and, in fact, to see the record as "more" than it has been taken to be.

At Cueto de la Mina, the possible activities and productive processes are only *implied by* the presence – that is, the listing – of the materials. Activities are also *implied by* the functionally-loaded terms given to the artifacts (e.g. scrapers, harpoons, bâtons), most of which derive from the typologies of the late nineteenth century and that tend to emphasize certain "tools" and related activities (e.g. hunting, leadership) that are (assumed to be) associated with males (cf. Kehoe 1987; Gero, this volume). What happens if one looks at the materials in one level of the site in terms of a much wider range of human activities that they may represent? What happens if we grant *any* division of labor?

Although Vega del Sella distinguished three Magdalenian levels B, C, D, representing an Upper Magdalenian (probably at least a Magdalenian V), a Middle Magdalenian, and the Cantabrian (Lower) Magdalenian, we need examine only level B to see how we can begin to infer activities and aspects of the social relations of production. It is not the point, however, to debate the chronological/temporal resolution represented by Level B. No one has ever explicitly claimed, much less demonstrated, that the Level B deposit represents a discrete occupational "event". But most researchers consider the Cueto de la Mina levels, as identified by Vega del Sella, to have enough integrity to be considered as viable analytical units – and somehow as representative of different Magdalenian (Upper, Middle, Lower) behavioral sets – whether for inferring diet (Freeman 1973), lithic technologies (Utrilla 1981), engraving styles (Conkey 1978), or resource exploitation strategies and regional population dynamics (Clark and Straus 1983; Freeman 1981).

The point here *is*, however, to note that in order to account for the specific materials in Level B – whether they accumulated during *an* occupation event or as a result of several – a great range of productive and therefore *social* processes must be invoked. Divisions of labor and social technologies had to have been "at work" in order for the level B materials to have come into existence as context-specific cultural products.

Cueto de la Mina B: inferring social relations of production

In this ˙Upper Magdalenian level, there are more than 200 whole or (mostly) fragmentary pieces of worked bone and antler, including the diagnostic harpoons with a single row of barbs (figure 3.5). Forty-six of

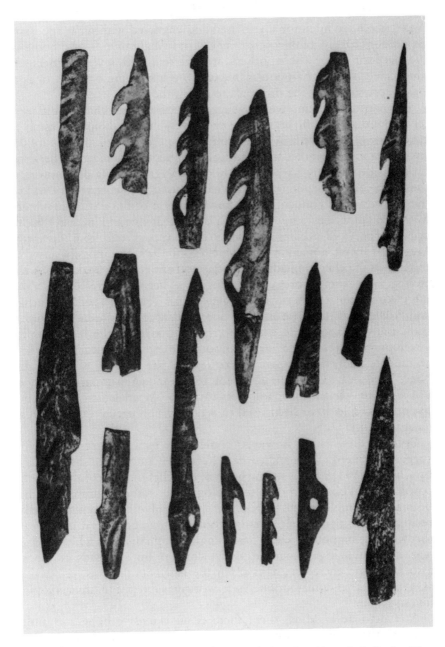

Figure 3.5 Harpoons from Level B, Cueto de la Mina (Asturias), Spain. Note the perforated ones, implying the use of cordage or lines. Note also the two on the far left, which are only partially fabricated, with the barbs not yet fully carved out. (Photo from Vega del Sella (1916, plate XLII), by kind permission.)

these pieces are intentionally incised and engraved with what appear to be predominantly geometric or suggestively figurative forms. Some of the harpoons are whole, others are broken, and several others are unfinished; that is, harpoon manufacturing was going on here, or is at least represented by the materials found in the level.

The harpoons themselves are suggestive of another entirely different technology and set of productive processes – the making and using of cord, string, line, even, by extension, perhaps weaving – because of the small perforation (rather than the more frequently found proturberance) on one side of many harpoons. Although Vega del Sella discusses how these perforated harpoons *must* have been used with cordage (1916: 55), there is very rarely much, if any, consideration of this entire domain of Magdalenian technologies. Although the appearance and intensive use of bone/antler eyed-needles has long been recognized as a distinctly Magdalenian phenomenon (Stordeur-Yedid 1979), the possible uses of thousands of other implements of bone and antler in the making of nets, cordage, or some sort of weaving has been underestimated and unexplored (but cf. Piette 1907: plate IV.3). The find (Leroi-Gourhan and Allain 1979) at Lascaux (Dordogne, France) of the impression of three-twined rope is the best empirical support for the technological development of cordage itself, although there are recent theoretical arguments and ethnographic analogues for the making of Paleolithic "lines" and related tool forms (Kehoe 1987), and an in-progress study of use wear on certain morphological forms of Magdalenian bone/antler hypothesized to have been used in working cordage or strings/thread (Dobres n.d.).

Both of these latter, however, come from feminist researchers who suggest that net-making and cordage have been ignored (or dismissed, as by Chollot 1964: 99) not so much out of disbelief that Paleolithic peoples could and did engage in such technologies but rather because there has been an overemphasis and privileging of the study of (presumably) male-related technologies such as stone-tool manufacturing, hafting, spear-throwing, or harpoons. There has been this emphasis even when cordage was not implicitly associated with women: but it tends to be so associated and therefore, as is often the case, devalued as an activity, as a productive contribution, as a worthy subject for archaeological investigation.

At Cueto de la Mina, then, there is an extensive bone and antler industry that, even without use-wear studies of awls or "crochet-like" pieces, implicates a cordage and line-making technology for the harpoons. There are also the many eyed-needles, mostly fragmentary but some intact, which also attest to another additive technology involving string or lines. As with the harpoons, there are incomplete needles in

Level B, suggesting that needle-making was taking place at the site. Thus, just a limited sample of the site's materials – harpoons, needles – can be taken to represent the manufacture *and* use of bone and antler implements *and* the making and using of cordage and lines for at least sewing and harpoon attachments.

Other materials from Level B include a fragment of worked hematite (a coloring pigment), perforated deer teeth and perforated shells, and three perforated engraved "bâtons" all about 16 cm long, made from the pointed antler tips of red deer, all with the perforation (about 2 cm or more) broken in about the same way, all incised with geometric and possible figurative (fish? ibex?) forms, and all found at the very same stratigraphic level within a four square meter area (Vega del Sella 1916: plate 39). There is also a "cache" of seven quartzite tools, six of which are of unusually large size, and also a large percussor. Other lithics include abundant scrapers of many varieties, points in quartzite, blades with marginal retouch, gravette bladelets, burins, and backed microliths.

The faunal remains are merely listed as follows (giving common names here). Mammals: bison, horse, red deer, roe deer, ibex (abundant), wolf, vole; Molluscs: four different species, including limpets (*Patella vulgata*) and with *Litorina litorea* as "abundant". No body parts (of mammals) nor counts of minimum number of individuals (or any more detailed information) is given.

From just this, however, there are many activities and productive processes represented at Cueto de la Mina B; many are directly implicated as having gone on at the site, such as manufacturing of harpoons, of needles; lithic working; sewing. Many other activities are implicated by recent functional analyses of certain classes of tools that are also in the Level B deposits: shaft-straightening (bâtons); hide-working (some scrapers); vegetation-processing (scrapers); engraving bone and antler (burins); making and use of compound tools (microliths, antler rods). Other Magdalenian activities had to have gone on, if not at the site itself: perforating shell and teeth; obtaining pigment; obtaining antler (either from kills or shed) and bone for the making of more than 200 bone and antler implements; and, of course, the hunting and gathering of an array of resources that meant some people had to have gone to/come from the coast, the woodlands and plains, and to the higher elevations. From these animal resources, one can expect that butchering and processing took place, as well as a variety of other potential processings to yield hide, bone, antler/horn, sinew, and so forth.

The activities and productive processes implicated by the repertoire of materials in Level B attest to a mobilization and yet a differentiation within the productive lives of "Magdalenian" peoples. This is not a material culture inventory that was monopolized by any one group or set of individuals; many different domains are represented and social differentiations, including sex-based differentiations had to have been "at work". Let's grant some particular divisions of labor to account for the archaeological materials, something that has never been done in discussions of these Magdalenian sites. Let's grant some particular divisions of labour, even if we start with some generalized (and stereotypic) notions from ethnographic accounts of hunter-gatherers as to how age and sex might be partitioned – such as males as the usual big mammal hunters, certain women as sewers – there can be elaborations on these limited notions of productive activities, there will be implications for the social relations of production, and there will be more human action – engendered social action – than in extant accounts of "the Magdalenian".[6] I am intentionally referring to women's activities and to men's activities in a first round of "peopling" the Magdalenian so as to stress the necessity of considering gender more broadly than just the traditional and unchallenged models of Magdalenians as (male) hunters, (male) technological innovators, and (male) artists.

I will use the "items" listed for the archaeological inventory and some baseline sex/age associations. I will assume, as well, that, in most instance, those who use certain tools and facilities in their tasks are likely to be those who are *primarily* (but not exclusively) engaged in the manufacture and maintenance of them. That is, we can set some baselines for generating "associational strings" of certain social groupings, tasks, resources, raw materials, implements, and even cultural meanings and symbolic values.

First, let's assume that adult women with young children were primarily the makers of cordage, nets, and "lines", and were primarily engaged in the activities associated with the use of these products: making of "clothing", storage bags or sacs, sewing sections of hide together for "tents"; collecting and transport of shellfish with nets; use of cords in harpoons for fishing; collecting plant resources for cordage; setting "net" fences and traps. Thus, these females would be making their own scrapers for hide-working, their own needles, and their own harpoons for fishing. This implies that they had to work at least some blanks of antler and flint or quartzite for such implements. From their involvement in shellfishing, these women would be associated with the perforating of shells for wearing, attaching to 'clothing', and/or exchange of shells that extend over great distances. In many of these tasks, prepubescent girls and boys would also participate.

Adult males would be primarily engaged in activities related to mammalian land resources, although cooperative work groups of *all* ages and both sexes would have been involved in hunting – by game drives –

the gregarious herd animals of the open plains and woodlands, such as red deer that is often the most abundant fauna in sites (cf. Freeman 1981: 160). Given the inferred strategies (Straus 1987) for ibex hunting from other Cantabrian (and Pyrenean) sites, I can envisage small groups of males and adult women without children staying away for several days to stalk and then process carcasses. Much bone and antler work, for example, could be carried out while waiting. These hunters would make their own hunting and processing implements – bone points, composite tools (e.g., with microliths, the shafts of spears, bows).

Two questions for a gendered approach might follow from these beginning notions about sexual divisions of labor. First, what can we say about the (necessary?) social partitions, the sexual divisions, that are suggested to come into play? Second, given these sketchy ideas about activities, what can we then say about the tensions and social negotiations that would be concomitant with such differentials?

At the particular locale of Cueto de la Mina B, there is tangible direct evidence of more than a dozen different productive and technological processes; many more such processes are directly implied (e.g. cordage). Not all of the implements or items were necessarily manufactured at the site, but given that most of the bone and antler objects are broken, one might argue that they were used, and broken, by the occupants of the site and then abandoned. Certainly the tangible evidence for many technologies – bone/antler working and engraving, cordage, lithic making and using, pigment use, shell/tooth perforation, food-processing and consumption (butchering animals, shellfish boiling, etc.) – implies many different sets of skills, a necessarily wide range of knowledge about and towards different materials, their properties, how to work them, and how to achieve certain intended "results".

If we take technologies in the broad sense – not merely as a means to exploit the environment but as sets of culturally-embedded conceptual frameworks, as sets of ideas and performances that are potentially sources for creating and maintaining symbolically-meaningful daily lifes, experiences, and as praxis – then the elucidation and detailing of these technologies provides more than a list of activities, more than a data set for making broad generalizations about regional hunter-gatherer adaptations.

These technologies involve the procurement and use of a wide variety of raw materials and of the knowledge and means whereby to transform the materials. Concomitant with the varied materials, the varied productive processes that transform them, and with the varied uses to which the "products" are put would be divisions of labor and social "categories" of producers and users. In a locale such as Cueto de la Mina, where one can easily envision some dozens of people coming and going, these technologies and productive processes transcend the smaller units that are intermingling here. These technologies, and all the cultural and symbolic, as well as operational aspects that go with them, are simultaneously partitioned by/among the occupants *and* generate partitionings that contribute to the social "orders" of the larger than usual groups.

But this is not necessarily a picture of easy accommodation and intragroup equilibrium. Certainly tensions and at least interpersonal differences arise; certainly one can imagine how the very partitionings of materials, labor, space, and time that generate the differential technologies are potentially as much a source of tension as of "order". Certainly there would have to have been discussions over the scheduling and timing of differential "work parties": when women, many children and some of the elderly would set off to the coast, then more than 5 km away, to return with nets or sacs of shellfish for preparation and consumption (boiling?), and for occasional perforating, and with coastal and estuary reeds and plants for various uses; when most adult males and some adult women would go off for big game, sometimes several days at a time; when women and young girls and boys would join the hunters for a large group size to effect a drive of a herd of red deer, or to set their net "fences".

When one group or set of individuals provides resources or labor to another, we might also imagine tensions. Tensions might arise, for example, if the young women did the fishing and provided their own nets and lines but relied on others to provide the harpoons; or if they didn't fish but provided the lines; or when flint or quartzite raw materials were somehow provided by a few for use by others; or when women needed sinew from animal kills for their "lines". Spatially, many activities had to be arranged: spear-shaft straightening probably works best near a fire; hide-working probably involves several square meters of space away from most activities because it can be quite "messy"; engraving and net-making/repairing is probably best done in daylight, whereas the cave itself is a good locale for caching large tools for future use, for storage of materials that could be damaged by rain or snow, such as grasses or reeds, unprocessed hides, etc. We can imagine that men and women had to have discussed, even negotiated, time and space, materials and labor.

Some structuralist-like gymnastics could move us from these hypo-thesized differentiations towards possible cultural sets of meaning. It is suggestive that, after lining up the different (and normativized) gender roles, we could easily generate an association of (maternal) women with the sea (shellfish) and water (fishing), with "lines" and connections (from net-making to shell exchange), with facilities (energy storage: sacs, nets, sewn clothing and "tents", cordage to tie things together). And there could be an association of men with the land (hunting), with "points" (see Kehoe 1987 for an original elaboration of "points" vs. "lines"), and with energy expenditure and separations or detachments (animals from the herd, dismembered body parts of prey, flakes from cores, and themselves from the matrifocal core of most women, children and the elderly, who constitute the social past and social future of the group).

Of course, these associations and divisions of labor are only imagined here (but cf. McGee 1977 for a similar kind of "reading" for the Thule), but they certainly allow a more dynamic, and *plausible*, set of interactive circumstances to have gone on at Cueto de la Mina. This *was* a place where people came together to take in various resources, to make and repair (and abandon) their materials, to process raw materials for their personal and group shelter and coverage, to engage with each other in the use of space, in the dynamics of scheduling, and in the sharing and provisioning of materials that surely had cultural meanings. One must imagine equally the tensions and the exchanges. The site becomes more than an inventory, more than an "archaeological record" to be used by us primarily as a data set (or as separate data sets, e.g. fauna, lithics, engraved bones) for making more inclusive (impersonal) inferences about a regional adaptation or about the development of some evolutionary sequence of resource exploitation strategies.

Some assessments

Although I have here brought in the possibility of "women's roles" at *a* particular Late Magdalenian locale, these are obviously very normalized and even enclosing (Elshtain 1986). I have not really challenged, either conceptually or with evidence, the taken for granted hunter-gatherer male/female division of labor. Women, in this account, may be responsible for a great deal of the site's archaeological materials and for what – as productive processes – is implied by them. But, on one hand, the variations in roles and experiences, and the social dynamics are still glossed over. On the other hand, "finding" women in the Magdalenian is not the primary point, either. What do we do about the problem raised here, about relying upon some stereotypical notions implicated by an all too pervasive man-the-hunter/woman-the-gatherer model that here, I hope, have, through elaboration, allowed for further conceptualizations and more inclusive engenderings? Yet, aren't the stereotypical notions further promoted and given credence? Or are they seen as just that, even for males – stereotypical, enclosing and homogenizing – when they are applied more broadly and extended to "women's roles"? Even if we have a more "peopled" account of a site – Cueto de la Mina – and even if we are very explicit about our baseline assumptions, can we and should we base our arguments for an engendered vision on some of the very notions that we hope to problematize?

Yet, if we want to make inferences about gender relations, about how different divisions of labour might work and be played out in a particular context, this might be a place and way to start, if only to put more of our hidden and covert assumptions about gender into sharper relief. If a sexual division of labor is not just the product of the groupings at these locales but, in fact, is one of the defining and constituting processes that "allow" a beyond-the-households grouping to take place, then we can begin with inquiries into these divisions of labor.

Even with data from very old excavations (such as at Cueto de la Mina), we can begin to see ways in which we might engender specific Upper Paleolithic contexts and locales. Can we not imagine what might be done with data that is now coming from modern excavations of Magdalenian sites (e.g. Enlène, Verberie), where we have better control over provenance and spatial patternings, source information on raw materials, specific counts and body parts of faunal remains, refitting of stone implements and even of bones from individual animals, and so forth? We can look forward to use wear studies to detect other "technologies", such as that of cordage, and to grounded structuralist inquiries into associations and patterns of contextually related materials. But unless these methodologies are *simultaneously* informed by a social theoretical framework that takes gender as an analytical concept, they will contribute primarily towards only a fuller inventory and a further buttressing of the evolutionary scenarios of a Eurocentric Upper Paleolithic – in which it is only men who hunt, make stone tools, paint cave walls, engrave bone, make female figurines (see e.g. the illustrations in Augusta and Burian 1960, Howell 1965, and almost any introductory prehistory and archaeology textbook).

What I wanted to do here is to try to convey a sense of why it is a challenge to turn a gender-sensitive approach onto the Upper Paleolithic of Europe, which has yet to be considered as a variety of socio-historical contexts and processes. And, as I discuss in the last section of the chapter, it is a challenge not merely because we lack direct historic ethnography or because we are so "deep" in prehistory. As one response to the challenges, what I have suggested here is that it may be at certain locales of the so-called Magdalenian that we may have the contexts and materials, and thus the inferential bases, for thinking about gender relations.

The sphere of social action at such locales would have been defined by social rearrangements and divisions of labor that surely involved, if not depended upon, differentiations of sex and age; and this sphere of social action would also be defined by the divisions of, and tensions over, time and space that are associated with divisions of labor. In this initial analysis, I have asked some questions about a particular site, Cueto de la Mina B, using just a few gender concepts. From this, I believe, we already have another picture; one that is richer and still plausible and supportable. It is a picture that invites further analysis of the possible social and even symbolic meanings of the roles and relations that generated what has come to be "the site". It is a picture that invites another reading of the prehistoric experience that must have gone on while simultaneously promoting another way for us to experience prehistory.

Afterword: The Conceptual Overburden of Research into the Upper Paleolithic

We have all too often treated the entire Upper Paleolithic of Eurasia (and especially of Europe) as a monolithic cultural bloc of some 25,000+ years (35–10,000 years ago) (cf. Conkey 1984; Conkey with Williams forthcoming). The imputed social homogeneity and continuity of the Upper Paleolithic has been perpetuated by the use of *a* stone tool typology (after de Sonneville-Bordes and Perrot 1954–6) to handle all Upper Paleolithic assemblages, by monolithic interpretations of Paleolithic "art", and by collapsing Upper Paleolithic hunter-gatherers into a "segment of ethnography" (Isaac 1976; see also Fagan 1983, whose prehistory book puts the Upper Paleolithic in the same chapter with ethnographic hunter-gatherers).

The peoples of the Upper Paleolithic (and especially the Magdalenians) have been constru(ct)ed as an Eskimo-like group of peoples (figure 3.6), and they have been stopped by us in their time space tracks to *stand for* the origins of art; for the appearance (like actors coming onto the evolutionary stage) of fully modern "men" with fully developed symbolic behaviors; to stand for the successful replacement of other hominids as dictated by the narrative structure of human evolutionary tales (Landau 1984), and thus to *stand for* the node at which "difference" is negotiated. The temporality of Upper Paleolithic lifeways has been denied by their spatialization: the Upper Paleolithic – and all the modernity it implies – is Eurocentric.

Although there are now serious challenges to the geographic centrality of Europe as a heartland for *Homo sapiens sapiens* (Lewin 1987; Mellars and Stringer 1989) and as an *early* locale where our species not only became established but flourished, there is no indication that the privileged and culturally rich status of the European Upper Paleolithic is

Figure 3.6 An artist's reconstruction to accompany an article by John Pfeiffer (1986) about Cro-Magnon peoples of the late Ice Age "who were really us: working out strategies for survival". The original caption reads: "Hunters surround reindeer as they ford an icy river, when they are most vulnerable. Cro-Magnon bands could kill an entire herd. Their weapons included harpoons, like the longest object at top left. It was carved from reindeer antler. The smaller ones, possibly fishhooks, were made from bird bone. Scrapers to flesh hides are at top right, while, at bottom, wild horses have been engraved on an antler baton" (Pfeiffer 1986: 79). Note here that the hunters are active and attributed with great prowess, although no European Upper Paleolithic site attests to the killing of "an entire herd". The material culture, however, is described using the passive tense, with no reference to the peoples who made or engraved these objects. Note also the way in which this scene is a composite of artifacts from many different sites and of attributes presumably "shared" by the European Ice Age and recent Eskimo caribou hunters, collapsing the distinctions between ethnographically documented hunter-gatherers and "our" Upper Paleolithic ancestors, and presenting their lifeways as a single homogenized "bloc". (Drawing by Lloyd K. Townsend with kind permission.)

being questioned. Not only are some of the earlier (90,000 years ago?) *Homo sapiens sapiens* peoples (but found outside of Europe) "still" making Middle Paleolithic tools, but the Eurocentric transformation appears all the more significant and even "explosive" in contrast to the now extended history of earlier *H.s.s.* It is even more apparent that modern men are "out of Africa": out of nature, out of women (with mitochondrial Eve as the "mother of us all").

In the narrative of human evolution, an "authorial subject and subjectivity is constructed: man evolves *from* nature (i.e., from animals, Africa, men of color, woman) to become sovereign, the hallmark of which is a large brain, capable of self-awareness" (Williams 1986: 12), which is securely in place with the Upper Paleolithic. The *result* of our origin (i.e. Upper Paleolithic Europe) "is neither 'Other' nor 'female/ human'; it is 'a not her' version" (Williams 1986: 12; see also Conkey with Williams forthcoming).

It is in this wider context that the last 5000+ years of the European Upper Paleolithic, which we have labeled the Magdalenian, has been situated. The Magdalenian is the cap to a wider biocultural evolutionary construction. The archaeo-logical result of 'our origin' has been presented as men as providers, men as tool-makers, men as artists; women as objects of art ("Venus figurines"), women as a means for reproduction, women as care-takers and food-processors: any artistic reconstruction and/or archaeological narrative of the Upper Paleolithic or of the Magdalenian will "show" you this.

The Magdalenian itself is, of course, only an "archaeological culture" – one of the primary interpretive devices of all archaeological inquiry. The Magdalenian has become a period within a period (the Upper Paleolithic); it should, therefore, be subject to scrutiny as to how we come to our periodizations (see Kelly-Gadol 1976) and as to the basis for our definitions of an "archaeologial culture". Most Paleolithic "cultures" are defined on the basis of lithic assemblages, although, in the case of the Magdalenian, bone and antler tool types also play a defining role (cf. Breuil 1912). It is a technological definition, a technological culture, an "industry"; there are no gender or social relations explicit in the concept and method of assemblages, except, of course, for the presumed association of all the tool-making with men/males (see Gero, this volume). All of our labels are embedded in techno-ecological concepts – the Upper Paleo*lithic*, the *Stone* Age, the *Ice* Age – and it should not be surprising that, with them, comes a techno-ecological (read male) vision of our past: hunting prowess, technological achievements; "Cro-Magnon hunters were really us, working our strategies for survival" (Pfeiffer 1986).

Life in Ice Age Europe has come to be ripe grounds and has provided a wealth of materials for "aesthetic colonization"; the past decade alone has witnessed the publication of six popular "Ice Age novels", two major museums shows, and several major films. The reconstructions from these have come to constitute a *simulacrum*: "the identical copy for which no original has ever existed" (see Jameson 1984; Baudrillard 1983). It is now possible, suggests Jameson,

to receive the narrative as though it were set in some eternal (Ice Age) beyond historical time. The approach to the present by way of the art language of the simulacrum or of the pastiche of the stereotypical past, endows present reality and the openness of present history with the spell and distance of a glossy mirage. (Jameson 1984: 68).

It will be particularly hard to intervene into this simulacrum of Ice Age Europe and to elucidate specific historical forces.

Thus, a very important and challenging aspect of turning a gender analytical framework onto the Magdalenian is to disengage (disembed!) the Magdalenian archaeological record and how it is used or interpreted from these wider conceptual predispositions. As we begin, we need to recognize "the extent to which archaeology has 'mythic' qualities, in the Barthesian sense of 'forms of representation which naturalize certain meanings and interests'" (Solomon 1989: 72, citing Moore's (1986: 3) citation of Barthes 1973).

The challenge is to extricate "the Magdalenian" from the grand inclusive scale of cultural evolution and from the vast collection of images as a "multitudinous photographic simulacrum" (figure 3.6), and to redefine it as a set of archaeological materials to be used in exploring some historically and contextually situated processes by which social lives (social formations) are constructed (after Scott 1986: 1075). Towards this end, I chose here to bring into our conceptual, and ultimately our analytical, frameworks the generative and constitutive processes – divisions of labor, relations of production, divisions of time and space associated with that labor and production – that both created the "aggregation" contexts and that surely involved and were effected by gender relations and conceptual categories of gender.

ACKNOWLEDGMENTS

Deep gratitude and thanks go to Joan Gero for her support and gentle proddings in our efforts to do The Wedge conference, for her many hours of work on conference logistics and on the volume, and for her insightful and articulate ideas about gender and archaeology; also, many thanks for Stephen's support of her time and for his wonderful cards, the gifts, and peanuts round the fire. Very special thanks to Les for his tolerance and support of all my time spent on this project and this paper. The Wedge conference participants were particularly helpful with their urging me to take up "any division of labor" for the Magdalenian materials, and I especially appreciated the call for imaginative empirical depth that "Sister" Pat Watson "laid on" me! A particularly helpful last round of critical comments from Kathy Bolen were an important impetus. And everyone should be as fortunate to have a colleague in everyday archaeology who is as sympathetic but incisive and inspirational as I have found Ruth Tringham to be.

NOTES

1   Despite the preference of Paleolithic archaeologists to allow "strategic locale" alone to be causal in the presumed aggregations, Riches (1982) shows how aggregations, as socially meaningful, are not guaranteed by such strategic locations and resource-related variables. Aggregations are social processes and social entities, whether resources are involved or not. It is interesting that the reasons usually given for a site to have been an aggregation locale are ecological and subsistence-related, often implying some sort of division of labor that, however, is never really discussed!

2   To suggest that gender has not figured in interpretations of Upper Paleolithic life is not completely accurate, given the path-breaking structural analysis of Leroi-Gourhan for the cave wall art. Originally, Leroi-Gourhan (e.g. 1965) postulated that a structural division of the Paleolithic universe into male and female domains was the underlying principle that generated the placement of specific images (e.g. horse or bison) in specific locales within any given cave. Thus, the fundamental valences of the "mythogram" were maleness and femaleness. This account, however, had nothing to do with the ways in which gender "worked" as particular historical and social forces in the daily lives of Paleolithic peoples. In his later writings (e.g. Leroi-Gourhan 1982), the reference to male/female as structuring principle is no longer in evidence.
    Other considerations of Paleolithic imagery have also had implications for our conceptualizations of gender, especially females, in the Upper Paleolithic. As has been shown (Conkey with Williams forthcoming; Bahn 1986; Handsman, this volume), these conceptualizations are subjective and androcentric, depending upon certain "identifications" of imagery as male/female genitalia or on certain twentieth-century presuppositions about especially the "female" imagery as cultural commodification. A more thorough approach to archaeologies of gender in the Upper Paleolithic must include taking these conceptualizations apart, taking them as problematics, and there is *much* to be done.

3   No one has ever really looked at Magdalenian archaeological contexts such as "aggregation sites" from the perspective of their having been collectivities of peoples engaging in several levels of *social* dynamics, drawing upon particular historical features of and meanings within their lives in order to do so. Almost no one has worked away at trying to understand the relations of particular (Magdalenian) cultural products and particular meanings, in the particular conditions of existence (such as an "aggregation" context), much less tried to advocate and elucidate that part of the meanings and part of the relations have to do with gender.

4   To argue the case for the existence of gender and gender relations is another step that should, of course, have preceded this kind of an inquiry; in any event, the existence should not be assumed. The more inclusive evolutionary questions about gender – has there always been gender? when and under what contexts and conditions does gender come into existence? – have yet to be argued.

5   The social lives of hunter-gatherers are more likely to be described in
    ethological terms than in the more traditional categories of ethnography.
    Their behaviors are viewed as more determined by biological (e.g. viable
    mating networks) and ecological (e.g. resource-procurement strategies)
    variables than by socially constructed frameworks (Collier and Rosaldo
    1982: 277).

6   For one account that is a slight exception to the dehumanized discussions of
    Paleolithic life, see Freeman (1981) who writes about "Magdalenian peoples"
    who, for example, "prepared their food", "began to use resources intensively",
    "might seasonally have entered the broken uplands of Cantabria to
    concentrate on capturing the 'alpine' species", and who "might have lived in
    smaller social units in base camps where the accumulated surpluses of the
    'seasonal harvests' were consumed." But these are all activities directly
    related to resources and subsistence and are discussed as generalized trends,
    even if reported in the active voice. Ceremonial activities, however, are
    reported on in the passive tense: "caves might have served as centers for
    ceremonial activities" (see also the original caption to figure 3.6, where
    material culture "was made" or "was engraved").

REFERENCES

Audouze, Françoise (1987). "The Paris Basin in Magdalenian Times." In *The
    Pleistocene Old World: Regional Perspectives*, Olga Soffer, ed. New York and
    London: Plenum Press, 183–200.
Augusta, Josef and Zdenek Burian (1960). *Prehistoric Man*. London: Hamlyn.
Bahn, Paul G. (1982). "Inter-site and Inter-regional Links During the Upper
    Paleolithic: The Pyrenean Evidence." *Oxford Journal of Archaeology* 1(3):
    247–68.
—— (1986). "No Sex, Please, We're Aurignacians." *Rock Art Research* 3(2): 99–
    120.
Barthes, Roland (1973). *Mythologies*. London: Paladin.
Baudrillard, Jean (1983). "The Procession of Simulacra." *Art and Text* 11: 3–47.
Breuil, Henri (1912). "Les subdivisions du Paléolithique supérieur et leur
    signification." In *Comptes rendus de 14ème Congrès International d'Anthro-
    pologie et d'Archéologie Préhistorique*. Geneva: 165–238.
—— (1954). "Bas-reliefs féminins de la Magdeleine [Penne, Tarn près Montauban
    (Tarn-et-Garonne)]." *Quaternaria* 1.
Burch, E.S., Jr (1980). "Traditional Eskimo Societies in Northwest Alaska." In
    Alaska Native Culture and History, Y. Kotani and W. Workman, eds. Osaka:
    National Museum of Ethnology, Senri Ethnological Studies 4, 253–304.
Cassell, Mark (n.d.) "Farmers of the Northern Ice, or, When is a Hunter-
    gatherer not a Hunter-gatherer?" Manuscript on file with the author,
    Department of Anthropology, State University of New York, Binghamton.
Chollot, Marthe (1964). *Musée des Antiquités Nationales: Collection Piette (Art
    mobilier préhistorique)*. Paris: Musées Nationaux.

Clark, Geoffrey A. and Lawrence G. Straus (1983). "Late Pleistocene Hunter-gatherer Adaptations in Cantabrian Spain." In *Hunter-gatherer Economy in Prehistory*, G. Bailey, ed. Cambridge: Cambridge University Press, 131–67.

Collier, Jane and Michelle Z. Rosaldo (1982). "Politics and Gender in Simple Societies." In *Sexual Meanings. The Cultural Construction of Gender and Sexuality*, Sherry Ortner and Harriet Whitehead, eds. Cambridge: Cambridge University Press, 275–329.

Conkey, Margaret W. (1978). "An Analysis of Design Structure: Variability among Magdalenian Engraved Bones from Northcoastal Spain." Unpublished Ph.D. dissertation, Department of Anthroplogy, University of Chicago.

—— (1980). "The Identification of Prehistoric Hunter-gatherer Aggregation Sites: The Case of Altamira." *Current Anthropology* 21(5): 609–30.

—— (1981). "What Can We Do with Broken Bones? Paleolithic Design Structure, Archaeological Research, and the Potential of Museum Collections." In *The Research Potential of Anthropological Museum Collections*, A.-M. Cantwell, J. B. Griffen, and N. Rothschild, eds. Annals of the New York Academy of Sciences 376, 35–52.

—— (1984). "To Find Ourselves: Art and Social Geography of Prehistoric Hunter-gatherers." In *Past and Present in Hunter-gatherer Studies*, Carmel Schrire, ed. New York: Academic Press, 253–76.

—— (1985). "Ritual Communication, Social Elaboration, and the Variable Trajectories of Paleolithic Material Culture." In *Prehistoric Hunter-gatherers. The Emergence of Cultural Complexity*, J. A. Brown and T. D. Price, eds. New York: Academic Press, 299–323.

—— (1987). "Interpretive Problems in Hunter-gatherer Regional Studies: Some Thoughts on the European Upper Paleolithic." In *The Pleistocene Old World: Regional Perspectives*, Olga Soffer, ed. New York and London: Plenum Press, 63–79.

—— (1989). "The Use of Diversity in Stylistic Analysis." In *Quantifying Diversity in Archaeology*, R. D. Leonard and G. T. Jones, eds. Cambridge University Press, 121–32.

—— (forthcoming). "Les sites d'agrégation et la répartition de l'art mobilier, ou: y a-t-il des sites d'agrégation magdalenien?" In *Le peuplement magdalenien: centenaire de la découverte de l'homme de Chancelade*, D. Gambier, H. Laville, J.-Ph. Rigaud, and B. Vandermersch, eds.

Conkey, Margaret and Joan Gero (1988). "Towards Building a Feminist Archaeology." Paper presented at 53rd annual meeting, Society for American Archaeology, Phoenix, AZ.

Conkey, Margaret with Sarah H. Williams (forthcoming). "Original Narratives: The Political Economy of Gender in Archaeology." In *Gender at the Crossroads of Knowledge: Feminist Anthropology in the Post-modern Era*, Micaela diLeonardo, ed. Berkeley and Los Angeles: University of California Press.

Delporte, Henri (1979). *L'image de la femme dans l'art préhistorique*. Paris: Picard.

Dobres, Marcia-Anne (n.d.). "The Social Organization of Prehistoric Labor: Mid-range Research and Beyond. Proposal submitted to Wenner-Gren

Foundation for Anthropological Research. Manuscript on file with the author, Department of Anthropology, University of California, Berkeley.

Fagan, Brian (1983). *People of the Earth: Introduction to World Prehistory* (4th edn). Boston: Little-Brown.

Elshtain, Jean B. (1986). "The New Feminist Scholarship." *Salamagundi* 70–1: 3–26.

Freeman, Leslie G. (1973). "The Significance of Mammalian Faunas from Paleolithic Occupations in Cantabrian Spain." *American Antiquity* 38: 3–44.

—— (1981). "The Fat of the Land: Notes on Paleolithic Diet in Iberia." In *Omnivorous Primates: Gathering and Hunting in Human Evolution*, Richard Harding and Geza Teleki, eds. New York: Columbia University Press, 104–65.

Gamble, Clive (1982). "Interaction and Alliance in Paleolithic Society." *Man* (n.s.) 17: 92–107.

—— (1986). "Hunter-gatherers and the Origin of States." In *States in History*, J. A. Hall, ed. Oxford: Basil Blackwell, 22–47.

Gaussen, Jean (1980). *Le paléolithique supérieur en plein air en Périgord. Industrie et structure d'habitat. Gallia Préhistoire*, Supplément 24. Paris: Éditions du C.N.R.S.

Howell, F. Clark (1965). *Early Man*. New York: Time-Life Books.

Isaac, Glynn Ll. (1976). "Stages of Cultural Elaboration in the Pleistocene: Possible Archaeological Indicators of the Development of Language Capabilities." In *Origins and Evolution of Language and Speech*, S. Harnard, H. Stekelis, and J. Lancaster, eds. New York: New York Academy of Sciences, 275–9.

Jameson, Frederic (1984). "Postmodernism or the Cultural Logic of Late Capitalism." *New Left Review* 146: 85–106.

Johnson, Gregory A. (1982). "Organizational Structure and Scalar Stress." In *Theory and Explanation in Archaeology. The Southampton Conference*, C. Renfrew, M. Rowlands, and B. A. Seagraves, eds. New York: Academic Press, 389–421.

Kehoe, Alice (1987). "Points and Lines." Paper presented at annual meetings, American Anthropological Association, Chicago.

Kelly-Gadol, Joan (1976). "The Social Relations of the Sexes: Methodological Implications of Women's History." *Signs: Journal of Women in Culture and Society* 1: 809–24.

LaFontaine, Jean S. (1978). "Introduction." In *Sex and Age as Principles of Social Differentiation*, Jean S. LaFontaine, ed. Association for Social Anthropological Monographs 17. New York: Academic Press, 3–20.

Landau, Miscia (1984). "Human Evolution as Narrative." *American Scientist* 72: 262–8.

Lee, Richard B. (1980). *The !Kung San. Men, Women and Work in a Foraging Society*. Cambridge: Cambridge University Press.

Leroi-Gourhan, André (1965). *Treasures of Prehistoric Art*. New York: Abrams.

—— (1982). *The Dawn of European Art*. Cambridge: Cambridge University Press.

Leroi-Gourhan, André and Michel Brezillon (1983). *Fouilles de Pincevent. Essai d'analyse ethnographique d'un habitat magdalenien. Gallia Prehistoire,* Supplément 7. Paris: Éditions du C.N.R.S.

Leroi-Gourhan, Arlette and J. Allain (1979). *Lascaux inconnu.* Paris: Éditions du C.N.R.S.

Lewin, Roger (1987). "Africa: Cradle of Modern Humans." *Science* 237: 1292–5.

Mauss, Marcel and H. Beuchat (1904). "Essai sur les variations saisonnières des sociétés eskimos." *L'Année Sociologique* 1904–5: 39–132.

McGhee, Robert (1977). "Ivory for the Sea Woman: The Symbolic Attributes of a Prehistoric Technology." *Canadian Journal of Archaeology* 1: 141–50.

Mellars, Paul and Chris Stringer, eds (1989). *The Human Revolution: Behavioral and Biological Perspectives on the Origins of Modern Humans.* Edinburgh and Princeton: The University Presses.

Miller, Daniel (1983). "THINGS Ain't What They Used to be." *Royal Anthropological Institute News* 59: 5–7.

Moore, Henrietta (1986). *Space, Text, and Gender: An Anthropological Study of the Marakwet of Kenya.* Cambridge: Cambridge University Press.

—— (1988). *Feminism and Anthropology.* Cambridge: Polity Press.

Otte, Marcel (forthcoming). "Processus de diffusion à longue distance." In *Le peuplement magdalenien, centenaire de la découverte de l'homme de Chancelade,* D. Gambier, H. Laville, J.-Ph. Rigaud, and B. Vandermersch, eds.

Pfeiffer, John (1986). "Cro-Magnon Hunters Were Really Us, Working Out Strategies for Survival." *Smithsonian*: 75–85.

Piette, Edouard (1907). *L'art pendant l'âge du renne.* Paris: Masson.

Pigeot, Nicole (1987). *Magdaleniens d'Etioles. Économie et organisation sociale. Gallia Préhistoire,* Supplément 25. Paris: Éditions C.N.R.S.

Riches, David (1982). *Northern Nomadic Hunter-gatherers: A Humanistic Approach.* New York: Academic Press.

Scott, Joan (1986). "Gender: A Useful Category of Historical Analysis." *American Historical Review* 91: 1053–75.

Shanks, Michael and Christopher Tilley (1987). *Social Theory and Archaeology.* Albuquerque: University of New Mexico Press.

Sieveking, Ann (1979). *The Cave Artists.* London: Thames & Hudson.

Simmonet, Robert (1987). "Notice sur l'exposition et les illustrations du catalogue." In *Art mobilier magdalenien dans les Pyrénées Centrales,* L'exposition au Musée de l'Ariège, Chateau de Foix, à l'occasion du 1er Colloque international sur l'Art mobilier paléolithique, November 1987. Conseil General de l'Ariège, Direction des Musées de France, Direction Regionale des Affaires Culturelles. Toulouse: Éditions d'Art Larrey, 4–32.

Solomon, Anne Catherine (1989). "Division of the Earth: Gender, Symbolism, and the Archaeology of the Southern San." Unpublished Master's thesis, Department of Archaeology, University of Capetown, South Africa.

de Sonneville-Bordes, Denise and Jean Perrot (1954–6). "Lexique typologique du paléolithique supérieur. Outillage lithique." *Bulletin de la Société Préhistorique Française* 51: 327–35; 52: 76–9; 53: 408–12, 547–59.

Spencer, R. F. (1959). *The North Alaskan Eskimo: A study in Ecology and*

Society. Bureau of American Ethnology, Bulletin 171. Washington: US Government Printing Office.

Straus, Lawrence G. (1975). "A Study of the Solutrean in Vasco-Cantabrian Spain." Unpublished Ph.D. dissertation, Department of Anthropology, University of Chicago.

—— (1987). "Upper Paleolithic Ibex Hunting in Southwest Europe." *Journal of Archaeological Science* 14: 163–78.

Stordeur-Yedid, Danielle (1979). *Les aiguilles à chas au paléolithique. Gallia Préhistoire*, Supplément XIII. Paris: Éditions du C.N.R.S.

Ucko, Peter and Andree Rosenfeld (1967). *Paleolithic Cave Art*. New York: McGraw-Hill.

Utrilla, Miranda P. (1981). *El Magdaleniense Inferior y Medio en la Costa Cantabrica*. Centro de Investigacion y Museo de Altamira, Monografia 4. Santillana del Mar.

de la Vega del Sella, Conde (1916). *Paleolítico de Cueto de la Mina*. Comision de Investigaciones Paleontologicas y Prehistoricas, Memoria numero 13. Madrid: Museo Nacional de Ciencias Naturales.

White, Randall (1985). "The Upper Paleolithic Occupation of the Périgord: A Topographic Approach." Oxford: British Archaeological Reports, International Series 253.

Wiessner, Polly (1977). "Hxaro: A Regional System of Reciprocity for Reducing Risk Among the !Kung San." Ph.D. dissertation, Department of Anthropology, University of Michigan. Ann Arbor: University Microfilms.

—— (1982). "Beyond Willow-smoke and Dog's Tails: A Comment on Binford's Analysis of Hunter-gatherer Settlement Systems." *American Antiquity* 47(1): 171–8.

—— (1984). "Reconsidering the Behavioral Basis of Style." *Journal of Anthropological Archaeology* 3: 190–234.

Williams, Sarah (1986). "Paleoanthropology and the Construction of Mankind: An Outline." Paper on file with the author, History of Consciousness Program, University of California, Santa Cruz.

4

Households with Faces: the Challenge of Gender in Prehistoric Architectural Remains

Ruth E. Tringham

Prologue: A Story

I begin this paper with a story. As with all good stories, I have created, exaggerated and stylized reality to improve the text.

I was taken kicking and screaming to the conference "Women and Production in Prehistory" in the marshes of South Carolina, convinced that gender differences were not visible in the archaeological record, least of all in the architectural remains of deep prehistory, with which I was most concerned. I was moreover at a loss as to how I should rework my current research strategy to face the question of what women were doing in the houses that I was so busy studying.

I had an "Aha" experience.

I presented a summarized version of my paper about investigating household organization and architectural remains in prehistoric southeast Europe to the 20 or so participants round the table. They listened politely – the archaeologists did – and worried about the validity of the data I presented for my conclusions.

And then someone said, "Yes, but how do you envisage these households?" It was Henrietta Moore, I think.

"You mean how do I imagine their composition?" thinking: Oh, heavens, she wants me to imagine their kinship structure, but I am interested in what households *did* not what they comprised . . .

Henrietta said "No, how do you envisage them going about their daily actions?"

You can imagine, I felt quite defensive. "Archaeologists don't do that. We don't go around envisaging people leading cows to pasture and gossiping around the household chores."

"Yes, but what *if* you were allowed to do it; just relax; no one will tell. Now, just tell us how you see them. What do they look like?"

"Well," I said, "there's a house, and cows, and pigs, and garbage . . ."
"Yes, but the people, tell us about the people."
"Well . . .," I said. And then I realized what I saw. "I see," I said, ". . . a lot of faceless blobs."

Figure 4.1 Households without faces in the Selevac fields, Yugoslavia. (Photo by Carol Spears)

And then it dawned on me what she wanted me to see. That until, as an archaeologist, you can learn to give your imagined societies faces, you cannot envisage gender. Or, in somebody else's terms (Conkey's?) you cannot engender prehistory.

And until you can engender prehistory, you cannot *think* of your prehistoric constructions as really human entities with a social, political, ideological, and economic life.

Ahaaaa!

Women in European Prehistory

The original plan of this contribution was to consider the question of how gender relations would be reflected in the remains of the built environment on archaeological sites. I had already been struggling for several years with the problem of how household organization would be reflected in the archaeological record, specifically its architectural domain, and thought that the question of gender could be treated as an

Figure 4.2 Households with faces in the Selevac fields, Yugoslavia. (Photo by Carol Spears)

extension, albeit a challenging one, of the "household" question. I realized, as I prepared myself for the original conference, that what I was attempting to do would be classed as a "remedial" feminist archaeology (Harding, 1987; Wylie, this volume). That is, that my theoretical and methodological framework based on the concept of material culture as a *passive* reflection of society's behaviour, would remain unchanged. I was merely going to "add women and stir".

In fact, in my original contribution to the conference papers at "The Wedge" I added a lot of household activities "and stirred", but there were very few women! I was still in my "phase" of embarrassed protest. My wish to retain respectability and credibility as a scientific archaeologist was stronger than my motivation to consider gender relations.

It is not as though gender had never been considererd in the area of my research – prehistoric Europe. There have been archaeologists who have explicitly envisaged women in prehistoric Europe. Two sets of these archaeologists are relevant to the discussions in this paper since they involve the archaeological record of architecture. These sets comprise, on the one hand, archaeologists working within the ideological framework of post-Revolutionary Soviet Union, and, on the other hand, one archaeologist – Marija Gimbutas – with a large non-archaeological following, who focused on the development and untimely destruction of what she has termed the "Civilization of Old Europe" in prehistoric Southeast Europe.

Both of these groups of archaeologists had strong, if not always explicit, agendas in constructing prehistoric society and focusing on the role of women in prehistory. Both groups envisaged women as an equalizing force in society, who mitigated competition between individuals and the dominance and exploitation of one group or individual by another. Such a society, in both cases, is seen as a universal ideal, which was destroyed by later male-dominated, competitive, production-for-profit motivated societies. The agenda in both groups has been to reconstruct the time-space framework of the prehistoric ideal and its destruction, and to suggest that the fulfillment of human social evolution and a truly human society will only be achieved by a return to this ideal. Both groups used the data on the Neolithic–Copper Age period of Southeast Europe (including the SW USSR) to propose that the early agricultural societies of Europe were organized on a matrilineal, matrilocal egalitarian basis in large households.

Archaeologists of the first group took it as their role to demonstrate such societies as one of the pre-capitalist stages of the unilinear scheme of social evolution suggested by Morgan, Marx, and Engels (e.g. Childe 1958; Engels 1972; Semenov 1980). The excellent excavations in the Soviet Union and elsewhere in East Europe that are characterized by a broad exposure of village house plans and careful attention in recording the spatial distribution of artifacts, furniture, and internal divisions in houses represent their field strategy to gather the primary data for this purpose (Dumitrescu 1965; Kričevski 1940; Passek 1949).

Marija Gimbutas has focused on those parts of the archaeological record which she feels will inform her on the values, the folklore, customs, ceremonies, rituals, and beliefs of the early agriculturalists. Gimbutas has used the prehistoric architectural data to provide evidence of what she sees as the context of the rich ceremonial and ritual life of Old Europe (Gimbutas 1980). But it is through the study in particular of clay anthropomorphic representations (figurines) from archaeological sites within their architectural context that she has shown to her own satisfaction (Gimbutas 1970, 1980, 1982) and to that of a broad public following (Eisler 1987), the contrast between the "peaceful character of most of these art-loving peoples"[1] of "the Civilization of Old Europe" and that of the society which destroyed it: the patriarchal, hierarchical, and war-loving Indo-European Kurgan invaders. "An equalitarian male-female society is demonstrated by the grave equipment in practically all the known cemeteries of Old Europe" writes Gimbutas. "She also notes the presence of numerous indicators that this was a matrilinear society. . . . Moreover, she points out that the archaeological evidence leaves little doubt that women played key roles in all aspects of Old European life" (Eisler 1987: 14). I shall focus at this point in the paper on one of the major problems inherent in these early attempts to discuss the role of women in prehistory; one, moreover, that has prevented not only these attempts but also the whole topic of gender relations to be taken at all seriously by Establishment (yes, undoubtedly male-dominated) archaeology in Europe.

The Morgan/Engels unilinear scheme of socioeconomic formations has been severely criticized from many different directions (e.g. Harding 1983; Leacock 1972; Thompson 1970; Trigger 1984). At the same time, archaeological research of the Anglo-American academic establishment from the late 1960s to the present, in its attempt to join the ranks of the scientific community at large, demanded rigorous testing and demonstration of hypotheses. In such an intellectual climate, the reconstruction of the role of men and women in economics, ideology, and social and political relations in prehistory was regarded as quite unvalidated and unvalidatable. It is not surprising, therefore, that many of the early Soviet reconstructions of the sexual division of labor amongst the early agriculturalists have been disregarded for their unscientific reasoning and lack of solid supporting archaeological data. At the same time, the work of Gimbutas has been heavily criticized for its inconsistencies and hasty inferences (Hayden 1986).

Explicit statements on the role of men and women in any walk of prehistoric life have virtually ceased to be presented by any archaeologists who wanted to be accepted by the archaeological Establishment of the dominant cultures of the West. Those who have dared to discuss the topic have confined themselves to the direct data on differences of sex, namely burial and other skeletal data (Gibbs 1987; Randsborg 1986; Sørensen 1987; Tilley 1981). Questions on gender in prehistory are not the only ones to have fallen victim to the "scientific method". The demise of social and political questions in general in prehistory in such a climate has been well described in a number of recent works (Hodder 1982; Shanks and Tilley 1987; Wylie, this volume).

Why have archaeologists produced a prehistory of genderless, faceless blobs? This question was originally considered by Conkey and Spector (1984). Now in this volume, the editors and Alison Wylie have suggested that a basic problem is a misunderstanding as to what an engendered prehistory should comprise. One of the beliefs leading to this misunderstanding is that the methodology of an archaeology of gender requires us to be able to identify gender in the archaeological record, that is to be able to attribute certain activities (e.g. ploughing, weaving) or material culture to males or females.

Expanding on this theme, it seems to me that, according to the methodology of logical positivism, the ability to assign the archaeological record directly or indirectly to behavior is what *enables* hypotheses about human social and economic behavior in the past (as well as about gender relations) to be testable with empirical archaeological data. For this reason it has always seemed an essential step in any engendered or *social* archaeology. Thus, the ability to assign the archaeological record to behavior represents the strength of scientific archaeological enquiry, allowing us to demonstrate "facts" within a framework established by the academic community. Yet it also represents a devastating weakness in that it *inhibits* us from using the riches of modern social theory to construct prehistory: suggesting that certain questions are "untestable" or "marginal".

My personal resolution to this seeming insoluble problem could have come from a number of directions. I could have retained my original research strategy, heavily restricted by the demands of testing empirical hypotheses with the archaeological data, and focused on those sets of data that would give me information on sexual attribution, if not gender. Burials and two- or three-dimensional representations of human figures with clearly diagnostic features of sex could provide such apparently unambiguous sets of data. But I have chosen to work with architecture – a body of data that is not regarded as unambiguous for this purpose. Or, again within my original research strategy, I could have chosen a set of data which was apparently less ambiguous by virtue of being close to or within a period in which historical records were present. Those working in near-historical periods have felt that they could more convincingly attribute architectural units to household units, and even gender, through ethnohistory and close direct historical analogy (Bawden 1982; Ciolek-Torrello 1985, 1989; Donley 1987; Hill 1970; Reid and Whittlesley 1982; Stanish 1989). But I have chosen to work in a period of prehistory – Southeast Europe at 6000–4000 BC – that is separated by many thousand years from any written sources.

My only alternative then, apart from giving up the idea of gender relations, was to change my research strategy, to one which has a different standpoint on ambiguity and the scientific method, one that has been elegantly described by a number of philosophers of science including Alison Wylie (1982, this volume) and Harding (1986, 1987). A requirement was also a recognition that material culture, including architecture, has a richer role to play in archaeology than a passive reflection of human behavior.

Thus, what started out as an unrequited attempt at writing a European prehistory of gender relations on the basis of architectural remains has exploded into a reconceptualization of what writing prehistory is about, including the use of the archaeological record and the engendering of prehistory. My contribution to this volume will try to indicate some of the directions that this explosion has taken me and, I hope, will take me and others in the future. Many will find most of these directions entirely unacceptable, others will find them disconcerting and unsettling.

I shall focus on the essential linkage between microscale archaeology – the archaeology of the household – and the study of prehistoric gender relations. This will take the form of a mild critique of the recently growing trend towards household archaeology, which is characterized by a lack of explicit consideration of gender relations. I will then discuss the kinds of linkages that can be made, along with the use of the architectural data in these considerations. At this point I shall introduce my field research on prehistoric households in Southeast Europe. The idea here is to avoid presenting this work in a traditional hypothetico-deductive context as a "case-study of a generalized concept/methodology". I shall introduce the field project – the excavation of Opovo, a Late Neolithic village in Yugoslavia – and the archaeological record, that has been created by myself and the team that works with me, within the framework of a dialogue of alternative historical trajectories for the prehistory of Southeast Europe. In each of these trajectories, gender relations are considered, but none can be considered an "engendered prehistory" of Southeast Europe. Thus, the challenge that is taken up in the last section of the paper is to show post-Wedge archaeology in action; to show whether, if at all, it differs from what we have done before.

The Household as Unit of Analysis in Archaeology

What has dominated the interest and energies of archaeologists in the (re)construction of prehistoric life has been what goes on beyond the household: for example, the corporate production of surplus goods, exchange and alliances on a regional and inter-regional scale, the struggle of humans to control the environment, the hierarchies and dominance structures between settlements. This is surprising in view of the pretensions of the discipline to be a social science. In the social sciences in general, the analysis of social change at a microscale of the household or coresidential group or family has long been recognized as an essential scale for the study of the social relations of production, including gender relations, especially in non-capitalist or pre-capitalist social formations (Goody 1958, 1972; Hammel and Laslett 1974; Laslett 1972; Netting, Wilk and Arnould 1984; Yanagisako 1979). It has also more recently been recognized as an essential aspect of understanding the feminist standpoint in the analysis of capitalist social formations (Beechey 1978;

Glazer-Malbin 1976; Hartmann 1981; Hartsock 1983; Rapp 1977; Smith 1978; Yanagisako 1979).

Such a reluctance seems extraordinary also in view of the fact that most archaeological excavation of settlements retrieve data which are most pertinent to the study of households and the products of domestic[2] labor (housework).

It seems to me that this lack of interest in the study of prehistoric households must reflect a willingness to accept the generalized assumptions concerning what goes on in and around the house. This focus on the "other" and the "outside" and a corresponding *lack* of interest in challenging the "givens" of social action at a microscale (along with a devaluation of women and their "labor") is characteristic of social archaeology of both Marxist (Bender 1985; Frankenstein and Rowlands 1978; Gilman 1981) and non-Marxist theoretical standpoints (Champion 1989; Renfrew and Shennan 1982), and is exactly what we can expect according to a "masculinist standpoint" in archaeology (Hartsock 1983).

Nevertheless there has been a growing – as yet still marginal – group of archaeologists who have chosen to carry out what is sometimes called "household archaeology". Since the initial study of households in the late 1970s and early 1980s this scale of analysis has been claimed to offer "a chance to archaeologists to examine social adaptation with direct reference to the empirical details of the archaeological record" (Flannery and Winter 1976); that is, with the methodology of scientific logical positivism, household analysis allows us to "bridge the existing 'mid-level theory gap' in archaeology" (Wilk and Rathje 1982: 617). In other words, the study of the archaeological record at this scale would allow us to attribute it to some sort of homogeneous social behavior.

But there are grave challenges in "household attribution", just as there are with "gender attribution". For every attempt to identify households in prehistory, there is an ethnographic or ethnoarchaeological cautionary tale to warn us of the dangers of linking architectural units with specific social units, such as with the "family" or "household" (Donley 1982; Hayden and Cannon 1982; Kramer 1982a, 1982b; Moore 1986, 1982; Watson 1978, 1979). The identification of units of cooperation is made more challenging archaeologically by the likelihood that cooperative action is being carried out at other levels as well: lineages, or villages (Hayden and Cannon 1982; Wilk and Rathje 1982: 621). Nevertheless, archaeologists have ploughed on in their endeavor. The Mesoamerican archaeologists, who have been particularly active in developing household archaeology, suggest that it is most important to understand what a household *does* rather than what its social form is (who lives there and how they are related) (Ashmore and Wilk 1988: 4–5; Wilk and Netting 1984; Wilk and Rathje 1982). Thus they suggest that we attribute the archaeological record to units of cooperative production – consumption, generational transmission, coresidence, reproduction – all functional and all without specific active humans – through analysis of architectural remains and associated features and material culture. This path to the attribution of the archaeological record to household organization in prehistory may be one way of dealing with the problem of validating hypotheses about households with scientific rigor. But it nevertheless leaves prehistory hanging in a cloudy nowhere-land of faceless, genderless categories.

The "household scale of analysis" is the vehicle with which we may possibly make the inivisible women of prehistory and their production visible, since at this level – the minimal unit of social reproduction – their presence can be guaranteed. And yet, even in those household studies that have been carried out by archaeologists, gender relations are rarely if at all explicated. My own studies of household organization in southeast Europe have been no less characterized by this phenomenon. I confess that I have been highly inhibited from making such links even as far as "household" – let alone gender relations – by the perceived methodo-logical difficulty of attributing architectural and associated data to household membership and gender. Even those working in historical and near-historical periods have generally balked at the topic of gender relations. There is no doubt, however, that, as with social archaeology at a more regional level, strong *implicit* assumptions about generic gender relations form the foundation to many theoretical formulations in "household archaeology" studies.

It is possible that the identification of units of cooperative production or coresidence will satisfy the ambitions of archaeologists working at this microscale of analysis. There are indications, however, that for the interest in and impact of "household archaeology" to be more sustained, it will need to be incorporated in a more ambitious theoretical program in archaeology (Freidel 1989). Such a theoretical program would challenge the search for universal categories of microscale social units in prehistory, such as the nuclear family, as it has been challenged in anthropology as a whole (Moore 1988; Yanagisako 1979), and would recognize the richness of the variability of the social context of domestic action. Thus, the fact that the definition and nomenclature of microscale social units have received anything but consensus from anthropologists and social theorists, who would recognize the Coresidential Domestic Group, the Household, the Housefull and last but not least the Family, should be treated as a constructive challenge for dialogue rather than as an inhibitor to research (Ashmore and Wilk 1988; Bender 1967; Goody 1972; Hammel and Laslett, 1974; Laslett 1972; Moore 1988; Yanagisako 1979). This is not the place to enter into the dialogue, but obviously an archaeologist must if he/she is to understand or contribute anything to the discussion of the transformation of the social relations of production and gender relations in prehistory.

In recognizing the rich variability of social arrangements, dominance structures, and tensions produced in the social relations at this "domestic" scale, we see immediately that it is necessary never to forget that action at a microscale is an essential part of the social relations of production at larger scales, such as the village and the region and the known (and unknown) world.

> Despite the great difficulties facing the analysis and interpretation of households, the resolution of really fundamental issues in the study of ancient civilization lies in this empirical arena. Large-scale hierarchical society survives through the constant renegotiation of relationships between those who provide power, the commoners, and those who wield it as elite. The language of such negotiation . . . derives from both sides; and so too do the success and failure of complex societies. (Freidel 1989)

The recognition of this linkage has led researchers of social formations with a Marxist standpoint, but especially those with a *feminist* standpoint, to a very different understanding of the nature and role of labor and social relations at a household level and, most importantly, by definition, the nature of women's labor and the tension of gender relations (Hartmann 1981; Hartsock 1983; Moore 1988; Yanagisako 1979). It seems to me that this is the only theoretical basis that is likely to sustain interest in microscale archaeology, since it at once lifts the household sphere out of its current position of "assumed general knowledge" and as marginal to the "great events" of prehistory and provides a richly based theoretical framework for a consideration/imagination of the role of women's labor.

A second direction that will certainly contribute to the development of microscale studies is in dealing with the archaeological record itself. There is no doubt that the architectural remains of prehistory can be used much more imaginatively (this is *not* the same as speculatively) than the studies most frequently met with, whose primary aim is to reconstruct function and technology of the buildings as reflecting past human behavior. Ethnographic and architectural data show that buildings and their associated material culture act and have acted as both context and media in domestic tensions, gender relations, and dominance structures (Blier 1987; Bourdieu 1973; Donley 1982, 1987; Douglas 1972; Hodder 1986; Moore 1986).

The architectural remains of the archaeological record provide a rich source of information if one can be freed, if only slightly, from the restrictive effects of the testing requirements of logical positivism and from the need to attribute the record to function, gender, or "domestic unit" before one can think further about the context of gender relations and household tensions. Thus, ethnoarchaeological studies and ethnographic observations of residential architecture may be used for more than cautionary tales. They can be used to help us formulate expectations in terms of variability in architectural remains that relate to and reflect changes in the role, relations and actions of men and women in the household in prehistory. They allow us to formulate empirical hypotheses and/or "read" the archaeological record on architecture and associated debris in a rich variety of ways.

It will be interesting to see if a division of labor develops in archaeology of the kind noted by Gero (this volume) as a result of the potential development in household studies in relation to gender relations and a feminist standpoint. Will we see (can we see already?) that there is a tendency for women professionals to focus on domestic production, households, housework, domestic architecture, microscale analysis with male professionals tending to focus on the "other", the "outside": trade, regional studies, inter-settlement studies, world systems, monumental architecture, elite architecture, surplus production?

Households, Gender and the Archaeological Record of Architecture

If one does not assume households to be faceless units of cooperation, and if one does not assume that housework is a given universal pattern of devalued at-home social action, and if one does not assume that the roles and relations of men and women in domestic space is more or less uniform, and if one does not assume that the built environment looks the same to prehistoric eyes as it does to ours, then where does one start? How far can you allow your imagination take you? Where and how do you draw the parameters of what *can* be said? How do you proceed with your archaeological investigation and construction of an engendered prehistory?

There is no quick recipe. Not even a recipe book!

The investigations of archaeological settlements that I have carried out in Yugoslavia are by no means good models of how to proceed. They reflect my own changing questions, theoretical framework, and epistemological basis of research. I offer them here as the example with which I am most familiar. The research at Opovo–Ugar Bajbuk, in Northeast Yugoslavia, north of the Danube (figure 4.3) was designed specifically to demonstrate the changing role and activities of households in the Late Neolithic/Early Eneolithic of Southeast Europe, by a relatively large exposure of domestic structures and detailed stratigraphic control (Tringham et al. forthcoming, Tringham, Brukner, and Voytek 1985). In designing the project at Opovo, I assumed that the study of production, and of the distribution and transmission of property and products in its social context through the detailed study of the built environment (i.e. architecture) is a key to understanding the social relations of production and household organization. I am still under that impression and would now extend its importance to the study of gender relations in prehistory.

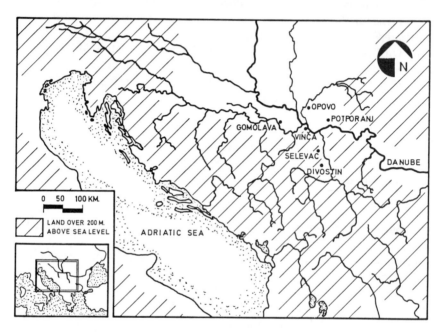

Figure 4.3 Map of Yugoslavia, showing geographical names and archaeological sites mentioned in the text.

At Opovo–Ugar Bajbuk in 1983–9, a clear microstratigraphic sequence of three phases of building activity and house overlapping and replacement has emerged in the 16×20 meter excavated block (figure 4.4). These comprise two building horizons, 1 and 3, with well preserved architectural remains of burned wattle-and-daub buildings, and one building horizon (2) whose architectural remains are less well preserved and/or existed outside the excavated block. The whole settlement demonstrates changes during a roughly 200-year period of the Late Neolithic/Early Eneolithic Vinča culture (ca.4400–4200 BC).

The original idea in 1983 – and it was innovative then for European prehistory – was that the architectural process reflected social processes

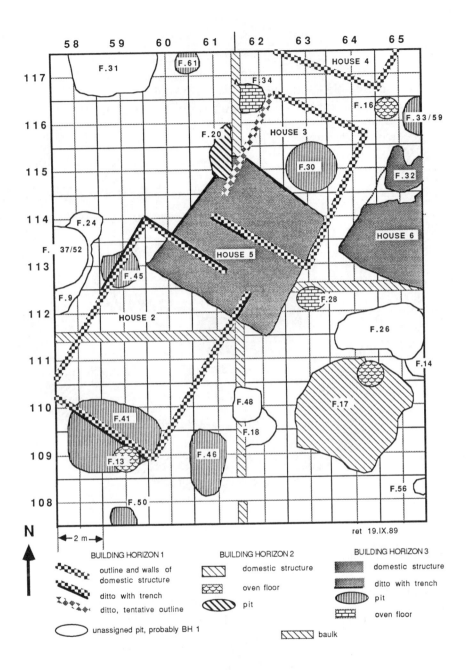

Figure 4.4 The sequence of building horizons at Opovo, showing the pattern of house replacement.

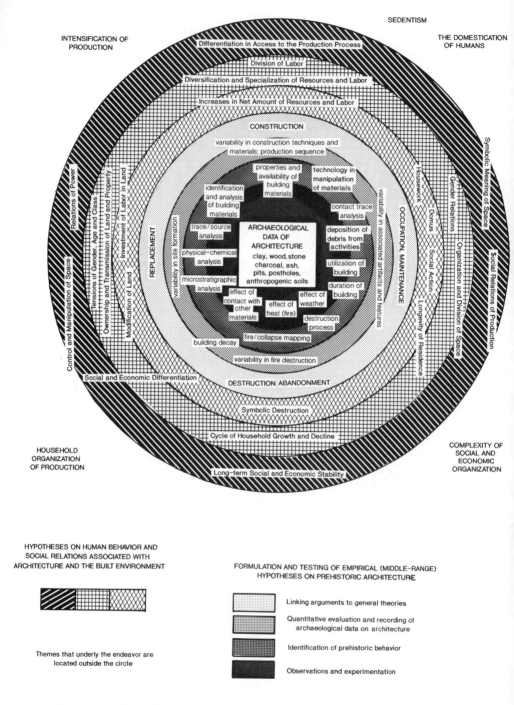

Figure 4.5 Chart for a middle-range research design to study archaeological architecture remains.

at a microscale (family, household, coresidential group) during the use-life of the buildings. This concept contrasted sharply with the more traditional prehistoric architecture studies that have focused on variability of the form and style of buildings as finished artifacts. In a series of complicated charts (figure 4.5) I plotted how these social processes could have been reflected in buildings at different stages of their use-lives (Tringham 1984). Ethnographic and ethnoarchaeological observations were synthesized and experimental studies of various kinds carried out to provide a series of test expectations of how different human actions would be reflected in the archaeological record (Stevanović 1984 and 1985). This whole enterprise may be described as leading towards a model of middle-range research design within the framework of a logical positivist scientific methodology of hypothesis testing (Binford 1981; Raab and Goodyear 1984; Tringham 1978, 1984).

The original aim of the study was to *attribute* certain architectural features and spatial patterns of associated materials, such as the recognition of discrete groups of complete production sequences, to units of economic and social cooperation (i.e. households); this would provide a first step in reconstructing the *transformation* of households at prehistoric Opovo. Thus, I fell smack into that trap of scientific restrictions that I warned against at the beginning of this paper. However, I do not wish, in a fit of self-critique, to denigrate this research design or the wealth of detailed data on construction, duration, utilization, maintenance, abandonment, destruction, and replacement of buildings that was collected as a result of it.

The middle-range research at Opovo has set basic material parameters of architectural variability at the site and provided information on the basis and nature of that variability that go beyond superficial appearance and association. The contrast between the original study and that beginning to be practiced now is that originally the information – on variability in materials, labor requirements and expenditure, external and internal elaboration of buildings, spatial arrangement of the built environment in general, the attempts to prolong a structure's use-life, its reuse, and the nature of its destruction and eventual abandonment – would have been assumed to provide a passive reflection of the actions and behavior of prehistoric households. Now, this same information is regarded as providing for us – the archaeologists – and for them – the prehistoric men and women – the *material context* of those actions and relations and tensions.

The underlying model of the transformation of Neolithic society in Southeast Europe of our original study prompted certain questions about the architectural record of the context of domestic life that went well beyond traditional questions of change in Southeast European prehistory. Envisaging the prehistoric settlement in terms of *household* organization allowed and encouraged me to think about the implications of the architectural changes on a small scale. It encouraged me to excavate and observe and take into account details of variability that I might otherwise have taken for granted as being the same from one domestic structure to another. It encouraged my efforts to establish contemporaneity or sequence of occupation of various buildings.

From the start, the site of Opovo presented some striking contrasts with what we had come to expect of the Late Neolithic Vinča culture settlements along the Danube river and in the fertile agricultural valleys and hills to its south. It is clear that there are differences in the material remains of the Upper and Lower Building Horizons, but neither horizon reflects the socioeconomic system of the large settlements of the Danube and Morava basin Vinča settlements to the south, nor those of the Tisza culture to the north.

When compared with the domestic structures in other Vinča culture settlements south of the Danube, those excavated at Opovo have many features of construction in common in terms of building materials (plank-post-wattling framework covered by clay daub) and detached quadrangular ground-plan. In the Late Neolithic/Early Eneolithic settlements of Southeast Europe, including Selevac, it had been observed that the anticipated and actual use-life of houses increased. We have interpreted this as provision being made for long-term residence of the "domestic groups" (households) and reflecting the emergence of stable long-lasting households as the main units of cooperative production and distribution (Chapman 1981; Kaiser and Voytek 1983; Sherratt 1982; Tringham 1971, 1990). For example, the addition of rooms onto the ends of dwellings in Neolithic Europe, making square structures rectangular and increasing the length of rectangular structures, has been hypothesized to reflect the growth of a household during its cycle of growth and decline (Coudart 1980; Startin 1978). The predominantly rectangular ground-plan of the Vinča culture houses, therefore, may be thought of as representing the dwellings of long-established households.

We expected Opovo to show a similar development, modified perhaps by the fact that it was not located in prime agricultural soils, but in a predominantly marshland environment with islands of the more difficult to cultivate chernozem soils. At Opovo, we were deliberately looking for information on planned and actual use-life of dwellings by studying the nature of the building materials, technique of construction of buildings and surrounding facilities, such as storage pits, in terms of the relative investment of labour and commitment made by a group in their modification of the landscape, maintenance of dwellings, and the use-life of artifacts associated with the occupation of the house.

Our overall impression of the houses at Opovo, however, is that they were less well prepared and less long-lived than the majority of Vinča culture houses, especially those of the latest building horizon (BH 1). This impression is provided by the lack of clay floor in BH 1, the wooden framework of houses of BH 1 and 3 (even that with two storeys) which comprised a dense network of small vertical poles rather than the thick deep posts noted in the large houses south of the Danube, and the fact that all domestic structures excavated at Opovo at 6–7 meters length are much shorter than the standard Vinča culture dwellings, although they have the same width (Tringham et al. forthcoming). Associated features such as a relative lack of storage facilities and vessels and a high percentage of wild animals among the faunal remains strengthened this impression.

The majority of Vinča culture settlements are characterized by a greater degree of complexity in the use of residential household space than preceding or succeeding settlements in the Danube and Morava basin (Chapman 1981). This complexity is expressed especially in the division of space as separate rooms within the buildings. It is traditionally suggested that separate rooms reflect a more elaborate division of household activities and tasks. Such complexity in the use of space is also thought to be reflected in an increasing number of facilities and activities, such as storage and food preparation and cooking, being moved within the walls of the dwellings. The reconstruction of room function and activities, based on the spatial patterning of the material record of production, consumption, and distribution on and around the house floors (e.g. Ciolek-Torrello 1985; Dodd 1984; Hill 1970; Kramer 1982b; Reid and Whittlesley 1982; Watson 1979), has been an important aspect of traditional architectural studies of Vinča culture settlements (Benac 1973; Stalio 1968) and Neolithic and Eneolithic settlements of Southeast Europe in general (Dumitrescu 1965; Kričevski 1940; Passek 1949).

The houses at Opovo are different from the Vinča pattern of increasing complexity in the use of space on all counts. There is only one example of an excavated dwelling at Opovo with an internal division into a room and with an internal oven. In Building Horizon 1, a low partition (30 cm high) separated a clay-floored area with a bread-oven and food-preparation facilities from the rest of the dwelling in House 2 (figure 4.6). Although not a complete physical separation of these tasks, the partition does reflect nevertheless a subdividing of space. In Building Horizon 3 (the earlier one), no such room subdivision existed on the floor of House 5 or 6, nor was any formal food-producing area identified, for example with an oven or built-in storage pot inside the house. Within House 5, however, there was a vertical subdivision of

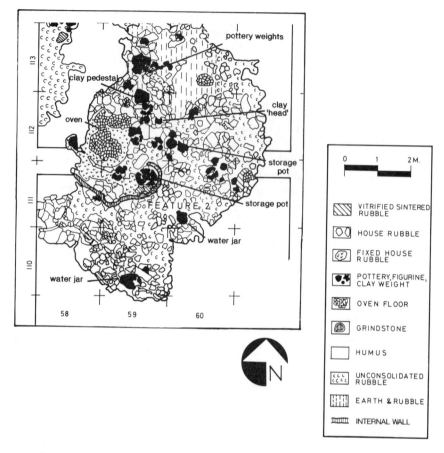

Figure 4.6 Ground-plan of House 2 of Building Horizon 1 at Opovo.

space provided by the construction of a partial second storey or loft (figure 4.7). Upper storeys have traditionally been interpreted as the location of internal food storage, rather than as provision of additional living space for a growing household or as specially segregated space for other purposes. Our conclusions as to the significance of the second storey of House 5 must await the subsequent analysis of associated materials, but I am trying not to assume that the loft was for grain storage. Second storeys have hardly ever been reported from other Late Neolithic settlements of Southeast Europe, but this is probably the effect of focusing excavation of house debris on clearing the floor and its contents, rather than on a detailed recording and excavation of the collapsed superstructural rubble (where the second storey is to be found), as we did in the Opovo project.

Our conclusion in a recent report (within the original theoretical framework of the project) as to the households represented in the excavated houses at Opovo is that they are shorter-lived and/or less well established than those in the large villages such as Selevac, Gomolava,

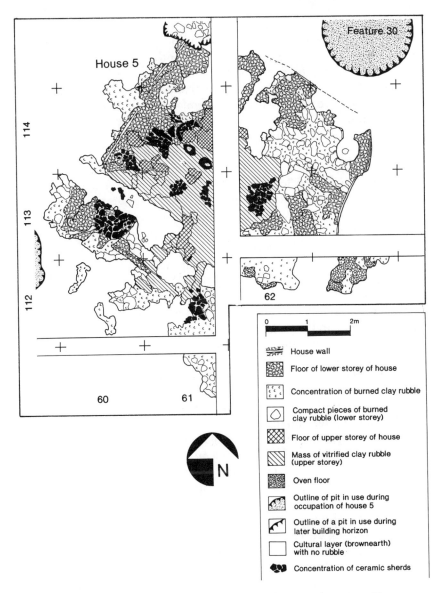

Figure 4.7 Ground-plan of House 5 of Building Horizon 3 at Opovo.

and Vinča in the primary agricultural regions of Southeast Europe at this time, and that their activities and/or size and complexity was very different from the latter (Tringham et al. forthcoming). Moreover, these differences became more marked during the later occupation of the village. Traditionally, archaeologists would have had no problem in explaining these differences by the fact that the "domestic" structures and the behavior of their occupants at Opovo represent an adaptive response to the special ecological conditions of the southwest Banat, more forested than the Hungarian Plain to the north, but marshier than the forested region further south in the Danube and Morava basins. But this model does not satisfy anyone interested in household organization, much less anyone interested in an engendered prehistory. What was such a population doing in this "inhospitable" area in the first place? What is the significance of the fact that they have much of the same cultural elaboration established in the Vinča culture settlements (ceramic decoration, figurines, etc.)? Why should their households or their houses necessarily have been less long-lived as an "adaptive response"?

Can we improve on the richness of this "adaptive response" model? No doubt of it, but if we do, then we run the risk of losing credibility in the world of Science, since any other models will take us away from the strict rigor of testability with the archaeological record. No matter.

Here is a dialogue (imaginary) of what four different archaeologists would make of our situation at Opovo: Marija Gimbutas, Ian Hodder, Andrew Sherratt, and myself. The dialogue is imaginary, partly because it has never taken place (and I am sure it never will), and partly because two of these archaeologists (Gimbutas and Sherratt) have not yet included a discussion of Opovo in their published works. But in general it is based on their published models (Gimbutas 1970, 1980, 1982; Hodder 1990; Sherratt 1981, 1984). This dialogue is really a medium by which to introduce their different scenarios of social and cultural change in Europe in the fifth to fourth millennia BC (calendric).

It is not my intention in this dialogue to set these eminent people up in competition as being more or less plausible (not even myself). They all make excellent usage of what is essentially the same body of data. But they do hold different underlying assumptions and beliefs about the world. Thus they selected different aspects of the data and even certain sets of data as deserving top priority. They attach greater significance to different sets of data in the advocation of their models. In other words they are creating different kinds of archaeological records (Patrik 1985). They will not talk about their models in detail in this short exposé. The point here is to show that they should be treated as a plurality – but a critically analyzed plurality – in the construction of prehistory, and that certain dimensions of the problem have hardly been considered.

A Radio Story

Interviewer: *Here is a picture of the ground of House 2 at Opovo (figure 4.6) What do you think of the "room"?*
AS: A pathetic attempt to recreate the grandeur of the great households in the aggregated villages of the south.
MG: A temple to the Goddess.
IH: A symbolic expression of the richness of the dramatus domesticus, women, domus.
RT: A separation of domestic labor from surplus production.

Interviewer: *Who built the houses of Opovo?*
AS: Men while women were hoeing.
MG: Men under women's (the Goddess's) direction.
IH: Women under men's direction.
RT: The coresidential cooperative productive unit.

Interviewer: *What did the women do at Opovo?*
AS: Hoed.
MG: Everything.
IH: Practiced a secret subversive power.
RT: I don't know; I can't say; I presume they participated in household cooperative action.

Interviewer: *Why do you think Opovo looks so different from other Vinča culture settlements?*
MG: I don't think it does. I think that they have exaggerated the differences. The influence of the Goddess is as strong at Opovo as she is elsewhere in the Vinča culture. These people have been demonstrated to be cooperative and peaceful. There is no evidence of the new wave of patriarchal war-loving Kurgans that destroyed the peacefulness of Old Europe. It is true that Opovo is poorer, and demonstrates fewer of the accomplishments of the civilization of Old Europe. But what else would you expect out there in the marshlands?

IH: I think that Opovo is similar enough to other Vinča culture sites that I can include it in a general treatment of symbolic and social life in those villages. In fact I can use Opovo as a well excavated site typifying a period when the domus was the central focus of life, when women were highly visible and when "individuals submitted themselves to the rules and constraints of larger . . . units" (1990 ch. 4, p. 21) in Europe. Yet it's true that Opovo shows an unusually high visibility of the "wild", the untamed, the uncontrolled, the outside. This could possibly be an early indication of the "collapse of the domus and the outside becoming the new discourse of social life" (1990, ch. 4, p. 28). Statistically, though, it is only one site.

RT: It is a well-known fact that I don't find the model of adaptation to the ecological context of the marshland of SW Banat satisfying. I prefer to interpret the situation at Opovo in the form of two possible scenarios. In one I think that Opovo was a special purpose, short-term, perhaps seasonal, settlement oriented toward a limited range of activities, such as the extraction of certain raw materials, for example antler, or carrying out exchange for minerals from the mountains on the northwestern margin of the marshlands. As an alternative I suggest that Opovo was a more permanent bud-off from one of the larger Danube Vinča culture sites, for example Vinča itself, of a "junior" or "disenfranchised" household(s) into the agriculturally marginal land north of the Danube. In both these alternative models we would expect to see much of the exchange network and symbolic expression and elaboration of the Vinča culture settlements intact at Opovo, as indeed we do. What is changed is that the full complement of production activities (tool production, storage) is not present at Opovo. In my opinion, the architectural evidence and the nature of the tasks selected and resources exploited favors the model of a more seasonal short-term specialized nature for the prehistoric village at Opovo. One of the important sources for enrichening our picture of the village will be the results of the current investigation on the nature of the household organization and the relocation of residence at Opovo in contrast to that of other Vinča culture and Tisza culture sites. We would expect the household to have a different form and activity according to each of these models. But in both cases they would look different from the well-established stable households of the aggregated villages in the Danube and Morava Valleys. According to model of seasonal specialized settlement, only a limited number of people would occupy the settlement, possibly being predominantly one gender, or one age group, so that one would not expect the kind of cooperation in production, distribution, and reproduction as on the larger sites. According to the model of "bud-off" settlement, we would expect to see fully developed stable household organization, with cooperation in production and distribution, but at the beginning of their developmental cycles and with strong ties of alliance with the "homeland" as well as new exchange patterns with other areas. According to the "adaptation response" model – the one I don't like – we would probably expect to see poorly formed household units, probably the loose kinds of cooperation as was described for the Early Neolithic situation in the Danube and Morava Valleys.

AS: What we see at Opovo is the Secondary Products Revolution in action. I think that Opovo is an early example of what became the norm in Southeast Europe in the succeeding Late Copper Age (Eneolithic), that is a small hamlet scattered in an area that should rationally be regarded as "marginal" to the previously occupied easily cultivated soils. Large aggregated villages such as Selevac and Vinča were the more typical form of Late Neolithic/Early Eneolithic settlement. The political community coincided with such villages in which several lineages would have been aggregated. The role and power of lineages in these villages were subordinated to cross-cutting institutions based on age grades, ritual groupings, etc. Villages such as Selevac and Vinča were "organized on an established territorial basis, with public rituals and symbolic analogies based on female images", and they were "characterized by stable flows of regionally-acquired goods" (Sherratt 1984: 132).

The later Copper Age villages, of which I think Opovo is an early example, by contrast, were dispersed settlements in conditions of unconstrained expansion in which genealogical units (wide-ranging lineages) were the primary units of political and productive and distributive cooperation. The individual head (male) of a lineage provided the focus of allegiances over a wider area and his power/political role is expressed in inter-regional symbols of rank. Along with this system of political control went a change to "a greater emphasis on exotic goods and longer distance trading contacts . . . in which information-carrying items took precedence over more basic commodities. Their territorial basis was less stable, their ethos was a competitive and self-aggrandizing one, with symbolic analogies based on the image of the warrior male" (Sherratt 1984: 132).

The change of settlement pattern represented by sites such as Opovo was ultimately the result of adaptive innovations in technology (plough, milk- and wool-production, wheeled transport) in response to modifications of the resource base caused by such factors as a reduction in soil fertility, growth of population beyond the carrying capacity of the site territory, and deforestation. I hypothesize, that, as part of the social adaptation to these ecological problems, there were marked changes in social and political organization, reflected as "a shift from societies organized primarily on the basis of community . . . to an increased emphasis on the potential of kinship for forming wider networks of alliance" (Sherratt 1984: 132), expressed in the declining importance of settlements and rising prominence of cemeteries (which map social relations symbolically that are no longer visible in residence patterns).

This imaginary dialogue has demonstrated I hope that none of the interviewees is practicing a feminist archaeology. Each, however, has something valuable to offer on the path to creating an engendered prehistory of Southeast Europe.

Marija Gimbutas's study, as mentioned earlier in this paper, is a "remedial feminist study" which has put women into the pot of archaeological interpretation and has stirred vigorously, but her basic epistemological framework and theoretical standpoint remains very much in the center of traditional Establishment archaeology in Europe, although certainly her work does not satisfy the rigors of the New Archaeology program of scientific hypothesis validation. Her ultimate aim is to write prehistory in large (macro) terms. Behavior is normatized on a large-scale in time and space to paint a picture of massive and

Figure 4.8 Fanciful but faceless reconstruction of House 5 at Opovo.

generalized change, for example from matriarchal to patriarchal, or from equalitarian to hierarchical.

Ian Hodder's is an example of "post-processual archaeology" which turns on its head the traditional "processual" passive reflective role of material culture into that of an "active" medium for and symbolic expression of, for example, the tensions of gender relations in material culture including architecture. This, as mentioned above, is one of the essential steps to viewing and creating the archaeological record from a plurality of standpoints, including that of the women of prehistory, that would characterize an engendered prehistory. Hodder professes to be interested in the social action of individuals within their social and political context. In practice, however, he focuses on the "domus" that has an abstract, emotional, almost psychic quality emphasizing the separation of the "domesti" from the "outside" (Ladurie, 1978). Within this context, the behavior of the actors, their household, their village become normatized as he extrapolates from one site (Opovo) to the whole region.

Andrew Sherratt focuses on the effect of long-term transformations of social and economic relations on regional settlement patterns in prehistory. In keeping with the mainstream of social archaeology, he sees that the most important factors in the transformational process involved demographic growth and increasing control of the material world:

changes in land-use, settlement pattern, subsistence and agricultural and other productive technology. These changes are typically at a macroscale and involve political decisions and power brokerage. It *is* essential to consider this scale of action, but here this is done at the expense of a consideration of variability in the domestic sphere itself. Gender relations are implied throughout his studies, but not specifically addressed. Both Hodder and Sherratt rely heavily on generalizations that correlate material culture with social forms and relations and with social divisions of labor (hoe/women; plough/men).

My own research of the social relations of production in prehistory, architecture, household organization, and domestic production, is the only one of these four that focused on the variability of social action at a microscale, and thus has contributed to this essential prerequisite for an engendered prehistory. In spite of its potential for an engendered prehistory of Southeast Europe, the essential aim of my study at Opovo *until now* has been to attribute aspects in the use-life of a building to a *faceless* unit of cooperative production and distribution and/or coresidence, a unit without gender, a unit without age, a unit without personae (figure 4.8).

The problem has been that "faces" are not demonstrable in the archaeological record, they cannot be "operationalized" archaeologically, they are not testable, and thus they cannot be taken seriously by respectable scientists. It moreover takes a great deal of effort and imaginative power to consider them. But they *are* there (figure 4.9). To "engender" my original topic of the transformation of households in prehistoric Southeast Europe means, in essence, to deal with this problem. It does *not* mean to search for the material correlates of gender roles in the architectural phenomena of deep prehistory as a primary research goal. Nor is it a "remedial" attempt to put women into prehistoric household cooperative action. The aim must be rather to produce a visibility of gender when I visualize such an elemental social unit as the household.

Archaeologists tend to base their visualization of gender relations and the sexual division of labor, either explicitly or enthymematically, on the cross-cultural generalizations about the family or household made by social anthropologists and social historians (Boserup 1970; Goody 1969; Laslett 1972). Such general correlations between social institutions and division of labor and levels of technology as hoe cultivation/women's labor/covert male power or plough cultivation/men's labor/overt male power have been severely criticized as treating the family and household as a social entity whose contextual variability and internal division of activity is not of crucial importance (Yanagisako 1979). These generalizations have also encouraged the highly criticized separation of the domestic sphere from the extra-domestic or public sphere (Moore 1988: 21–4).

The generalizations about gender relations are somehow more attractive and easier to deal with (can be grasped on a superficial basis more quickly by archaeologists who are always desperate for a quick entrée into social theory, especially those not trained in it from the start of their careers) than those that emphasize variability and the investigation of the social organization at a microscale in a specific historical context (e.g. Moore 1988). Archaeologists need some solid "givens" to hang on to. For prehistorians, at least, the historical context is not given, we have to create it. If household activity and gender relations are also not a given, predictable entity, then where do we start our construction of prehistory? One answer lies with the material culture itself (Hodder 1986).

The solution to "adding faces" to the prehistoric households, however, lies (contrary to the opinion of many of my empiricist friends) *in enriching the archaeologists' models and general knowledge* of gender relations within household and families. The anthropological/ethnographic and historical literature is rich with details of the variability of gender relations at a microscale and the essential relationship of these to

Figure 4.9 The reconstructed House 5, with faces, thanks to Pieter Bruegel.

macroscale contexts. It is rich in examples that illustrate the importance of "domestic" labor in household production and the negotiating and political power that women and families have beyond that of physical reproduction (Moore 1988; Yanagisako 1979). We do not have to "identify" this rich variability in the archaeological record but we must be aware of it. Why simplify prehistory?

To engender prehistory allows and encourages us to go much further in our understanding of architectural variability in terms of the dominance relations and tensions between males and females, between siblings, between neighbors, between age-groups as they move within and between the space that we call the built environment. A significant change in the archaeological pattern of settlement, such as, for example, that of which Opovo might be a part at the end of the Neolithic in Southeast Europe, is the dispersal of settlement on agriculturally marginal lands. This has considerable implications for labour access and resource procurement for a household as a whole, but an interest in gender relations enables us to broaden these implications to include a rapid decrease in the pooling of labor between households and extra-kin support especially for the female members of the households.

Death of the House and the End of the Household Cycle

One way in which the archaeological record can be transformed by the richer set of theoretical formulations that is stimulated by an interest in household organization and gender relations in prehistory is to study the relationship of a household to a locus or loci through time. House replacement, that is the placing of buildings in relation to each other in time as well as in space, has always been an important aspect of archaeological research, usually disguised under the dehumanized title of "chronological sequence of building or occupation horizons". This aspect of the archaeological record, however, takes on new significance when viewed within the context of the rich body of ethnographic observations and historical records of the ownership and inheritance of land. There is much evidence for links between the treatment of the dwelling in the latter days of its use-life and the placing of a new house on the one hand and the ownership and inheritance of property, especially land, as well as gender relations that focus on land on the other hand (Moore 1986: 91–102). The distributive role of the household between generations by inheritance comprises a most important factor in determining the size and nature of a household and its built environment (Goody 1969, 1972; Laslett 1972).

For those who wish to take their prehistory beyond the variability of the household to the very heart of the transformation of gender relations, one must grasp the richness and complexity of modeling links between domestic organization, forms of inheritance, and the sexual division of labor (Boserup 1970; Goody 1976; Moore 1988: 45). In European prehistory the modeling of changes in inheritance systems has closely followed the generalizations of Goody and Boserup, mentioned above, that are linked to general models of socioeconomic transformation. It has been suggested, for example, that a Neolithic–Early Eneolithic social formation characterized by a hoe cultivation/women's labor/covert male power/control of labor/inheritance through the household correlation was replaced by a Late Eneolithic–Bronze Age social formation that was characterized by a plough cultivation/men's labor/overt male power/ control of land/interest in land ownership and inheritance/inheritance through extra-household units correlation (Bradley 1984; Hodder 1984, 1990; Sherratt 1981, 1984). The point is here that these questions of significant social transformation are considered always on a macroscale. If considered at all at a microscale, it has only been by observation of archaeological burials and grave-goods. The question of inheritance has never been linked either conceptually or analytically to changes in the destruction, abandonment, and replacement of houses.

In Southeast Europe, the period of greatest intensification of production and permanence of settlement, as well as the universal practice of burning of houses described below – the Late Neolithic and Early Eneolithic – coincides with the practice of rebuilding a new structure in a completely new location using completely new foundations (figure 4.10) (Chapman 1981; Tringham 1990). At Selevac, for example, such horizontal displacement over a 200–300-year period resulted in occupational materials being spread over a 53-hectare area of the site (Tringham 1990). What is the significance of a change to horizontal displacement of new buildings in a period of supposed decrease in availability of new land as has been hypothesized in the Late Neolithic of Southeast Europe (Chapman 1990; Sherratt 1984)?

A most interesting topic from the point of view of ownership and inheritance of land for the prehistory of Southeast Europe is the variability in the distribution of mound ("tell") settlements and flat settlements (Davidson 1976; Kosse (Krudy) 1968; Rosen 1986; Tringham 1990). What is interesting is that horizontal displacement is not mutually exclusive of the formation of a "tell". The "tell" settlements of Southeast Europe, e.g. Vinča, Gomolava, Karanovo, usually involve a certain amount of horizontal displacement of consecutive buildings, in contrast to those of the Near East, which are characterized by vertical superimposition of buildings (Banning and Byrd 1987). The traditional explanation for the concentration of deposits in mounds or "tells" in

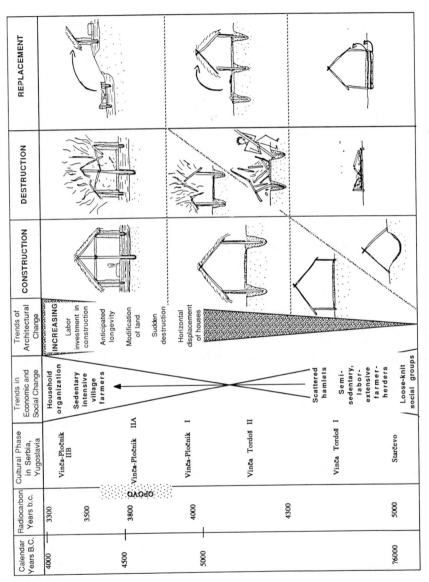

Figure 4.10 Pattern of change in house replacement and socio-economic transformation in Neolithic–Eneolithic Southeast Europe.

Europe is in terms of adaptive response to particular topographic restrictions on settlement, such as river or marshland. But there are certainly many other reasons to restrict residence locus, such as unequal social access to and ownership of land for residence. Thus the nature of the relationship between house replacement and "tell" formation is obviously more complex than is usually assumed.

At Opovo, the deposits of different building horizons piled up to form a low mound over what was already a natural island in the marshes. It is possible that the area for residence was restricted by the surrounding marshland but we can imagine many other restricting factors, such as household ownership and inheritance of specific loci for residence. The two well-preserved building horizons (BH1 and BH 3) at Opovo are not chronologically contiguous and display a certain amount of (but not complete) horizontal displacement (figure 4.4). Nevertheless, the builders of the BH 1 structures were probably well aware of the remains of earlier building horizons, and knew their exact locations, either through tradition or direct observation on or near their occupation surface. For example, they used these remains to their advantage in the construction of their dwellings, as a way of providing a stable foundation layer, probably without themselves having to go to the effort of preparing a clay floor.

What was the end of the use-life of a house at Opovo like? During the Late Neolithic/Early Eneolithic period, the settlements of Southeast Europe, including those of the Vinča culture, are characterized by burned remains of houses which surpass in terms of their volume and their universality on the settlements those preceding and succeeding this period and those found anywhere else in Europe. It is this fact that is responsible for the preservation of excellent settlement data in this period. Opovo is no exception to this pattern.

Explanation of this "Burned House Horizon" in European prehistory has traditionally been based on intuitive common-sense reasoning: accidental fires resulting from the increased use of fire within houses or the denser crowding of houses within the villages; deliberately set fires, either individually or as a whole village, due to inter-settlement competition, unrest, raiding, and even invasion. Because of the coincidence of the apparently universal occurrence of house-fires with socio-economic changes such as the intensification of production, permanence of settlement, and organizational importance of autonomous households, the systematic investigation of their causes has taken up much of the research effort in the architectural sphere at Opovo. Our preliminary results show that there were no houses that did not burn. In addition, the lack of burned materials in the areas between houses indicates that the houses burned in separate fires.

The houses burned at temperatures that in some parts of each house reached over 1000 °C. Such temperatures are regarded as very high for accidental fires of wattle-and-daub houses and indicate that the fires are likely to have been "helped" by deliberate fueling and tending (Kirk 1969). For example, the central part of House 5 at Opovo is characterized by a massive area (ca 3×3 m) of vitrified structural clay and ceramics, indicating a fire of high intensity at this point; this represents the rubble of the upper storey, which collapsed along with its melted pots which were fused to the floor in the heat of the combustion, and fell onto the lower floor along with the collapsing side walls burying, burning, crushing, and preserving the ceramics, stone, and other contents (including textile and string) of the lower floor (figure 4.7).

There are many reasons why dwellings might be destroyed deliberately in separate fires, for example, to eradicate pests, insects, disease. It is also likely that the burned houses of the "Burned House Horizon" should be explained by a multitude of causes. In some sites in Southeast Europe they may be the result of village-wide fires resulting from accident or deliberate arson. Some of us are gently suggesting, however, that the destruction of a house by burning in the Late Neolithic/Early Eneolithic period was frequently a deliberate act carried out at the death of the household head as a symbolic end of the household cycle. This is certainly an "attractive" hypothesis to me in view of the suggested importance of autonomous households as units of socioeconomic cooperation at this time in Southeast Europe. But how would this idea fit into our engendered prehistory of Opovo?

Efforts were made in prehistoric Opovo, evidently immediately after the burning events, to flatten the burned remains of the houses and deposit some of it in pits, in one case filling a probable well, and in other cases topping off garbage pits. My general impression, however, is that the pattern of house replacement at Opovo conforms to the pattern of house replacement in contexts where the land available or preferred for residence seems to be more restricted, that is the "tells" such as those at Vinča and Gomolava, on the banks of the Danube and Sava respectively. In this respect, the houses at Opovo reflect a continuity of land use and (possibly) land ownership.

Many dramatic changes in social life undoubtedly accompanied those terms that we write so blithely: "the household in the decline and at the end of its cycle" and "the end of the use-life of a house". It is tempting to envisage the whole process of abandoning old houses and locating and constructing new ones coldly and objectively. Recent ethnographic and non-Western architectural studies, however, abound with accounts of the significant impact that these processes have on the lives of the men and women involved. A "house" is part of their social lives, with a life-cycle of its own, even to the extent of being a person (Alexander 1979; Blier 1987: 118).

Fantasy>Fact: How to End the Use-life of a House

She watched the house burn.

He had died. He's strung up in the tree now, safe. Now it's time to kill the house.

Finally after all these years living in these godforsaken marshlands. Stuck in this place, with no one to turn to or to help, except him, or worse, *her.*

It was alright for him, he could escape *that* one by running off to the village. "Time to take the deer timber down there" or "my turn to tell the story to the new ones down there." And off he'd go. Leaving me. And her. And the others, but they don't count.

It's burning nicely now. What a crummy house they built. Nothing but kindling for its bones. Only an outer skin. I'm surprised the loft didn't fall down on our heads, with all his pots and her rugs up there. Well it doesn't take long to collapse and kill it. They wouldn't think much of this house down in the village. You can't kill a house by yourself down there. But then you can't do anything by yourself down there.

Here it goes! Watch the flame! Look at it burn! Yellow, purple, sunlight, moonlight, orange, marshlight. Ugh! What's that smell? Must be her clothes! Or maybe he was hiding something else up there. Ooops, step back a little. My hair's scorching. It makes my eyes water. I'm crying! I haven't done that for a long time.

What a roaring! It sounds like those dreadful other men – the deer – when they come looking for us – the women. Why do they always have to fight? There go his pots. All killed. Finally! They seem to be throbbing in the middle there.

Mustn't let the fire die, or he'll come back. More wood. Pile it up a bit more here. Let in some more air! A house must breathe to die. Push the air into its cavity. That's better. Flaming again! Burn his pots! Kill his stuff! Now I'm in charge. The circle is complete. I can go back to the vilage. Away from the heat, away from the creatures that torture and bite. Back to village noise, complaints, shrieks, laughter, gossip, friends, life.

Afterword

Microscale archaeology of the social relations of production in pre-history – the study of residential architecture and household organization and production – is an essential prerequisite for an engendered prehistory and, I would argue, any kind of social archaeology. When carried out with a feminist standpoint it allows us to engage in the study of a prehistory "with faces", faces behind which lie gender, age, hopes, fears, aspirations, "the whole catastrophe" as Zorba has described to us. Such faces may be less visible to those who prefer to study only large general trends and patterns of adaptive processes, but they are certainly not irrelevant to the trajectory of human transformation.

NOTES

1 The quotations have been taken from a secondary source, Eisler 1987: 13–14. The book from which they are supposedly quoted is Gimbutas's *The Early Civilization of Europe* (1980), Monograph for Indo-European Studies 131, UCLA. I have not seen this book. It is not listed in Books in Print. Nor is it listed in the long bibliography of Gimbutas's works in her Festschrift: S. Skomal and E. Polomé, eds (1987) *Proto-Indo-European: The Archaeology of a Linguistic Problem*, Institute for the Study of Man. I imagine that Eisler has seen the monograph in manuscript form. In this case, however, I am not sure how reliable are her quotation skills, since she has surely misquoted Gimbutas who, according to Eisler (p. 14), in chapter 2, p. 32–3 of this non-circulating book, describes "the 53-grave cemetary [sic] of Vinča, (in which) hardly any difference in wealth of equipment was discernible between male and female graves . . ." Gimbutas certainly knows that only 11 graves have been found at Vinča that date to the period of her "Old Europe" and that, in the Vinča culture as a whole, no more than 23 graves were ever found together in a cemetery. Perhaps Eisler misread Varna (in northeast Bulgaria) for Vinča. However, this is the only place where Gimbutas sets out her ideas of the nature of Old European society, and for that reason I am using it here.

2 The use of the term "domestic" from this point in the paper will return at frequent intervals. As with many terms that try to express social action at a microscale in more humanistic ways, "domestic" is as fully loaded with meaning for us as are the terms "house", "household", and "family". I have sometimes, however, not been able to avoid the use of the word. In doing so I refer the reader to a discussion of the term "domestic" in Spector's contribution to this volume with which I concur fully. I am also aware of the danger of its usage in leading towards an implicit acceptance of a whole set of dichotomies such as domestic/public, inside/outside. Since it is just these dichotomies which I am trying to avoid in my engendering of the prehistory

of Europe, I would also refer the reader to the excellent discussion of the use of this term in Moore (1988: 21).

REFERENCES

Alexander, C. (1979). *The Timeless Way of Building.* Oxford: Oxford University Press.
Ashmore, W. and R. Wilk (1988). "House and Household in the Mesoamerican Past: An Introduction." In *Household and Community in the Mesoamerican Past*, R. Wilk and W. Ashmore, eds. Albuquerque: University of New Mexico Press, 1–28.
Banning, E. B. and B. F. Byrd (1987). "Houses and the Changing Residential Unit: Domestic Architecture at PPNB 'Ain Ghazal, Jordan." *Proceedings of the Prehistoric Society* 53: 309–25.
Bawden, G. (1982). "Community Organization Reflected by the Household: A Study of pre-Columbian Social Dynamics." *Journal of Field Archaeology* 9: 165–81.
Beechey, V. (1978). "Women and Production: A Critical Analysis of Some Sociological Theories of Women's Work." In *Feminism and Materialism*, A. Kohn and A.-M. Wolpe, eds. London: Routledge & Kegan Paul, 155–97.
Benac, A. (1973). "Obre II, a Neolithic settlement of the Butmir Group at Gornje Polje." *Wissenschaftliche Mitteilungen des Bosnisch-Herzegowinischen Landesmuseums* III(A): 5–191.
Bender, B. (1985). "Prehistoric Developments in the American Midcontinent and in Brittany, Northwest France." In *Prehistoric Hunter-Gatherers*, D. Price and J. Brown, eds. New York: Academic Press, 21–57.
Bender, D. (1967). "A Refinement of the Concept of Household: Families, Co-residence, and Domestic Functions." *American Anthropologist* 69: 493–504.
Binford, L. R. (1981). *Bones: Ancient Men and Modern Myths.* New York: Academic Press.
Blier, S. P. (1987). *The Anatomy of Architecture: Ontology and Metaphor in Batammaliba Architectural Expression.* Cambridge: Cambridge University Press.
Boserup, E. (1970). *Women's Role in Economic Development.* London: George Allen & Unwin.
Bourdieu, P. (1973). "The Berber House." In *Rules and Meanings: The Anthroplogy of Everyday Knowledge*, M. Douglas, ed. Harmondsworth: Penguin Books, 98–110.
Bradley, R. (1984). *The Social Foundations of Prehistoric Britain.* London: Longman.
Champion, T. (1969). "Introduction." In *Centre and Periphery*, T. Champion, ed. London: Unwin, Hyman, 1–21.
Chapman, J. (1981). *The Vinča Culture.* Oxford: BAR International Series 117.
—— (1990). "Regional Study of the North Šumadija Region." In *Selevac: A Prehistoric Village in Yugoslavia*, R. Tringham and D. Krstić, eds. Los Angeles: UCLA Institute of Archaeology Press.

Childe, V. G. (1958). *The Prehistory of European Society*. London: Penguin Books.

Ciolek-Torrello, R. (1985). "A Typology of Room Function at Grasshopper Pueblo, Arizona." *Journal of Field Archaeology* 12: 43–63.

—— (1989). "Households, Floor Assemblages and the 'Pompei Premise' at Grasshopper Pueblo." in S. M acEachern, D. Archer, and R. Garvin, eds. *Households and Communities*, Calgary, Alberta: Chacmool, 201–8.

Conkey, M. and J. Spector (1984). "Archaeology and the Study of Gender." In *Advances in Archaeological Method and Theory*, vol. 7, M. Schiffer, ed. New York: Academic Press, 1–38.

Coudart, A. (1980). "A propos de la maison néolithique danubienne." Paper presented at the conference Le Néolithique de l'Est de la France, Sens.

Davidson, D. A. (1976). "Processes of Tell Formation and Erosion." In *Geoarchaeology; Earth Sciences and the Past*, D. A. Davidson and M. Shackley, eds. London: Duckworth, 255–66.

Dodd, W. A. (1984). "The use of domestic space by sedentary households: some organizing principles." Paper presented at the 49th Annual Meeting of the Society for American Archaeology, Portland, Oregon.

Donley, L. (1982). "House Power: Swahili Space and Symbolic Markers." In *Symbolic and Structural Archaeology*, I. Hodder, ed. Cambridge: Cambridge University Press, 63–73.

—— (1987). "Life in the Swahili Town House Reveals the Symbolic Meaning of Spaces and Artefact Assemblages." *The African Archaeological Review* 5: 181–92.

Douglas, M. (1972). "Symbolic Orders in the Use of Domestic Space." In *Man, Settlement, and Urbanism*, P. Ucko, R. Tringham and G. W. Dimbleby, eds. London: Duckworth, 63–73.

Dumitrescu, V. (1965). "Cascioărele: A Late Neolithic Settlement on the Lower Danube." *Archaeology* 18: 34–40.

Eisler, R. (1987). *The Chalice and the Blade*. San Francisco: Harper & Row.

Engels, F. (1972). *The Origin of the Family, Private Property and the State*. New York: International Publishers Co.

Flannery, K. and M. Winter (1976). "Analyzing Household Activities." in *The Early Mesoamerican Village*, K. V. Flannery, ed. New York: Academic Press, 34–47.

Frankenstein, S. and M. Rowlands (1978). "The Internal Structure and Regional Context of Early Iron Age Society in South-western Germany." *Bulletin of the Institute of Archaeology, London* 15: 73–112.

Freidel, D. (1989). Review of *Household and Community in the Mesoamerican Past*, R. Wilk and W. Ashmore, eds (1988). *Science*, 19 May, 863–4.

Gibbs, L. (1987). "Identifying Gender Representation in the Archaeological Record: A Contextual Study." In *The Archaeology of Contextual Meanings*, I. Hodder, ed. Cambridge: Cambridge University Press, 79–89.

Gilman, A. (1981). "The Development of Social Stratification in Bronze Age Europe." *Current Anthroplogy* 22(1): 1–23.

Gimbutas, M. (1970). "Proto-Indo-European Culture: The Kurgan Culture During the 5th to the 3rd Millennia B.C." In *Indo-European and Indo-*

Europeans, G. Cardona et al., eds. Philadelphia: University of Pennsylvania Press, 155–98.

—— (1980). "The Temples of Old Europe." *Archaeology* 38: 41–50.

—— (1982). *The Goddesses and Gods of Old Europe* (2nd edn). Berkeley: University of California Press.

Glazer-Malbin, N. (1976). "Housework." *Signs: Journal of Women in Culture and Society* 1(4): 905–22.

Goody, J. (1958). *The Developmental Cycle in Domestic Groups*. Cambridge: Cambridge University Press.

—— (1969). "Inheritance, Property and Marriage in Africa and Eurasia." *Sociology* 3: 55–76.

—— (1972). "The Evolution of the Family." In *Household and Family in Past Time*, P. Laslett and R. Wall, eds. Cambridge: Cambridge University Press, 103–24.

—— (1976). *Production and Reproduction*, Cambridge: Cambridge University Press.

Hammel, E. and P. Laslett (1974). "Comparing Household Structure over Time and between Cultures." *Comparative Studies in Society and History* 16: 73–109.

Harding, S. (1983). "Why has the Sex/gender System Become Visible Only Now?" In *Discovering Reality*, S. Harding and M. Hintikka, eds. Dordrecht: Reidel, 311–24.

—— (1986). *The Science Question in Feminism*. Ithaca: Cornell University Press.

—— (1987). "Introduction: Is There a Feminist Method?" In *Feminism and Methodology: Social Science Issues*, S. Harding, ed. Bloomington: Indiana University Press, 1–14.

Hartmann, H. (1981). "The Family as the Locus of Gender, Class, and Political Struggle: The Example of Housework." *Signs: Journal of Women in Culture and Society* 6(3): 366–94. (Reprinted in Harding 1987: 109–34.)

Hartsock, N. (1983). "The Feminist Standpoint: Developing the Ground for a Specifically Feminist Historical Materialism." *Discovering Reality*, S. Harding and M. B. Hintikka, eds. Dordrecht: Reidel, 283–310.

Hayden, B. (1986). "Old Europe: Sacred Matriarchy or Complementary Opposition?" In *Archaeology and Fertility Cult in the Ancient Mediterranean*, A. Bonnano, ed. Amsterdam: B. R. Gruner Publishing, 17–30.

Hayden, B. and A. Cannon (1982). "The Corporate Group as an Archaeological Unit." *Journal of Anthropological Archaeology* 1(2): 132–58.

Hill, J. N. (1970). *Broken K Pueblo: Prehistoric Social Organization in the American Southwest*. Tucson: Anthropological Papers of the University of Arizona 18.

Hodder, I. (1982). "Theoretical Archaeology: A Reactionary View." In *Symbolic and Structural Archaeology*, I. Hodder, ed. Cambridge: Cambridge University Press, 1–46.

—— (1984). "Burials, Houses, Women and Men in the European Neolithic." In *Ideology, Power and Prehistory*, D. Miller and C. Tilley, eds. Cambridge: Cambridge University Press, 51–68.

—— (1986). *Reading the Past*. Cambridge: Cambridge University Press.

—— (1990). *The Domestication of Europe*. Oxford: Basil Blackwell.

Kaiser, T. and B. Voytek (1983). "Sedentism and Economic Change in the Balkan Neolithic." *Journal of Anthropological Archaeology* 2: 323–53.

Kirk, P. (1969). *Fire Investigation*. New York: John Wiley & Sons.

Kosse (Krudy), K. (1968). "Settlement Types of the Early Neolithic Karanovo-Starčevo-Körös-Linear Cultures in S.E. Europe." Unpublished MA thesis, University of Edinburgh.

Kramer, C. (1982a). "Ethnographic Households and Archaeological Interpretation." In R. Wilk and W. Rathje, eds. *American Behavioral Scientist* 25(6): 663–76.

—— (1982b). *Village Ethnoarchaeology: Rural Iran in Archaeological Perspective*. New York: Academic Press.

Kričevski, E. Y. (1940). Tripolskiye ploščadki (po raskopkam poslednikh let). *Sovetskaya Arkheologiya* VI: 20–45.

Ladurie, E. L. (1978). *Montaillou: The Promised Land of Error*. New York: Vintage Books.

Laslett, P. (1972). "Introduction: The History of the Family." In *Household and Family in Past Time*, P. Laslett and R. Wall, eds. Cambridge: Cambridge University Press, 1–89.

Leacock, E. B. (1972). "Introduction." In *F. Engels: The Origin of the Family Private Property and the State*, E. B. Leacock, ed. New York: International Publishers Co., 7–69.

Moore, H. (1982). "The Interpretation of Spatial Patterning in Settlement Residues." In *Symbolic and Structural Archaeology*, I. Hodder, ed. Cambridge: Cambridge University Press, 74–9.

—— (1986). *Space, Text, and Gender*. Cambridge: Cambridge University Press.

—— (1988). *Feminism and Anthropology*. Minneapolis: University of Minnesota Press.

Netting, R., R. Wilk, and E. Arnould, eds. (1984). *Households: Comparative and Historical Studies of the Domestic Group*. Berkeley: University of California Press.

Passek, T. (1949). *Tripolskiye poseleniye*. Moscow–Leningrad: Materiali i Issledovanya 10.

Patrik, L. (1985). "Is There an Archaeological Record?" In *Advances in Archaeological Method and Theory*, vol. 8, M. Schiffer, ed. New York: Academic Press, 27–62.

Raab, L. M. and A. C. Goodyear (1984). "Middle-Range Theory in Archaeology: A Critical Review of Origins and Applications." *American Antiquity* 49(2): 255–68.

Randsborg, K. (1986). "Women in Prehistory: The Danish Example." *Acta Archaeologica* 55: 143–54.

Rapp, R. (1977). "Gender and Class: An Archaeology of Knowledge Concerning the Origin of the State." *Dialectical Anthropology* 2(4): 309–16.

Reid, J. J. and S. M. Whittlesley (1982). "Households at Grasshopper Pueblo." In *Archaeology of the Household: Building a Prehistory of Domestic Life*, R. Wilk and W. Rathje, eds. *American Behavioral Scientist* 25(6): 687–704.

Renfrew, A. C. and S. Shennan, eds. (1982). *Ranking, Resource and Exchange.* Cambridge: Cambridge University Press.

Rosen, A. M. (1986). *Cities of Clay: The Geoarchaeology of Tells.* Chicago: University of Chicago Press.

Semenov, Y. I. (1980). "The Theory of Socio-economic Formations and World History." In *Soviet and Western Anthropology*, E. Gellner, ed. London: Duckworth, 29–58.

Shanks, M. and C. Tilley (1987). *Social Theory and Archaeology.* Albuquerque: University of New Mexico Press.

Sherratt, A. (1981). "Plough and Pastoralism: Aspects of the Secondary Products Revolution." In *Pattern of the Past*, I. Hodder, G. Isaac, and N. Hammond, eds. Cambridge: Cambridge University Press, 261–301.

—— (1982). "Mobile Resources: Settlement and Exchange in Early Agricultural Europe." In *Ranking, Resource and Exchange*, C. Renfrew and S. Shennan, eds. Cambridge: Cambridge University Press, 13–26.

—— (1984). "Social Evolution: Europe in the Later Neolithic and Copper Ages." In *European Social Evolution*, J. Bintliff, ed. Bradford: University of Bradford, 123–34.

Smith, P. (1978). "Domestic Labour and Marx's Theory of Value." In *Feminism and Materialism*, A. Kuhn and A. Wolpe, eds. London: Routledge & Kegan Paul, 198–220.

Sørensen, M. L. S. (1987). "Material Order and Cultural Classification: The Role of Bronze Objects in the Transition from Bronze Age to Iron Age." In *The Archaeology of Contextual Meanings*, I. Hodder, ed. Cambridge: Cambridge University Press, 90–101.

Stalio, B. (1968). "Naselje i stan neolitskog perioda." In *Neolit Centralnog Balkana.* Beograd: Narodni Muzej, 77–106.

Stanish, C. (1989). "Household Archaeology: Testing Models of Zonal Complementarity in the South Central Andes." *American Anthropologist* 91(1): 7–24.

Startin, W. (1978). "Linear Pottery Culture Houses: Reconstruction and Manpower." *Proceedings of the Prehistoric Society* 44: 143–59.

Stevanović, M. (1984). "Middle Range Analysis of the Use-lives of Neolithic Domestic Building in Yugoslavia." Paper presented at the 83rd Annual Meeting of the American Anthropological Association, Denver.

—— (1985). "Construction and Destruction of Houses in the Vinča Culture: An Experimental Archaeological Investigation." Unpublished MA thesis, University of Belgrade.

Thompson, M. W. (1970). "Postscript to: Archaeology in Britain – A Marxist View, by Leo S. Klein." *Antiquity* 44: 302.

Tilley, C. (1981). "Conceptual Frameworks for the Explanation of Sociocultural Change." In *Patterns in the Past*, I. Hodder, G. Isaac, and N. Hammond, eds. Cambridge: Cambridge University Press, 363–86.

Trigger, B. (1984). "Marxism and Archaeology." In *On Marxian Perspectives in Anthropology*, J. Maquet and N. Daniels, eds. UCLA: Undena Publications, 59–97.

Tringham, R. (1971). *Hunters, Fishers and Farmers of Eastern Europe, 6000–3000 b.c.* London: Hutchinson.

—— (1978). "Experimentation, Ethnoarchaeology and the Leapfrogs in Archaeological Methodology." In *Explorations in Ethnoarchaeology*, R. Gould, ed. Albuquerque: University of New Mexico Press, 169–99.

—— (1984). "Architectural Investigation into Household Organization in Neolithic Yugoslavia." Paper presented at the 83rd Annual Meeting of the American Anthropological Association, Denver.

—— (1990). "Selevac and the Transformation of Southeast European Prehistoric Society." In *Selevac: A Prehistoric Village in Yugoslavia*, R. Tringham and D. Krstić, eds. Los Angeles: UCLA Institute of Archaeology Press.

Tringham, R., B. Brukner, and B. Voytek (1985). "The Opovo Project: A Study of Socio-economic Change in the Balkan Neolithic." *Journal of Field Archaeology* 12(4): 425–44.

Tringham, R., B. Brukner, T. Kaiser, K. Borojević, N. Russell, P. Šteli, M. Stevanović and B. Voytek (forthcoming). "The Opovo Project: A Study of Socio-economic Change in the Balkan Neolithic. 2nd Preliminary Report." *Journal of Field Archaeology*.

Watson, P. J. (1978). "Architectural Differentiation in Some Near Eastern Communities, Prehistoric and Contemporary." In *Social Archaeology: Beyond Subsistence and Dating*, C. Redman et al., eds. New York: Academic Press, 131–58.

—— (1979). *Archaeological Ethnography in Western Iran.* Washington: Smithsonian Institution, Viking Fund Publications in Anthropology 57.

Wilk, R. and R. Netting (1984). "Households: Changing Forms and Functions." In *Households: Comparative and Historical Studies of the Domestic Group*, R. Netting, R. Wilk, and E. Arnould, eds. Berkeley: University of California Press, 1–28.

Wilk, R. and W. Rathje (1982). "Household Archaeology." In *Archaeology of the Household: Building a Prehistory of Domestic Life*, R. Wilk and W. Rathje, eds. American Behavioral Scientist (25(6): 617–40.

Wylie, A. (1982). "Epistemological Issues Raised by a Structuralist Archaeology." In *Symbolic and Structural Archaeology*, I. Hodder, ed. Cambridge: Cambridge University Press, 39–46.

Yanagisako, S. (1979). "Family and Household: The Analysis of Domestic Groups." *Annual Reviews of Anthropology* 8: 161–205.

5

Gender, Space, and Food in Prehistory

Christine A. Hastorf

Introduction

If we take "gender" to mean socially constructed male and female categories, can we study gender relations in the archaeological record? Can studies of food systems and how people interact via the food they eat and discard lead us to new understandings of how human social relations operated in past cultures? Many scholars have proposed that there is a direct relationship between food systems and social relations, just as economic relations are part of food production (Bourdieu 1979; Douglas 1984; Mead 1943; Sahlins 1972). I propose that since the use and distribution of food can express political, social, and economic relations as well as nutrition, it also expresses the development and maintenance of gender relations in the past. To initiate this pilot study, I present several archaeological approaches that link food and culture.

While paleoethnobotanical data should be able to be linked to women's activities in the past with sufficient supporting evidence, it has rarely been used to discuss women's or men's roles in past societies. Plant remains are often considered a poor data set and therefore not important in most archaeological investigations. This might be related to the current, unspoken assumption that women's activities are commonly linked to plants and to cooking and therefore are not of importance in the study of "larger" issues. Although the ethnographic literature often shows women playing some role in these domains, these activities are not always women's work. No matter whose domain the kitchen is, however, the expression of relations between men and women necessarily operate wherever food is produced, prepared, served, or disposed. The study of food remains should inform us about the development and maintenance of gender relations which, in turn, should improve our interpretation of food deposits.

132

To find interpretable links between food systems and social relations I begin by examining some ethnographic relationships between food and gender in the realms of economics as well as politics. I then focus on interpretations of food and diet in the archaeological record with special reference to paleoethnobotanical data. Here I propose two complementary approaches. First I explore spatial distributions of food deposited and/or stored as they reveal the roles of men and women through the use of space. I assume that food remains can, in their spatial distribution, portray aspects of social relations within the residential house (Ardener 1981: 12). In the second approach I look at dietary intake of males and females to understand how access to different foods might signify different social positions. Both approaches are illustrated using botanical distributions in domestic compounds and burial data for the Sausa, a group in the central Andes of Peru.

Studies of gender in the prehistoric record have concentrated on female burials that can be sexed, on female imagery in paintings or figures (Gibbs 1987; Pollock, this volume), on artifactual associations and ethnographic analogies (Marshall 1985), or on spatial patterning of gender associated activity areas (from artifacts) in structures (Clarke 1972; Flannery and Winter 1976). Gender identification in material distribution is one of the challenging goals for archaeological research, for the data must be linked before the meanings of the distributions can be considered or the tasks can be discussed in terms of control and social interaction. Ethnoarchaeological studies that describe the contents of domestic areas could be productive in linking gender relations and artifact distributions as long as care is taken in interpretation (Gould 1978; Gnivecki 1987; Kent 1984, 1987; Kramer 1979). Yet almost none of these ethnoarchaeological studies have considered plant deposition let alone gender.

Food and Gender

Gender is created out of more general relations within the family through division of labor, differential access to goods, social negotiation, production, and reproduction. All are created from cultural ideas and cultural symbols that are seen in the use and placement of material items in space within the residential house (Ardener 1981; Bourdieu 1973; Cunningham 1973). Hence, if gender is created in the residence, then food should be a significant medium for determining and maintaining gender relations. Food and eating are central to these processes, as ethnographies about gender and family relations are often about food. Durkheim (1961) and Radcliffe-Brown (1977) note that most social activities center on food, and both functionalists (Malinowski (1961) and structuralists, (Lévi-Strauss 1988) have written about the importance of food, its categorization, and preparation. Hartmann (1981) suggests that the creation of gender developed out of the division of labor in food production. More than a necessary nutritional requirement to keep living things alive, food is a focus of social interaction for family and community as seen in the many cultural dimensions in which food is central; in food procurement and distribution, in exchange, tribute, as well as in food taboos (Goody 1982). While each food-related activity can be associated with specific implements and activity areas, linking these tasks to a gender is not easy or universal.

In ethnographically documented contexts, women are often reported to be in charge of the preparation and serving of food (Afshar 1985; Friedl 1975). In many cases, women's power surrounds the distribution of food. Because of this, women are regularly associated with hearths, grinding equipment, cooking pots, and processing food (in the New World see Cushing 1920; Hayden and Cannon 1984; Weismantel 1988). They can also regularly be associated with the refuse from cooking, hearth ash, and food rubbish (Hodder 1987; Moore 1986). Female involvement with production and storage, however, is more variable, especially in their control of the means of production and the yields, both *de facto* and *de jure*. It is in just these spatial distributions of production/storage and preparation/disposal that I hope to find social relationships. I am concerned therefore not so much with linking a gender with an activity, as much as gaining evidence of differential control in how the activities are performed.

Material correlates for women's positions in a society may be evident from spatial distributions such as boundedness of work spaces and material deposits (Ardener 1981; Arnold 1989; Kus and Raharijaona n.d.). When women can be linked to artifacts and activities in specific cultural settings, the artifactual distributions may suggest social relationships among members of a residence but also in the greater society. Patterns of artifactual distribution in space perhaps might provide a way to view the daily life of social relations. Let us begin with a few ethnographic examples before focusing on the Andes.

Several studies of societies where women enjoy some degree of economic independence show a pattern of spatially discrete storage of goods. Among the Kofyar of the Nigerian Jos Plateau, for instance, women control all the food they have grown, storing it in their own houses and selling it as they wish (Netting 1969). This is also seen on the coast of Tanzania where Caplan (1984) found that women retain their private property and their own income in marriage. Here, both partners have their own resources which are kept separate, exchanging goods and labor when needed. Women's control over resources gives them power and is reflected materially through controlled and restricted access to storage space.

An example of space, women, and relations, is seen in the ethnographic study among the Marakwet by Henrietta Moore (1986) where she claims that opposing gender interests are manifested in the spatial locations of food preparation, refuse deposition, and food storage. Control and restrictions in these areas defines and provides social meaning for the Marakwet. The female domain of control is restricted within discrete locations of the residence, centered around the hearth and associated with specific food-related objects such as ash and chaff refuse (while animals and animal dung are male). Women are in control of the harvest, the stores, and the provisioning of food, but this constitutes little status or value in the larger society. Women, subordinate to men, are considered dangerous in that they can destroy the social unit and are instructed and constrained in how they dispose of house refuse such as ash from the fire. Moore's study shows how the spatial distribution of objects in the home is the product of as well as constitutes gender relations in that society.

Another approach to gender through food is through investigations of specific foods, their meanings, and their uses over time. Food symbolism and meaning depend on the cultural setting, who prepared the food, how it was prepared, who served it, and what it was served with (Lévi-Strauss 1988). In every society plant foods have specific connotations. Some foods may change meanings by context, while other foods may have a constant meaning throughout all contexts. Specific foods, their uses, and associations communicate, reaffirm, and aid in the construction of the cultural system, acting as a system of signs containing social messages (Barthes 1973). Thus, the meal as a group of food types portrays a set of meanings that the viewer and consumer internalize through repetition. In this way, dietary practices become a collective tradition that maintains and reinforces the culture by the co-occurence of material artifacts. This should allow us to link certain prehistoric food remains with certain meanings.

How can we learn about internal contestation through food use? One avenue is to study the use and restriction of highly symbolic foods. Although Douglas (1966) writes mainly of sexual taboos this can include taboos of food, for hunger and sex are two powerful drives that often become the locus of power and control. Food restrictions circumscribe and maintain boundaries in marginal, dangerous, or socially sensitive arenas, often relating to the act or results of sex (1966: 127). Douglas proposes a dichotomy of cultural dynamics surrounding sex (and food). In cultures where the males have fairly clear control over the social relations and moral codes (including power over the sexuality of women and their marriage), such as among the Walbiri of central Australia, food and sex taboos tend to be absent (Douglas 1966: 141). Social relationships are controlled directly by the males as subordinate subgroups (females) do not have avenues to contest (Goodale 1971; Hiatt 1965).

On the other hand, in cultures where dominance is contested, Douglas notes that ambiguous and contested power between genders is often translated into food taboos that involve restrictions on specific foods. These groups may have taboos on food consumption, on certain activities (speech), and on timing of sexual activity (abstinence during menstruation), thus delimiting areas of control (e.g. the Enga or Wamira of New Guinea). In this way, women have some control over themselves but it is bounded (Hamilton 1981). If there are gender differences in consumption restrictions we might be able to link them to social contestation. Certain subgroups are constantly at odds with each other and so rules are made (and challenged) in an attempt to maintain control over what is considered important.

Relating food use to contestation between genders, Miriam Kahn (1986) studies gender expression through food consumption amongst the Wamira of New Guinea. She found that food, especially certain highly valued types of food (sea food and oily food), expresses and manipulates social relationships and tensions between men and women. Both food and sex are acknowledged as creative forces for the Wamira and must be controlled to maintain society. One of the fundamental issues that give Wamira women independence is the power they derive from their creative potential through childbirth. Women gain this position naturally while men must achieve an equivalent procreative power. This power is created and controlled through rituals of masculinization and food restrictions for males and females – but mainly females! (Kahn 1986: 149; Newman 1965). The male procreative rituals revolve around food. Taro for men is analogous to children for women. In producing taro, men claim they gain productive forces like women.

There are a series of food taboos surrounding childbirth for the Wamira. Men who are cultivating taro and women who are pregnant or nursing are not allowed to eat foods that might cause the "fetus" to slip; salty foods (sea food), greasy foods (pork), or coconut cream, all are highly prized foods (Kahn 1986: 116). This of course makes female food restrictions much more extensive then males, as pregnancy lasts for nine months and nursing after birth continues for well over a year, whereas taro cultivation happens only in short spurts, a day or two at a time (Kahn, personal communication). There are different levels of consumption between males and females of these prized foods.

Restrictions of and contradictions in power between the genders are complex and operate on many levels. Yet, with careful study, I hope to begin to infer social negotiations similar to these examples in the archaeological record from spatial distribution of or access to certain food items. Ethnographic studies suggest that we might be able to see different spatial patterning of artifacts, in storage contexts, in food preparation loci (surrounding hearths), in refuse disposal areas, in or near the domestic structures (Bourdieu 1973; Kus and Raharijaona n.d.; Moore 1986; Sikkink 1988; Vogt 1969), and in different diets (Douglas 1966; Kahn 1986). As they change over time we can see shifts in the relative control of space and diet.

We can begin to propose links that exist in many societies between gender relations, spatial distributions, and food taboos. Relating these issues to archaeology, the problem becomes which artifact distributions imply meaningful interpretation of control or contestation? If one assumes that gender is a structuring principle in human life and is reaffirmed through practice (Barthes 1973), the material aspects of gender relations *should* be present in archaeological assemblages.

The Pre-Hispanic Sausa of Peru

Cultural background

Although there are many relevant studies in Andean society that pertain to women's positions and their social negotiations (Bourque and Warren 1981; Silverblatt 1987; Skar 1981), I briefly mention only a few social traits that I think could be particularly illustrative in a study of pre-Hispanic Andean gender relations. While there are indications that women have not been equal to men in all domains, especially in political realms, there are suggestions that women were not always so subordinated as they are today.

Today dual complementarity, a division into two parts, is important in highland life (Bastien 1978; B. J. Isbell 1978). It is tempered by inequality within the division between upper/right/male and, lower/left/female. This symbolically places the woman as the lesser partner, suggesting the female has her own sphere of influence but that it is smaller and less valued than the male. These dualities are present in many aspects of social life seen spatially in communities and village plans (Bastien 1978; Skar 1981). In some regions, females pass on land-use rights or animals to their female children, and men do the same to male children. This bilateral inheritance and parallel descent gives autonomy to women within their household, as both males and females gain their own resources and membership in their same-sex parent's *ayllu* (Arnold 1989;

Zuidema 1973, 1977: 240). It is through this connection to the *ayllu*, a political unit with territory control, that each individual holds rights to the means of production.

Andean society is clearly gendered, but it is also dependently reciprocal. This is so in domestic as well as cosmological realms. There is a sexual division of labor in the household but it is flexible (Harris 1982). Different people completing tasks lead to different valuation of the tasks. For many agricultural tasks, men and women work together, often completing the same activities. On the other hand, there are also some clearly gendered aspects to agriculture, that reflect differential control. Today, women are in charge of the seeds and the planting of the seeds. Men, on the other hand, must plow. In some areas, women are in charge of processing and storing the harvest, thus they have control over the produce for consumption and sale (Arnold 1989; S. Radcliffe, personal communication; Skar 1981: 41). Andean women make decisions about the kitchen and the storage areas, located in the roofed structures off the patios. Ethnohistoric documents mention tasks that are associated with highland women (Cobo 1964; Garcilaso 1960; Murra 1980; Moria 1946). These include weaving, spinning, cooking, brewing *chicha* (maize beer), planting seeds, child rearing, hoeing, weeding, and carrying water (Arriaga 1968: 33–5; Cobo 1964; Garcilaso 1960; Guaman Poma 1956).

There is little information about the wider network of women. Women are known to be curers as well as traders who travel (G. Delgado, personal communication). Today they are often sellers in the local markets, though these did not exist before the conquest. Women have close contact with their kin group and members of their *ayllu*, rarely moving far from their family's home with marriage. Today they rarely hold political office. There are hints in the ethnohistoric documents, however, that Andean women occasionally held political positions during Inka times (Espinoza Soriano 1978: 338; Oberem 1968). Perhaps the choosing of local leaders (*curacas*) from certain lineages resulted in the occasional circumstance where a woman was the next person in line. Silverblatt (1987: 19) comments that the scant evidence of female political leaders in the documents may be because the Spanish chroniclers did not recognize the female leaders.

Males have discrete tasks as well: plowing, loading the pack animals, and organizing transport of the crop to the house. During Inka times, men were obliged to be warriors and complete state *mit'a* labor away from their homes (Guaman Poma 1956). Today, once married, men are responsible for the household labor tax owed to the community (*faena*), they often are the traders, hold the community political offices, and leave periodically for work (B. J. Isbell 1978; Skar 1982). And, so, highland men operate more in the sphere outside the home than women.

As Silverblatt (1987) has suggested, the social restructuring that began with the Inka conquest was amplified by the Spanish, diminishing the social position of women in Andean society. What we see today is that Andean women exercize their power and influence from within the household, over familial issues.[1] Has the social position of women altered over time and can we track it?

The pre-Hispanic data

The material used in this study comes from the intermontane central Andes, where the Upper Mantaro Archaeological Research Project (UMARP) has been investigating the pre-Hispanic Sausa, a subgroup of the Wanka (Earle et al. 1980, 1987; Hastorf et al. 1989). The Sausa's ancestors have been residing for several thousand years in an area of the northern part of the intermontane Mantaro Valley where there is an array of indigenous crops that are produced including maize (*Zea mays*), Andea tubers (potato *Solanum tuberosum*, oca *Oxalis tuberosa*, ulluco *Ullucus tuberosus*, and mashua *Tropeaolum tuberosum*), quinona (*Chenopodium quinoa*), and legumes (tarhui *Lupinus mutabilis* and beans *Phaseolus vulgaris*). Of particular note are the many historic and modern references that describe the sacred and ritual importance of maize (Rowe 1946; Murra 1960; Rostworowski 1977: 240; Morris 1978). Maize is often converted into beer (*chicha*) and is consumed at all ritual, political, and social meetings (Skar 1981). We know that the Inka focused much of their agricultural work projects on increasing maize production (Murra 1982). Potatoes, the other highland staple, although an important component in the Andean diet, do not have the symbolic value of maize. The other crops are vegetable-like and supplement these two staples.

We have excavated domestic compounds dating back to at least the Early Intermediate Period (AD 200–600). These pre-Hispanic compounds are composed of one or more circular structures entering onto a curved walled courtyard area. The walls and internal divisions throughout all eras suggest that residents desired to divide their space into different units where different activities could occur. Ethnographic and archaeological evidence indicates that the range of domestic activities in the compounds has continued to be the same.

Much of our research has focused on the later pre-Hispanic record, just before the Inka, Wanka II (AD 1300–1460) and during Inka control, Wanka III (AD 1460–1532). In Wanka II times the local population seemed to have been organized into politically differentiated groups numbering in the thousands. This organization is inferred from the settlement pattern, artifact distribution, and agricultural systems at large centers and small associated satellites (LeBlanc 1981; Hastorf 1990a).

In the Wanka III times, the Sausa society was transformed through imperial conquest and incorporation into the Inka state (D'Altroy 1981, 1987; D'Altroy and Earle 1985; Espinoza Soriano 1971; Murra 1980). As part of this transformation the population returned to small valley settlements. We know that the Inka restricted access to some goods such as silver, while influencing crop production and consumption of some crops (Hastorf 1990b). What were the dynamics of social relations in the Wanka II and the Wanka III home? Was there a differential impact on men and women with the Inka arrival? How did women's social position change?

The spatial distribution of artifacts

This is an application of the idea that artifact distributions, reflecting processing, consumption, and disposal, either at refuse dumps or in activity areas, are linked to gender relations. From a modern household study in the central Andes, we learn that certain locations are used in specific ways by individuals while other multipurpose zones can be used by any member of the household such as "ungendered" patio areas (Sikkink 1988). Some tasks concentrate in specific locations indoors; cooking, eating, storage, ritual offerings, and sleeping, while others occur anywhere, such as tool production, mending, and processing. The artifactual evidence supports this behavioral evidence, although it is not a simple relationship. The plant distributions collected by Sikkink are patterned. Charred seeds are less dense where many different activities occurred, in the patios and in outer walled enclosures, with more charred material deposited in the more specialized activity areas such as the kitchen and the storage areas, both of which today are located inside the structures or the refuse-compost piles in the walled patios. Taxa diversity is greatest in the kitchen, with charred food remains most highly concentrated in the cooking areas, it is less dense in the storage areas (Lennstrom and Hastorf forthcoming). From what we know about the Andean house, women are closely connected with food preparation and storage. These "female" activities are directly reflected in botanical data, hearth, food processing, and storage locations.

We cannot infer too much from Sikkink's three households with respect to gender relations, but it is intriguing to note that the one household with a female head had crop seeds more frequently in patio locations as well as inside her kitchen structure. It is possible, given the type of relationships between food and gender discussed above, that this family has less need to control the preparation and deposition of food because there is no contestation between genders, with no male head of the household. So, one might propose in the Andes that restricted crop distributions reflect more constraints on female activities, while less restrictions on the distributions would suggest less social (gendered?) pressure to contain crops to specific activity areas.

To initiate a study of the distribution of plant remains and how the use of space informs us about gender, I present paleoethnobotanical data from two pre-Hispanic compounds. I assume that paleoethnobotanical data in general reflects production rather than consumption (Dennell 1976). The Wanka II compound, J7 = 2, is from the 25 ha single occupation knolltop site of Tunánmarca. The Wanka III compound, J54 = 2, is from the 33 ha site of Marca some 4 km from Tunánmarca on a lower hilltop (Earle et al. 1987). These compounds were chosen because they are well preserved, have evidence of domestic occupation, are well dated, and much of each compound has been excavated. Both compounds display evidence of single occupation, with two floors in only one structure at J7 = 2 (structure 6). J7 = 2 is a large enclosed six-structure compound, centrally located on the site with no evidence of rebuilding over the some 100 years of occupation (Earle et al. 1987: 23). Three structures contained hearths, each with an above average density of food remains and grinding stones. J54 = 2 is smaller with only one well-associated structure and one hearth in the southeastern corner of the patio. The Wanka III occupation would have only been used for approximately 70 years and there is no evidence of rebuilding in this compound.

I plotted the botanical domestic food taxa from all 88 soil samples collected throughout the J7 = 2 compound (figure 5.1 with figure 5.2 displaying the sample number locations) and 68 samples from J54 = 2 (figure 5.3, with figure 5.4 displaying the sample locations; see table 5.1 for raw counts). The charred plant remains are from point provenienced soil samples that were separated out by water flotation (see Earle et al. 1987 for a description of the procedure). The pie charts on figures 5.1 and 5.3 are generated from specimen counts adjusted to a standardized weight of 6 kg. Samples where there were no botanical remains have their flotation sample number. The pie diagrams come in four sizes, illustrating increasing densities of the food remains. This provides the relative presence of the food crops across each compound as well as a picture of their relative densities. While these pie charts are biased in a number of ways, there should be little post-depositional effect as each site was abandoned rapidly and the walls were pushed over, covering the domestic areas and protecting them from the elements. Each crop has its own rate of deterioration and likelihood of survival which should be kept in mind when viewing the data (Schiffer 1976). The soft tissue in tubers degrade most quickly, while maize, legumes, and quinoa are more durable.

At J7 = 2 in figure 5.1, the density of charred plants is much higher

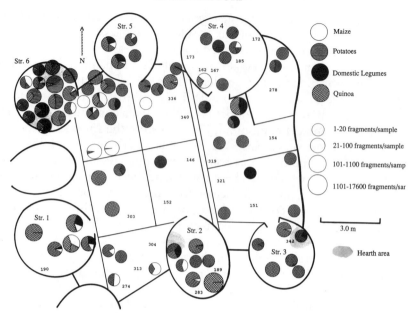

Figure 5.1 Patio J7 = 2 on Tunánmarca with the four adjusted food plant frequencies represented in pie charts. Soil sample locations plotted as pie charts or numbers. Numbers are samples that have no food crops.

and more diverse in the structures than in the patio areas (larger pie diagrams). This is the pattern for the charred remains in modern household examples (Sikkink 1988). This pattern can be partially explained by the hearth locations, found only in the structures. In the patios, rubbish-compost piles, processing, and industrial activity waste could have been burned, but it would have occurred more sporadically since no discrete hearths were found in the patio.

Dense and diverse food clusters in the J7 = 2 structures suggest that the houses were zones of use, storage, and deposition. This is seen in the higher tuber presence in structures 5 and 6, with more of everything in structure 1. The plant, artifact, and human bone deposits in structure 1 are jumbled up, suggesting that it might have been a dump or compost area (Kadane and Hastorf 1988). Hearths in structures 2, 3, and 6 each have an above average density of food remains and grinding stones (Earle et al. 1987). Structure 4 has the least amount of charred food and other plant matter with no hearth, but it does have a lot of animal dung (presumably used for fuel). Based on an array of artifactual data from the structures, I infer that the structures were used primarily for cooking, eating, sleeping, food and fuel storage, and some refuse, especially ash

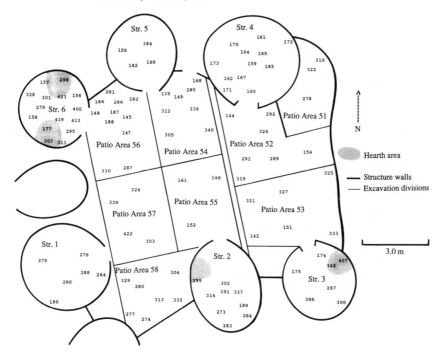

Figure 5.2 Patio J7 = 2 on Tunánmarca with soil sample locations plotted by the flotation number.

disposal, today retained for fertilizer (Earle et al. 1987: 23–4). This makes structures the likely candidates for womens' domains. I conclude then that at least four of these structures would have been primarily a female domain.

The densities in figure 5.1 show that the botanical taxa are not evenly distributed throughout the patio as there are some dense clusters in individual locations. Yet crops are found in 77 per cent of the patio samples. Samples without crops predominate in the center of the patio where more foot traffic would occur (identified by sample numbers). Plant food remains occur throughout the patio. With more tubers in the north and more maize in the west, crops seemed to spill out from the structures, as the densest crops cluster outside of structures 4, 5, and 6, and at the compound entrance. Maize tends to be found in the patio area. Because maize is such a special and sacred crop and is relatively uncommon in this cultural phase (Hastorf 1990b), the maize in the patio suggests group efforts at food processing (such as beer production) and/ or group consumption.

The patio data suggest that the space was used for many different activities including tool manufacture, processing, preparation, metal production, and midden deposits, but not for everyday cooking and food storing. It is along the patio walls where most of the lithics and ceramics were found. While this area is multipurpose, women's activities are present as crop processing remains are scattered throughout the patio.

Looking at the next phase illustrated by J54 = 2, figure 5.3 displays a slightly different picture. First of all, the plant diversities and densities are lower. Despite regular sampling, the one structure definitely in the compound did not yield many plant remains, as only 63 per cent of the samples contained crops. Unlike the samples in the J7 = 2 structures, these samples are not very mixed but contain pure plant taxa with an unusual dominance of maize, as three of the samples are 100 per cent maize.

The pie diagrams show more maize in this Wanka III compound than is present in the Wanka II compound, especially in the one structure. There are however almost no potatoes, the Andean staple. Relative to the earlier compound, this gives us a sense of more maize processing and of

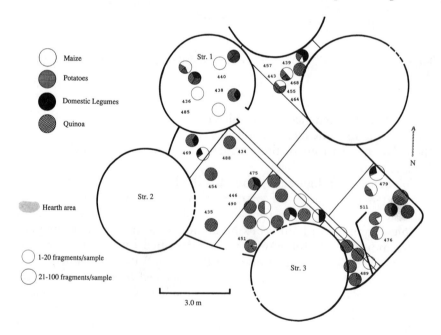

Figure 5.3 Patio J54 = 2 on Marca with the four adjusted food plant frequencies represented in pie charts. Soil sample locations plotted as pie charts or numbers. Numbers are samples that have no food crops.

concentrated activities with little burning in the structure. It is very possible also that the most common form of maize consumption is as beer.

In the J54 = 2 patio, there is also a very low density of plant matter scattered across the compound, with the greatest densities in the corners of the patio, near the compound entrance, and in the walled-off corner where the hearth is. The hearth area in the patio suggests that the occupants were cramped for discrete activity zones, creating a makeshift structure in the corner for food preparation and eating. Again, there are no potatoes in this walled-in zone. In general, the patio crop remains seem restricted in clusters up against the compound walls. Only 57 per cent of the patio samples contained crop remains in contrast to 77 per cent of the Wanka II patio samples. While this is only one example from each phase, it begins to suggest that there was more restriction in crop deposition in this Wanka III patio when compared to the Wanka II patio distributions.

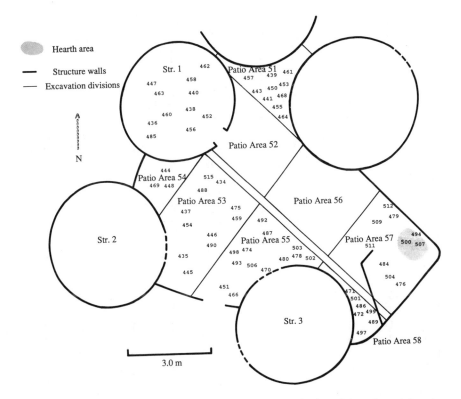

Figure 5.4 Patio J54 = 2 on Marca with soil sample locations plotted by the flotation number.

Table 5.1 Charred agricultural product counts from J7 = 2 and J54 = 2 by flotation sample number. Counts made from 6 kgs of soil per sample.

J7 = 2

No.	Maize	Potato	Quinoa	Legumes	No.	Maize	Potato	Quinoa	Legumes
139	0	0	14	1	264	7	2	25	14
142	0	0	2	0	273	2	0	29	0
144	0	5	0	3	274	0	0	0	0
145	0	0	4	3	275	0	0	133	1
146	0	0	0	0	276	13	2	56	24
147	0	0	1	0	277	1	0	1	0
148	1	0	0	0	278	0	0	0	0
149	0	1	2	0	279	0	25	10	0
151	0	0	0	0	280	0	0	1	0
152	0	0	0	0	281	0	0	10	0
154	0	0	0	0	282	0	0	12	0
155	3	4	10	6	283	0	0	0	0
156	1	50	4	0	284	2	90	17465	0
157	0	14	2	0	285	2	4	45	0
158	0	9	2	0	286	1	29	9	0
159	0	0	7	0	287	225	0	5	0
160	0	0	1	0	288	41	21	45	1
161	0	4	0	0	289	0	0	3	0
162	0	0	0	0	290	3	0	33	2
164	0	3	0	0	291	0	0	3	0
165	1	1	3	0	292	0	0	48	37
167	0	0	0	0	295	0	9	14	0
168	0	0	2	0	297	0	0	2	0
169	0	0	1	0	298	2	112	96	39
170	0	0	2	0	299	0	0	19	9
171	48	5	13	0	300	0	0	1	0
172	0	0	0	0	301	2	5	8	3
173	0	0	0	0	302	0	6	51	2
174	1	0	22	0	303	0	0	0	0
175	0	2	14	0	304	0	0	0	0
177	0	4	1	0	305	0	0	1	0
181	0	0	5	0	307	0	0	3	13
182	4	15	26	24	310	0	0	1	0
184	1	2	5	0	311	2	1	12	37
185	0	0	0	0	312	1	0	0	0
186	0	0	12	0	313	0	0	0	0
187	21	10	18	3	314	2	0	3	0
188	1	4	2	1	319	0	0	0	0
189	0	0	0	0	321	0	0	0	0
190	0	0	0	0	322	0	7	5	0

No.	Maize	Potato	Quinoa	Legumes	No.	Maize	Potato	Quinoa	Legumes
324	0	1	2	0	456	12	0	0	0
325	0	0	13	0	457	0	0	0	0
326	0	1	3	6	458	1	0	0	0
327	0	0	0	3	459	0	1	2	2
328	3	1	3	0	460	5	0	0	0
329	2	0	9	0	461	1	0	2	5
330	65	2	3	0	462	0	3	1	0
332	2	0	1	0	463	0	1	1	1
333	0	0	3	0	464	0	0	0	0
336	0	0	0	0	466	1	2	16	0
337	0	0	14	0	468	0	0	0	0
339	0	0	38	0	469	0	0	0	0
340	0	0	0	0	470	0	0	2	0
342	0	0	0	0	471	3	0	0	0
396	0	0	22	0	472	0	0	4	0
400	2	5	24	1	474	2	0	2	0
407	0	0	7	2	475	0	0	0	0
413	2	0	3	0	476	0	0	0	0
419	0	37	32	1	478	0	0	2	0
422	0	0	20	0	479	0	0	0	0
423	1	989	79	1	480	1	0	2	2
					484	1	0	4	0
					485	0	0	0	0
		J54 = 2			486	0	0	1	0
					487	0	0	5	0
434	0	0	0	0	488	0	0	0	0
435	0	0	0	0	489	0	0	0	0
436	0	0	0	0	490	0	0	0	0
437	0	0	1	0	492	0	0	1	0
438	0	0	0	0	493	0	0	1	0
439	0	0	0	0	494	0	0	36	0
440	0	0	0	0	497	0	0	3	0
441	1	1	1	0	498	0	0	2	0
443	0	0	0	0	499	3	0	0	0
444	0	0	2	1	500	0	0	5	3
445	0	0	1	0	501	0	0	2	0
446	0	0	0	0	502	3	0	0	3
447	3	1	1	0	503	1	0	0	0
448	10	1	0	3	504	2	0	3	0
450	2	1	1	0	506	1	0	0	0
451	0	0	0	0	507	0	0	5	0
452	0	0	2	1	509	4	2	1	0
453	0	0	1	0	511	0	0	0	0
454	0	0	0	0	512	18	0	1	6
455	0	0	0	0	515	0	0	9	0

Using Sikkink's (1988) modern study as a comparison, one would expect charred food plants in the cooking area, the processing area, and the compost/ash dump areas; other activity areas or generalized space should not yield as many crop remains. Clustered remains might suggest a more designated use of space or more regular/intensive activity. Food remains commonly scattered throughout a residence suggests that it might not have been important to keep the burned hearth and refuse remains in discrete locations.

The dense pre-Hispanic botanical distributions around the hearths and ash pits links the greatest amount of charred crop remains to the female domain. Crop plant refuse is not restricted to these areas however, as it is distributed both within all structures and throughout the patio, though this is more evident in the Wanka II patio. This lack of discrete spatial deposition in the $J7 = 2$ patio and structures (see especially structure 1 at $J7 = 2$ as contrasted with structure 1 at $J54 = 2$) might suggest less strain between individuals or genders during that time when compared to the Wanka III patio. If we assume that an increase in control over the daily household activities is tied to more constraints on individuals, including women, this relationship might have been changing during the Wanka III times.

Being bold for a moment and perhaps over-interpreting this information, I would propose that we might be seeing an increased circumscription of female activities in the Inka phase of Sausa life. In addition dense but restricted Wanka III maize distributions also suggest increased intensification of female processing labor, representing an escalation of women's labor to support social-political activities, which are predominantly male activities.

Access to specific foods

The second approach to gender relations through food investigates food consumption, access, and meaning. Food communicates, reaffirms, and builds a cultural "way of life". In every society plant foods have specific connotations. It is the recurring use of food items and their contexts that gives certain foods meaning, allowing us to interpret prehistoric food use (Barthes 1973). Dietary practices become a collective tradition that maintains and reinforces the cultural order.

Here I look at Sausa food use and meanings through dietary evidence, using stable isotopic[2] analyses of sexed skeletons from the Wanka II and III phases. Stable isotopic analysis, as Murray and Schoeniger (1988) and Price (1989) demonstrate, provides an important method for studying gender and class through dietary differences. Isotope values for individuals reflect a cumulative picture of food consumption.

The consumption data from Wanka II and III human skeletal material are presented as stable carbon and nitrogen isotope delta values, calculated from geochemical procedures (DeNiro 1987; van der Merwe 1982). There are many aspects of biochemical isotopic research that are still in the process of refinement due to the problems of contamination and diagenetic changes in the amino acids from which the isotopes are measured. Tests on the samples completed thus far demonstrate that they are valid (M. DeNiro, personal communication).

The way to interpret isotope values from extracted bone collagen is to plot each sample's delta values in relation to the ideal values for the major food types, illustrated by the boxes in figures 5.5 and 5.6. Each box represents the isotopic values of the biochemical plant group assessed from modern regional plants. The right C4 box reflects the range of stable isotopic values for a pure C4 (maize) diet, ranging between −8.5 to −11.00 parts per mil (thousand). The left C3 box reflects 100 per cent non-leguminous C3 plant (tubers, quinoa) consumption, with a range between −22.00 and −28.00 parts per mil. For the Sausa, the farther right along the horizontal axis the more maize was consumed, the farther left, the less maize and the more tubers and quinoa.

Meat consumption is also reflected in the isotope values. Animals are not as easy as plants to place on an isotopic chart because their diet can vary. Overall, camelids were the dominant animal food source for the pre-Hispanic Sausa (Earle et al. 1987: 86; Sandefur 1988). In general, the delta N values below 10.5 parts per mil reflect a terrestrial herbivorous diet, while above 10.5 is a terrestrial carnivorous diet. For the animals in this region, the delta C value reflects grazers towards the C4 end versus browsers towards the C3 values. The camelid (*Lama* spp.) values reflect a mixed herbivorous diet of grazing and browsing with a delta C value around −17 parts per mil. The human isotopic values suggest that animal meat was a portion of the Sausa diet, decreasing slightly the amount of maize consumption.

When we view the isotopic values of the sexed burials from the Wanka II and Wanka III time periods, we see intriguing social and political results. Figure 5.5 presents the Wanka II sexed adult delta values. Unfortunately to date, there are only seven skeletons that could be unquestionably sexed from good Wanka II contexts, two females and five males. This makes the discussion of these data very tentative. The mean male delta C value is −18.03, and the mean female value is −18.01, suggesting no difference between male and female diets in the Wanka II times.

This Wanka II diet parallels the local production data, as one of mainly tubers and quinoa with a lesser amount of maize (Hastorf 1990a). In addition, the isotope data suggest that men and women were *not*

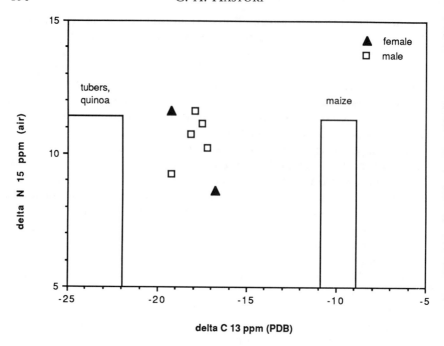

Figure 5.5 Carbon and nitrogen isotopic values for Wanka II adults.

consuming plant food differentially, including maize. This is of particular interest because maize is often consumed in the form of *chicha*, the crop of ritual and political gatherings, suggesting that both genders participated equally in ritual, community, and political events though this was done with women's labor (Skar 1981). What was processed seems to have been shared.

With the Inka's entrance into Sausa society, the diets changed. There are 21 human skeletons from good Wanka III contexts (figure 5.6), 9 females and 12 males. One can immediately see the delta C value differences between males and females. Whereas the female population has a mean delta C value of −16.41, the males have a mean value of −14.18. Both have more maize in their diet than before, but 50 percent of the male diets are significantly enriched in maize beyond the female diets. While the female data suggest a diet similar to the Wanka III botanical production data (a fairly even mix of tubers/quinoa, and maize, Hastorf 1990b), the male diet is 1.5 parts per mil enriched in maize. This enrichment suggests that under the Inka hegemony, while the women were producing more *chicha*, it was only certain men in the Sausa community who were consuming more maize outside the house and the community food exchange networks. Additionally, most males also have higher delta N values than females, suggesting increased meat consumption as well. The diets of the two genders were no longer the same. This is of special interest since there is no difference between the two identified economic classes of this time period (Hastorf 1990b).

Differential consumption could have taken place in the home, in the community, or on state business. Supporting evidence suggests that this was stimulated by the Inka's new political organizations, including state work parties as well as increased local political negotiations among the Sausa themselves (D'Altroy and Earle 1985; Murra 1980; Rowe 1982: 110; Salomon 1986). Because there was no unifying regional organization before the Conquest, the Inka had to create one. In particular, Rowe (1982) notes from native testimony that the Inka had to create a regional government for the Wanka (Levillier 1940: 19–20). This suggests that the Sausa were incorporated into the Wanka regional system of political hierarchies based on existing principles like exchange and mutual obligation. This political sphere would have included gatherings, rituals, and obligatory work forces, hence more meat and maize beer consumption for the participants, and more *chicha* production. The isotopic data suggest that this participation was for Sausa men rather than for Sausa women. While the women were working harder producing beer, they

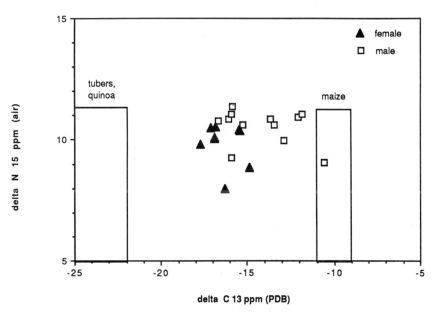

Figure 5.6 Carbon and nitrogen isotopic values for Wanka III adults.

did not join in the extra-house political consumption. In this way we again see how the women's position outside the home was more restricted in the Wanka III times.

A hallmark of the Inka state was the obligatory *mit'a* labor tax that generated surplus production. All populations worked periodically for the Inka throughout the year in their home territories (LeVine 1987: 15). Although there is agreement that the taxation was levied on the married male household-head, there is some debate about exactly who completed the labor. For certain specialized tasks like state *chicha* brewing or weaving, women were moved into Inka centers (Morris 1982). The most common *mit'a* services were considered male tasks: agriculture and military service, often taking men away from the home for short periods.

As part of the Andean ethic of exchange, the state institutionalized a symbolic exchange for the *mit'a* work by feeding laborers. One chronicler, Vilca Cuitpa, gives us a typical example of this stating that those who worked for the Inka were fed "meat and maize and cornbeer" (Murra 1982: 256). Therefore it seems that males actually did complete most of what was labelled *mit'a* service, by receiving more maize in their diet. These activities separated the two genders physically, politically, and symbolically.

The symbolism of maize and the differential access to it seem to have played an important role in the construction of gender during the period of the Inka state. Through maize we see how women became the focus of tensions as they produced more beer while at the same time they were more restricted in their participation in society. The isotopic and ethnohistoric data also suggest that during Inka rule, the Andean women's political position diminished. This seems to have been initiated not through specific internal politics within the Sausa, but through the newly imposed state political structures. At the same time, the Sausa women probably did not lose their means of domestic production at home. Surely these dynamics altered the gender relations in the Sausa community.

Summary

By studying the shifts in material over time, we can begin to make women and men visible in the archaeological record, albeit in this case it is watching women's political position diminish as they focus on the domestic sphere. From these independent data sets related to food, we can begin to see the change in women's position in an Andean community. Overall, with the entry of the Inka state, women, while maintaining autonomy in some domestic tasks, probably were under more social strain. Interestingly enough, the two approaches complement each other and provide a picture of changing social relations. Exploratory as these examples are, I hope they illustrate a potential for the study of social relations in the archaeological record through the dynamics of food.

Although much is left unexplained in these archaeological examples, I have tried to demonstrate the importance of food in the study of social and gender relations in prehistory and in particular, women in the Andes. Two approaches are proposed, one focusing on the spatial distribution of material within domestic settings and its reflections of interpersonal negotiation and control. The second approach is to look at gender relations through differential access to food. More specifically, I attempted to test the usefulness of these approaches by presenting first, Andean food systems and botanical frequencies within domestic compounds, and second, skeletal evidence for gender differences in diet.

With conscious effort, both ethnographically and archaeologically, I think much can be gained through the study of boundedness and control over things and space, especially viewing changes in spatial distributions over time. Great care must be taken labeling genders with artifacts, activities, and foodstuffs in the archaeological deposits however.

Food systems, in many ways, are the bases of societies, essential to sustenance, division of labor, control, and social symbolism. Despite our archaeological fascination with how people got their food, we must not miss the ability of food to inform us about the equally important cultural dynamics. The use of botanical data has its limitations, but it also has important potential to view social and political relations. Paleoethnobotanical data should not be confined only to what people ate, but should help in investigating broader social and political relationships. My goal in this paper was to try to provide a new perspective from which to study gender in prehistory, using such unlikely data as charred plant remains. In the archaeological examples from Peru, I hope that the connection between food, gender, access, and control has been sufficiently highlighted to attract the attention of other investigators.

ACKNOWLEDGMENTS

I would like to thank very much both Joan Gero and Meg Conkey for inviting me to participate in the Women and Gender in Prehistory conference. It was challenging and very exciting. I wish to thank Michael DeNiro for the stable isotope analysis completed at UCLA, and Heidi Lennstrom, along with the members of the Archeobotany Laboratory at the University of Minnesota, for help in plant analysis and especially the graphics. The field and laboratory

154   C. A. HASTORF

research has been supported by the National Science Foundation grants BNS 8203723 and BNS 8451369. Part of the data analysis was completed while a fellow at the Center for the Advanced study in the Behavioral Sciences, with partial support by BNS 8411738. Special thanks goes to the Instituto Nacional de Cultura for allowing us to excavate and study in the Mantaro region and to export the macrobotanical and bone data for these analyses. This paper, being an experiment for me, was helped greatly by the comments discussions, and encouragement of Meg Conkey, Russ Handsman, Ian Hodder, Beth Scott, Janet Spector, and Patty Jo Watson. All of the analysis and conclusions however are my own responsibility. This paper is dedicated to Rosalyn Hoyt who struggled long and hard to gain some control of her life in a man's world.

NOTES

1   Although the use of the concept household has been correctly criticized in many parts of the world (Moore 1988: 54), it actually works quite well in the Andes for the working unit based in a residential compound, as community work is organized by household.
2   Isotopes are varieties of elements with different amounts of neutrons. They occur in living systems in different ratios due to different reaction times when the isotope ratios of the products are different from the ratios of the reactants. The two stable isotopes in this study are nitrogen and carbon. Among terrestrial plants, carbon isotopes can separate C4 (tropical grasses), C3, and CAM plants. The nitrogen isotope is more complex, but in terrestrial situations nitrogen isotopes can separate nitrogen-fixing plants (legumes) from non-legumes, as welll as identifying 3 to 4 parts per mil enrichment up the food chain (Schoeniger and DeNiro 1984). From experimental data, it has been shown that different plant foods have different isotope ratios (DeNiro and Epstein 1978, 1981; DeNiro and Weiner 1988). Hence, all animals take up the isotopic ratios of the food they consume, making it possible to infer from skeletal collagen, for example, what the average lifelong diet was for the individual under investigation (van der Merwe and Vogel 1977). These isotopic values are notated as delta values in parts per mil (thousand), or as the difference in the amount of 13C isotope to 12C isotope or 15N isotope to 14N isotope. These two isotopic ratios can then be graphed together to show values that correlate to food types.

REFERENCES

ueztbAfshar, Haleh, ed. (1985). *Women, Work, and Ideology in the Third World.* New York: Tavistock.
Ardener, Shirley, ed. (1981). *Women and Space.* London: Croom Helm.
Arnold, Denise (1989). "The House as Dungheap, the House as Cosmos: The Aymara House in its Social Setting." Lecture at the Centre of Latin American Studies, Cambridge, England (February 2, 1989).

Arriaga, Father Pablo José de (1968). *The Extirpation of Idolatory in Peru* [1621], Tr. L. Clark Keating. Lexington: University of Kentucky Press.

Barthes, Roland (1979). "Toward a Psychosociology of Contemporary Food Consumption." In *Food and Drink in History*, R. Forster and O. Ranum, eds. Baltimore; Johns Hopkins University Press.

Bastien, Joseph W. (1978). *Mountain of the Condor*. Prospect Heights, IL: Waveland Press.

Bourdieu, Pierre (1973). "The Berber House." In *Rules and meanings*, M. Douglas, ed. Harmondsworth: Penguin Books, 98–110.

—— (1979). *La distinction, critique social du jugement*. Paris: Éditions de Minuit.

Bourque, Susan C. and Kay Barbara Warren (1981). *Women of the Andes*. Ann Arbor: University of Michigan Press.

Caplan, Patricia (1984). "Cognatic Descent, Islamic Law and Women's Property on the East African Coast." In *Women and Property, Women as Property*, R. Hieschon, ed. London: Croom Helm, 23–43.

Clarke, David L. (1972). "A Provisional Model of an Iron Age Society." In *Models in Archaeology*, D. L. Clarke, ed. London: Methuen, 801–70.

Cobo, Bernabe (1964) *Historia del nuevo mundo* [1653], 2 vols. Madrid: Bibloteca de autores Espanoles.

Cunningham, Clark E. (1973). "Order in the Atoni House." In *Right and left*, R. Needam, ed. Chicago: University of Chicago Press, 204–38.

Cushing, Frank (1920). *Zuni Breadstuff*. Washington: Smithsonian Institution.

D'Altroy, Terence N. (1981). "Empire Growth and Consolidation: The Xauxa Region of Peru under the Incas." Ph.D. dissertation, Department of Anthroplogy, UCLA. Ann Arbor: University Microfilms.

—— (1987). "Transitions in Power: Centralization of Wanka Political Organization under Inka Rule." *Ethnohistory* 34(1): 78–102.

D'Altroy, T. N. and T. K. Earle (1985). Staple Finance, Wealth Finance, and Storage in the Inka Political Economy. *Current Anthropology* 25(2): 187–206.

Dennell, Robin W. (1976). "The Economic Importance of Plant Resources Represented on Archaeological Sites." *Journal of Archaeological Science*: 1: 257–65.

DeNiro, Michael J. (1987). "Stable Isotopy and Archaeology." *American Scientist* 75: 182–91.

DeNiro, M. J. and S. Epstein (1978). "Influence of Diet on the Distribution of Carbon Isotopes in Animals." *Geochimica et Cosmochimica Acta* 42: 495–506.

—— (1981). "Influence of Diet on the Distribution of Nitrogen in Animals." *Geochimica et Cosmochimica Acta* 45: 341–51.

—— DeNiro, M. J. and S. Weiner (1988). Chemical, enzymatic, and spectroscopic characterization of collagen and other organic fractions in prehistoric bones. *Geochimica et Cosmochimica Acta* 52: 2197–2206.

Douglas, Mary (1966). *Purity and Danger: An Analysis of Concepts of Pollution*. New York: Praeger.

—— ed. (1984). *Food in the Social Order*. New York: Russell Sage Foundation.

Durkheim, Émile (1961). *The Elementary Forms of Religious Life* [1912]. New York: Collen Books.

Earle, T. K., T. D'Altroy, C. LeBlanc, C. Hastorf, and T. LeVine (1980). "Changing Settlement Patterns in the Yananmarca Valley, Peru." *Journal of New York Archaeology* 4(1).

Earle, T. K., T. D'Altroy, C. Hastorf, C. Scott, C. Costin, G. Russell, and E. Sandefur (1987). *Archaeological Field Research in the Upper Mantaro, Peru 1982–1983: Investigations of Inka Expansion and Exchange.* Institute of Archaeology, UCLA, Monograph 28.

Espinoza Soriano, Waldemar (1971). "Los huancas, aliados de la conquista." *Anales cientificos de la universidad de centro del Peru* I: 3–407.

—— (1978). "Dos casos de senorialismo feudal en el imperio Inca." In *Los modos de produccion en el imperio de los Incas*, W. Espinoza Soriano, ed. Lima: Mantaro-Grafital, 329–56.

Flannery, Kent and Marcus Winter (1976). "Analyzing Household Activities." In *The Early Mesoamerican Village*, K. Flannery, ed. New York: Academic Press.

Friedl, Ernestine (1975). *Women and Men: An Anthropologist's View.* New York: Holt, Rinehart & Winston.

Garcilaso de la Vega, "el Inca" (1960). *Commentarios reals de los Incas* [1609], 3 vols. Jose Durand, ed. Lima: Universidad Nacional Mayor de San Marcos.

Gibbs, Liv (1987). "Identifying Gender Representation in the Archaeological Record: A Contextual Study." In *The Archaeology of Contextual Meanings*, I. Hodder, ed. Cambridge: Cambridge University Press, 79–89.

Goodale, Jane (1971). *Tiwi Wives.* Seattle: University of Washington Press.

Goody, Jack (1982). *Cooking, cuisine, and class.* Cambridge University Press.

Gould, R. A., (ed.) (1978). *Explorations in Ethnoarchaeology.* Albuquerque: University of New Mexico Press.

Gnivecki, Perry (1987). "On the Quantitative Derivation of Household Spatial Organization from Archaeological Residues in Ancient Mesopotamia." In *Method and Theory for Activity Area Research*, S. Kent, ed. New York: Columbia University Press, 176–235.

Guaman Poma de Ayala, Felipe (1956–7). *La nueva cronica y buen gobierno* [1613], 3 vols. Tr. into modern Spanish by Luis Bustios Galvez. Lima: Editorial Cultura.

Hamilton, A. (1981). "A Complex Strategical Situation: Gender and Power in Aboriginal Australia." In *Australian Women: Feminist Perspectives*, N. Grieve and P. Grimshaw, eds. Oxford: Oxford University Press, 69–85.

Harris, Olivia (1982). "Labour and Produce in an Ethnic Economy, Northern Potosi, Bolivia." In *Ecology and Exchange in the Andes*, D. Lehmann, ed. Cambridge University Press, 70–96.

Hartmann, Heidi (1981). "The Family as the Locus of Gender, Class, and Political Struggle: The Example of Housework." *Signs* 6(3): 366–94.

Hastorf, Christine A. (1990a). A path to the heights: The negotiation of political inequality. In *Political evolution and the communal mode.* Edited by S. Upham, Cambridge University Press.

—— (1990b). "The Effect of the Inka State on Sausa Agricultural Production and Crop Consumption." *American Antiquity* 55(2): 262–90.

Hastorf, C., T. Earle, H. E. Wright, L. LeCount, G. Russell, C. Costin, and E. Sandefur (1989). "Settlement Archaeology in the Java Region of Peru: Evidence from the Early Intermediate Period through the Late Intermediate Period: A Report on the 1986 Field Season." *Andean Past* 2: 81–129.

Hayden Brian, and Audrey Cannon (1984). *The Structure of Material Systems: Ethnoarchaeology in the Maya Highlands*. Washington: Society for American Archaeology.

Hiatt, L. R. (1965). *Kinship and Conflict*. Canberra: Australian National University.

Hodder, Ian (1987). "The Meaning of Discard: Ash and Domestic Space in Baringo." In *Method and Theory for Activity Area Research*, S. Kent, ed. New York: Columbia University Press, 424–48.

Isbell, Billie Jean (1978). *To Defend Ourselves*. Austin: Institute of Latin American Studies, University of Texas.

Isbell, William (1978). "Cosmological Order Expressed in Prehistoric Ceremonial Centers." *Actes XII Congrès International des Americanestes* 9: 269–99. Musée de l'Homme, Paris.

Kadane, Joseph B. and Christine A. Hastorf (1988). "Bayesian Paleoethnobotany." In *Bayesian Statistics III*, J. Bernards, M. DeGroot, D. V. Lindley, and A. M. F. Smith, eds. Oxford: Oxford University Press, 243–59.

Kahn, Miriam (1986). *Always Hungry, Never Greedy*. Cambridge: Cambridge University Press.

Kent, Susan (1984). *Analyzing Activity Areas: An Ethnoarchaeological Study of the Use of Space*. Albuquerque: University of New Mexico Press.

—— ed. (1987). *Method and Theory for Activity Area Research*. New York: Columbia University Press.

Kramer, Carol, ed. (1979). *Ethnoarchaeology*. New York: Academic Press.

Kus, Susan and Victor Raharijaona (n.d.). "Domestic Space and the Tenacity of Tradition among some Betsileo of Madagascar." In *Architecture and the Use of Space – An Interdisciplinary Cross-cultural Study*, S. Kent, ed. MS in author's possession.

LeBlanc, Catherine (1981). "Late Prehispanic Huanca Settlement Patterns in the Yanamarca Valley, Peru." Ph.D. dissertation, Department of Anthropology, UCLA. Ann Arbor: University Microfilms.

Lennstrom, H. and C. A. Hastorf (forthcoming). "Homes and Stores: A Botanical Comparison of Inka Storehouses and Contemporary Ethnic Houses." In *Storage in the Inka Empire*, Terry Y. LeVine, ed. University of Oklahoma Press.

Levillier, Roberto (1940). *Don Fransciso de Toledo, supremo organizador del Peru: su vida, su obra (1515–1582)*, Tomo II, *Sus informaciones sobre los Incas (1570–1572)*. Buenos Aires: Espasa-Calpe.

LeVine, Terry Yarov (1987). "Inka Labor Service at the Regional Level: Functional Reality." *Ethnohistory* 34(1): 14–46.

Lévi-Strauss, Claude (1988). *The Origins of Table Manners*. New York: Harper & Row.

Malinowski, Bronislaw (1961). *Argonauts of the western Pacific* [1922]. New York: E. P. Dutton.

Marshall, Yvonne (1985). "Who Made the Lapita Pots? A Case Study in Gender Archaeology." *The Journal of the Polynesian Society* 94(3): 205–33.

Mead, Margaret (1943). *The Problem of Changing Food Habits, 1941–1943.* Washington: National Academy of Sciences, National Research Council, Bulletin 108.

Moore, Henrietta (1986). *Space, Text and Gender.* Cambridge: Cambridge University Press.

—— (1988). *Feminism and Anthropology.* Cambridge: Polity Press.

Morris, Craig (1978). "The Archaeological Study of Andean Exchange Systems." In *Social Archaeology*, C. Redman et al., eds. New York: Academic Press, 315–27.

—— (1982). "Infrastructure of Inka Control in the Central Highlands." In *The Inca and Aztec States*, G. A. Collier, R. I. Rosaldo, and J. D. Worth, eds. New York: Academic Press, 153–71.

Moria, Martin de (1946). *Historia del origen y geneologia real de los Incas [1590].* C. Bayle, ed. Madrid: Consejo superior de investigaciones cientificas, Instituto Santo Toribio de Mogrovejo.

Murra, John V. (1960). "Rite and Crop in the Inca State." In *Culture in History*, S. Dimond, ed. New York: Columbia University Press.

—— (1980). *The Economic Organization of the Inka State.* Ph.D. dissertation, 1955 Greenwich, CT: JAI Press.

—— (1982). "The Mit'a Obligations of Ethnic Groups to the Inka State." In *The Inca and Aztec States*, G. A. Collier, R. I. Rosaldo, and J. D. Wirth, eds. New York: Academic Press, 237–62.

Murray, M. L. and M. J. Schoeniger (1988). "Diet, Status, and Complex Social Structures in Iron Age Central Europe; Some Contributions of Bone Chemistry." In *Tribe and Polity in Prehistoric Europe*, D. B. Gibson and M. N. Gelselowitz, eds. New York: Plenum Press, 155–76.

Netting, Robert McC. (1969). "Women's Weapons: The Politics of Domesticity among the Kofyar." *American Anthropologist* 71: 1037–45.

Newman, Philip (1965). *Knowing the Gururumba.* New York: Holt, Rinehart & Winston.

Oberem, Udo (1968). "Amerikanistische Angaben aus Dokumenten des 16. Jahrhunderts." *Tribus* 17: 81–92.

Price, T. Douglas ed. (1989). *The Chemistry of Prehistoric Human Bone.* Cambridge University Press.

Radcliffe-Brown, A. R. (1977). *The Social Anthropology of Radcliffe-Brown*, A. Kuper, ed. Boston/London: Routledge & Kegan Paul.

Rostorowski de Diez Canseco, Maria (1977). *Etnia y sociedad.* Lima: Instituto de Estudios Peruanos.

Rowe, John Howland (1946). "Inca Culture at the Time of the Spanish Conquest." *Handbook of South American Indians*, Bureau of American Ethnology, Bull. 143(2): 183–330.

—— (1982). "Inca Policies and Institutions Relating to Cultural Unification." In

The Inca and Aztec States, G. A. Collier, R. I. Rosaldo, and J. D. Wirth, eds. New York: Academic Press, 93–118.

Sahlins, Marshall (1972). *Stone Age Economics*. Chicago: Aldine.

Sandefur, Elsie (1988). "Andean Zooarchaeology: Animal Use and the Inka Conquest of the Upper Mantaro Valley." Ph.D. Dissertation, UCLA, Archaeology Program. Ann Arbor: University Microfilms.

Salomon, Frank (1986). *Native Lords of Quito in the Age of the Incas*. Cambridge: Cambridge University Press.

Schiffer, Michael (1976). *Behavioral Archaeology*. New York: Academic Press.

Schoeniger, M. J. and M. J. DeNiro (1984). "Nitrogen and Carbon Isotopic Composition of Bone Collagen from Marine and Terrestrial Animals." *Geochimica et Cosmochimica Acta* 48: 625–39.

Sikkink, Lynn (1988). "Traditional Crop-processing in Central Andean Households: An Ethnoarchaeological Approach." In *Multidisciplinary Studies in Andean Anthropology*, V. J. Vizthum, ed. Ann Arbor: Michigan Discussions in Anthropology 8, 65–87.

Silverblatt, Irene M. (1987). *Moon, Sun, and Witches*. Princeton: Princeton University Press.

Skar, Harold O. (1982). *The Warm Valley People*. New York: Columbia University Press.

Skar, Sarah L. (1981). "Andean Women and the Concept of Space/time." In *Women and Space*, S. Ardener, ed. London: Croom Helm, 35–49.

van der Merwe, Nick J. (1982). "Carbon isotopes, Photosynthesis, and Archaeology." *American Scientist* 70: 209–15.

van der Merwe, Nick J. and J. C. Vogel (1977). "Isotopic Evidence for Early Maize Cultivation in New York State." *American Antiquity* 42: 238–42.

Vogt, E. Z. (1969). *Zinacantan: A Maya Community in the Highland of Chiapas*. Cambridge, MA: Belknap Press.

Weismantel, Mary (1988). *Food, Gender, and Poverty in the Ecuadorian Andes*. Philadelphia: University of Pennsylvania Press.

Zuidema, R. Tom (1973). "Kinship and ancestor cult in three Peruvian communities. Hernandes Principe's account of 1622." *Bulletin de l'Institut Français d'Études Andines* 2: 16–33.

—— (1977). "Inca Kinship." In *Andean Kinship and Marriage*, R. Bolton and E. Mayer, eds. Washington: American Anthropological Association, Special Publ. 7, 240–81.

Part III

Material Aspects of Gender Production

6

Genderlithics: Women's Roles in Stone Tool Production

Joan M. Gero

The most traditional technology of all, in every society, is the social technology of the division of labor which leaves woman with the most labor-intensive responsibilities of child and food production, and which defines her role as one that does not require tools. . . . What is most urgently needed is to begin to define women as tool-makers and tool-users – which they have always been.

E. Boulding, "Women, Peripheries and Food Production" (1978)

Introduction: Did Women Make Stone Tools?

Stone tool production, the bashing of rock against rock, is a male province by all accounts. "The most visible activity in the archaeological record is stone tool fabrication, an exclusively male endeavor" (Thomas 1983: 439). Or from a National Science Foundation reviewer,

> I would hardly have the temerity, in these enlightened times, to deny that there has been androcentrism in the reconstruction of the past (and in the recruitment of those chosen to do that reconstruction). Yet I remain unconvinced that there is any significant misunderstanding as to the fact that most prehistoric lithic production (unarguably the material with which we must work for the first million years or so) was produced by males. No doubt women made bags and baskets and cloths of numerous sorts for just as long . . . [and] in most cultures, past and present, ceramics were and are made by women. . . . No doubt also there are some historically documented reversals of these traditional sex roles, but . . . certainly there is no indication of a technological breakthrough that would require a seriously revisionist archaeology . . . (Anonymous, 1988)

This paper challenges the assumption that males alone are responsible for producing the stone tools that comprise so much of the archaeological

163

record for extended periods of prehistory. My critique, involving no technological breakthrough that allows sex to be assigned to artifacts, attempts a seriously revisionist archaeology with another kind of breakthrough: a theoretical perspective that recognizes gender as a dynamic and critical construct in social life and one that provides entry into studying the organization of prehistoric social labor. It will be a significant outcome of this study to show that engendering tool production does more than map females onto the prehistoric record; it also provides a framework for reconstructing gender relations as they are mediated by material culture.

The logic of this paper proceeds as follows. I begin by examining the current use and loading of the term "stone tool", turning then to question why males are so widely assumed to be the producers of this broad category of material culture and offering, finally, arguments for women's participation in stone tool production. In the second half of the paper I inspect a sequence of changes in stone tool technology from the highlands of Peru to identify women's roles in tool production and to interpret their significance.

What is a Stone Tool? Where Did This Definition Come From?

The study of stone tools, the material remains most closely associated with evolving hominids, speaks directly to the validation of being human. It is not coincidental that the early studies of stone tools and tool-makers (Holmes 1897; Wilson 1899) occurred in the heady flush of newly accepted evolutionary theory (Kehoe 1987); while ethnologists analyzed contemporary savages and barbarians for evidence of the successive ages and stages through which humanity had evolved and progressed, archaeologists unearthed direct evidence of brutish early man from the material record (Kehoe (1987: 3). Spearheads and axes, weapons and implements fashioned out of stone, were identified as the essence of man's rude beginnings, savage, indeed, as beginnings must be, but also full of the clever promise that makes them appropriate hallmarks of human ability. Accompanying this early attention to the forms of stone tools were the related attempts to understand their technology of manufacture, and different tool forms were frequently replicated in experimental undertakings during the late nineteenth and early twentieth century (Hester and Heizer 1973; Johnson 1978), to identify the nature and capacity of early man. (And note please: "man" is not a semantic generalization – such tools were seen, without doubt, as the products of male labor.)

The definition of what constitutes a tool, then, is intimately wrapped up in how Man-the-Toolmaker demonstrates his human-ness. Tools are the standard by which Mankind can be measured. "Tools provide a thermometer for measuring intellectual heat" (Laughlin 1968: 318), as though making tools is what man does and, once made, these tools have completed their function: to bear testimony to man's abilities. Today's lithic analysis has not completely outgrown these beginnings but still focuses on the production and final forms of elaborately finished tools, with only secondary regard to the range of economic and cultural goals accomplished by tools. The most primary distinctions in lithic analysis are still made between the end-products of the manufacturing sequence, "tools", and the by-products of manufacture, cores and debitage, so that the production sequence rather than use-applications still predominates in tool analysis. These distinctions are underscored by further classifactory groupings: artifacts that were obviously used but that had not been subjected in the productive stages to being made into a standardized shape are referred to not as "tools" but as "utilized flakes", or even more emphatically as "unretouched flakes", with the emphasis retained on the amount of production – or lack of it. Tools, it is clear, is a term retained for categories of elaborated retouched artifacts with formal structure, although the question is clearly begged: when does one "use a tool" and when does one "utilize a flake"?

In fact, of course, "utilized flakes" *are* tools, although in the literature, "tools" are still frequently comprised of only standardized, classifiable, reproduced forms of worked stone. Thus, Hayden writes that among the Australian aborigines he was surprised to confront "the unbelievable lack, or rarity, of what the archaeologist calls 'tools'. At first I saw Aborigines using only unretouched primary flakes for shaving and scraping wood, and unmodified blocks of stone for chopping wood. None of these would have been recognized archaeologically as 'tools'" (Hayden 1977: 179). Or again, Binford and Binford categorize Middle Paleolithic artifacts in five general classes: Levallois flakes, non-Levallois flakes, cores, waste flakes, and utilized flakes, and then they *exclude* the final category of utilized flakes from their graphed results "because they are not diagnostic and because their quantity is such that they tend to distort the graph" (Binford and Binford 1966: 263–4).

As Hayden suggests, part of the conventional loading of the term "tool" towards elaborated and retouched forms derives from the real difficulty that archaeologists have had in recognizing unretouched flakes that may have been used as tools. In lithic studies expressly designed to detect artifact use, the term "tool" (or tool-edge) is applied much more generally to any stone that exhibits evidence of having been used, and a much broader, more inclusive range of artifact forms is covered by the "tool" term. In functional analysis, and especially in use-wear studies where microscopic analysis of an artifact's edge may reveal evidence of how it was used, the identifying criteria are turned around and *use* defines tool-ness, clarifying the distinction between unused flakes and tools.

But microscopic use-wear evidence is the exception and is relatively recent, and in general the flake vs. tool distinction upholds the larger archaeological paradigm; lithic studies are most frequently undertaken to erect a simple classification system that can be used as an adjunct to other spatio-temporal approaches, another tool, as it were, to sort culture groups on the basis of material culture correlates, to "measure intellectual heat", to erect a culture history of "man". Tools are identified on the basis of their typological characteristics and their redundant features in order to partition prehistoric time into knowable, comprehensible units. In so doing, lithic analysis has ignored large bodies of data consisting of *ad hoc* or expediently produced flake tools, the non-classifiable, not formally redundant tools that lack elaborate retouch. Adopting a broader definition of "tools" not only refines one of archaeology's central tenets but proves fundamental to a feminist analysis of tool use in prehistory.

Why is Making Stone Tools Perceived as a Male Activity?

If males making elaborated tools have been linked to the progress of mankind, other biases in modern lithic analysis also reinforce the equation of tools with male makers and users. Lithic studies have served as a venue for male and female archaeologists alike, and indeed, a relatively large number of women archaeologists have built reputations on, and made significant contributions to, the study of ancient lithic technologies (e.g. Juel Jensen 1982, 1988; Johnson 1977; Knudson 1973, 1979; Leudtke 1979; Montet-White 1974; Moss 1983, 1986; Purdy 1975, 1981; Torrence 1983, 1989; Tringham et al. 1974). But studies undertaken by women are not representative of the range of interests in lithics, and entire areas of modern lithic studies include virtually no women investigators. Most notably perhaps, flint knapping, where archaeologists replicate lithic production techniques, is exclusively a male arena (e.g Bonnichsen 1977; Bordes 1968; Bradley 1975; Bryan 1960; Callahan 1979; Clarke 1982; Crabtree 1967, 1972; Flenniken 1981, 1984; Kelterborn 1984; Madsen 1984; Neill 1952; Newcomer 1971; Sheets and Muto 1972; Sollberger 1969; Titmus 1984; Tsirk 1974; Witthoft 1967; Young and Bonnichsen 1984). While many women archaeologists have learned to knap (e.g. personal experience), there is virtually no published literature by women as flint knappers: knapping is publicly male territory.

Not only do only male archaeologists make stone tools, but the tools experimentally reproduced by modern (male) flint knappers duplicate the narrow definition of tools as highly formalized, elaborately retouched and morphologically standardized. As noted by Johnson (1978: 355), the single most frequently replicated artifact is the projectile point, especially the fluted point. After the point come other technically demanding tool forms such as Egyptian predynastic flint knives, prismatic blades, Levallois cores, polished celts and axes, all technologically difficult and requiring a long sequence of manufacturing steps and, usually, a high quality raw material. The male gender-loading on tool production is maintained by modern males reproducing only the conventionally circumscribed range of tools by which Man-the-Tool-maker is evaluated and measured.

It is also exclusively male archaeologists who experimentally use replicated, standardized tools in modern, analogical activities (in contrast to research such as Tringham et al. 1974, or Juel Jensen 1982, which test fresh flake edges for micro-wear). Note too that the modern man-made tools are used in highly selected activities to recreate ancient man/"real man". Fastened into reconstructed haftings, attached to spears, arrows, darts, and shafts, these experimental testing programs have in common an overwhelming emphasis on tool use in exaggeratedly "male" activities, especially hunting (Flenniken and Raymond 1986), butchering (Elliott and Anderson 1974; Hester et al. 1976; Odell 1980), spear throwing (Odell and Cowan 1986; Spencer 1974), and the particularly popular combined "research" endeavor of throwing projectiles into, and carving up, modern analogs to big game (Butler 1980; Frison 1989; Huckell 1982; Park 1978; Rippeteau 1979; Stanford 1979), as well as felling trees (Coutts 1977; White 1977) and making bows or arrows (Miller 1979; White 1977). This research often oversteps the fine line dividing imaginative science from popular ideas of the past, filled with rugged men doing primal things – and the media coverage responds accordingly; shooting arrows into newly killed and (importantly!) still warm boar strung up in wooden frames (Fischer et al. 1984) illustrates a particularly lurid design in which only males participate. (In contrast to males' programs, women's experimental lithic studies focus on such things as nutting (Spears 1975), leatherworking (Adams 1988), grain harvesting (Korobkova 1981), and woodworking (Price-Beggerly 1976), all of which are done with unelaborated and non-standardized stone tools.) If male archaeologists are replicating anachronistic stone technologies for purposes other than reiterating an elemental association of males with stone tool production and use, their reenactments nevertheless project and keep alive, as *male*, the reduction of nature through stone.

A final area of lithic studies that consistently underrepresents both female investigators and female tool-makers/users is the ethnoarchaeological observation of "stone age" peoples. Based on males' ethnographic observations, it is again almost invariably males who are observed producing and using stone tools (Holmes 1897; Miller 1979; White 1967, 1969, 1977) in a narrow range of male-related productive tasks. Ethnomales are recorded or filmed making projectile points, fashioning arrow shafts, felling trees, grinding axes.

Ethnographically observed tool-making women occasionally figure into these scenarios as secondary players. For example, Richard Gould's study of Australian Aborigines notes that both males and females pick up and use sharp flakes for butchering and other domestic tasks (1977: 164). But even after pointing this out, Gould reverts to a study entirely devoted to males, and it is still only males and male tasks that are systematically observed:

> . . . approximately 20 of these flake knives are used by one person each year. Of course, women use these as much as men, and I might add here that women sometimes take a hand in the final finishing of wooden bowls too. Thus I am being arbitrary in referring to use of stone tools as male tasks, and I think it best to say so. (Gould 1977: 166)

But the recognition of female tool-makers and users is thereafter ignored, and data is tabulated as "Total amounts of lithic raw material needed *per man* per year" (Gould 1977: 166, emphasis mine), although we have been told that women use flake knives *as much as men*!

The point here is not accusatory but expository; male bias is systematically imposed on archaeological interpretations of tool manufacture and use, as constructs of archaeological interpretation interact with modern gender ideology. Modern, western males generally make tools and women don't. It is sometimes even postulated that only males are strong enough to make stone tools (but see Geis 1987). Modern gender ideology is underwritten by male archaeologists undertaking lithic studies that illustrate males making and using stone tools, appropriating this productive arena as male for as far back as humanity can be extended. The restrictive and self-fulfilling definition of stone tools as formal, standardized tools central to male activities leads to an anthropological overstatement about the importance attached to weapons, extractive tools, and hunting paraphernalia. The "maleness" of "tools" derived in this fashion ties back to control over the techno-eco/ environment, as part of the same logical system that tacitly accords priority to technoenvironmental factors to account for cultural change and human evolution (Meg Conkey, personal communication; Gero forthcoming).

Considerations for Women as Likely Stone Tool Producers

In contrast to the male-dominated areas of lithic studies that focus on (some) tool forms and on how (some) tools are made, a very different line of investigation asks how tasks were carried out with stone tools. And it is female investigators who, in disproportionate numbers, have worked from a functional perspective to study how tools were used, at the level of microwear analysis (e.g. Adams 1988; Bienenfeld 1985; Juel Jensen 1982, 1988; Lewenstein 1981, 1987; Mansure-Franchomme 1983; Moss 1983, 1986; Olausson 1980; Price-Beggerly 1976; Sale 1986; Unger-Hamilton 1984), macrowear analysis (e.g. Cantwell 1979; Knudson 1973; Stafford 1977), or assemblage composition (e.g. Arundale 1980; Gero 1983a, 1983b).[1] In doing so, women study the flake tools, the "non-standardized", "non-curated", "expedient" tools that are in almost all regards held to be inferior, based on contemporary values attached to time and form and ranking, and on the male-biased standards for tools that pervade lithic studies. If women's work has been observed cross-culturally to be devalued, in archaeology it is put to the study of the devalued "utilized flakes".

I now wish to examine the proposition that women in prehistory made stone tools. I will argue that women, at the very least, made many of the flake tools on which modern female archaeologists focus their studies and which modern female archaeologists replicate in experimental procedures. In the course of this argument I believe we will recognize much potential for women making a wider range of tools as well.

Let us start with the simplest assumptions: females comprised approximately half of all prehistoric populations, and these women carried out productive activities at prehistoric sites. We suspect, moreover, that women were especially visible and active in household contexts where they played significant roles in household production and household management (Moore 1988: 32). Almost ironically, women can be expected to be most visible and active precisely in the contexts that archaeologists are most likely to excavate: on house floors, at base camps and in village sites where women would congregate to carry out their work. Prehistoric women are probably disproportionately represented in densely concentrated areas of household refuse, and archaeological materials from the central areas of base-camp or house-floor excavations are at least *likely* to be associated with women's work.

As women work in association with such living areas, they need tools for the tasks they carry out. Although the kinds of tools women need would clearly vary from culture to culture and from task to task, it is inconceivable that they sat and waited for a flake to be produced, or that they set out each time to borrow one. Women clearly required ready access to efficient working edges in their routine work, and they must have manufactured them as needed. Since the user of a tool is in the best position to judge its adequacy, it makes sense that women produced many of their own tools, and indeed it would be most inefficient for them to rely on men for these needs.

Finally, women are both strong and smart enough to produce stone tools. The ethnographic, ethnohistoric, and experimental archaeology literature amply illustrates (or implies) that women make tools, although the unspectacular, routine nature of such activity mitigates against its being recorded as a distinctive undertaking: "[Women] undertake all the work except that alone of the grand chase" (*Jesuit Relations* 3: 101), although we also know that women in some contexts hunt as well (cf. Estioko-Griffin and Griffin 1981). The ethnohistorical observations of stone-using societies illustrate that women both make and use stone tools; in addition to flake tools and core tools made by Australian aboriginal women (Gould 1977: 166; Hamilton 1980: 7; Hayden 1977: 183, 185; Tindale 1972: 246), Tiwi women made axes (Goodale 1971: 155) and, in at least one instance, a companion to the Lewis and Clark expedition reporting seeing "squaws chipping flakes into small arrow points, holding the flake in their left hand, grasped between a piece of bent leather, and chipping off small flakes by pressure, using a small pointed bone in the right hand for that purpose" (Holmes 1919: 316).

Like men's tools, the kinds of tools made by women would be determined by a range of historical, material, economic, social, political, and symbolic factors; to generalize further about women's tools would be to reduce the category "woman" to one so broad and homogenized that it would be meaningless. We must be wary of reducing and simplifying the variations on gender divisions manifest in different societies, and even within single societies, as they relate to the production of technological artifacts. It is obvious that the division of productive activities by gender varies enormously from group to group, that what is exclusively males' work in one setting is females' work in another, and that women's control over a specific task in one context tells us little about that work falling to women in all comparable contexts. In addition, feminist scholarship has contributed important insights into how gender interacts with age classes and status rankings as relationships that organize productive activities (Gailey 1987; Moore

1988), and it is this richness in gender systems that makes gender a dynamic variable in social and productive relations.

To avoid an argument that would simply assign men to some tasks and women to others, we can better examine some of the common constraints on tool production for their gender implications; I will here consider four: scheduling, access to appropriate raw materials, biological strength and, finally, the symbolic significance of production.

Scheduling

Judith Brown argues (1970: 1077) that women's child-care responsibilities tend to restrict women to "repetitive, interruptible, non-dangerous tasks that do not require extensive excursions", thus setting up universal task restrictions for nursing mothers or for women with children three years of age or younger. Such universal prescriptions are widely debated and in fact rejected today, especially in reference to generalizations such as "women's roles" or "women's experiences" (see Coward 1983); certainly women in many societies share responsibilities for child care with other household members or other household units. Even if one were to accept Brown's argument, this hardly eliminates women's participation from stone tool production. Producing expedient tools requires only a single blow to a core and virtually no time at all. Even working formalized tools is not time consuming: an "average sized" projectile point is finished by a practised knapper in about 30 minutes (Holmes 1919: 313 and 328). If flying debitage is considered dangerous around young children, special tool preparation areas are easily arranged at a short remove from the house floor, and young children can always congregate elsewhere. There is every reason to believe that women in many stone-using contexts could regularly have found time and space to produce tools, and that tool production would have been localized within camps or villages or, many times, even within structures.

Access to lithic raw materials

"Accessing" or "gaining access to" lithic raw materials frames the problem of procuring stone in terms of obstacles, restrictions, and constraints; one gains access *despite* such barriers as distance, knowledge of sources, claims of ownership, payments, transport, divisibility of what's been acquired. In contrast, the idea of "control over" lithic raw materials renders such constraints invisible and suggests an immediate correspondence between wanting stone and having it. Clearly, who "accesses" stone and who "controls" stone provides a semantic loading

that is easily genderized in modern categories; women are allowed to
access sources of stone while men control the flows of lithic material.
   In fact, of course, the matter of attributing gender to stone procurement is difficult in any case, and the amount of women's control over
appropriate raw lithic materials is difficult to reconstruct and probably
highly variable. Ethnographic reports of stone-using people have often
been interpreted to illustrate a pattern of male control over exotic stone.
Gould, for instance, reports that among the Australian aborigines,

> quarries occur at or near sacred sites – that is, totemic "dreaming" places.
> People [men – J.G.] who believe themselves to be descended patrilineally
> from the particular totemic being at one of these sites will make special
> trips to the quarry to secure stone there. A man places a high value on
> stone from a site of his dreamtime totem . . . Because of his patrilineal
> relationship to the site, a man sees the stone as part of his own being – a
> fact which motivates him to carry the stone to other, distant sites . . .
> (1977: 164, emphasis mine)

   This spiritual justification for why men and not women control the
rare, imported, traded, or quarried stone materials is paralleled in other
Australian contexts to rationalize male control over foreign interactions
and exchanges: "Among the Yankuntjara people that I worked with, it
appeared that there was a prohibition against women using crypto-
crystalline rocks. . . . A similar prohibition was recorded in Central
Australia by Spencer and Gillen [1912: 373, 376]" (Hayden 1977: 183).
   A third observation focuses on the acquisition of grindstones in the
western zones of the Australian desert regions where stone represents a
scarce resource: "Men travelled to the known sources of stone, utilizing
kinship ties with people in these areas. [The grindstones] were then
handed over to their wives . . ." (Hamilton 1980: 8).
   But other Australian accounts clearly report that while men flake the
stone at quarry sites, it is women's work to carry it away (Jones and
White 1988: 61 and 83). Thus, women clearly do partake in long-distance
trade for "exotic" rock and certainly could have controlled such stone
once it arrived "back home".[2] We also know that quarry sites were often
visited by larger residential groups, presumably of both sexes, and that
camps were established over longer time periods where huge quantities
of flakes and partially reduced bifaces were removed (e.g. references to
tipi circles associated with quartzite quarries of eastern Wyoming, or the
evidence for habitations at Flint Ridge, Ohio, in Holmes 1919: 178 and
211). These reconstructions surely allow ample access for women to
highly-sought, high-quality stone. Finally, the ethnographic glimpses of
male-dominated trade for distant stone materials fail to address the
question of control over local stone sources for tool production, and of

course it is the flake tools of local materials that represent a vast majority of tools in the archaeological record.

Biological strength

Already alluded to, the issue of strength is addressed here because it is raised so regularly in discussions of sex roles, and because it lurks as an implicit objection to women's participation in stone tool production. Sex differences in upper body strength, significant in modern populations even when normalized for lean body mass (Fausto-Sterling 1985: 217, but see Lowe 1983), could be thought to have ramifications in tool production.

In fact, upper body strength is not an issue in making tools, where technique rather than force is determinate (John Clark, personal communication). Moreover, differential upper body strength gives us no reason to expect an activity like tool production should fall either to males or to females; we don't expect the division of sex roles to follow our own cultural categories of either rational efficiency or fairness. Women in fact are often found carrying out heavier labor tasks than males, as in the transport of heavy goods to market locations or gathering and transporting firewood. We can't even assume that stone tool manufacturing will always be divided by gender rather than by age or class or ability. Divisions or labor not only vary in all these dimensions but also in the degree of task specialization, that is, in how production sequences are divided up into specified tasks. A more meaningful question might ask, what stages of stone tool production could be divided between males and females in the course of producing specific tool types and, even more importantly perhaps, as played out in specific socio-historic contexts.

The issue of upper body strength might be significant only in very specific areas of lithic production: in quarrying raw stone from bedrock sources, in breaking apart large cobbles or large blocks of quarried stone to produce primary flakes, and in some pressure-flaking techniques, especially using an indirect punch. Female disadvantage in these areas could be significant enough for them regularly to fall to men. This presents more interesting alternatives for how gender might have been played out in stone tool production: under what circumstances would females and males have separate charge of distinct production spheres (for what types of tools? in which quarrying contexts?), and under what circumstances would gender tasks be specialized and complementary, towards a shared production goal?

The social value of tool production

It is in the realm of meaning, or social value, that women's participation in tool production must ultimately be considered. That women *can* and *do* make stone tools has already been shown. The questions of where and when women make tools, the kinds of tools they make, and the task-specialized jobs they perform within tool production, are more complex matters and will vary in different socio-historic contexts. Recognizing that social value is always attached to specific labor tasks and that males' labor is generally more highly valued that females', brings us directly to the question of how gender systems work: how do males control the labor that is more socially valued, and how do these gender roles in production activities come into being? Is some labor valued principally *because* it is performed by males? And how do we account for the apparent invisibility of women's labor? Finally, what social value would accompany the production of different classes of stone tools?

Flake tools by definition lack the investment of energy that we today, using a modern value system, accord greater symbolic and social importance. Where women regularly perform undervalued work, it is relatively simple today to associate the production of flake tools with women, with base-camp operations, with local materials, with simple production sequences. Devoid of social meaning, the common, expedient "utilized flake" naturally falls within a larger class of productive activities that women are not only allowed to perform but that are often associated by modern gender ideology with their lot. We find it easy to believe that women were allowed to do, perhaps were *only* allowed do, "meaningless" work, work without social value, such as flake tool production.

But these value loadings on stone tools can be questioned for prehistoric times. Terms like an *"investment of energy"* smack so thickly of modern values that we are forced to question the assumption that tools with more retouch automatically carried greater social status or importance than effective, reliable (throw-away? "expedient"?) flake tools. Are we sure that elaborately worked bifaces were necessarily more highly valued? Or does this "investment of energy" only today produce the expectation that formal "tools" were high class and made by men? Most central to this issue, would women have made elaborately retouched tools?

Everything we have considered up to this point suggests that they could have and probably did. It certainly can be argued that the implicit ranking (based on "energy investments") of projectile points at the top, other bifacially produced tools in the middle, and flake tools at the bottom, is a recent construct. Moreover, even if this value system held in prehistory, there is no reason to exclude women's roles as producers of finely finished tools. We have ample evidence of other wealth items and highly decorated items that women were charged with producing. Schneider (1983: 106–9), for instance, discusses Plains Indian women making and dressing the ritual Sun Dance Dolls among the Crow, or doing the quillwork on high-status Pawnee shirts; Blackfeet women decorate tipis with paintings of war and hunting, and Gros Ventre women made beaded moccasins. Gailey depicts Tongan chiefly women as the makers of all *koloa*, valuables or wealth objects: "[Women-made] valuables were always superior to things made by men . . . Chiefly women's production of valuables validated other chiefly persons' status throughout life" (Gailey 1987: 97). In societies where female–male relationships are characterized by reciprocity and complementarity rather than by hierarchy and dominance, and where women are known to have held positions of power and respect, there is no reason to believe that women did not produce elaborate worked stone tools.

This brings us to the final query: are projectile points in a category by themselves? Do men have to have made the arrow heads? We have already noted one ethnographic example of women chipping arrow points, suggesting that the partitioning of labor is not determined solely by what it is that is being made. Instead, the division of labor will be conditioned by the context of social relations, and by the social and symbolic value placed on what is made. The projectile point in and of itself has no universal meaning. It *can* represent the cunning and danger of the hunt, where hunters are highly esteemed and where projectile points speak to control over the means of production, in meat as well as in stone. In such cases, projectile points may indeed provide a means of reproducing the male status as hunter and may be made by men. But this is not all cases. In other contexts, especially agricultural societies, small-game hunting is divested of these meanings and is conducted as an ancillary, secondary subsistence enterprise. Projectile points in these contexts convey neither cunning nor danger, dominance nor male status . . . nor would projectile points have to have been made by men.

What then do we know? Unilateral male control over lithic production, from flake to point, has crumbled in light of sociological, historical, experimental, and ethnographic evidence. Women can be suspected of making as many stone tools as men, and of leaving even more tools than men do in recoverable concentrations where archaeologists usually dig. Indeed, in hindsight it is illogical that the medium of stone should, by itself, have been thought to have deterministic power over the sex of those who would work it. Gender systems, deeply embedded in social relations of complementarity and/or hierarchy, cooperation and/or dominance, override any particular artifact medium.

J. M. GERO

There are no compelling biological, historical, sociological, ethno-graphnic, ethnohistorical, or experimental reasons why women could not have made – and good reason to think they probably *did* make – all kinds of stone tools, in all kinds of lithic materials, for a variety of uses and contexts. On the other hand, direct gender attribution of individual tools remains problematic; women, like men, can't easily be sought at the level of individual tool producers. Thus, for purposes of elucidating the bare minimum level of female participation in stone tool production, I suggest we look at lithic assemblages that are (1) from dwelling or habitation areas where, because of occupation over many days, weeks or months, we are most likely to find evidence of maintenance tasks related to food, clothing, child-rearing; (2) made of locally available raw materials, to avoid arguments for or against differential male/female mobility; and (3) of "expedient" flake tools, leaving aside the highly retouched tools which, from our cultural perspective, conform to formal standards of tool morphology and are granted high social value. It is at this most minimal analytical and contextual level, which probably constitutes 90 percent of the archaeological record of stone tool manufacture, that we will surely "see" women. The remainder of this paper examines a particular context of stone tool production and use in the highlands of Peru, arguing that the work of women can be detected in this lithic tradition, and that the meaning of gender can be approached by these means.

Stone Tools at Huaricoto, Peru

Context of study

The lithic assemblages used in this study were excavated from the site of Huaricoto, a formative period temple with associated occupational components located in the Callejón de Huaylas intermontane valley of northcentral highland Peru.[3] The data have previously been analyzed to assess the potential of stone tools for carrying messages of social status and group identity (Gero 1983a, 1989). Here, changes in lithic technology will be reviewed to see how an explicitly gendered analysis refocuses the interpretation.

The site of Huaricoto is located at 2740 m on a small promontory on the eastern side of the Rio Santa, a north flowing river that is bounded by two parallel but contrastive mountain chains (figure 6.1). Both Cordilleras exhibit extensive post-glacial change, but outwash and erosional deposits are considerably more pronounced on the eastern, Cordillera Blanca side of the Callejón, a function of its higher, steeper slopes. Rapid glacial

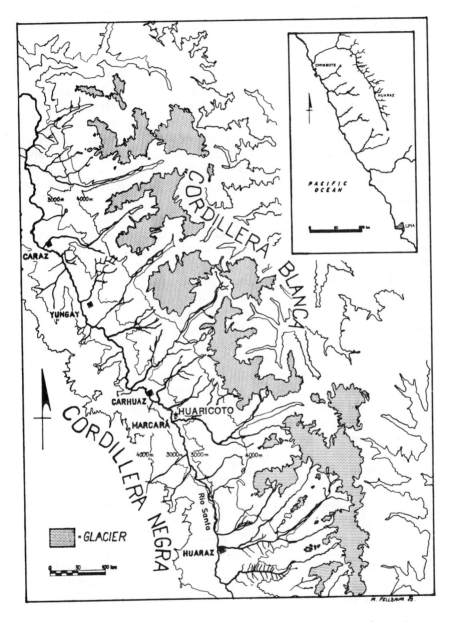

Figure 6.1 Callejón de Huaylas region showing location of site of Huaricoto.

melting has further contributed to these processes, depositing materials derived from the Cordillera Blanca on the valley floor where they accumulate in terraces running parallel to the mouths of the rivers emptying upper glacial lakes. It is on such a terrace of unsorted sands and gravels that Huaricoto is situated.

Occupation of the site spans approximately 2500 years, from the late preceramic period around 2000 BC through the Early Intermediate period/Middle Horizon at AD 600 (Burger and Salazar-Burger 1980). The earliest levels have exposed a ceremonial platform covered with yellow clay and constructed with several carefully prepared, sunken, clay-lined ceremonial hearths (Burger and Salazar-Burger 1985). Burger and Salazar-Burger (1980) interpret this stage as an unoccupied ceremonial zone that was visited and used only intermittently by mobile hunters and gatherers.

The introduction of ceramics at the site at about 1700 BC does not seem to accompany other large scale socio-cultural changes. Rather, a series of enlargements of the temple area through regular construction and filling of ceremonial hearths appears to continue out of the preceramic levels through the Initial period and Early Horizon phases. Terraces that buttressed the growing temple mound have been traced around the northern perimeter of the temple, and large elliptical areas defined by the erection of 3 m high dressed boulders ('huancas') were constructed during the later Chavin phases, setting apart an open plaza area in front of the temple and defining other ritual areas on the other side of the main structure as well (figure 6.2).

Because excavations at Huaricoto were largely directed to defining the temple and ceremonial areas of the site, the residential components are less well understood. Starting in the Early Intermediate period (EIP), however, large amounts of midden accumulation are apparent in the northernmost excavation sector, representing dense concentrations of domestic refuse from the rapidly expanded village that now reaches its maximum extent of 3 ha. This EIP development of a permanent village settlement associated with an older, strictly ceremonial area is paralleled at other highland sites.

Lithic materials from Huaricoto were collected from four excavation sectors (figure 6.2), which are detailed elsewhere (Gero 1983a, 1989). The four site sectors contributed unequally to the total lithic assemblage as well as to the representations of each cultural period. Sector I, the open plaza east of the temple, spanned the entire occupation of the site with particularly interesting quartz materials coming from two preceramic ceremonial hearths in the lowest levels. Sector II, the central temple area, yielded a low density of lithics and lacked the EIP strata corresponding to the residential occupation found elsewhere at the site for this time.

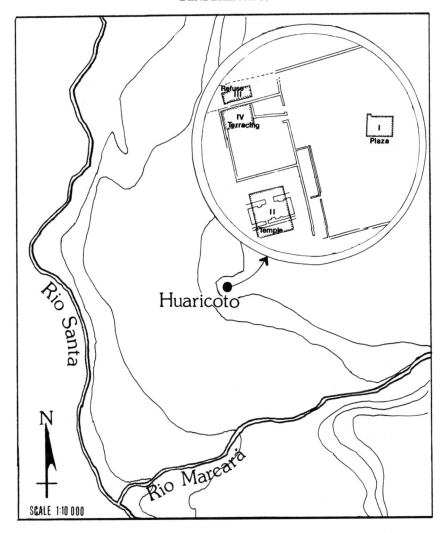

Figure 6.2 Huaricoto, showing distinct excavation sectors (inset courtesy of R. Burger).

Chipped and ground slate bifaces are noted throughout Sector II levels, mostly in a disfunctional broken or exhausted state, accompanied by a thin scatter of barely modified flake tools. Sector IV, represented by a series of supporting terraces north of the temple, apparently dates only to the middle period of Huaricoto's occupation: the two lower terraces are Initial period, and there is one upper Early Horizon terrace. Of special interest, the lowest terrace of Sector IV contained a well-defined lithic workshop area, apparently corresponding to the production of bifaces recovered from Initial period occupations at Huaricoto. Finally, Sector III, the deep refuse area on the extreme northern edge of the temple mound, dates predominantly to the last (EIP) period of site occupation. This sector contained the greatest density of artifactual material in its midden strata, with few projectile points and an over-whelming proportion of expediently produced flake tools, while the lowest levels revealed a preceramic component of carefully prepared hearths and a few tools. Tool frequencies by cultural periods for the entire site are given in table 6.1.

Table 6.1 Size and structure of the Huaricoto lithic assemblage based on 1014 artifacts

	Flake tools	Bifaces and projectile points
Early Intermediate Period (n = 622)	636 (96%)	26 (4%)
Early Horizon (n = 74)	57 (77%)	17 (23%)
Initial Period (n = 247)	221 (89%)	26 (11%)
Preceramic Period (n = 31)	27 (87%)	4 (13%)
TOTALS	941	73

Inspection of the Huaricoto stone tools focuses on the three dimensions of lithic assemblages identified earlier as areas in which gender roles appear to interact with lithic production and use. Again, while none of these represents a simple correspondence of archaeological artifact with sex, each area has gender implications:

1 *Lithic raw materials.* Gender can obviously be used as a category to limit control over different types of workable stone.
2 *Degree of preparation of tool forms.* Gender has already been shown to be associated with "energy investments" in tool production, although we suspect this is largely a modern association. Minimally, women have certainly contributed extensively to flake tool production.
3 *Context of tool preparation and use.* Gender has spatial implications, with certain contexts and ranges of tool applications at least loosely suggesting female work areas.

Lithic raw materials

If we take the view that women enjoyed access to abundant local lithic materials rather than depending on imported quarried materials, we can evaluate the Huaricoto lithic assemblage for the accessibility of the stone materials represented at the site.

As tabulated in figure 6.3, "local" materials are readily accessible from river cobbles or surface outcroppings close at hand: sandstones, quartzites, granites, and metamorphosed sedimentary rocks. These probably were taken from the nearby riverbeds of the Rio Santa, just 500 m below and to the west of the site promontory, or from the Rio Marcará flowing 500 m southeast of the site.

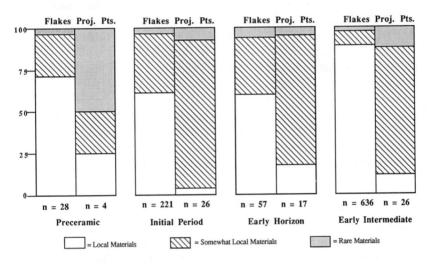

Figure 6.3 Artifacts grouped in categories of relative rareness of raw material.

"Somewhat local" materials include volcanic stones (tuffs, rhyolites, and andesites) derived from at least approximately 5 km away and from the other side of the Rio Santa (Wilson et al. 1967: 44–6). In addition, this group includes materials that occur in the Cordillera Blanca but are more difficult to obtain than the "local" materials because they are derived from lower geological beds and outcrop less frequently: rhyolites and tuffs, shale, slate, and caliz.

Finally, "rare" materials were imported from outside the Callejón de Huaylas or, minimally, were unevenly and sparsely available within the wider local region; these include obsidian, quartz crystals, and high-quality chert. Chert sources can only be identified in the Marañon drainage at significant remove (Wilson et al. 1967: 26–7), while Burger and Asaro (1977) report that Callejón obsidian was imported from Quispisisa in Huancavelica, several hundred miles to the south.

The data in figure 6.3 indicate first, that although rare stone was used more often to produce bifaces than flake tools (12% compared to 2%), no cultural component at Huaricoto exhibits a significantly high proportion of rare materials, with the possible exception of the unreliably small preceramic biface sample.

On the other hand, the pattern of using somewhat local materials for complex tools, and local materials for expedient tools, is apparent for all cultural periods; bifaces made of local materials show up as only 4% up to 25% of each biface sample, while the flake tools of local materials are never represented by less than 60% and reach as high as 89% of the flake tool assemblages. As well, somewhat local and rare materials account for between 82% and 96% of all the biface samples, while the same materials only account for between 11% and 40% of the flake tools.

A third trend somewhat obscured in the grouped data of figure 6.3 is the strong tendency towards the adoption of a single local material, a metamorphosed sedimentary rock here called "metashale", as the standard material for flake tools. During earlier periods of site occupation, metashale represented only 35% to 40% of the flake tool material while in the last EIP period, metashale dominated the flake tool assemblage with a representation of 62%. We return to interpret these findings after looking at the other lithic dimensions.

Degree of tool preparation

Tool preparation at Huaricoto can be assessed initially by a separation of "expedient" flake tools from the carefully worked bifaces that occur throughout the sequence. Table 6.1 showed that bifaces comprise between 4% and 23% of the total assemblage for any period, and that while the Early Horizon representation of bifaces is unexpectedly high, it is the dramatically low frequency of bifaces in the EIP that is most noticeable. Whereas in earlier periods, bifaces comprised between 23% to 11% of the assemblages, in the EIP only 4% of the lithics are represented by bifaces.

Not only do bifaces almost disappear in the later, more residential EIP sample, but even the flake tools exhibit less preparation. Measuring the percentage of flake tools with cortex remaining on the surface shows an increase of residual cortex in the EIP: 57% of flake tools retain some cortex, compared to measures of 43%, 49%, and 63% in the three earlier periods.

Finally, the amount of retouch per flake tool was calculated for a sub-set of the Huaricoto materials and can be simply summarized (cf. Gero 1983a: 139): a slight but consistent trend demonstrates that tools from later occupational periods show less retouch, measured both by shaping and thinning flake scars, than tools from the earlier periods. A fair summary of the amount of investment in tool preparation over time at

Huaricoto is simply that *more tools* are made expediently, and tools are made *more expediently*.

Context of tool preparation and use

The contextualization of Huaricoto lithics rests on recognizing the overarching change in site function from the preceramic/Early Horizon occupations when the site was dominated by its ceremonial aspects, to the later EIP occupation associated with a village population and residential functions. All time-transgressive trends must be interpreted in light of this contextual shift.

Projectile points and bifaces are overrepresented in the earlier strata and, significantly, in the "ceremonial sectors" of temple and plaza (Table 6.1). Most of these were recovered in a much reduced or broken, expended state although a number of unbroken points recovered from ceremonially prepared hearths exhibit virtually no use at all (figure 6.4). In the later EIP village context, flake tool assemblages replace bifaces and appear to be produced on-site more often than before; the amount of cortex remaining on debitage flakes (see Gero 1983a) provides a crude

cms

Figure 6.4 Projectile points recovered from ceremonial contexts of Huaricoto.

measure of river cobble material that was worked (or reworked) at the site rather than at the river or quarry location. The fact that, after the unrepresentative preceramic sample, proportions of debitage with cortex rise steadily and reach a full 25% of all debitage in the EIP, suggests that more tools are being produced, or reworked, on site than earlier, a finding that fits comfortably with the EIP rise in frequency of expedient tools and with the replacement of the ceremonial area with a village economy.

Gender shifts in tool production and use at Huaricoto

To recapitulate, the major trends that accompany the shift from ceremonial center to village settlement include: (1) a consistent pairing of flake tools with local raw materials, while bifaces are made of less accessible materials; (2) both bifacially prepared tools and flake tools of the later EIP occupation manifest less retouch and more cortex on tool surfaces (less tool preparation) than in earlier periods; and (3) a dramatic increase in flake tools (and the virtual disappearance of bifaces), together with the homogenization of local raw materials, characterizes the EIP village (non-temple) phase. How are gender systems operating to produce these data?

It is questionable whether the lower proportions of bifacial tools in later phases is because the preceramic, Initial period and Early Horizon economies were so much more intensely focused on hunting or even on meat-eating. In fact, camelid domestication most likely dates to the late EH, and meat preparation and consumption would probably have increased in the EIP (Burke 1990). The change in the ratio of lithic forms and raw materials follows more closely from the shift from a ceremonial to a residential context. We recognize that the carefully finished biface of exotic material in the restricted context of the ceremonial center is *equivalent* to the flake tool in the residential setting, and the flake tool performs many of the same actions unceremoniously that bifaces perform in a ritualistic setting: cutting, scraping, sawing, skinning, and whittling (Ahler 1970: 88–98). Bifaces recovered from restricted, sacred contexts may have been constrained by more formal, standardized morphological definitions and by the value of exotic raw materials from which they were made, to contribute to the legitimation of a restricted and sacred context: the Huaricoto preceramic and Initial period temple.

The high proportions of expended projectile points from the early ritual contexts at Huaricoto probably refer to meat consumption (or offerings) at ceremonial feasts; there is ample evidence for meat preparation in Huaricoto's ritually prepared, ash-filled hearths that are full of splintered bone and tiny flake spalls. At the same time, the examples of dedicatory and apparently unutilized (or underutilized) projectile points recovered from ceremonial hearths in the early Huaricoto temple suggest that the projectile point was also offered up, in addition to or as a substitute for ceremonial meat. In the earlier occupations at Huaricoto, we can speculate that we are observing rituals in which meat played an important role, with males possibly providing this highly valued food, and probably actually hunting it, in an economy that lacked domesticated animals until late in the Early Horizon.

It may be, too, that men manufactured the Huaricoto bifaces recovered from the early ceremonial and dedicatory contexts; the narrowly restricted conditions that associate men with the production of projectile points (e.g. when such tools carry the social meanings of, and reflect directly on the prestige of hunting and meat production) could apply in this circumstance. Women, however, are likely to be directly associated with the use of these tools in the Huaricoto temple context and most probably participated in the rituals in the preparing, cooking, and serving of the ceremonially important meat.

It also can be seen that the conditions suggesting women's participation in stone tool production and use increase with time, especially in conjunction with the appearance of a residential settlement at Huaricoto after the Early Horizon. When flake tools replace bifaces and become more expedient in their production, and when local raw materials increase in representation, it is not necessarily because a new economic base is creating new uses for stone tools. Rather, the demands on stone tools as sacred and prestigious have changed with the cessation of the temple complex, and social meanings attached to ritual hunting paraphernalia have shifted.

In the village context, stone tools fulfill a much broader range of functions than in the temple area, with less focus specifically on meat preparation and less social loading on tool morphology. Conditions are created that concentrate women's secular work in household production and management, and in the process, encourage the making and using of expedient flake tools produced from abundant local raw materials. The precise activities carried out at Huaricoto by EIP women using flake tools is still not well defined; the quality of locally available lithic materials precludes fine-grained microwear analysis and we are left with gross functional interpretations: working wood, defleshing cactus, butchering and skinning animals, perhaps leather work. In general, the flake tools show little tendency toward task specialization, and the same tool proves to have been used in a wide variety of work actions (Gero 1983a: 152–61).

While males may also be making and using flake tools, male status is no longer linked to lithic production but is tied up in newly defined prestige goods in other media, some of which are probably commissioned (e.g. the elaborated Recuay ceramics of the EIP (Gero 1990)) and/or made by women (e.g. fancy textiles). Males are increasingly involved in activities that accompany early state formation and that take males into wider socio-political spheres but whose definition lies outside the bounds of this inquiry.

Our understandings of gender relations as they operated in Huaricoto tool production are still very incomplete, and indeed, the question "Did women make stone tools?", although it can now be answered affirmatively, will hardly produce compelling insights into how gender systems operated in Formative Peru. To understand the constitution and operation of gender systems, a focus on a single material technology such as lithics is not necessarily fruitful, and to a great extent the argument presented here is constrained by an archaeological paradigm that would, at least implicitly, assume a simple correspondence between one productive process and one sex. To elucidate gender systems and relations, we will need to trace the convergence of many lines of material evidence. But we have had to put such interests on hold until gender is accepted as a constitutive element of all social relations and as a primary means of signifying relationships of power (Scott 1986). As a new axis of investigation, gender is only beginning to accumulate the analytic power to address (and change) existing archaeological categories, to shift our specialized focus from stones, shells, or sherds to men and women.

ACKNOWLEDGMENTS

Many thanks to the participants of "The Wedge" conference for their wise and supportive comments on this work, and to Meg Conkey for her careful, insightful critique that got to the heart of alternative structures. Liz Brumfiel kindly supplied the epigram. John Clark, Alice Kehoe, and Morgan Maclachlan offered thoughtful comments along the way, and Kathy Bolen contributed diligent research, all of which I very much appreciate and much (but not all) of which I used.

NOTES

1 In contrast to the 100% sample of males in flint knapping research, the ratio of women to men involved in microwear studies appears to be approximately 1:1, compared to an overall ratio of 1:5 women to men employed as full-time archaeologists in anthropology departments listed in the *AAA Guide* (Kramer and Stark 1988: 11).

2 Note that the associational chains that build up and give value to tools as
   standardized, curated, and elaborately retouched, also include tools of
   "exotic" (vs. "common") materials, all associated with male production and
   use. Note how different these values sound when "exotic" materials are
   called "low density" materials and "common" materials are "high density".
   In whose terms do we rationalize the high- and low-value terms placed on
   stone tool dichotomies?
3 Research on the lithic materials of Huaricoto was carried out from 1978 to
   1980 with the generous help of a Fulbright-Hays pre-dissertation award,
   administered by the Comisión para Intercambio Educativo entro los Estados
   Unidos y el Perú. A 1982 Sigma Xi Grant-in-Aid supported the computeri-
   zation of the flake tool data. The assemblages considered here are restricted
   to lithics collected in 1978 and 1979 and owe much to the generous
   cooperation of Dr Richard Burger, Lucy Salazar-Burger, and Abelardo
   Sandoval, project directors.

REFERENCES

Adams, Jenny L. (1988). "Use-Wear Analysis on Manos and Hide Processing
   Stones." *Journal of Field Archaeology* 15: 307–15.
Ahler, Stan (1970). *Projectile Point Form and Function at Rodgers Shelter,
   Missouri.* Missouri Archaeological Society Research Series No. 8.
Arundale, Wendy H. (1980). "Functional Analysis of Three Unusual Assem-
   blages from the Cape Dorset Area, Baffin Island." *Arctic* 33: 464–86.
Bienenfeld, Paula (1985). Preliminary Results from a Lithic Use-Wear Study of
   the Swifterbant Sites, S-51, S-4, and S-2. *Helinium* 25: 194–211.
Binford, Lewis R. and S. Binford (1966). A Preliminary Analysis of Functional
   Variability in the Mousterian of Levallois Facies. *American Anthropologist* 68:
   238–95.
Bonnichsen, Robson (1977). *Models for Deriving Cultural Information from
   Stone Tools.* Ottowa: Mercury Series Paper No. 60, National Museum of
   Man.
Bordes, Francois (1968). *The Old Stone Age.* New York: World University
   Library.
Boulding, Elise (1978). "Women, Peripheries and Food Production." Consortium
   for International Development, "International Conference on Women and
   Food," January 8–11, 1978. Vol. I, Tucson: University of Arizona, 22–44.
Bradley, B. A. (1975). "Lithic Reduction Sequences: A Glossary and Discussion."
   In *Lithic Technology: Making and Using Stone Tools*, E. Swanson, ed. The
   Hague: Mouton, 5–13.
Brown, Judith (1970). "A Note on the Division of Labor by Sex." *American
   Anthropologist* 72: 1073–8.
Bryan, A. L. (1960). "Pressure Flaking: The Problem of Identification." *Tebiwa*
   3: 29–30.
Burger, Richard L. and Frank Asaro (1977). "Analisis de rasgos significativos en

la obsidiana de los Andes Centrales." *Revista del Museo Nacional* (Lima) 43: 281–325.

Burger, Richard L. and Lucy Salazar-Burger (1980). "Ritual and Religion at Huaricoto." *Archaeology* 33: 26–32.

—— (1985). "The Early Ceremonial Center of Huaricoto." In *Early Ceremonial Architecture in the Andes*, Christopher Donnan, ed. Washington: Dumbarton Oaks Research Library and Collection, 111–38.

Burke, Robin (1990). "The Llama Figurine in Andean Prehistory: Analysis of Examples from the Callejón de Huaylas, Peru." Unpublished MA Thesis, Department of Anthropology, University of South Carolina.

Butler, William B. (1980). "Penetrating Elephant Hide with Wood Atlatl Darts." *Plains Anthropologist* 25: 353–6.

Callahan, Eric (1979). "The Basics of Biface Knapping in the Eastern Fluted Point Tradition: A Manual for Flintknappers and Lithic Analysts." *Archaeology of Eastern North America* 7.

Cantwell, Anne-Marie (1979). "The Functional Analysis of Scrapers: Problems, New Techniques and Cautions." *Lithic Technology* 8: 5–11.

Clark, John E. (1982). "Manufacture of Mesoamerican Prismatic Blades: An Alternative Technique." *American Antiquity* 47: 355–76.

Coutts, P. J. F. (1977). "Green Timber and Polynesian Adzes and Axes." In *Stone Tools as Cultural Markers*, R. V. S. Wright, ed. Canberra: Australian Institute of Aboriginal Studies, 67–82.

Coward, Rosalind (1983). *Patriarchal Precedents*. London: Routledge & Kegan Paul.

Crabtree, Don E. (1967). Notes on Experiments in Flintknapping: Tools Used for Making Flaked Stone Artifacts. *Tebiwa* 10: 60–73.

—— (1972). *An Introduction to Flintworking*. Boise: Idaho State University Museum Occasional Papers 28.

Elliott, W. J. and R. Anderson (1974). "A Butchering Experiment with Flaked Obsidian Tools." *Archaeology in Montana* 15: 1–10.

Estioko-Griffin, Agnes and P. Bion Griffin (1981). "Woman the Hunter: The Agta." In *Woman the Gatherer*, Frances Dahlberg, ed. New Haven: Yale University Press, 121–51.

Fausto-Sterling, Anne (1985). *Myths of Gender*. New York: Basic Books.

Fischer, Anders, P. V. Hansen, and P. Rasmussen (1984). "Macro and Micro Wear Traces on Lithic Projectile Points." *Journal of Danish Archaeology* 3: 19–46.

Flenniken, J. Jeffrey (1981). *Replicative Systems Analysis: A Model Applied to the Vein Quartz Artifacts from the Hoko River Site*. Washington State University Laboratory, Anthropology Report No. 59.

—— (1984). "The Past, Present and Future of Flintknapping: An Anthropological Perspective." *Annual Review of Anthropology* 13: 187–203.

Flenniken, J. Jeffrey and Anan Raymond (1986). "Morphological Projectile Point Typology: Replication Experimentation and Technological Analysis." *American Antiquity* 51: 603–14.

Frison, George C. (1989). "Experimental Use of Clovis Weaponry and Tools on African Elephants." *American Antiquity* 54: 766–84.

Gailey, Christine Ward (1987). *Kinship to Kingship: Gender Hierarchy and State Formation in the Tongan Islands.* Austin: University of Texas Press.

Geis, Maureen (1987). "Lithic Flake Production Analysis: Another Fly in the Ointment." Paper presented at the 15th Annual Meeting of the Northeast Anthropological Association, Amherst, MA.

Gero, Joan M. (1983a). "Material Culture and the Reproduction of Social Complexity: A Lithic Example from the Peruvian Formative." Unpublished Ph.D. dissertation, Department of Anthropology, University of Massachusetts.

—— (1983b). "Stone Tools in Ceramic Contexts: Exploring the Unstructured." In *Investigations of the Andean Past*, D. Sandweiss, ed. Ithaca: Cornell University Latin American Studies Program, 38–50.

—— (1989). "Stylistic Information in Stone Tools: How Well do Lithics Measure Up?" In *Time, Energy and Stone Tools*, Robin Torrence, ed. Cambridge: Cambridge University Press, 92–105.

—— (1990). "Pottery, Power and Parties! at Queyash, Peru." *Archaeology*, March/April: 52–6.

—— (forthcoming). "Facts and Values in the Archaeological Eye." In *The Powers of Observation*, S. Nelson and A. Kehoe, eds. American Anthropological Association Publication No. 2.

Goodale, Jane C. (1971). *Tiwi Wives.* Seattle: University of Washington Press.

Gould, Richard A. (1977). "Ethno-archaeology; Or, Where do Models Come From?" In *Stone Tools as Cultural Markers*, R. V. S. Wright, ed. Canberra: Australian Institute of Aboriginal Studies, 162–77.

Hamilton, Annette (1980). "Dual Social Systems: Technology, Labour and Women's Secret Rites in the Eastern Western Desert of Australian." *Oceania* 51: 4–19.

Hayden, Brian (1977). Stone Tool Functions in the Western Desert." In *Stone Tools as Cultural Markers*, R. V. S. Wright, ed. Canberra: Australian Institute of Aboriginal Studies, 178–88.

Hester, Thomas R. and Robert F. Heizer (1973). *Bibliography of Archaeology I: Experiments, Lithic Technology, and Petrography.* Reading, Massachusetts: Addison-Wesley Module in Anthropology No. 29.

Hester, T., L. Spencer, C. Busby, and J. Bard (1976). "Butchering a Deer with Obsidian Tools." *University of California Archaeological Research Facility Contributions* 43: 33–75.

Holmes, W. H. (1897). "Stone implements of the Potomac–Chesapeake Tidewater Province." In *15th Annual Report of the Bureau of Ethnology*, J. W. Powell, ed. Washington; Government Printing Office, 13–152.

—— (1919). *Handbook of Aboriginal American Antiquities: Part I. The Lithic Industries.* Washington: Bureau of American Ethnology, Bulletin 60.

Huckell, Bruce (1982). "The Denver Elephant Project: A Report on Experimentation with Thrusting Spears." *Plains Anthropologist* 27: 217–24.

Jesuit Relations and Allied Documents: Travels and Explorations of the Jesuit Missionaries in New France, 1610–1791, Father Pierre Biard, *Relations of New France, of its Lands, Nature of the Country and of its Inhabitants* Vol. III: Acadia, 1611–1616.

Juel Jensen, Helle (1982). "A Preliminary Analysis of Blade Scrapers from

Ringkloster, a Danish Late Mesolithic Site." *Studia Praehistorica Belgica* 2: 323–7.

—— (1988). "Functional Analysis of Prehistoric Flint Tools by High-Power Microscopy: A Review of West European Research." *Journal of World Prehistory* 2: 53–88.

Johnson, Lucy Lewis (1977). "A Technological Analysis of an Aguas Verdes Quarry-Workshop. "In *The Individual in Prehistory: Studies of Variability in Style in Prehistoric Technologies*, J. N. Hill and J. Gunn, eds. New York: Academic Press, 205–29.

—— (1978). "A History of Flint-knapping Experimentation, 1838–1976." *Current Anthropology* 19: 337–72.

Jones, Rhys and Neville White (1988). "Point Blank: Stone Tool Manufacture at the Ngilipitji Quarry, Arnhem Land, 1981." In *Archaeology with Ethnography: An Australian Perspective*, Betty Meehan and Rhys Jones, eds. Canberra: Australian National University, 51–87.

Kehoe, Alice (1987). "Points and Lines." Paper presented at the Annual Meeting of AAA, Chicago.

Kelterborn, Peter (1984). "Towards Replicating Egyptian Predynastic Flint Knives." *Journal of Archaeological Science* 11: 433–53.

Knudson, Ruthann (1973). "Organizational Variability in Late Paleo-Indian Assemblages." Unpublished Ph.D. dissertation, Washington State University.

—— (1979). "Inference and Imposition in Lithic Analysis." In *Lithic Use-Wear Analysis*, B. Hayden, ed. New York: Academic Press, 269–81.

Korobkova, G. F. (1981). "Ancient Reaping Tools and Their Productivity in the Light of Experimental Tracewear Analysis." In *The Bronze Age Civilizations of Central Asia*, Philip L. Kohl, ed. Armonk, NY: M. E. Sharpe, 325–49.

Kramer, Carol and Miriam Stark (1988). "The Status of Women in Archaeology." *Anthropology Newsletter*, (American Anthropological Association) 29(9): 1, 11–12.

Leudtke, Barbara (1979). "The Identification of Sources of Chert Artifacts." *American Antiquity* 44: 744–57.

Laughlin, William (1968). "Hunting: An Integrative Biobehavior System and its Evolutionary Importance." In *Man the Hunter*, Richard Lee and Irven deVore, eds. Chicago: Aldine, 304–20.

Lewenstein, Suzanne (1981). "Mesoamerican Obsidian Blades: An Experimental Approach to Functions." *Journal of Field Archaeology* 8: 175–88.

—— (1987). *Stone Tool Use at Cerros: The Ethnoarchaeological and Use-Wear Evidence*. Austin: University of Texas Press.

Lowe, Marian (1983). "The Dialectic of Biology and Culture." In *Woman's Nature: Rationalizations of Inequality*, Marian Lowe and Ruth Hubbard, eds. New York: Pergamon, 39–62.

Madsen, Bo (1984). "Flint Axe Manufacture in the Neolithic: Experiments with Grinding and Polishing of Thin-Butted Flint Axes." *Journal of Danish Archaeology* 3: 47–62.

Mansure-Franchomme, Maria Estela (1983). "Scanning Electron Microscopy of Dry Hide Working Tools: The Role of Abrasives and Humidity in Microwear Polish Formation." *Journal of Archaeological Science* 10: 223–30.

Miller, Tom O., Jr (1979). "Stonework of the Xetá Indians of Brazil." In *Lithic Use-Wear Analysis*, Brian Hayden, ed. New York: Academic Press, 401–7.

Montet-White, Anta (1974). "The Significance of Variability in Archaic Point Assemblages." *Plains Anthropologist* 19: 14–24.

Moore, Henrietta (1988). *Feminism and Anthropology*. Cambridge: Polity Press.

Moss, Emily (1983). *The Functional Analysis of Flint Implements. Pincevent and Pont d'Ambon: Two Case Studies from the French Final Paleolithic*. Oxford: BAR International Series No. 177.

—— (1986). "What Microwear Analysts Look At." In Owen, L. and G. Unrath, ed. "Technological Aspects of Microwear Studies." *Early Man News* (Tübingen) 9–11: 91–6.

Neill, Wilfred T. (1952). "The Manufacture of Fluted Points." *The Florida Anthropologist* V(1–2): 9–16.

Newcomer, Mark H. (1971). "Quantitative Experiments in Handaxe Manufacture." *World Archaeology* 3(1): 85–93.

Odell, George H. (1980). "Butchering with Stone Tools: Some Experimental Results." *Lithic Technology* 9: 39–48.

Odell, George H. and F. Cowan (1986). "Experiments with Spears and Arrows on Animal Targets." *Journal of Field Archaeology* 13: 195–212.

Olausson, Deborah Seitzer (1980). "Starting from Scratch: The History of Edge-Wear Research from 1838–1978." *Lithic Technology* 9: 48–60.

Park, Edwards (1978). "The Ginsberg Caper: Hacking it as in Stone Age." *Smithsonian* 9: 85–94.

Price-Beggerly, Patricia (1976). "Edge Damage on Experimentally Used Scrapers of Hawaiian Basalt." *Lithic Technology* 5: 22–4.

Purdy, Barbara A. (1975). "Fractures for the Archaeologist." In *Lithic Technology: Making and Using Stone Tools*. Earl Swanson, ed. Chicago: Aldine.

—— (1981). *Florida's Prehistoric Stone Technology*. Gainesville: University Presses of Florida.

Rippeteau, Bruce (1979). "The Denver Elephant Project: A Personal and Semi-Preliminary Report." In *Megafauna Punchers' Review*, vol. 1, B. Rippeteau, ed. Denver: Office of the Colorado State Archaeologist, 1–8.

Sale, Irene Levi (1986). "Use Wear and Post Depositional Surface Modification: A Word of Caution." *Journal of Archaeological Science* 13: 229–44.

Schneider, Mary Jane (1983). "Women's Work: An Examination of Women's Roles in Plain Indian Arts and Crafts." In *The Hidden Half: Studies of Plains Indian Women*, P. Albers and B. Medicine, eds. Lanham, MD: University Press of America, 101–21.

Scott, Joan W. (1986). "Gender: A Useful Category of Historical Analysis." *American Historical Review* 91: 1053–75.

Sheets, Payson D. and Guy Muto (1972). "Pressure Blades and Total Cutting Edge: An Experiment in Lithic Technology." *Science* 175: 632–4.

Sollberger, J. B. (1969). "The Basic Tool Kit Required to Make and Notch Arrow Shafts for Stone Points." *Texas Archaeological Society Bulletin* 40: 232–40.

Spears, Carol S. (1975). "Hammers, Nuts and Jolts, Cobbles, Cobbles, Cobbles: Experiments in Cobble Technologies in Search of Correlates." In *Arkansas*

Eastman Archaeological Project, C. Baker, with contributions by C. Spears, C. Claassen and M. Schiffer. Fayetteville: Arkansas Archaeological Survey, 83–110.

Spencer, L. (1974). "Replicative Experiments in the Manufacture and Use of a Great Basin Atlatl." In *Great Basin Atlatl Studies*, T. R. Hester, M. P. Mildner, and L. Spencer, eds. Ramona, CA: Ballena Press Publications in Archaeology, Ethnology and History No 2, 37–60.

Spencer, W. B. and F. J. Gillen (1912). *Across Australia*. London: Macmillan.

Stafford, Barbara D. (1977). "Burin Manufacture and Utilization: An Experimental Study." *Journal of Field Archaeology* 4: 235–46.

Stanford, Dennis (1979). "Carving up a 'Mammoth' Stone Age Style." *National Geographic* 155: 121.

Thomas, David H. (1983). *Gatecliff Shelter*. New York: Anthropological Papers of the American Museum of Natural History 59, part 1.

Tindale, N. B. (1972). "The Pitjandjara." In *Hunters and Gatherers Today*, M. G. Bicchieri, ed. New York: Holt, Rinehart & Winston, 217–68.

Titmus, Gene L. (1984). "Some Aspects of Stone Tool Notching." In *Stone Tool Analysis: Essays in Honor of Don Crabtree*, J. Woods, M. G. Plew, and M. G. Pavesic, eds. Albuquerque: University of New Mexico Press, 243–63.

Torrence, Robin (1983). "Time Budgeting and Hunter-Gatherer Technology." In *Hunter-Gatherer Economy in Prehistory: A European Perspective*, G. Bailey, ed. Cambridge: Cambridge University Press, 11–22.

—— (1989) (ed.) *Time, Energy and Stone Tools*. Cambridge: Cambridge University Press.

Tringham, Ruth, Glenn Cooper, George Odell, Barbara Voytek, and Anne Whitman (1974). "Experimentation in the Formation of Edge Damage: A New Approach to Lithic Analysis." *Journal of Field Archaeology* 1: 171–95.

Tsirk, Are (1974). "Mechanical Basis of Percussion Flaking: Some Comments." *American Antiquity* 39: 128–30.

Unger-Hamilton, Romana (1984). "The Formation of Use-Wear Polish on Flint: Beyond the 'Deposit vs. Abrasion' Controversy." *Journal of Archaeological Science* 11: 91–8.

White, J. Peter (1967). "Ethno-archaeology in New Guinea: Two Examples." *Mankind* 6(9): 409–14.

—— (1969). "Typologies for Some Prehistoric Flaked Stone Artifacts of the Australian New Guinea Highlands." *Archaeology and Physical Anthropology of Oceania* 4(1): 18–46.

—— (1977). *Axes and Aré: Stone Tools of the Duna*. Forty-one minute documentary film.

Witthoft, John (1967). "The Art of Flint Chipping." *Journal of the Archaeological Society of Maryland* 3: 123–44.

Wilson, John, L. Reyes, and J. Garayar (1967). *Geología de los Cuadrangulos de Mollebamba, Tayabamba, Huaylas, Pomabamba, Carhuaz y Huari*. Lima: Servicio de Geología Minería, Boletín 16.

Wilson, Thomas (1899). "Arrowpoints, Spearheads, and Knives of Prehistoric Times." Report of the U.S. National Museum 1897, Part 1, 811–988.

Young, David and Robson Bonnichsen (1984). *Understanding Stone Tools.* Orono: University of Maine, Peopling of the American Process Series No. 1.

7

Women's Labor and Pottery Production in Prehistory

Rita P. Wright

Feminist theory does not call on us exclusively, or even primarily, to pay more attention to women in the history of technology. Rather, it urges us to pay more attention to gender: to those ideologies that have attributed certain characteristics to men and others to women. It alerts us that beliefs about sex differences exert so pervasive and profound an influence that we must take account not only of the ways in which gender assumptions have shaped technology historically, but also of the ways in which gender notions shape the way we write technology's history.

J. A. McGaw, "No Passive Victims, No Separate Spheres: A Feminist Perspective On Technology's History." (1989)

Introduction

Although pottery is among the most longstanding of human technical achievements, the history of the development of pottery production and the organization of its production is a topic that is only just beginning to be written in any detail. In prehistoric South Asia, the archaeological area discussed here, the appearance of pottery roughly coincides with the first settled communities in the seventh millennium BC. From that point onwards, even into the present, pottery occupies a central place as an essential commodity. The coincidence of settled communities and pottery, both in South Asia and in other prehistoric contexts, has provided an invaluable resource to archaeologists for establishing relative chronologies and for linking cultures regionally and inter-regionally. Until recently, however, archaeologists have been less interested in the technical aspects of pottery production and its organization than in exchange networks (Stark 1985: 159); moreover, even when technical information has been available, it has rarely been integrated into the questions of social process that are so compelling to contemporary

archaeologists (but see, for example, De Atley 1986, van der Leeuw 1977, van der Leeuw and Pritchard 1984; Peacock 1981, 1982; Rice 1981; Shepard 1965, 1976).

Aside from the admittedly difficult problems associated with integrating the work of specialists into archaeological site reports, there are other reasons why pottery technology has been neglected. One of these pertains to strong gender biases, which are themselves rooted in the ethnographies on which archaeologists rely for their reconstructions. Typically, these ethnographies have associated the earliest prehistoric pottery with women as potters whose work was confined to domestic consumption and to practicing a technology that required only the most rudimentary techniques (Brew 1956: 126; Briffault 1927: 470, 471; Chapple and Coon 1942: 124). For the ethnographers, early pottery technology is portrayed as a "labor intensive and time-consuming" task in which absolute production was necessarily limited (Foster 1959: 100). When they describe how production later became mechanized under circumstances of commercialization, the vocabulary changes dramatically and takes a more active form: "The wheel greatly shortened the time necessary to make a vessel . . . and simultaneously eliminated women from pottery work, thus commercializing a home craft. Greatly increased production stimulated the development of trade and markets" (Ibid.: 100). At the heart of this reconstruction is the assumption that labor extensive activities with low economic yields are engaged in by (all) women, whereas labor intensive activities are innovative and lead to commercialization, the (exclusive) domain of men.

In this chapter I present a different view. The history of pottery technology must be seen as an invention of major historic significance, and as one in which women played an active part, although the technical knowledge they possessed to do so was never only rudimentary. I hope to show that the basis of statements such as the ones quoted above is an expression of an ideology of "separate spheres", an ideology that has had a pervasive influence on our understanding of the organization of labor, both in our own society and in other cultures. This ideology, which grew out of the specific alignment of the historical events of the eighteenth and nineteenth centuries and the development of social science itself (Collier and Yanigisako 1987, Jordanova 1980, McGaw 1989, Rosaldo 1980) defined work and the workplace as occurring in separate spheres for men and for women. And while this separation may hold for recent American society, it also has greatly influenced, if not predetermined, the way we have viewed non-western ones. There is now consensus among anthropologists that dichotomies of this kind (for example, nature/culture or domestic/public formulations) are not universal (cf. Mukhopadhyay and Higgins 1988: 479ff.). As McGaw has put it:

separate spheres designated the public arena as masculine, making the public records on which we so often rely not merely public but also masculine . . . Likewise, the doctrine of separate spheres meant that men and women very rarely worked at the same jobs or even in the same places . . . We need not accept home and work, women's activities and men's labor, as separate simply because Americans chose historically to separate them spatially and rhetorically. (1989: 178)

One of the focuses of this chapter, then, is to demonstrate how contemporary concepts of gender and the workplace have worked to bias not only our understanding of prehistoric pottery production but also our interpretation of its development. Our understanding of the prehistoric or historic record is better served, not by taking "separate spheres" as an unquestioned given, but by raising the question: are gender spheres separate? If so, what "social functions" might such separation – or lack thereof – have served (ibid.: 178)?

How are we to tackle these issues in an archaeological context? Here, I view this topic from several angles. First of all, my point is not to provide definite *answers* or "truths" on whether women actually did invent, innovate, and produce pottery, since this kind of positivist linkage between individual social groups and particular productive activities is difficult, if even possible, for most prehistoric contexts (see Introduction, this volume). Nor is it my point here to define those social conditions under which they may have done so, although this question is explored. Rather, I want to *raise questions* about the extant ethnographic literature and current reconstructions of the role of women in pottery production in prehistory, which should reveal more specifically that it is not the case that women have been left out of these reconstructions, but rather that interpretations of their dynamic role in it have been biased by our contemporary gender ideology and by modern models of the workplace.

There are many ways to approach the sources and implications of gender bias in studies of potters and pottery technology, but a most direct route is to examine both the ethnographies and various conceptual frameworks that are concerned with the anthropological study of work and with the divisions and organizations of labor and production. Obviously, the two literatures are related; the theoretical literature dealing with the epistemology of women's occupational status and roles in different societies (Silverblatt 1988: 428) can be useful in reassessing the traditional ethnographies. At the same time, however, it draws heavily on ethnographic sources as a way to inquire into or to establish the claim that there is a link between the diminished status accorded to female activities and a radical reordering of the organization of production that is taken to be a central feature of the development of complex societies (Gailey 1987; Moore 1988; Silverblatt 1988). Because the development of pottery technology does, in many historical circumstances, seem to have taken place in some association with the emergence and development of complex societies, it will be particularly interesting to look at this theoretical literature in conjunction with a specific instance of the development of pottery production.

Thus, the chapter will proceed as follows: first, I will consider in more detail the way in which women have been associated or marginalised with respect to ethnographies of pottery production; next, I will consider just some of the general approaches taken to understanding divisions of labor and the organization of work, with particular emphasis on two approaches – the ecological and the evolutionary – that have been central to many archaeological discussions. In the final section, I will discuss in some detail the development of pottery production and pottery technologies leading to and contemporary with the Harappan civilization, a period from ca.6000–1800 BC. This discussion will demonstrate that the development of pottery constitutes a major innovation and improvement over previous technologies, that it was most likely a highly valued craft, and that in the Harappan case there are many particular factors that support the idea that women were involved in the entire developmental sequence and elaboration of pottery technology. In fact, the development of pottery technology and the way in which its production was organized at the sites discussed here does not support the exclusive association of males with innovations and with state intervention in pottery production, as suggested for the emergence of other complex, prehistoric states.

The Ethnography of Pottery Production and Gender

A paper by Murdock and Provost (1973) establishes a convenient base line for many current assumptions regarding both contemporary and prehistoric pottery production. In their study a list of 50 technological activities was defined for a sample of 185 societies taken principally from the cross-cultural files developed by Murdock (1937). Each of the 50 activities, then, was ranked in descending order according to the degree of participation by males. Indices of male participation were then calculated by weighting different degrees of participation. These indices subsequently were broken down into clusters with distinct statistical characteristics (Murdock and Provost 1973: 206) and on that basis pottery was ranked as a "swing activity" (ibid.: 209), in that it was not clearly correlated with one gender or another. When males were involved in pottery production, their participation was associated with a complex division of labor and high degree of occupational specialization (ibid.: 213), intensification of agriculture (ibid.: 215), and complexity of technology (ibid.: 216).[1] In contrast, the data suggest that women are the principal producers of pottery where there is a low degree of occupational specialization and division of labor.

However, other statistics in the same paper by Murdock and Provost indicate that pottery making is more commonly a female activity at all levels of complexity. Arnold (1985: 102), for example, has interpreted the same data to support his conclusion that in most of the societies studied women devote significant amounts of their time to pottery production. Only seven other activities had more female participation than pottery production – gathering of wild vegetal foods, dairy production, spinning, laundering, water fetching, cooking, and preparation of vegetal foods – suggesting that it is a major female activity worldwide. The difference between the two interpretations clearly reflects on Arnold's more female-focused view of the data but also suggests that in many societies, although women were present and "counted", they were "invisible", as a result of terminological biases that distort the "reality" of pottery production. These biases relate both to discrepancies in the terminology used in the ethnographies and in the ethnographers' conceptions of the workplace.

In virtually all studies of pottery production, the word *potter* has been equated with the individual who *forms* pots, that is with the person who shapes the clay while it is in its plastic state. This means that individuals who perform other tasks in the production sequence (e.g. procuring and processing clay, decorating finished vessels, collecting wood and loading kilns, marketing final products) are not counted as "potters" despite Kramer's finding (1985: 84) that potters sometimes work in groups, and that often different parts of a production sequence are executed by more than one individual. Thus to equate "the potter" – then used as a statistic – with only one (or even a few) of the many potential and necessary stages in a production sequence is extraordinarily misleading.

The problematic implications of "invisible" producers are many: For example, when either males or females participate in pottery production, discrepancies may occur in reporting which sex/gender is the "producer". Men often are recorded as sole producers even though women (almost always family members) engage in essential pottery-making tasks. Daniel Miller (1985: 110) refers to census reports of village potters in India in which, although in all households women paint designs on pottery, "the pot is still known as the potter's [male], and not the painter's product."[2] This also is the case in the reporting of agricultural labor, where "real" work is sowing and threshing and male-dominated, and "peripheral" work, such as weeding, is female-dominated (ibid.: 110). Rye and Evans (1976), in a study of potters in Pakistan who produce pottery for non-household consumption, similarly describe all potters as men, despite their explicit recognition that with the exception of one potter, all of the potters studied are assisted either by family members or apprentices. One potter, for example, is described as "the only potter in this small village" (ibid.: 27); but later on they write that "the women of his household help with the unskilled work . . . and with the more skilled task of applying red slip" (ibid.: 27).[3] The reverse, the exclusion of men, occurs elsewhere, as in Mexican communities where women who produce pottery for non-household consumption are described as the potters, although men gather firewood and help with firing and marketing (Rice 1987: 187).[4]

These examples suggest an overly simplified interpretation of gender roles in a craft in which there is a technological division of labor, as attention is not given to the organization of tasks within production sequences. The complex reality of how gender interacts with and supports production sequences is glossed by a simple gender ideology that holds that pottery production is a male activity whereas, in fact, it is a male and female activity. They also illustrate that pottery production is a craft that, more often than not, is dependent upon a cooperative labor force, in that in many societies – especially those that are small in scale and where production is for the market or non-household consumption – it is participated in by a group and not a lone producer. Although individual producers have been documented ethnographically, they are more rare than situations in which several workers are engaged in varying parts of the production sequence. This is especially true where vessels are formed consistently by one gender or the other, "where children and adults of the opposite sex often participate in the productive process" (Kramer 1985: 79). This suggests that, in addition to their gender biases, anthropologists have carried with them western assumptions about individualism and the organization of production and distribution that have biased their accounts.

In summary, not only can pottery be both a male and female craft with women usually integral to its production, but there also is little basis for the stereotype that when pottery is produced for non-household consumption, women no longer participate in it. Rather, it appears that, although there clearly are societies in which women do not produce pottery, in many, because of reporting procedures and the ideology of separate spheres, they are "invisible" producers.

Gender – Adaptation or Ideology?

It is issues such as these that have led some anthropologists to investigate the basis on which a division of labor and the organization of work develop. Some investigators view a division of labor in pottery production as an adaptive response to ecological conditions (e.g. Arnold 1975, 1985; Matson 1965), while others, who deal more generally with an evolutionary perspective account for sex role differences based on ideological factors and changing socio-political relations, with the development of complex societies (e.g. Engels 1972; Gailey 1987; Leacock 1972; Rapp 1977; Sacks 1974; Silverblatt 1988). Both approaches rely on ethnographic sources to establish those critical junctures at which there are significant shifts in the division of labor and the organization of production in society.

Using empirical data from ethnographic sources, Arnold (1985), for example, explains variations in male and female participation in pottery production based upon ecological factors.[5] These factors include resources, weather and climate, scheduling conflicts, degree of sedentariness, demand for products and "man/land" relationships. Thus he accounts for gender differences in pottery producers – differences that may favor one gender or the other as producers – based upon the ecological parameters listed and the importance of agriculture. Scheduling problems occur when "good weather and climate for pottery production" coincide with agriculture in societies in which agriculture is a major subsistence activity (Arnold 1985: 100). A solution to these conflicts is for households to broaden their productive base through a division of labor. In this scenario, men take over subsistence activities and women become the primary pottery producers.

Arnold follows the ethnographic literature in assuming that when scheduling conflicts occur between agriculture and other activities, men will assume responsibility for agriculture. Several factors are relevant. When viewed cross-culturally, there is evidence that men engage in activities more distant from their homes than women, who, in contrast, work closer to home (Burton et al. 1977: 250). Some researchers believe that childcare responsibilities are the major factor in this choice; Arnold (1985) favors this explanation, since he believes that childcare and pottery production are compatible "household" activities (ibid.: 101).[6] In one of the earliest papers on gender bias, Brown pointed specifically to childcare as central to this type of division of labor in that non-childcare activities would have to fit in with women's central role as mothers (1970: 1077). Nevertheless, as numerous scholars have subsequently shown, although there is an obvious link between women and childcare, there does not appear to be a set pattern on how individual societies arrange "appropriate" childcare. Mukhopadhyay and Higgins (1988: 475) review many studies that support the claim that various strategies may be adopted, such as what we would call "substitute" childcare taken on by others in the society. Whether or not these substitute arrangements are developed (or are even considered "substitutes" to what western scholars highly value as the "real" childcare) is obviously a culturally-specific and specifically cultural decision.

These interpretations suggest that, although there are exceptions, there is a cross-cultural pattern among sedentary agriculturalists for women to engage in activities near their home, but that this choice is not due, at least exclusively, to childcare responsibilities. In fact, all of the tasks documented cross-culturally by Murdock and Provost (1973) for which there was a low index of male participation (e.g. gathering foods, dairy production, spinning, laundering, water fetching, cooking, and preparation of plant foods) may occur near dwellings. In order to account for this pattern, it seems appropriate to turn to the ecological factors that may account for the division of labor. In particular, Arnold has emphasized seasonal overlaps that may occur between agricultural and pottery production as important ecological variables that should be observable in the archaeological record.[7]

Another approach that is potentially useful in sorting out the conditions under which women are active participants in pottery production is an evolutionist perspective. Scholars who take this perspective have been most provocative and successful at addressing the ideology of gender by outlining the differences that separate western, capitalist society from non-western, precapitalist ones. Although the capitalist–precapitalist separation, as a topic, has a long history, it offers gender studies a new angle from which to observe long-term changes in the division of labor and status differentiation. In this view, although gender is taken to have its basis in social relationships constructed by individual societies, there is also a long-standing concern with what appears to be a more general phenomenon, namely a shift to the subordination of women with the evolution from a pre-state to state level society. Leacock (1972, 1978, 1981, 1983), for example, even views these changes as universal in that they occurred with the shift from small-scale societies to large, complex ones (but cf. Moore 1988: 31ff. for a critique of this position). The fundamental point is that the organization of production and work in small-scale societies is based on a kinship mode of production; there, roles are defined according to age and the life cycle and the organizing principles are simultaneously public, economic, and political. The separation of, and the according of differential status to, these domains occurs as a consequence of state formation, at which point kinship organization is attenuated.

More recently, Gailey (1987), building on Leacock's interpretation, has suggested that "the turmoil of class formation itself" is the key to women's subordination. Kinship groups are subverted through political strategies carried out by elites in order to gain access to labor previously organized along kinship lines. The importance of these shifts to the development of the state cannot be overemphasized because the erosion of kinship-based production and the possible imposition of a division of labor and differentiated labor force erodes the wider power of kinship groups, where indeed the roles and powers of women are well documented. "The *state*, then, represents a rough, crisis-ridden series of institutional mediations between producers, on the one hand, and those who benefit from the forcible extraction of goods and labor, on the other" (Gailey 1987: 28).

These concepts appear to have some validity in understanding the social dynamics of craft and pottery production in some prehistoric states. For example, if we look at the early state-level society in Mesopotamia, particularly with regard to craft production, we can see some evidence for the association of males with pottery production and with a positive cultural value. We know that in Mesopotamia men and women were employed in many crafts, but some types of pottery production may only have been conducted by men. The word for potter, *bahar* (Sjoberg 1988: 46), as is often the case with names of professions, makes no specific reference to either male or female. However, in texts dating from 2066–2010 BC, potters are included among a list of masculine crafts (Waetzoldt 1987: 121). This does not necessarily indicate that only men produced pottery; it more reasonably reflects biases in the written documents. Yet it does suggest that some pottery production was concentrated or at least located in temples or households (centrally administered) and that it was mainly carried out by males.[8]

More importantly, compensation in Mesopotamia for one's labor varied not only according to profession but also, and most obviously, according to sex (ibid.: 122). Payment or "rations" were in the form of barley allotments; the normal allotment for women was between 30 and 40 liters per month, whereas 60 liters per month was normal for men (ibid.: 121).[9] This difference in wages is not the most obvious sign that we have that women's labor was valued less than men's. Large numbers of women and children were taken as prisoners of war and incorporated into a dependent labor force, as workers in textile production (Gelb 1972; Zagarell 1986). As Adams has pointed out, that some women were deployed as dependent and forced laborers would, no doubt, "have had pervasive effects on the entire social system, but especially on the status of women" (1984: 116). This kind of reconstruction for aspects of Mesopotamian life does support ethnohistoric and ethnographic analyses (e.g. Silverblatt 1988; Gailey 1987) that make a case not just for a reorganization of work and gender status with the emergence of the state, but also the subordination of women and their status.

It is obvious from the above discussion that there have been major upheavals in the development of theories of state formation during the past two decades with respect to gender (see especially Silverblatt 1988 for a bibliography). While the views represent different theoretical perspectives, there is consensus that the separation of genders into different activities is culturally and locally determined and not universally decreed; that the division of labor and organization of production in small-scale societies, although culturally determined, is predominantly based on kinship (but cf. Kramer 1985: 84), and that it is only with the formation of states that new forms of organization of production develop which may exclude women and reorder kinship relations.

In some respects these revisions have served as an important corrective to the bias of previous male-centred analysis. But while some researchers, including feminists (e.g. Gailey 1987; Silverblatt 1988) have found that there still remains some basis for viewing the transformation of kinship-based societies to states as a locus and context within which women as a group tend to lose power and status, others remind us that this "fact" may still be an artifact of our observational frames and analytical categories (for example McGaw 1989). However, the very revisions of more androcentric thinking about the state and the fact that women's status in early states is now subject to investigation rather than a given has important implications for our conceptual reorientations. In particular, they allow a new set of frameworks to be applied in our inquiry into the origins and development of pottery.

In the foregoing discussion I have examined a number of issues of specific relevance to women's labor and pottery production. First, the cross-cultural evidence, when modified to correct the underreporting of their participation, indicates that women are major producers of pottery. In addition, there appears to be a link between the activities in which women participate and the importance of agriculture in a society. When viewed from an ecological perspective, the dominant pattern in sedentary societies is one in which there is a division of labor that favors men as the primary agricultural producers. In many pottery producing societies, a strategy for continued engagement of households in both activities, when peak periods for the two coincide, is to have women continue to produce pottery and to reduce the time they spend on agriculture. Second, there clearly is no basis for the assumption that women do not engage in pottery production for non-household consumption. The documented cases of commercialized production by women as well as the underreporting of their participation in it argues against this assumption. This underreporting results from a lack of understanding of pottery production sequences and the dependence of some potters' workshops on the labor of several individuals as well as contemporary ideological biases in which women's labor is not recorded. And finally, although there is an extensive and persuasive literature on dramatic changes in the division of labor that occur with the formation of states, there remain questions concerning whether this interpretation is free of the biases which have been discussed here. The Harappan case can now be examined in the light of these findings.

Origins, Technology and Cultural Context

The following discussion focuses on the origins and technology of pottery production in the Harappan civilization and its antecedents during the period 6000–1800 BC. The Harappans lived in cities, towns, and villages along the Indus River and its tributaries, and although they are best known from two major cities, Mohenjo-daro and Harappa, the civilization was widespread (figure 7.1). In fact, the best location from which to view the development of pottery production is along the western edges of the Harappan civilization in Baluchistan at the site of Mehrgarh, where we can trace its earliest antecedents (Jarrige and Meadow 1980) and where we have our most complete sequence. For later periods, the discussion will shift to Mohenjo-daro and Harrappa.[10]

Origins and technology

Understanding the complexity of the technical knowledge required of ancient potters is integral to the argument being presented. As indicated earlier, little atttention has been paid to the importance of pottery production as a major technological development, perhaps as a result of a general bias that characterizes potters and pottery production as conservative and unimaginative. I have suggested that this bias is rooted in the association of women with the craft, particularly with its beginnings as a technological addition. In the following I present a different perspective that emphasizes innovations over time, the complexity of technological developments, and the organization of production as it pertains to women. Although in this section I concentrate on pottery and on technology, my point in doing so is to provide a visible demonstration of the ways in which women may have contributed to it.

Among the ways in which pottery production represents both a practical advance and a social one relates to its impact on other activities and to the development of the technology itself after its initial discovery. Perhaps most important are improvements in storage and cooking-related activities. Superior to basketry and other non-ceramic containers, ceramics have the potential of broadening the range of food resources by

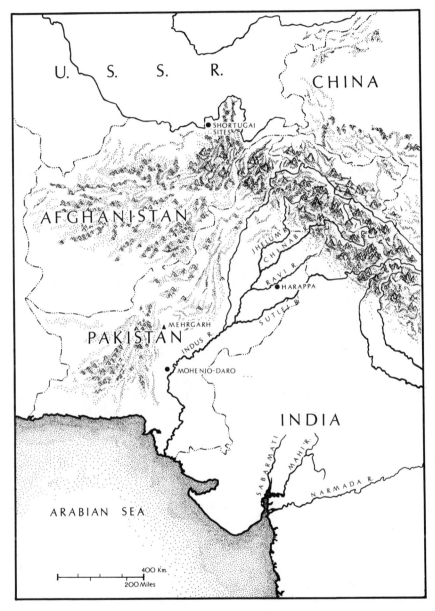

Figure 7.1 Archaeological settlements referred to in the text. The site of Mehrgarh is pre- to Early Harappan; other sites are Mature Harappan.

enhancing the digestibility and palatability of foods consumed. Ceramics hold these advantages over basketry and stone boiling due to refractory properties that make it possible to cook food at higher temperatures in a sustained heat. Cooked in this way food can be left unattended for longer periods of time than cooking with baskets or other containers such as hide, wood, and stone, but most importantly toxins in certain foods can be reduced (Arnold 1985: 128).[11] Thus ceramics have the potential of significantly changing cooking methods and increasing the range of foods that could be consumed. Other improvements would be in preserving techniques and in enhancing the nutritional value of plant foods. Moreover, the plasticity of clay makes it possible to form a greater variety of vessels in a relatively shorter period and of longer lasting quality than the production of basketry or stone vessels (Arnold 1985: 28ff.). These improvements go hand-in-hand with the continuous refinement of the craft as better clays are discovered, compositions of paste are refined, efficiency of production methods increased through the use of mechanical devices, pigments for slips and other decorative purposes developed, and more efficient kilns are introduced (Shepard 1965: 84). Changes also potentially affect social and economic developments such as the transformation of production from household to non-household consumption, the development of specialization due to exceptional skills required in the production process, and the establishment of trade or exchange networks (ibid.: 86).

The use of clay and its transformation from a pliable and fragile medium to one of some durability and hardness in South Asia coincides roughly with the first known settled communities and appears to have been an indigenous invention, developing independently in a variety of locations and contexts. Its development occurred as a two-stage process in which clay objects initially were formed by hand and were unfired. This use of clay occurred in the pre-Harappan period sometime during the seventh millennium BC, a period during which human and animal figurines, small containers (Jarrige and Meadow 1980: 126), mudbrick architecture, ovens, and compartmented storage pits were in use (Jarrige and Lechevallier 1979: 469). In a second stage, which occurred in the first half of the sixth millennium BC, straw-tempered, low-fired ceramic vessels appeared (ibid.: 477). Within a few centuries other clay products appeared, finer wares to which a slip was applied and burnished (ibid.: 478), terracotta nails, bangles, figurines, clay rattles, seals, and pendants. A similar sequence from unbaked to kiln-fired objects occurred in adjacent regions in the Near East, for example at Ganj Dareh, where unbaked objects precede fired ones by several centuries. Although the sequence at Ganj Dareh (ca.7000 BC) begins earlier than at Mehrgarh, the obvious experimentation with clay as a precursor to fired objects is more suggestive of local innovation at Mehrgarh and Ganj Dareh than it is of diffusion from either place.

In order to understand the innovative process of the development of pottery technology, crafts can be viewed as associated sets of technical developments, as Ruth Amiran (1965) has done. Speaking of developments elsewhere in the Old World, she specifically pairs the "making/ cooking of bread/porridge" with pottery production. In particular, she points to the close association of clay-lined depressions in floors with ovens and hearths in household courtyards. The proximity of "preparing-cooking-baking" and these immovable basins may have resulted in an accidental firing of mud clay to pottery. She states: "The resemblance which exists between the two, both in the processes together – preparing, grinding, mixing with water, kneading, shaping, and firing – and in the auxiliary instruments, has been taken as a basis for grouping the two crafts together" (ibid.: 240).

This same association of materials is present at Mehrgarh, where in the earliest sector of the site "circular ovens lined with moulded bricks baked by the fire" have been found; on the surface of this area many similar circular firing places were found in association with "a very large number of grinding stones" (Jarrige and Lechevallier 1979: 469), suggesting that Amiran's reconstruction may hold for developments at Mehrgarh.[12]

After the initial invention of baked clay, improvements and innovations in pottery production can be seen with every archaeological level throughout the sequence at Mehrgarh and they include a number of technological breakthroughs which can only be summarized here, but which I have dealt with in more detail elsewhere (Wright 1989b). With respect to selection and processing, as I have indicated, the early chaff-tempered wares were quickly replaced by a grit temper which enhanced the plasticity and pyrotechnical stability of the wares. This also expanded the range of vessel shapes in that it was now possible to produce finer and thinner vessels. Manipulation of clays while in the plastic state became increasingly sophisticated, perhaps as potters were challenged by the new clay pastes but also in response to questions of "efficiency" or at least production quantities, as pottery became an item of exchange. At Mehrgarh the potters' wheel appeared early in the record (ca.4000 BC), even though slabbed, pinched, and other hand-building techniques continued to be used. The invention of a slow wheel, used to trim pots after they were leather hard, seems to be a logical prototype to the potters' wheel (Amiran 1965: 246).[13] This innovation had considerable advantages since forming pots on the potter's wheel speeds up production.[14]

The earliest shapes found in the pre-Harappan are bowls and circular, flat dishes which are undecorated, but jar forms appeared soon after.

Jars, no doubt, revolutionized the repertoire of containers for liquids; some vessels were slipped and burnished, presumably to enhance their impermeability. In fact, the invention of slips and paints occurred almost simultaneously with the first pottery and required a fairly sophisticated knowledge of colorants and their alteration under different firing conditions (Wright 1986).

At Mehrgarh a series of advances in the use of slip/paints gradually evolved into a mastery of a variety of colors achieved through combining different paint recipes and manipulating the atmospheric conditions in kilns. These advances were accompanied by increasing sophistication in the types of kilns that were used in an apparent shift from open firings (Audouze and Jarrige 1979: 219; Jarrige and Meadow 1980: 129) to enclosed and single-chambered kilns (Santoni 1989: 176). The development of enclosed kilns would have increased the number of days during the year in which pottery could be fired (Arnold 1985: 215). Another possible advantage to enclosed kilns was that higher temperatures could be reached, a factor that would enhance the durability of the final product over lower-fired vessels.

The use of fired pottery for vessels became widespread by the fifth millennium and continued through the end of the sequence at Mehrgarh. Although other crafts were produced at Mehrgarh, pottery appears to have been a major commodity, especially in the last two periods of occupation when enormous heaps of broken pottery and "elegant examples of fine craftsmanship" have been found (Jarrige and Meadow 1980: 130). Thus the initial invention and continued development of new techniques outlined here suggests that potters were neither static nor conservative in experimenting with new techniques, as is often portrayed in ethnographic and archaeological accounts.

When we turn to the urban periods of the Harappan civilization which occurred at ca.2500 BC, some 3,000 years after the introduction of ceramic vessels, potters had acquired a sizable repertoire of techniques, yet they continued to develop new ones. Throwing pots "on the hump" was an innovation that occurred in the Early Harappan period (ca.3500–2500 BC), but it became the predominant method in use during the Mature Harappan, suggesting a desire or need to produce pots quickly, since the technique made it possible to produce several vessels off of a single lump of processed (wedged) clay. Similarly, the use of molds in forming clay in its plastic state, although not as rapid a technique as throwing, also took less time than previous methods and increased the range of vessel forms that could be produced. In addition, potters systematized sets of production sequences, taking advantage of each of them to make a range of vessels. For example, during the Mature Harappan period at Harappa, there were over 60 different pottery types but less than eight production sequences that were used to produce them, yielding a variety of pottery types that ranged from miniatures to large jars.[15]

The techniques used in producing Harappan forms required considerable scheduling, planning, and control, as many Harappan vessels consisted of individual pieces that were produced separately and then joined together. The technique of joining sections of vessels required a mastery of the clay system and a concern with fit, measuring and standardization of tasks, as the components of pots were built upon each other, joins were smoothed over and surfaces paddled and clays stretched. Procedures involved a lot of scraping and adding of clay as different parts of vessels became weakened during production.[16] These componential techniques unquestionably indicate that several potters worked together on individual pots and cooperated in a fairly precise system of scheduling, planning and control of the production sequence.

Cultural context

There are several factors to consider in assessing how technical advances in pottery production may have complemented or enhanced other cultural developments and how they pertain to women. First, we can look at associated sets of technical achievements, in particular cooking and wild plants that were domesticated. Second, we can investigate spatial arrangements of production areas and speculate on whether or not women were likely to have participated in production. And finally, we can examine the question of commercialization and whether women in prehistoric contexts participated in this type of production.

With respect to the first factor, the invention of pottery clearly parallels advances in food production. Although it is impossible to document specific changes in cooking that occurred as a result of the availability of ceramic vessels, there are plant foods in the botanical record at Mehrgarh whose toxicity would have been reduced or destroyed by heating in ceramics. Among them are barley (various subspecies of *Hordeum vulgare*), wheat (*Triticum* sp.), oats (*Avena* sp.), peas (*Pisum* sp.), and sorghum (*Sorghum* sp.) (Meadow 1989: Table 6.1), which contain various toxins that can be broken down through heating at sufficiently high temperatures (Arnold 1985: table 6.1, 129ff.). In addition, ceramics would have been effective containers for use in brewing and fermentation of grains or fruits, for example dates (*Phoenix dactylifera*) and grapes (*Vitis vinifera*), because of their durability during fermentation and storage. Although studies of the residues in containers have not been conducted at Mehrgarh (or at any other Harappan site), the slipped and burnished jars that were produced throughout the pre- to

Mature Harappan periods would have been suited for these uses, as well as for storage of milk products and grain. The intervention and use of ceramics, therefore, at least had the potential of enhancing food resources. Evidence for the presence of domesticated plants that required prolonged and sustained heating strongly indicates that the development of ceramics may have been integral to the process. The association of women with both cooking (see p. 198) and pottery production suggests that experimentation and development of the two technologies occurred hand-in-hand.

There are a number of spatial indicators of pottery manufacture that provide evidence for the organization of production. A traditional method for identifying pottery workshops is to look for spatial features, such as settling vats, clay storage and preparation areas, containers for water, firing areas, rotary devices, wheel pits, platforms, benches, niches, storage rooms (DeBoer and Lathrap 1979: 104ff.; Kramer 1985: 80) or associated tools and debris such as levigated clay, polishing stones, molds, lumps or pigment for slips, and over- or underfired wasters (Stark 1985: 168ff.). These features, when clustered in specified ways, make it possible to define organizational units within an archaeological context as Stark (ibid.: 160) has done "as a first step for an analysis of several economic and social aspects of pottery production". Although there is an extensive literature[17] on the different types of workshops in which production may take place, her units are more easily identified than others in an archaeological context. The units are based on spatial and economic considerations, as follows (ibid.: 160): (1) household production refers to production associated with domestic (dwelling) areas "and for the household"; (2) workshop production is associated with domestic areas and for household consumption and exchange "or some other economic system"; and (3) separate workshops represent more than one household and are "not integrated into a domestic area". Although the assumed coincidence of the term "household", a social unit, with domestic areas or dwellings, a physical structure, is problematic, since households differ from society to society (Wilk and Rathje 1982: 618), this typology can at least provide a preliminary assessment of the organization of production.

At Mehrgarh numerous pottery production areas have been identified, and they overwhelmingly are found in association with dwellings. One locus that has been extensively documented was inhabited during the last two periods of occupation of the site (Santoni 1989). It consists of large dwellings with several rooms enclosed by an exterior wall. In it, large quantities of debris associated with pottery-making (wasters, unbaked pottery) and potter's tools (flint blades with microtraces for cutting baked pottery (Vaughan forthcoming)), ochre for decorating pots, stones for grinding pigments, and pebbles used for burnishing were found. Also in the production and dwelling area, there were storage rooms that contained from 150 to 200 vessels (Santoni 1989: 176). In addition, several enclosed kilns with large firing chambers were found.

Based on the spatial features discussed and using Stark's typology, ceramic production would fall within the category of a household or workshop production, since it occurred in production areas integrated with dwellings rather than in separate workshops outside of domestic areas. Production was large in scale and suggestive of production beyond household consumption. Moreover, the presence of large quantities of pottery found in small "storerooms", within residential areas (even though we do not understand the purpose of these caches or inventories) suggests that pottery was an important item of exchange, a factor that will be discussed in more detail below.

If we return to our original question concerning gender and pottery production, we have every reason to expect that women continued to be involved as producers. As I have described, the documented cases for pottery production at Mehrgarh indicate that pottery manufacture occurred in the context of workshop production and while, admittedly, it is difficult to leap from this formal similarity to a specific organization of production, the small units described are at least suggestive of producers related through family or close community ties. This interpretation is the most reasonable for two reasons: first, there is an absence of any indication of a hierarchically-based society or of a formal authority structure, such as chiefs (Shaffer 1987), to coordinate production; second, on analogy with the ethnographic evidence, our best reconstruction would be production units in which several individuals participated in various aspects of production.

Although the organization of production units can take a variety of forms, ecological variables provide one basis on which to reconstruct how production was organized. As Claassen has pointed out elsewhere in this volume and as I have discussed, a major factor would have been coordinating the several activities carried out within households. Given the overlap of subsistence practices and optimal times for pottery production in this region, a division of labor within household units would have been a reasonable solution to the continuation of farming, husbandry, and craft production.

And finally, another way in which the development of ceramic technology complemented other cultural processes was the apparent high demand for ceramic products as evidenced by the storage facilities but also by their distribution within the region and within communities. The archaeological record at Mehrgarh and at other Early Harappan sites attests to the exchange of pottery between communities. At first, this exchange was confined to intra-regional distribution. By the end of the occupational sequence, contacts included both intra-regional and inter-regional exchange, which has been documented through trace element analyses (Wright 1985, 1989a).

This reconstruction contradicts concepts derived from some of the ethnographic literature in that trade and "commercialization" frequently have been correlated with an automatic shift of production from the household to separate workshops and by extension from a domain in which females figured predominantly to one assumed to be primarily male. In fact, even in the latest period in the sequence (ca.2800 BC) when there was an expansion of inter-regional exchange to regions 700 km distant, pottery production continued to be organized in workshops associated with dwellings. If we retain the traditional association of women with residentially-based ceramic production, the evidence from Mehrgarh suggests that they continued to be involved in pottery production, production that was destined, in part, for exchange.

During the Mature Harappan period, we see a continuation of the pattern of long-range exchange. A number of standardized types are found broadly distributed within the civilization itself, but there also is Harappan pottery at non-Harappan sites.[18] For example, large storage jars have been found on the Oman Peninsula (George Dales, personal communication), which are identical to Harappan types, suggesting that ceramics continued to be important in the development of exchange networks.

The context of production and distribution is complex during this period. First, the componential techniques described unquestionably indicate that several potters were working together on individual pots. Second, the spatial data, based on Stark's typology, indicates that there may have been changes in the organization of production. At Mohenjo-daro, there is evidence for craft production (but not specifically pottery production) in courtyards and open spaces within residential areas (Jansen 1983: 57), a pattern which may be similar to the household and workshop contexts at Mehrgarh. A second production context represents a new urban phenomenon. It occurs on the edges of the city, where alignments of debris may represent rows of separate workshops for the production of various crafts, possibly a craft quarter (Bondioli et al. 1983: 9ff.).[19] Although small in scale, artifacts associated with these separate workshops include numerous seal impressions and graffiti. Seal impressions and graffiti have been interpreted as evidence for administrative control of production (Halim and Vidale 1983: 96).

Other archaeological evidence for pottery production is from the site of Harappa, where a "specialized production area", consisting of kilns and associated debris has recently been discovered (Kenoyer 1989: 13).

Using ethnographic examples from South Asia, Kenoyer has argued that this area represents a "non-centralized intra-community aggregation of specialized craft production" (ibid.: 1) in contrast to the centrally adminstered craft quarter at Mohenjo-daro. He cites three factors: first, the range of ceramic types found in the production area is restricted to specific types of vessels, which suggests specialization; second, there is a continuous use of the area for pottery production from the Early to the Mature Harappan periods, suggesting possible hereditary ownership of land or segregation by a civic authority; and third, although to date excavations have not shown a direct association with habitation areas, there is no evidence for direct control of production (seal impressions or graffiti). Using ethnographic analogies from contemporary South Asia, his interpretation leaves open the possibility that pottery production at Harappa was conducted by "kin related communities" that engaged in cooperation and sharing of resources (ibid.: 5).

If the interpretations discussed above are correct, they indicate that production occurred within at least two and possibly three different contexts: in the small-scale, workshop units that follow the tradition already established for the towns and villages in Baluchistan; in separate workshops located in segregated craft quarters administered by a centralized authority; and in separate workshops administered by kinship groups. None of these contexts necessarily excludes women from pottery production: in the case of household or workshop production, we "assume" the presence of women, while in the separate workshops at Harappa, its localization and the absence of evidence for formal administrative control also leaves open the possibility that production continued to be organized in the urban setting as it had been in previous periods. Moreover, there is nothing about early (or late) urban life to necessarily preclude women from being mobile and active in the segregated craft quarter. Thus we have no reason to exclude either women or men from these units.

Conclusions

In attempting to resolve the issue of women's labor and pottery production in prehistory, there are many questions that must be left unanswered, underscored by my discomfort in depending on documentation from modern times, the only contrastive set of observations, given the problems of previously male-centred views (see Ardener 1975 and Ortner 1974 for cultural anthropology; Conkey and Spector 1984 for archaeology). As I have suggested, serious revisions are necessary in our recording procedures and in our attention to the variety of producers and the tasks they perform. Nonetheless, I have been able to show that the strong gender bias in ethnographies has wrongly excluded women from commercialized pottery production, thereby undermining their inclusion in archaeological interpretations. Similarly, there is every reason to assume their participation in production and in innovation in reconstructing the development of pottery technology in that when women are discussed ethnographically as potters or as involved with pottery production – which is surely an *underreporting* – they are associated with all levels of production, both mechanized and non-mechanized, small and large scale, for household and for external consumption.

Thus, I have shown that assumed concepts regarding the passivity of women and by association, their activities, have been responsible for a perspective in which the early developments of pottery are viewed as stagnant, even though the archaeological record, for South Asia, and most likely for other regions, strongly supports the contrary. My discussion of the archaeological record has concentrated on the *innovative* aspects of pottery technology as a corrective against these previous and pervasive interpretations. Pottery vessels were and remain a unique type of container, which even today is highly valued in both western and non-western settings. From its earliest appearance, it very likely involved women's labor and its development occurred hand-in-hand with other economic activities, such as the domestication process and trade. Thereafter, it remained a significant factor in social and economic changes.

A third common stereotype suggests that when pottery production became an "essential" economic activity, women no longer contributed to it or participated in it. This scenario cannot be taken as necessarily the case, much less as *a* universal, because there is little empirical basis for this either in the ethnographic or archaeological evidence. Pottery appears to have been a major activity for women, even though in many social and economic contexts, women's labor in the production of pottery for non-household consumption may not be counted.

One point that cannot yet be resolved, which I have not addressed, and that admittedly is most critical to any social reconstruction, is the ideological underpinnings for the division of labor that existed in Harappan society and the value attached to gender assignments (Conkey and Spector 1984: 16). It is only through an understanding of the ideology that we can claim knowledge of whether innovative or not, pottery and potters were accorded a high status and where women fit into these "rankings". Given our evidence that small-scale production persisted in the urban periods and that there is very little evidence that it was state controlled, we cannot assume that it was taken out of the hands of small, household production units. This suggests that, when the Harappan evidence is better understood, evolutionary models on the state and its relationship to kinship groups may need revision. As I have shown, here and elsewhere (1989b: 56), although the evolutionist view fits the evidence from Mesopotamia, it cannot account for the Harappan data. The kind of basic shifts in social and economic relations believed by evolutionists to be a universal in the formation of states appears not to have occurred here and provides a different type of state configuration that requires investigation and reworking of evolutionary concepts.

This reconstruction, then, contributes to the claim that gender is an issue in technology studies and that it must be factored into questions about the production process and the organization of work. The most fruitful avenue that we have open to us is the continued examination of archaeological, ethnographic, and ethnoarchaeological studies. A first step, which is what I have attempted here, is to reexamine these sources and their cultural biases, to document the participation of women in pottery production and to restore the dynamic qualities of the early invention of pottery to the archaeological record.

ACKNOWLEDGMENTS

Several individuals provided me with helpful comments in the course of writing this paper. I wish to thank Anita Feldman, Philip Kohl, and Wilma Wetterstrom for their helpful comments and suggestions. Virginia Kerns discussed various aspects of the paper with me as it progressed and provided me with stimulating and informative discussions, as well as bibliographic suggestions. But primarily, I thank Joan Gero and Meg Conkey for inviting me to contribute to this volume. Their generosity in taking the time to provide challenging commentary, numerous insights and editorial comments on several drafts of the paper is appreciated. In addition to being an enthusiastic and resourceful audience, they made writing the paper an intellectually stimulating experience. I also thank Tracey Whitesell, my research assistant, for her invaluable assistance. Throughout the paper I have drawn on my field work and ceramic studies at Mehrgarh and at Harappa; I want to thank Jean-François Jarrige, Director of the French Archaeological Mission to Pakistan, and George Dales, Director of the University of California, Berkeley team at Harappa, for allowing me to participate in these important excavations.

NOTES

1 Murdock and Provost (1973: 216) state that the general principle applies that greater technological complexity (undefined) is associated with a shift in

sexual allocation of the more complex tasks from females to males. The term "technological complexity" does not refer to pottery technology specifically but more generally to a variety of technologies, although it appears to concentrate on subsistence practices.

2 Painters of pottery in these workshops were female members of the family; wife and mother of the male reported (Miller 1985: 110).

3 Rye and Evans (1976) studied 20 potters in the NWFP, Panjab, and Sind. Of these 16 provided information on the organization of work. In 15 of the potteries more than one person was engaged in production; in 11, producers were related, but for 5 there was no information; in 8 potteries, women worked as producers, but for 3 there was no information. Women performed a variety of tasks: in 8 cases they performed what were described as "unskilled" activities, such as moving pots while drying or gathering firewood for kilns, but in 5 of these cases they decorated the pottery, although, again, the activity was described as unskilled work. The women either were wives or daughters of the "potter"; in 10 of the studies workshops were combined with dwellings or courtyards, in 2 in workshops separated from dwellings, but for 4 there was no information.

4 As a more general phenomenon, this bias emerges as a critical problem in third world development, as women's participation in production may go unnoticed in census-taking or even in more qualitative studies. In Egypt, for example, Lynch (1984: 1) states: "A major stumbling block has been acceptance by women as well as men of definitions of work which omit, from statistics compiled, productive activities within the domestic domain, as well as much of women's unpaid family labour in trading [handicrafts] and agriculture. Thus an impression is given that women's contribution to production and 'development' is mainly confined to 'housework', subsistence and child-rearing." This underreporting of women is pervasive; Moore states the problem succinctly: "The apparent invisibility of women's work is a feature of the sexual division of labour in many societies, and it is reinforced by the ethnocentric assumptions of researchers and policy-makers, and by indigenous gender ideologies" (1988: 43).

5 The idea of "ceramic ecology" was first introduced to archaeology by Frederick Matson (1965). Drawing on the works of Julian Steward (1955), Matson proposed that cultural ecology would be a useful framework for studies of ceramic technology in that one facet of cultural ecology was the attempt "to relate the raw materials and technologies" that people who engaged in crafts had at their disposal (1965: 203). The advantage of the approach is that it attempts to draw out relationships between ecological factors and sociocultural changes (Rice 1987: 314).

6 Arnold lists several reasons why pottery production is compatible with childcare: it is not dangerous or hazardous; it is monotonous and does not require concentration; it can be interrupted; it is compatible with cooking and spare time (1985: 101). I really cannot agree, however, that pottery production does not require concentration nor that it is non-hazardous. Descriptions of factors related to scheduling (Lacovara 1985: 84) and the importance of establishing a rhythm of work (Fournier 1977: 190) argue for

considerable skill and the importance of timing and concentration in pottery production. Nash for example, specifically mentions the regularity of the rhythm of work, even among women who care for children under three years of age and whose children may be nursing (1985: 49). Also, there are a number of safety factors especially during firings (Rhodes 1981: 241ff.), which indicates that at least during some parts of the production sequence, there are significant hazards. And finally, it seems almost too obvious to mention that the reproductive and childcare functions of women are governed by the life cycle, leaving numerous years when child care is not an issue.

7 There is an extensive literature on ecological variables that affect the division of labor. They include cereal crop agriculture since cereal crops require large amounts of time to process, leaving some members of the household (women) with less time to engage in agriculture (Martin and Voorhies 1975 cited in Burton and White 1984: 569); time spent caring for a permanent household, especially obtaining water and fuel and "more time spent on child care because children's labor is more valuable" (Nag 1962; White 1973 cited in Burton and White 1984: 570). Burton and White themselves stress ecosystem transformation (modification of the natural ecosystem as a result of agriculture), especially an increase in the use of female labor for the keeping of animals, again a strategy for spreading risks among household producers when seasonal windows for agriculture and husbandry coincide. This is especially the case with cattle-complex animals (as opposed to pigs) which may be due to feeding habits and the by-products of these animals, such as dung (ibid.: 580). This finding should be of interest to archaeologists and merits examination in an archaeological context.

8 Or does this voice from the past reflect the census problems of the day!

9 The discrepancy of wages in Mesopotamia is even greater when one considers that the rate of compensation was scaled according to specific tasks. According to Waetzoldt, whereas "a man could rise very high in the scale of compensation . . . women workers always remained on a relatively low level." In exceptional instances women with unusual weaving skills could earn as high as 100 liters per month, but men could earn much higher rates. For example, craftsmen earned as high as 300 liters/month; boat captains, 510; herdsmen, 900 liters; agricultural supervisors, 1200; scribes, 300 and *even* 5000! (1987: 123).

10 For purposes of this discussion, I have divided the Harappan sequence as follows: pre-Harappan: 6000–3500 BC; Early Harappan: 3500–2500 BC; Mature Harappan: 2500–1800 BC. These dates are approximate; for a more detailed chronology, see Shaffer (forthcoming).

11 For a bibliography on this topic, see Arnold's excellent discussion of the technological advantage of clay vessels; in particular see his outline of toxicity for specific plants and how they can be reduced through the use of ceramics (1985: 128ff.).

12 Other technologies that have been linked to the invention of pottery are the coiling technique used in basketry (Fairservis 1956) and pise and mudbrick architecture (Braidwood and Howe 1960: 40).

13 Opinions on the invention of the potter's wheel fall into two categories. One group follows Amiran's reconstruction from "slow wheel" to the true potter's wheel, which had been developed and extensively discussed in an earlier paper by Foster (1959) and is favored by most archaeologists. A second, non-evolutionary group of scholars favors a "transfer of principle" from the cart wheel to the turntable and potter's wheel. Their logic suggests that since the potter's wheel is associated with males, it seems more likely that a "male" tool was its original source. Moreover, they believe that it is inconceivable that a turntable (the slow wheel) that was used by women could have developed into a wheel used by men! (Van Gennep 1911, referred to in Foster 1959: 116). In taking the position that the potter's wheel is a process of evolution from the slow wheel, Foster admits that "The correlation between male potters and the wheel admittedly is one of the mysteries of history" (ibid.: 116), or as Herskovits put it, one of those "irrationalities in culture" (quoted in ibid.: 116). These origins aside, Kramer reports a consistent association of male potters with the "fast" wheel, although she finds it implausible that the reason for this is that women are "ill equipped" to use the potter's wheel (1985: 79). Recent general discussions of biological factors suggest that there are only a few forms of work for which women could not qualify; moreover, numerous female, contemporary potters, some of whom use non-electric wheels, are examples of the validity of Kramer's statement.

14 From time allocation studies which he conducted among potteries in Guatemala, Arnold has reported the number of bowls per hour that individual potters in Guatemala can produce as "50 bowls per hour using the wheel . . . over a three-week period, three potters can produce 5000 such wheel-made bowls" (1985: 208). This represents one-third to one-sixth of the time it takes a potter to make vessels using a two-piece mold.

15 Production sequences for prehistoric pottery are reconstructed through macroscopic study of surface characteristics, such as evidence of manufacture when the clay was plastic or of areas where parts of vessels have been joined or added, and through microscopic studies of paste characteristics, paint composition, levels of temperatures reached and atmospheric conditions in kilns. Once manufacturing processes are understood for each stage of production, production sequences can be developed for individual pottery types. For an extensive discussion of pottery production and the reconstruction of production sequences, see Rye (1981).

16 Dales and Kenoyer (1986) have described many of these techniques for Harappan pottery found at Mohenjo-daro.

17 See for example the discussions of Arnold (1985: 225ff.) and Rice (1987: 184ff.). Arnold, following van der Leeuw (1976) defines four possibilities: household production, household industry, workshop industry, large-scale industry. Each change represents increased specialization, demand, scale of production, increased division of labor by gender and diminished involvement of subsistence and control of pottery production by individual household units. Rice, following van der Leeuw (1977, 1984) but also Peacock (1981, 1982) uses a slightly different terminology: household

production, household industry, individual workshop industry, nucleated workshop, and state controlled production. Variables that differentiate each category are "frequency and seasonability of production; number of workers; age, sex, status, and relationships of the workers; degree of labor division; kind and extent of investment in special space or tools; variability in raw materials and products; and size and proximity of consuming groups" (Rice 1987: 184).

18 Laboratory analysis of the entire corpus of ceramics at Harappa is currently in process.

19 At Mehrgarh there is evidence for pottery production at the nearby site of Lal Shah. This area may represent a separate workshop associated with Mehrgarh; however, only one kiln has been excavated, although the results are unpublished. Moreover, it may be that when areas adjacent to the kiln are excavated, dwellings will be found in association with it. The kiln at Lal Shah is the only structure that could possibly be construed as a separate workshop in the Mehrgarh sequence that is known to me.

REFERENCES

Adams, Robert McC. (1984). "Mesopotamian Social Evolution: Old Outlooks, New Goals." In *On the Evolution of Complex Societies. Essays in Honor of Harry Hoijer 1982*, Timothy Earle, ed. Malibu: Undena Publications, 79–129.
Amiran, Ruth (1965). "The Beginnings of Pottery-Making in the Near East." In *Ceramics and Man*, F. R. Matson, ed. Chicago: Aldine, 240–7.
Ardener, Edwin (1975). "Belief and the Problem of Women." In *Perceiving Women*, S. Ardener, ed. London: Dent, 1–17.
Arnold, Dean E. (1975). "Ceramic Ecology of the Ayacucho Basin: Implications for Prehistory." *Current Anthropology* 16: 183–205.
—— (1985). *Ceramic Theory and Cultural Process*. Cambridge: Cambridge University Press.
Audouze, Françoise and Catherine Jarrige (1979). "A third Millennium Pottery-Firing Structure at Mehrgarh and Its Economic Implications." In *South Asian Archaeology 1977*, vol. I, M. Taddei, ed. Naples: Istituto Universitario Orientale Seminario di Studi Asiatici, 213–22.
Bondioli, Luca, M. Tosi, and M. Vidale (1983). "Craft Activity Areas and Surface Survey at Moenjodaro. Complementary Procedures for the Evaluation of a Restricted Site." In *Interim Reports*, vol. 1, M. Jansen and G. Urban, eds. Aachen: Forschungsprojekt, Mohenjodaro, 9–38.
Braidwood, Robert and Bruce Howe (1960). *Prehistoric Investigations in Iraqi Kurdistan*. Chicago: University of Chicago Press.
Brew, J. O. (1956). "The Metal Ages: Copper, Bronze and Iron." In *Man, Culture, and Society*, H. L. Shapiro, ed. New York: Oxford University Press, 111–38.
Briffault, Robert (1972). *The Mothers. A Study of the Origins of Sentiments and Institutions*, vol. I. London: George Allen & Unwin Ltd.

Brown, Judith K. (1970). "A Note on the Division of Labor by Sex." *American Anthropologist* 72(5): 1073–8.

Burton, Michael L., Lilyan A. Brudner, and Douglas R. White (1977). "A Model of the Sexual Division of Labor." *American Ethnologist* 4: 227–51.

Burton, Michael L. and Douglas R. White (1984). "Sexual Division of Labor in Agriculture." *American Anthropologist* 86: 568–83.

Chapple, Eliot D. and Carleton S. Coon (1942). *Principles of Anthropology.* New York: Holt.

Collier, J. F. and M. Yanagisako (1987). *Gender and Kinship: Essays Toward a Unified Analysis.* Stanford: Stanford University Press.

Conkey, Margaret and Janet Spector (1984). "Archaeology and the Study of Gender." In *Advances in Archaeological Method and theory*, vol. 7, Michael Schiffer, ed. New York: Academic Press, 1–38.

De Atley, Suzanne P. (1986). "Mix and Match: Traditions of Glaze Paint Preparation at Four Mile Ruin, Arizona." In *Ceramics and Civilization*, vol. 2, W. D. Kingery, ed. Columbus: The American Ceramic Society, 297–330.

DeBoer, Warren R. and Donald W. Lathrap (1979). "The Making and Breaking of Shipibo-Conibo Ceramics." In *Ethnoarchaeology: Implications of Ethnography for Archaeology*, Carol Kramer, ed. New York: Columbia University Press, 102–38.

Dales, George F. and Jonathan Mark Kenoyer (1986). *Excavations at Mohenjo Daro, Pakistan: The Pottery.* Philadelphia: The University Museum, University of Pennsylvania.

Engels, Friedrich (1972). *The Origin of the Family, Private Property, and the State* [1884]. New York: International Publishers.

Fairservis, Walter (1956). *Excavations in the Quetta Valley, Pakistan.* New York: Anthropological Papers of the American Museum of Natural History, vol. XLV, 2: 169–402.

Foster, George M. (1959). "The Potter's Wheel: An Analysis of Idea and Artifact in Invention." *Southwestern Journal of Anthropology* 15: 99–119

Fournier, Robert (1977). *Illustrated Dictionary of Practical Pottery.* New York: Van Nostrand Reinhold.

Gailey, Christine Ward (1987). *Kinship to Kingship. Gender Hierarchy and State Formation in the Tongan Islands.* Austin: University of Texas Press.

Gelb, I. J. (1972). "The *arua* Institution." *Revue d'Assyriologie et d'Archéologie Orientale* 66: 1–21.

Halim, M. A. and Massimo Vidale (1983). "Kilns, Bangles and Coated Vessels." In *Interim Reports*, vol. 1, M. Jansen and G. Urban, eds. Aachen: Forschungsprojekt, Mohenjodaro, 63–98.

Jansen, Michael (1983). "Theoretical Aspects of Structural Analyses at Mohenjo-daro." In *Interim reports*, vol. 1, M. Jansen and G. Urban, eds. Aachen: Forschungsprojekt, Mohenjodaro, 39–62.

Jarrige, Jean-François and Monique Lechevallier (1979). "Excavations at Mehrgarh, Baluchistan: Their Significance in the Prehistorical Context of the Indo-Pakistan Borderlands." In *South Asian Archaeology 1977*, vol. 1, M. Taddei, ed. Naples: Instituto Universitario Orientale Seminario di Studi Asiatici, 463–536.

Jarrige, Jean-François and Richard H. Meadow (1980). "The Antecedents of Civilization in the Indus Valley." *Scientific American* 243(2): 122–33.

Jordanova, L. J. (1980). "Natural Facts: A Historical Perspective on Science and Sexuality." In *Nature, Culture and Gender*, C. P. MacCormack and M. Strathern, eds. Cambridge: Cambridge University Press, 42–69.

Kenoyer, Jonathan Mark (1989). "Harappan Craft Specialization and the Question of Urban Segregation and Stratification." Paper presented at the Annual Meeting, Society for American Archaeology, Atlanta, April 1989.

Kramer, Carol (1985). "Ceramic Ethnoarchaeology." *Annual Review of Anthropology* 14: 77–102.

Lacovara, Peter (1985). "The Ethnoarchaeology of Pottery Production in an Upper Egyptian Village." In *Ceramics and Civilization*, vol. I, W. D. Kingery, ed. Columbus: The American Ceramic Society, 51–60.

Leacock, Eleanor (1972). "Introduction to F. Engels." In *The Origin of the Family, Private Property, and the State*, F. Engels. New York: International Publishers.

—— (1978). "Women's Status in Egalitarian Society: Implications for Social Evolution." *Current Anthropology* 19(2): 247–75.

—— (1981). "History, Development, and the Division of Labor by Sex: Implications for Organization." *Signs* 7(2): 474–91.

—— (1983). "Interpreting the Origins of Gender Inequality: Conceptual and Historical Problems." *Dialectical Anthropology* 7: 263–83.

Lynch, Patricia D. (with Hoda Fahmy) (1984). *Craftswomen in Kerdassa, Egypt. Household Production and Reproduction*. Geneva: International Labour Office.

McGaw, Judith (1989). "No Passive Victims, No Separate Spheres: A Feminist Perspective on Technology's history." In *History and the History of Technology. Essays in Honor of Melvin Kranzberg*, Stephen H. Cutcliffe and Robert C. Post, eds. Bethlehem: Lehigh University Press, 172–91.

Martin, M. Kay and Barbara Voorhies (1975). *Female of the Species*. New York: Columbia University Press.

Matson, Fred R. (1965). "Ceramic Ecology: An Approach to the Study of the Early Cultures of the Near East." In *Ceramics and Man*, F. R. Matson, ed. Chicago: Aldine, 202–17.

Meadow, Richard H. (1989). "Continuity and Change in the Agriculture of the Greater Indus Valley. The Paleoethnobotanical and Zooarchaeological Evidence." In *Old Problems and New Perspectives in the Archaeology of South Asia*, Jonathan M. Kenoyer, ed. Madison: Wisconsin Archaeological Reports 2: 61–74.

Miller, Daniel (1985). *Artefacts as Categories: A Study of Ceramic Variability in Central India*. Cambridge: Cambridge University Press.

Moore, Henrietta L. (1988). *Feminism and Anthropology*. Minneapolis: University of Minnesota Press.

Mukhopadhyay, Carol C. and Patricia J. Higgins (1988). "Anthropological Studies of Women's Status Revisited: 1977–1987." *Annual Review of Anthropology* 17: 461–95.

Murdock, George P. (1937). "Comparative Data on the Division of Labor by Sex." *Social Forces* 15: 551–3.

Murdock, George P. and Caterina Provost (1973). "Factors in the Division of Labor by Sex: A Cross–cultural Analysis." *Ethnology* 12: 203–25.

Nag, Moni (1962). *Factors Affecting Fertility in Nonindustrial Societies: A Cross-cultural Study.* New Haven: Yale University Publications in Anthropology No. 66.

Nash, June (1985). *In the Eyes of the Ancestors. Belief and Behavior in a Mayan community.* Prospect Heights, IL: Waveland Press.

Ortner, Sherry (1974). "Is Female to Male as Nature is to Culture?" In *Woman, Culture, and Society.* M. Rosaldo and L. Lamphere, eds. Stanford: Stanford University Press, 67–88.

Peacock, D. P. S. (1981). "Archaeology, Ethnology and Ceramic Production." In *Production and Distribution: A Ceramic Viewpoint*, H. Howard and E. Morris, eds. Oxford: BAR International Series 120, 187–94.

—— (1982). *Pottery in the Roman World: An Ethnoarchaeological approach.* London: Longman.

Rapp, Rayna (1977). "Gender and Class: An Archaeology of Knowledge Concerning the Origin of the State." *Dialectical Anthropology* 2: 309–16.

Rhodes, Daniel (1981). *Kilns. Design, Construction and Operation*, 2nd edn. Radnor, PA: Chilton Book Co.

Rice, Prudence M. (1981). "Evolution of Specialized Pottery Production: A Trial Model." *Current Anthropology* 22(3): 219–40.

—— (1987). *Pottery Analysis. A Sourcebook.* Chicago: The University of Chicago Press.

Rosaldo, Michelle Z. (1980). "The Use and Abuse of Anthropology: Reflections on Feminism and Cross-cultural Understand." *Signs* 5: 389–417.

Rye, Owen S. (1981). *Pottery Technology. Principles and Reconstruction.* Washington: Taraxacum Inc.

Rye, Owen S. and Clifford Evans (1976). *Traditional Pottery Techniques of Pakistan.* Washington: Smithsonian Contributions to Anthropology No. 21.

Sacks, Karen (1974). "Engels Revisited: Women, the Organization of Production, and Private Property." In *Woman, Culture and Society*, M. Rosaldo and L. Lamphere, eds. Stanford: Stanford University Press, 107–22.

Santoni, Marielle (1989). "Potters and Pottery at Mehrgarh during the Third Millennium BC (Periods VI and VII)." In *South Asian Archaeology 1985*, K. Frifelt and P. Sørensen, eds. London: Curzon Press, 176–85.

Shaffer, Jim G. (1987). "Reurbanization: The Eastern Punjab and Beyond." Paper presented at the symposium, Urban Form and Meaning in South Asia: The Shaping of Cities from Prehistoric to Precolonial Times. National Gallery of Art, Washington.

—— (forthcoming). "The Indus Valley, Baluchistan and Helmand Traditions: Neolithic through Bronze Age." In *Chronologies in Old World Archaeology*, 2nd rev. edn, Robert W. Ehrich, ed. Chicago: University of Chicago Press.

Shepard, Anna O. (1965). "Rio Grande glaze-paint Pottery: A Test of Petrographic Analysis." In *Ceramics and Man*, F. R. Matson, ed. Chicago: Aldine, 62–87.

—— (1976). *Ceramics for the Archaeologist*. Washington: Carnegie Institution.

Silverblatt, Irene (1988). "Women in States." *Annual Review of Anthropology* 17: 427–60.

Sjoberg, Ake W. (1984). *The Sumerian Dictionary*. Philadelphia: The University Museum.

Stark, Barbara L. (1985). "Archaeological Identification of Pottery Production Locations: Ethnoarchaeological and Archaeological Data in Mesoamerica." In *Decoding Prehistoric Ceramics*, B. A. Nelson, ed. Carbondale: Southern Illinois University Press, 158–94.

Steward, Julian (1955). "The Concept and Method of Cultural Ecology." In *Theory and Culture Change*, J. H. Steward. Urbana: University of Illinois Press, 30–42.

van der Leeuw, S. E. (1976). *Studies in the Technology of Ancient Pottery* (2 vols). Amsterdam.

—— (1977). "Towards a Study of the Economics of Pottery Making." *Ex Horreo* 5: 68–76.

van der Leeuw, S. E. and A. C. Pritchard, eds (1984). *The Many Dimensions of Pottery: Ceramics in Archaeology and Anthropology. CINGULA 7*. Amsterdam: Institute for Pre- and Proto-history, University of Amsterdam.

Van Gennep (1911). "Études d'ethnographie algérienne. III. Les poteries kabyles." *Revue d'ethnographie et de sociologie* 2(1–2): 277–331.

Vaughan, Patrick (forthcoming). "Microtraces on stone blades at Mehrgarh." In *Mehrgarh 1974–1985*. Paris: ADPF.

Waetzoldt, Hartmut (1987). "Compensation of Craft Workers and Officials in the Ur III Period." In *Labor in the Ancient Near East*, M. A. Powell, ed. New Haven: The American Oriental Society, 117–43.

White, Benjamin (1973). "Demand for Labor and Population Growth in Colonial Java." *Human Ecology* 1: 217–36.

Wilk, Richard R. and William J. Rathje (1982). "Household Archaeology." In *Archaeology of the Household*, R. R. Wilk and W. J. Rathje, eds. American Behavioral Scientist 25, 617–39.

Wright, Rita P. (1985). "Technology and Style in Ancient Ceramics." In *Ceramics and Civilization*, vol. 1, W. D. Kingery, ed. Columbus: The American Ceramic Society, 5–25.

—— (1986). "The Boundaries of Technology and Stylistic Change." In *Ceramics and Civilization*, vol. 2, W. D. Kingery, ed. Columbus: The American Ceramic Society, 1–20.

—— (1989a). "New Tracks on Ancient Frontiers: Ceramic Technology on the Indo-Iranian Borderlands." In *Archaeological Thought in America*, C. C. Lamberg-Karlovsky, ed. Cambridge: Cambridge University Press, 268–79.

—— (1989b). "The Indus Valley and Mesopotamian Civilization: A Comparative View of Ceramic Technology." In *Old Problems and New Perspectives in the Archaeology of South Asia*. Jonathan M. Kenoyer, ed. Madison: Wisconsin Archaeological Reports 2: 145–56.

Zagarell, Allen (1986). "Trade, Women, Class, and Society in Ancient Western Asia." *Current Anthropology* 27(5): 415–30.

8

Weaving and Cooking: Women's Production in Aztec Mexico

Elizabeth M. Brumfiel

Ethnohistoric documents from sixteenth-century Mexico suggest that weaving and cooking were the most common productive activities for Aztec women. According to Sahagún's native informants, "the good middle-aged woman [is] a skilled weaver, a weaver of designs, an artisan, a good cook, a preparer of good food" (1950–69: bk 10, ch. 3). Rulers' daughters were exhorted, "Look well to the drink, to the food: how it is prepared, how it is made . . . Apply thyself well to the really womanly task, the spindle whorl, the weaving stick . . . Pay good attention to the spindle whorl, the weaving stick, the drink, the food" (ibid., bk. 6, ch. 18). These texts are supplemented by pictorial documentation of women cooking and weaving, and girls being instructed in these arts (ibid. bk. 10, illus. 3, 21, 104, 105, 106 (see figure 8.1); *Codex Mendoza* 1964, Lám. LIX–LXI).

The documents provide a helpful initial definition of women's production in Aztec society, but their value is limited. For one thing, they are too narrowly focused. Having defined women's work as weaving and cooking, they do not comment upon the ties between these activities and other demographic, economic, and political structures in sixteenth-century Mexico. Secondly, the documents are oversimplified. As Nash (1976: 356) points out, the illustrations that accompany Sahagún's text indicate many other activities for women including healing and marketing (cf. Hellbom 1967). Finally, the documents have no time-depth; they indicate neither how women's production contributed to the transformation of Aztec society and culture during the thirteenth, fourteenth, and fifteenth centuries, nor how women were affected by this change.

A particularistic and ahistorical ethnohistoric record is especially regrettable because it plays to our own cultural prejudices. Since weaving and cooking occurred mostly (but not entirely) in a domestic setting, we

Figure 8.1 Women weaving and cooking. (After Sahagún 1950–69: bk 10, chs 1, 10, 14)

are likely to apply to the Aztec culture our own customary separations of "private" from "public", "homemaking" from "work", and "maintenance" from "production". Thus, the ethnohistoric record conspires with Western culture to encourage us to treat women's production as a nondynamic element in Aztec history, a constant to be acknowledged and then ignored in reconstructing the process of social change.

To dismiss women's production in Aztec Mexico would, of course, be a mistake. Even if the products of women's labor had not circulated beyond the household, such products were essential to population reproduction and growth. Sanders, Parsons, and Santley (1979: 184–6) document a ten-fold increase in the population of the Valley of Mexico during the last four centuries of the prehispanic era. This truly impressive demographic performance was crucial to the developing Aztec political economy. Population growth made possible the large-scale development of labor-intensive *chinampa* agriculture in the southern Valley of Mexico which, in turn, supported urbanization and political centralization in the Aztec capital (Parsons 1976; Parsons et al. 1982). Population growth also enabled the Aztecs to field large armies, which ensured their military success and the success of their tribute-based polity (Armillas 1964: 324; Hassig 1988: 101). Population growth was the product of a successful household economy, and women's work was essential to it.

In addition, the products of women's labor circulated beyond the household. Aztec women wove cloth, and cloth circulated through the market system and the tribute system and the redistributive economy of the palaces. Quantities of woven mantles, loincloths, blouses, and skirts were paid as tribute to local lords and to imperial tax stewards (Berdan 1975; Guzmán 1938; Hicks 1982: 238–41; Mólins Fábrega 1954–5). They were distributed to ritual and administrative personnel, craft specialists, warriors, and other faithful servants of the state (Berdan 1975: 126–9; Broda 1976: 41–2). Cotton mantles served as a unit of currency in the regional market system (Motolinía 1971: 374). Woven articles of clothing served as markers of social status (Anawalt 1981: 27–30), and clothing served as an idiom of political negotiation (Brumfiel 1987b: 111–12). Thus, cloth was a primary means of organizing the flow of goods and services that sustained the Aztec state, and cloth production was women's work.

This paper examines the production of cloth and food in Aztec Mexico. It offers a reconstruction of the work processes involved in weaving and cooking, based on ethnohistoric and ethnographic records of women's work in Central Mexico. Such reconstruction establishes the context within which women's production occurred and provides some idea of the amount of labor involved. Moreover, familiarity with the work processes establishes what evidence of weaving and cooking might be encountered in the archaeological record.

Having established this evidence, the paper examines the archaeology of women's work both within and outside the Valley of Mexico. Within the Valley of Mexico, data are examined from three Late Postclassic communities: Xico, Huexotla, and Xaltocan (figure 8.2). These three communities occupied rather different environmental zones, and they held different political statuses prior to Aztec conquest. Xico, an island in the middle of Lake Chalco, was in the heartland of the ridged-field (*chinampa*) agricultural zone that came to serve as the breadbasket of the Aztec capital. Xico was politically unimportant, subordinant to the autonomous kingdom of Cuitlahuac. Huexotla was located in a prime area for rainfall farming on the broad piedmont slopes of the middle valley. Before Aztec dominance, it was a powerful independent domain.

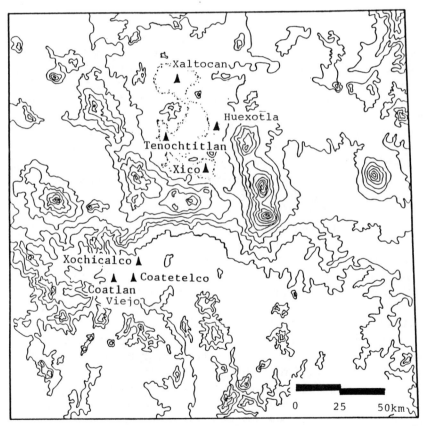

Figure 8.2 Late Postclassic sites in Central Mexico mentioned in text. (Modified from Smith and Hirth 1988)

Xaltocan was an island in the more brackish waters of the northern lakes; it possessed some agricultural *chinampas*, but agricultural production here was more limited than at Xico or Huexotla. Before Aztec dominance, Xaltocan was the capital of an imperial domain that was even more extensive and powerful than Huexotla. After 1430, all three communities fell under Aztec rule.

An examination of the frequencies of artifacts associated with weaving and cooking at these sites (and others located in the Valley of Morelos) reveals the complexity and dynamics of women's work, the strategies devised by women for exploiting the possibilities of environment and geography and for dealing with the demands of the expanding Aztec state.

Weaving

Work processes

Cloth was woven from two different fibers in Aztec Mexico. One was *ichtli* fiber extracted from the leaves of the maguey cactus. Maguey could be grown in thin soils; it was also tolerant of early frosts and long droughts, both common in the Valley of Mexico. The plant was highly valued not only for its fibers, but also for its sap which was drunk in fermented form as *octli* or reduced to a thick, sweet syrup (*necutli*) (Gonçalves de Lima 1956; Parsons and Parsons 1990). Maguey was planted in quantities on the piedmont slopes ringing the Valley of Mexico, and maguey fiber was a readily available local product.

The extraction of fiber from maguey leaves is a lengthy process (Manrique 1969; Parsons and Parsons 1990). The leaves are cut from the plant and beaten or buried in an earth oven for several days to loosen the flesh from the fiber. The leaves are then placed on a plank and the flesh scraped away. The remaining fiber is washed and whitened with a maize-dough application. It is then ready for spinning.

Maguey fiber can be spun into a coarse or fine thread. The fineness of the thread is controlled by the spinner who spins by hand working with a weighted spindle. While threads of different thicknesses can be woven with a spindle of a given weight, lightly weighted spindles facilitate the production of fine thread, and more heavily weighted spindles speed the production of coarse thread. In general, the Aztecs considered maguey fiber textiles inferior to those of cotton cloth, but some were quite fine, soft, and elaborately decorated (Anawalt 1981: 29). The thread was woven into cloth on a back-strap loom (figure 8.3).

Cotton was also woven. Cotton could not be grown in high mountain valleys like the Valley of Mexico, but it could be obtained by trade with

Figure 8.3 A mother teaches her daughter to weave. (After *Codex Mendoza* 1964: Lám. LXI)

nearby temperate regions in Morelos and Puebla and with more distant tropical lowlands. Highland rulers would sometimes provide their towns with the raw cotton needed to meet their tribute assessments in cotton textiles (Alva Ixtlilxochitl 1975–7: I,327; Zorita 1963: 187). The shorter cotton fibers required only a lightly weighted spindle. When spinning cotton, it was customary to support the end of the spindle in a small ceramic bowl to obtain greater control (Smith and Hirth 1988).

Spinning and weaving served three ends. The first was to provide clothing for household members. For commoners, this required only the production of maguey-fiber textiles; cotton textiles were reserved for the nobility (Durán 1971: 200). Second, textiles were produced to meet tribute assessments. Loads of cloth were demanded by both local rulers and Aztec tribute collectors on a regular schedule: once, twice, or four times a year (Berdan 1975: 105–8; Carrasco 1977; Guzmán 1938; Hicks 1982). Few details are available concerning how a town's collective assessment was allotted to individual families. Tribute was paid in either maguey-fiber or cotton textiles (Paso y Troncoso 1979: 73, 213, 221, 228, 233–4). The textiles for tribute were produced in standardized sizes and carried specified designs (Anawalt 1981: 29; Berdan 1975: 354). According to the *Matricula de Tributos* (Barlow 1949), the imperial tribute in textiles, alone, amounted to 125,000 loads of cotton textiles and 17,000 loads of maguey-fiber textiles.

Beyond the needs of family and state, textiles may also have been produced for market sale. A profusion of maguey-fiber and cotton textiles were available in urban markets (Cortés 1970: 63; Díaz 1956: 216; Durán 1971: 279). However, it may be that much of the cloth in the market was tribute cloth that had entered the market system (Brumfiel 1976: 209; Litvak 1971: 118; Molíns Fábrega 1954–5: 329–30); little cloth may have been produced specifically for market sale.

Under Aztec rule, women's workloads would have probably increased substantially because of the increased tribute assessments to which conquered peoples were subject. Conquest entailed the production of great quantities of cloth for imperial tribute. In addition, it appears that local rulers increased their own demand for tribute once they fell subject to Aztec rule. For example, the people of Tepexpan remembered the history of their tribute assessments as follows:

> In the time of their heathendon they were, the natives say, an autonomous republic. They paid no tribute to their rulers, they just gave them recognition by giving them hares and rabbits and quail and snakes and other game birds daily; they were *chichimecs*, until several years later a chief named Axoquauzin came to rule, of somewhat greater sophistication, to whom every eighty days they contributed four loads of maguey-fiber mantles, each of twenty mantles, and eighty loincloths of maguey-fiber and another four loads of finer maguey-fiber cloths called *ayates*. And later, fifty years before the reign of Montezuma, ruler of Mexico, Tencuiozin held the rule of Tepexpa to whom the natives of the said town began to pay tribute and every eighty days they paid him in tribute fifty cotton mantles, four lengths wide and eight spans long, and another thirty cotton mantles four spans long and four lengths wide, and another forty mantles embroidered with dyed rabbit's hair for clothing and twenty loads of cocoa beans of 24,000 beans per load from Xoconusco, and forty skirts and as many blouses and twenty loads of chili and as many of pumpkin seeds. (Paso y Troncoso 1979: 233–4)

Archaeological Evidence

Archaeological evidence of women weaving is provided by spindle whorls, the perforated ceramic disks used to weight the spindle during spinning (figure 8.4; Parsons 1972; Smith and Hirth 1988). Spindle whorls are readily identifiable and almost imperishable. Their frequencies in archaeological contexts provide a good gauge of the intensity of cloth production in ancient Mexico.[1]

Spindle whorls vary in terms of diameter, weight, and hole size. Parsons (1972) has demonstrated that they fall naturally into two categories. Small spindle whorls weigh 10 g or less and have hole

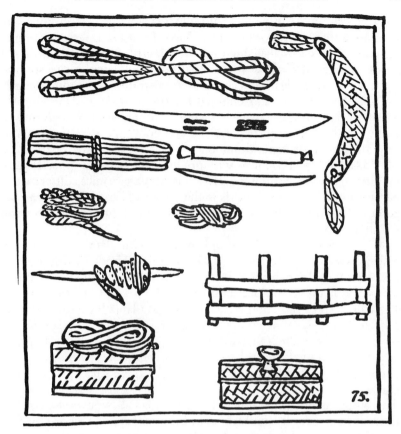

Figure 8.4 Weaving and spinning equipment from the chapter "How the (noble) women were trained." Note the ceramic spindle whorl on the end of the spindle. (After Sahagún 1950–69: bk. 8, ch. 16)

diameters of 2–4 mm. Large spindle whorls weigh more than 10 g with hole diameters of 6–12 mm. Parsons suggests that the small and large spindle whorls were used to spin different fibers: the small light whorls would have been used on the shorter, finer cotton fiber and the large heavy whorls would have been used on the longer, coarser maguey fiber. This suggestion has been validated by recent ethnoarchaeological research (Parsons and Parsons 1985), and it is widely accepted (e.g Mason 1980; Smith and Hirth 1988).

Representative samples of spindle whorls are available from several Late Postclassic sites in Central Mexico (figure 8.2). Huexotla, Xaltocan, and Xico have all been sampled using intensive systematic surface survey (Brumfiel 1976, 1980, 1986, 1987b). Sample sizes at the three sites varied from 1 percent in the urban core at Huexotla to 11 percent in Huexotla's piedmont sector, at Xaltocan, and at Xico. Even the 1 percent sample is large enough to supply reliable estimates of artifact populations. The 11 percent samples also allow for the definition of internal site structure since they were collected according to a stratified random sampling procedure (cf. Jermann and Dunnell 1979).

Huexotla's, Xaltocan, and Xico were all occupied prior to Aztec rule (i.e. the "Early Aztec" period, AD 1150–1350); they were also occupied during the period of Aztec dominance (i.e. the "Late Aztec" period, AD 1350–1521). When collections with predominantly Early Aztec ceramics are compared with predominantly Late Aztec ceramics, differences in the frequencies of spindle whorls in the early and late collections provide a good indication of the changing intensity of cloth production within the Valley of Mexico.

This information can be supplemented with data from Morelos. Coatlan Viejo is a Late Aztec site in Morelos, about 90 km from the Aztec capital of Tenochtitlan. It has also been investigated by means of intensive systematic surface collection; 25 percent of the site was collected (Mason 1980). Some data are also available from excavations at Xochicalco and Coatetelco (Smith and Hirth 1988). These sites are somewhat closer to the Valley of Mexico (80 km from Tenochtitlan), and they were occupied both before and during the period of Aztec dominance. Spindle whorl frequencies for all these sites appear in table 8.1.

The ethnohistorical documents suggest that all women wove cloth. This leads us to expect a uniform distribution of spindle whorls at Aztec sites. Within sites, this is true. Spindle whorls are scattered in low but even frequencies across sites with no particularly dense concentrations that would suggest specialized cloth production. The spindle whorl distribution within sites suggests that spinning and cloth production were common household activities.

There are, however, noticeable differences in the frequencies of spindle whorls between sites. Large (maguey-fiber) spindle whorls range from a high frequency of 3.1 per 1000 rim sherds at Early Aztec Huexotla to none at Late Aztec Xico. Small (cotton-fiber) spindle whorls range from a high of 22.0 per 1000 rim sherds at Coatlan Viejo in Morelos to a low of 0.4 per 1000 rim sherds at Aztec Xico. In addition, at least within the Valley of Mexico, spindle whorl frequencies are higher for the Early Aztec period than for the period of Aztec dominance. This clearly contradicts our expectation that cloth production increased after Aztec dominance. These data require some explication.

Prior to Aztec dominance, the intensity of cloth production seems to have been inversely related to the intensity of the agricultural production.

Table 8.1 Spindle whorl counts and frequencies for five Central Mexican sites. Figures in parentheses are frequencies per 1000 rim sherds. Asterisked figures in parentheses are frequencies per 1000 "quantified sherds".

	Early Aztec	Late Aztec
Valley of Mexico		
Huexotla		
Large spindle whorls	11 (3.1)	44 (1.6)
Small spindle whorls	10 (2.8)	37 (1.3)
Total rims	3582	27,720
Xaltocan		
Large spindle whorls	7 (1.0)	2 (0.3)
Small spindle whorls	6 (0.9)	7 (1.1)
Total rims	6661	6418
Xico		
Large spindle whorls	1 (0.2)	0
Small spindle whorls	5 (1.0)	1 (0.4)
Total rims	5062	2247
Morelos		
Xochicalco and Coatetelco[a]		
Large spindle whorls	3 (1.2)*	2 (0.4)*
Small spindle whorls	2 (0.8)*	12 (2.8)*
Total Quantified sherds	2402	5006
Coatlan Viejo[b]		
Large spindle whorls		13 (2.4)
Small spindle whorls		119 (22.0)
Total rims		5408

[a] Smith and Hirth 1988
[b] Mason 1980

Thus Xico, in the heart of the labor-intensive *chinampa* zone, spun almost no maguey and very little cotton. Huexotla, in the heart of the rainfall agricultural zone on the eastern side of the Valley of Mexico, produced significant quantities of maguey-fiber cloth, probably from locally grown maguey, and almost as much cotton cloth from imported cotton. The same was true for Xaltocan. With only a limited area of labor-intensive agricultural *chinampas*, Xaltocan appears to have imported both cotton from the (Huastec?) lowlands and maguey-fiber from the dry northern Valley of Mexico. A plausible explanation for the inverse relationship of intensive agriculture and cloth production is that these represented alternative employments for women's labor. When women resided on *chinampas*, they were more inclined to cultivate; where they did not, they took on more spinning and weaving.

Once under Aztec rule, both Xico and Huexotla show a sharp decline in spindle whorl frequency. At Xaltocan, large (maguey-fiber) whorls show a similar decline while the cotton whorls remain at pre-Aztec levels. This is astonishing. Certainly there was no decline in the need for clothing by the people, and certainly the demand for tribute in cloth increased. I would argue that the less intensive production of cloth was made possible by increasing participation in market exchange. By selling foodstuffs in the urban markets, rural households in the Valley of Mexico were able to purchase the textiles they needed to meet their tribute payments. Given a steady demand for food in the urban centers and an ample supply of finished textiles, the shift away from cloth production in rural households would represent a rational reallocation of labor (Brumfiel 1980).

There must have been a steady demand for food in Tenochtitlan's market. Calnek (1978: 100) estimates that only one-quarter to one-third of the city's population could have been supported by foodstuffs paid in tribute. Parsons (1976: 250) estimates that the food paid in tribute would have fed up to one-half of the population. Either way, between 80,000 and 150,000 people would have relied upon the regional market system for food supplies. The Tenochtitlan market must also have held ample supplies of cloth. Tremendous quantities of cloth entered the city as tribute payments, and much of it was redistributed by the Aztec ruler to nobles and commoners who had served the state. It seems probable that a good proportion of the redistributed tribute cloth was eventually taken to the market where it was exchanged for food and other needed goods (cf. Sahagún 1950–69: bk 2, ch. 29, 33; bk 3, ch. 1; bk 6, ch. 23).

If food was produced for sale in urban markets, we should find evidence of intensified food production, and more particularly, intensified food processing from Early to Late Aztec times. Such evidence is in fact present in the data from Huexotla and Xico (tables 8.2 and 3). At Huexotla, Late Aztec collections from the piedmont zones contain high frequencies of three artifact types associated with the collection and processing of maguey sap: plano-convex obsidian scrapers used to scrape the cavity in the maguey plant where the sap accumulated; high-neck jars used to transport the sap from the field to the household; and thick wide-mouth jars possibly used to boil the sap until it was reduced to a thick, sweet, nonperishable syrup (Brumfiel 1976: 105–7).

At Xico and Xaltocan, Late Aztec collections contain high frequencies of fabric-marked pottery, a ceramic ware associated with the production and transport of salt (Charlton 1969). The abundance of fabric-marked

Table 8.2 Counts for maguey sap processing artifacts at Huexotla, by residential sector. Figures in parentheses are frequencies per 1000 rim sherds.

	Early Aztec	Late Aztec
Urban core		
Plano-convex scrapers	4 (1.1)	15 (1.7)
High-neck jars	71 (19.8)	161 (18.4)
Thick, wide-mouth jars	17 (4.7)	40 (4.5)
Total rims	3582	8737
Piedmont		
Plano-convex scrapers		120 (7.2)
High-neck jars		774 (46.2)
Thick, wide-mouth jars		600 (35.8)
Total rims		16,736
Lakeshore		
Plano-convex scrapers		2 (0.9)
High-neck jars		62 (27.6)
Thick, wide-mouth jars		12 (5.3)
Total rims		2247

pottery does not match the quantities found at salt-producing locales in the Valley of Mexico (cf. Mayer-Oakes 1959), and so rather than indicating high levels of salt production, the fabric-marked pottery at Xaltocan and Xico must indicate high levels of salt use.

Current practices at Xaltocan suggest that salt was used extensively in commercial fish processing. Today, fish processing is a major industry in Xaltocan (Abundio Hernández, personal communication, 1987). Since the lake surrounding the community has been drained, Xaltocanos travel

Table 8.3 Counts for fabric-marked pottery at four Central Mexican sites. Figures in parentheses are frequencies per 1000 rim sherds.

	Early Aztec	Late Aztec
Huexotla	30 (8)	792 (26)
Xaltocan	1244 (187)	922 (144)
Xico	372 (73)	407 (181)
Coatlan Viejo		349 (64)

to Mexico City to purchase fresh fish in the urban produce market. Returning to Xaltocan, they salt the fish heavily, roast it in corn husks or maguey-leaf parchment, and take it to sell in the market towns such as Zumpango, Otumba, and Pachuca. The ratio of salt to fish is high: one kilo of salt to every ten to fifteen kilos of fish (Margarita Ramites, H. personal communication, 1987); there is little doubt that the salt prolongs the market life of the fish. The tradition of corn-husk roasted fish is widespread in the Valley of Mexico; it is reported in Pérez's ethnography of fishing in the chinampa community of San Luis Tlaxialtemalco (1985: 119). The tradition also has considerable time depth; Sahagún (1950–69: bk 10, ch. 22) reports that the vendor of fish sold "toasted fish wrapped in maize husks, fish wrapped in maize husks and cooked in an olla."

Thus, evidence of less intensive cloth production in the Valley of Mexico is accompanied by evidence of more intensive food processing. However, this pattern holds only for areas within the immediate hinterlands of Tenochtitlan where proximity to the city and access to water-borne transport encouraged specialization in bulky, low cost foodstuffs (Brown 1980; Hassig 1985; Rojas 1986). Transportation costs increased rapidly away from the Valley of Mexico lake system, making the production of food for urban sale less attractive. In these more distant hinterland regions we might expect that cloth production instead of cloth purchase served as a means of meeting tribute payments. If so, spindle whorl frequencies in these areas should be quite high.

This is, in fact, the case. The frequency of small spindle whorls increases from Early to Late Aztec times at Xochicalco and Coatetelco, and at Late Aztec Coatlan Viejo the frequency of small spindle whorls reaches an incredible 22.0 per 1000 rim sherds, about ten times more frequent than large and small spindle whorls combined at Valley of Mexico sites.[2]

Thus, the archaeological evidence suggests that despite the emphasis upon women as weavers in the ethnohistoric record, women in the Valley of Mexico turned from weaving to market-oriented productive activities during the period of Aztec dominance. Only outside the Valley of Mexico, where distance prevented access to the Tenochtitlan market, did women produce great quantities of the tribute cloth with which the Aztec empire transacted its business. In both cases, however, women's workloads must have increased substantially. We now turn to an examination of cooking to see if women altered their domestic routines to cope with the state's demands upon their labor.

Cooking

Work processes

Earlier in this century in rural Mexico, four items were essential to every household: the hearth, the griddle, the grinding stone, and the pot (Redfield 1930: 35). Interestingly, all four appear in the *Codex Mendoza* (1964: Lám. LXI (see figure 8.5); Coe 1985, 21: 46–7) where a mother instructs her daughter in the art of making tortillas. Because of the basic techniques of maize processing, food preparation in the sixteenth century, as in the twentieth, must have consumed much time and energy.

Most maize was processed into a lime-treated maize dough (*nextamalli*) before it was cooked. Shell maize was placed in a pot (*nexcomitl*) together with water and lime and brought to a boil. The mixture was allowed to cool several hours or overnight, during which time the maize softened, the hulls were loosened from the kernels, and the niacin in the

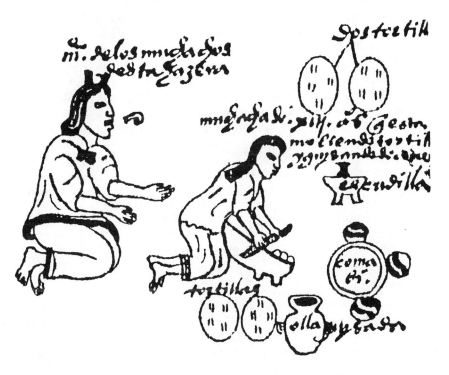

Figure 8.5 A mother teaches her daughter to make tortillas. Note the jar containing soaked corn and the griddle on a three-stone hearth waiting to receive tortillas. (After *Codex Mendoza* 1964: Lám. LXI)

maize was released making it available to human digestion (Katz, Hediger, and Valleroy 1974). The maize was drained and rinsed, placed on the grinding stone (*metlatl*) and ground to a fine dough. Grinding was time-consuming. Before the introduction of mechanized maize mills, a woman spent six to eight hours daily grinding maize into dough for her family (Chiñas 1973: 41; Lewis 1951: 99; Redfield 1930: 87; Whetten 1948: 305).

Making tortillas from dough took additional time. Balls of dough had to be patted into thin sheets and placed on a ceramic griddle (*comalli*) to cook over a three-stone hearth (*tlecuilitl*). Today, making tortillas from machine-ground maize takes an hour per meal, two or three hours a day (Foster 1948: 48; Lewis 1959: 25, 52; Swanson 1979: 383). One way a woman can save time is by making a few large tortillas instead of many smaller ones to feed her family (Foster 1948: 48). In the seventeenth century, Clavigero (1945: II, 355) observed that some tortillas were thick and three or four times larger than the average, but that Indian nobles, who had servants in their kitchens, ate thin small tortillas. The large tortillas depicted in the *Codex Mendoza* (1964: Lám. LIX–LXI) may indicate that women were being forced to cut corners under the stress of a heavy work load.

Variety was introduced to the tortilla-based diet in two ways. First, the tortilla itself was sometimes enriched by adding honey, eggs, or amaranth seed into the tortilla dough (Sahagún 1950–69: bk 10, ch. 19). Second, tortillas were accompanied by various sauces and stews. The sauces (*molli*), made by grinding chili peppers with other vegetables, seeds, and herbs, came in endless variation:

> . . . sauces of juices, shredded [food] with chili, with gourd seeds, with tomatoes, with smoked chili, with hot chilis, with yellow chilis, with mild red chilis, with an early variety of chili, with green chilis, with large tomatoes . . . bean sauce, toasted beans, mushroom sauce, sauce of small gourds, sauce of large tomatoes, sauce of ordinary tomatoes, sauce of various kinds of sorrel, avocado sauce. (Sahugún 1950–69: bk 10, ch. 19)

The basic implements for making sauces were the bowl-shaped, three-legged, stone or ceramic mortar (*molcaxitl*) and a small stone pestle (*texolotl*). A ceramic mortar and stone pestle appear in the scene of tortilla making in the *Codex Mendoza* (1964: Lám. LXI). Stews (*tlemolli*) showed even greater variety. Often only a pot of beans, stews were also prepared from fresh vegetables (nopales, squash or squash blossoms, mushrooms, tender maize, and greens) or meats (rabbit, gopher, birds, fish, frogs, tadpoles, turkey, or dog) (Sahagún 1950–69: bk 8, ch. 13). These were simmered with sauces in an earthenware pot (*comitl*).

Pots were also used to prepare *atolli*, the starchy liquid of boiled, strained maize dough (Hernández 1888: 198). The atole could be flavored by adding kernels of tender maize, toasted maize or amaranth, fermented maize dough, ground beans, chia, chili peppers, or honey (Sahagún 1950–69: bk 8, ch. 13; bk 10, ch. 26). Atole was a breakfast food (Clavigero 1945: II, 356; Hernández 1888: 198), but it was also taken at other meals in the company of other foods. Atole was thought to have medicinal powers, and it seems to have been consumed at the start of each day to strengthen the body against illness (Hernández 1888: 198; Sahagún 1950–69: bk 10, ch. 28).

In addition to these staples of the Mexican diet, there were two special purpose foods. Tamales (maize dough dumplings) require more time and labor than any other native Mexican foods. The dough must be beaten for a long time before it is ready for cooking (Redfield 1929: 176), and dumplings must be individually wrapped in corn husks. This is probably why tamales were most commonly eaten by nobles (Paso y Troncoso 1979; Sahagún 1950–69: bk 8, ch. 15) whose kitchens were staffed by women fulfilling their tribute obligations (Hodge 1984: 44, 65, 108). Commoners, then as now, made tamales only on ritual occasions, often staying up all night in female work parties to get the job done (*Codex Mendoza* 1964: Lám. LXIX; Redfield 1929: 176–8; Sahagún 1950–69: bk 2, ch. 27, 28, 34, 38 (figure 8.6); bk 3, ch. 1; bk 4, ch. 37; bk 6, ch. 23; bk 8, app. B). Appearing in ritual contexts, tamales may have been equated with human flesh (Sahagún 1950–69: bk 2, ch. 22, 24, 29, 32, 34). The pot (*comitl*) in which tamales were steamed was regarded as a symbolic womb (Sahagún 1950–69: bk 5, ch. 8).

War provisions were another special purpose food. They included finely ground toasted maize and chia seeds (*pinolli*) and dried maize dough, both of which could be reconstituted with water, and toasted tortillas (Sahagún 1950–69: bk 8, ch. 10). Griddles were used to parch the seeds and toast the tortillas.

The basic cooking vessels, then, were the griddle and the pot. These different vessel types produced different dishes: tortillas and pinolli on the one hand; stews, atoles, and beans on the other. Differing ratios of these vessel types can inform us of changes in patterns of food preparation. As Blanton et al. (1981: 71–2) suggest, patterns of food preparation may be sensitive to changes in the schedules of household members.

Archaeological evidence

Differences in the ratios of cooking pots to griddles signal changes in the pattern of food preparation in Central Mexico. They signal changes in

Figure 8.6 Tamales and meat stew served at a feast honoring the birth of a child. (After Sahagún 1950–69: bk 2, ch. 37)

the proportion of wet and dry foods in the diet: stews, atoles, and beans as opposed to tortillas and pinolli. Differences in the time spent in food preparation are also indicated. With the exception of tamales, an infrequent ritual food, cooking pots produce labor-saving "one-pot" meals while griddles are used for more labor-intensive foods: tortillas prepared in individual portions or slowly roasting cracked maize. Also indicated are changes in the portability of goods; wet foods are less easily carried and consumed away from home and dry foods more easily so (Blanton et al. 1981: 71). Finally, the pot-to-griddle ratio reflects people's ability to indulge the Mexican preference for foods cooked in pots, foods that traditionally carried positive symbolic connotations. As mentioned above, atole was thought to have curative powers, the steamed corn meal of the tamale symbolized human flesh, and pots were thought of as symbolic wombs. Clearly, the pot-to-griddle ratio is fraught with cultural meaning!

For the purposes of this study, pots include the rims of all types of thin to medium-walled, short-neck jars. Specifically excluded are the high-neck jars associated with maguey sap collection and the thick wide-mouth jars associated with maguey sap reduction. Even so, our category "pot" is probably a heterogeneous category that could in the future be greatly refined (cf. Costin 1986: 198–211; also Foster 1948: 81–4; Reina and Hill 1978: 24–8). Tortilla griddles present no problems of classification; they are a functionally homogeneous, highly distinctive ceramic form: nearly horizontal plates with well-burnished upper surfaces and roughened bottoms.

The ratios of pots to griddles at Huexotla, Xaltocan, and Xico are presented in table 8.4. The data for Huexotla are very stable. Ratios in the site's elite urban core are essentially the same for both Early and Late occupation. Similar ratios occur outside the urban zone in the piedmont and lakeshore sectors. In all the Huexotla collections, the pot-to-griddle ratio is close to 33:100. In contrast, the data for Xaltocan and Xico reveal a clear-cut temporal pattern. The ratio of pots to griddles decreases dramatically from Early to Late Aztec times, at Xaltocan from 62:100 to 29:100, at Xico from 155:100 to 30:100.

In some ways, these data are surprising. The uniformity of pot-to-griddle ratios at Huexotla across both the elite urban and lower class piedmont and lakeshore sectors is unexpected given the temporal and social differences apparent in other aspects of the Huexotla data. In addition, the falling pot-to-griddle ratios at Xaltocan and Xico indicate a move away from labor-saving pot foods and toward labor-intensive griddle foods which is somewhat surprising, given the intensification of tribute demands under the Aztec state. Finally, the pot-to-griddle ratios at Xaltocan and Xico during Late Aztec times fall very close to the 33:100 ratio which occurs at Huexotla.

Following Blanton et al. (1981: 71), I would suggest that the convergence of all these collections on relatively low pot-to-griddle ratios can be explained by the portability of dry griddle foods, the ease with which dry foods can be carried and consumed away from home. The decline in the ratio of pots to griddles suggests, then, domestic adjustments to a more mobile labor force. In making tortillas, women used their domestic labor to facilitate work activity carried out at some distance from the home.

A part of this work might have consisted of labor drafts imposed by imperial rulers. Men and women who supplied labor to the palaces of local rulers were fed from palace kitchens (Cortés 1970: 64; Díaz 1956: 210–11; Sahagún 1950–69: bk 9, ch. 13), but when responding to calls for labor on large public works (coatequitl), men may have carried their own provisions (although Zorita 1963: 203–4 implies they did not). Dried provisions were also prepared for men going off to war (Sahagún 1950–69: bk 8, ch. 19). But most commonly, they might be supplied to family members working away from the home to procure raw materials or to market household produce. One of the effects of Aztec dominance was to draw labor away from the household context; women's work in food preparation subsidized this labor mobilization.

At Huexotla, this pattern was achieved prior to Aztec rule, perhaps as a consequence of Huexotla's early incorporation into a pre-Aztec

Table 8.4 The ratio of pots to griddles at three Central Mexican sites. Figures in parentheses are frequencies per 100 rim sherds.

	Early Aztec	Late Aztec
Huexotla		
Urban Core		
Pots	192 (5.4)	481 (5.5)
Griddles	579 (16.2)	1518 (17.4)
Pots:Griddles	33:100	32:100
Piedmont		
Pots		1239 (7.4)
Griddles		3599 (21.5)
Pots:griddles		34:100
Lakeshore		
Pots		190 (8.4)
Griddles		596 (26.5)
Pots:griddles		32:100
Xaltocan		
Pots	758 (11.4)	456 (7.1)
Griddles	1213 (18.2)	1558 (24.3)
Pots:griddles	62:100	29:100
Xico		
Pots	722 (14.3)	170 (7.6)
Griddles	467 (9.2)	562 (25.0)
Pots:griddles	155:100	30:100

imperial system focused on nearby Texcoco, and its participation in a pre-Aztec market system unifying the central Valley of Mexico (Alva Ixtlilxochitl 1975–7: I, 321; Brumfiel 1986: 269). Xaltocan and Xico converged on this pattern of food preparation only after the two communities had fallen under Aztec rule with the demands for labor and tribute goods which such dominance implied.

Work away from the home appears to have been correlated with market procurement of tribute cloth. At all three Valley of Mexico sites discussed above, spindle whorl frequencies during Late Aztec times were relatively low, as were pot-to-griddle ratios. In contrast, at the Late Aztec site of Coatlan Viejo, high spindle whorl frequencies are accompanied by high ratios of pots to griddles (well over 100:100, cf. Mason 1980: 120–1). There is a certain logic to this. Within the Valley of Mexico, extra-domestic institutions lightened the work of women in meeting tribute assessments, but these institutions required a more mobile labor force, supported by more labor-intensive patterns of food preparation. Outside the Valley of Mexico, labor was more closely linked to the household. The burden of tribute cloth production fell squarely upon female members of the household units who retained less labor-intensive methods of food preparation.

Conclusion

The most striking thing about these data on women's production in Central Mexico is their variability. The variability exists despite very large sample sizes which suggests that it cannot be attributed to random error. The variability is real. I have accounted for this variability by relating it to factors such as the presence of agricultural *chinampas*, proximity to urban markets, degree of social status, and dominance by an imperial state. The suggestion is, then, that women's work is affected by the same broad range of ecological, economic, social, and political variables that affect the work of men. The household setting of much women's work in Central Mexico did not insulate women from the world beyond their patios.

A high degree of variability in women's work might be anticipated on the basis of recent discussions of the household. These discussions have presented the household as a flexible social institution, differing in structure and operation according to the opportunities and constraints afforded by its environment (McGuire, Smith, and Martin 1986; Rapp 1978a; Smith, Wallerstein, and Evers 1984). If this is so, then in settings of great ecological and social complexity such as late prehispanic Central Mexico, both households in general and women's work in particular would be expected to display considerable diversity according to local circumstances.

The variability of women's work that is visible archaeologically contrasts sharply with the narrow stereotypes presented in the ethno-historic literature. On closer examination, it becomes apparent that the documents present more of a "model for" than a "model of" women's work. The presentation of women as weavers and women as cooks, though based in reality, was also a cultural ideal. In many symbolic contexts, women were equated with weaving (Anawalt 1981: 13). For instance, newborn baby girls were presented with the symbols of womenhood: "the spinning whorl, the battan, the reed basket [for unspun fiber], the spinning bowl, the skeins, the shuttle, her little skirt, her little blouse" (Sahagún 1959–60 bk 6, ch. 37 (figure 8.7). A woman's weaving equipment was also placed with her when she died. Anawalt also comments upon the unpleasant sanctions that encouraged women to become competent weavers.

Figure 8.7 A baby is washed and given the symbols of its gender. The emblems of war or the tools of craftsmen were presented to male infants. Female infants received a broom and weaving equipment. (After *Codex Mendoza* 1964: Lám. LIX)

Weaving and cooking were also considered occupations of high social status; marketing was a metaphor for poverty. Rulers' daughters were exhorted to apply themselves to weaving and cooking, while marketing was disparaged: "The herbs, the wood, the strands of chili, the cakes of salt, the nitrous soil are not thy desert, not thy gift . . . because thou art a noblewomen" (Sahagún 1950–69: bk 6, ch. 18). Other contexts make it clear that selling vegetables, firewood, and salt in the marketplace was regarded as a sign of acute destitution (Alva Ixtlilxochitl 1975–7: II, 131; Sahagún 1950–69: bk 2, app. 2).

The idealization of cooking and weaving as women's roles may be related to the political significance of these activities. Pre-Aztec Mexico was an open, highly competitive political field, and within this field, clothing and food served as idioms of political negotiation (Brumfiel 1987a). Women who cooked and wove competently were women who were most capable of advancing men's claims to positions of status and power (figure 8.8). Later, under Aztec rule, cloth continued to serve political ends. Allocated to servants of the state, cloth became a means of maintaining centralized political control.

Figure 8.8 A man discharges his obligations to his associates by presenting them with the products of a woman's labor: woven cloth, food, and drink. Behind him, his wife dutifully spins. (After *Codex Mendoza* 1964: Lám. LXIX)

In addition, since women's status emerges as a central issue in all efforts to extend state power or to resist such extensions (Gailey 1985; Rapp 1978b; Silverblatt 1988), the idealization of cooking and weaving is almost certainly related to the broader process of Aztec political development. Gailey argues that, in emerging states, control over the determination and allocation of labor and products is the battleground of kin/civil conflict. Women's work becomes a particular focus of attention because women are both makers of goods and makers of people: "Control of women's dual potential becomes an obvious metaphor for the appropriation of kin group continuity" (Gailey 1985: 83). We might expect that such important issues would affect the way in which women and women's work are presented in the ethnohistorical sources. The sixteenth-century documents were produced by men of the native ruling class to instruct men of the Spanish ruling class, and they project an image of women's labor attuned to the needs of the state.

This image was contested by a second view, set forward in popular folklore. Here, cooking and weaving served as symbols of human reproduction. As mentioned above, tamales and cooking pots were associated with pregnancy and birth; spinning and weaving carried similar connotations (McCafferty and McCafferty forthcoming; Sullivan 1982). For example, the Aztec goddess Tlazolteotl-Ixcuina was both the "Great Spinner and Weaver" and the "Mother Goddess", the great giver of life (Sullivan 1982: 14). In humor and in ritual, spinning and weaving served as metaphors for female life-cycles, human sexuality, and childbirth (McCafferty and McCafferty forthcoming). The popular images linking women's work with human reproduction contested and possibly limited the appropriation of household labor by political elites. Calling attention to the dependence of reproduction upon the availability of labor for commoners' self-maintenance, such images may have contributed to the high status enjoyed by women in Aztec society (cf. Kellogg 1988; McCafferty and McCafferty 1988).

The images of women's work presented in the ethnohistorical literature and in popular folklore were parts of an ideological discourse over the disposition of productive and reproductive labor. As such, the images put forward were necessarily abstract and generalized. After all, the issue at stake was fairly simple: what were the limits of state exactions of goods and labor? However, while the simplified images presented by ethnohistory and folklore were adequate for the conduct of an ideological debate, they do not satisfactorily convey the complex reality of women's work.

Mexican women found themselves in a wide range of economic, social, and political contexts. They responded to the constraints and opportunities that surrounded them by working out a number of different strategies for managing the demands of both family and state. We must agree with Soustelle (1961: 185) that "The Mexican woman . . . had a great deal to do."

But Mexican women were not passive victims of emerging political power. They participated in the definition of its limits, and they devised strategies to deal with the changing circumstances that it created. Aztec women were flexible, adaptive, and dynamic elements in a dynamic system. While the ethnohistoric record limits us to a narrow, ahistorical stereotype of women's production, archaeology forces us to recognize the realities of women's production, characterized by variability and change.

ACKNOWLEDGMENTS

My thanks to Meg Conkey, Joan Gero, Cathy Costin, Geoffrey McCafferty, Sharisse McCafferty, Mike Smith, and Alison Wylie, for their very helpful comments on earlier versions of this paper. In writing it I benefited greatly from access to unpublished work by Frances Berdan, Geoffrey and Sharisse McCafferty, Mike Smith and Ken Hirth. I am grateful for their generosity. Fieldwork at Huexotla, Xico, and Xaltocan was supported by grants from the National Science Foundation (GS-38470), the Mellon Foundation, and the H. John Heinz III Charitable Trust.

NOTES

1   The archaeological context of some spindle whorls suggests that men may have participated in cloth production under different circumstances. For instance, Geoffrey and Sharisse McCafferty (personal communication 1988) report "In a recent excavation of a mass burial in San Andres Cholula by Arqlgo, Sergio Suarez of the Centro Regional de Puebla, 50 individuals were buried around a central pair. Many spindle whorls were found as offerings, associated with both male and female interments. That both males and females were buried with spindle whorls suggests that they may have been involved in textile production. Perhaps in this particular case the scale of production was sufficiently great relative to household production, that males also participated."

Spinning by males has also been reported by the Mexican ethnographer Mendizábal (1947: 162).

2   Smith and Hirth (1988: 356) have been able to date the initiation of the elevated spindle whorl frequencies at Coatetelco-Xochicalco to the first half of the Late Postclassic period, AD 1350–1485. On this basis they deny the relationship between Aztec imperialism and increased cloth production in Morelos: "the shift in the locus of textile production . . . took place nearly a century *before* the formation of the Aztec empire." Elsewhere, however, Smith (1986: 77) documents the likelihood of imperial conquests in the Coatetelco-Xochicalco region by the Tepanecs who preceded the Aztecs as an imperial, tribute-extracting power within the Valley of Mexico and beyond. Thus, although the initiation of elevated spindle whorl frequencies at Coatetelco-Xochicalco may precede the formation of the Aztec empire by a century, they may still coincide with the initiation of (Tepanec) imperial dominance in the region.

REFERENCES

Alva Ixtlilxochitl, Fernando de (1975–7). *Obras Históricas*, 2 vols, E. O'Gorman, ed. México: Universidad Nacional Autónoma de México. [orig. 1600–40].

248 E. M. BRUMFIEL

Anawalt, Patricia (1981). *Indian Clothing Before Cortes.* Norman: University of Oklahoma Press.
Armillas, Pedro (1964). "Northern Mesoamerica." In *Prehistoric Man in the New World,* J. D. Jennings and E. Norbeck, eds. Chicago: University of Chicago Press, 291–329.
Barlow, Robert H. (1949). *The Extent of the Empire of the Culhua-Mexica.* Berkeley: University of California Press.
Berdan, Frances F. (1975). "Trade, Tribute and Market in the Aztec Empire." Ph.D. dissertation, Anthropology Department, University of Texas.
Blanton, Richard E., Stephen A. Kowalewski, Gary Feinman, and Jill Appel (1981). *Ancient Mesoamerica: A Comparison of Change in Three Regions.* Cambridge: Cambridge University Press.
Broda, Johanna (1976). "Los Estamentos en el Ceremonial Mexicana." In *Estratificación Social en la Mesoamérica Prehispánica,* P. Carrasco et al., eds. México, D. F.: Instituto Nacional de Antropología e Historia, 37–66.
Brown, Kenneth L. (1980). "Comments on Brumfiel's 'Specialization, Market Exchange, and the Aztec State: A View from Huexotla.'" *Current Anthropology* 21: 467–8.
Brumfiel, Elizabeth M. (1976). "Specialization and Exchange at the Late Postclassic (Aztec) Community of Huexotla Mexico." Ph.D. dissertation, Department of Anthropology, University of Michigan.
—— (1980). "Specialization, Market Exchange, and the Aztec State: A View from Huexotla." *Current Anthropology* 21: 459–78.
—— (1986). "The Division of Labor at Xico: The Chipped Stone Industry." In *Economic Aspects of Prehispanic Highland Mexico,* B. L. Isaac, ed. Greenwich, CT: JAI Press, 245–79.
—— (1987a). "Elite and Utilitarian Crafts in the Aztec State." In *Specialization, Exchange, and Complex Societies,* E. M. Brumfiel and T. K. Earle, eds. Cambridge: Cambridge University Press, 245–79.
—— (1987b). "Informe al Instituto Nacional de Antropología e Historia Sobre el Proyecto Xaltocan Azteca." Paper on file, Department of Anthropology and Sociology, Albion College and the Instituto Nacional de Antropología e Historia, México, D.F.
Calnek, Edward E. (1978). "El sistema de mercado en Tenochtitlan." In *Economía Política e Ideologia en el México Prehispánico,* P. Carrasco and J. Broda, eds. México, D.F.: Nueva Imagen, 97–114.
Carrasco, Pedro (1977). Los Señores de Xochimilco en 1548. *Tlalocan* 7: 229–65.
Charlton, Thomas H. (1969). "Texcoco Fabric-marked Pottery, Tlatels and Salt Making." *American Antiquity* 34: 73–6.
Chiñas, Beverly L. (1973). *The Isthmus Zapotecs: Women's Roles in Cultural Context.* New York: Holt, Rinehart & Winston.
Clavigero, Francisco Javier (1945). *Historia Antigua de México* [1780–1], 3 vols. México, D.F.: Porrua.
Codex Mendoza (1964). "Codex Mendoza." In *Antigüedades de México Basadas en la Recopilación de Lord Kingsborough,* J. Corona Nuñez, ed. Mexico, D.F.: Secretaria de Hacienda y Crédito Público, vol. I: 1–149.

Coe, Sophie (1985). "Aztec Cuisine." *Petits Propos Culinaires* 19: 11–22, 20: 44–59, 21: 45–56.
Cortés, Hernan (1970). *Cartas de Relación* [1519–26]. México, D.F.: Porrua.
Costin, Cathy L. (1986). "From Chiefdom to Empire State: Ceramic Economy Among the Prehispanic Wanka of Highland Peru." Ph.D. dissertation, Anthropology Department, University of California at Los Angeles.
Díaz del Castillo, Bernal (1956). *The Discovery and Conquest of Mexico* [1568]. A. P. Maudslay, tr. New York: Noonday Press.
Durán, Diego (1971). *Book of the Gods and Rites and the Ancient Calendar* [1570]. F. Horcasitas and D. Heyden, tr. Norman: University of Oklahoma Press.
Foster, George M. (1948). *Empire's Children: The People of Tzintzuntzan.* Washington: Smithsonian Institution.
Gailey, Christine Ward (1985). "The State of the State in Anthropology." *Dialectical Anthropology* 9: 65–89.
Gonçalves de Lima, Oswaldo (1956). *El Maguey y el Pulque en los Códices Mexicanos.* México, D.F.: Fondo de Cultura Económica.
Guzmán, Eulalia (1938). "Un Manuscrito de la Colección Boturini que Trata de los Antiguos Señores de Teotihuacán." *Ethnos* 3: 89–103.
Hassig, Ross (1985). *Trade, Tribute and Transportation: The Sixteenth-Century Political Economy of the Valley of Mexico.* Norman: University of Oklahoma Press.
—— (1988). *Aztec Warfare: Imperial Expansion and Political Control.* Norman: University of Oklahoma Press.
Hellbom, Anna-Britta (1967). *La Participación Cultural de las Mujeres: Indias y Mestizas en el México Precortesiano y Postrevolucionario.* Stockholm: The Ethnographical Museum, Monograph Series No. 10.
Hernández, Francisco (1888). *Cuatro Libros de la Naturaleza y Virtudes Medicinales de las Plantas y Animales de la Nueva España* [1571]. A. León, ed. Morelia: Escuela de Artes.
Hicks, Federic (1982). "Texcoco in the Early 16th century: The State, the City and the *Calpolli*." *American Ethnologist* 9: 320–49.
Hodge, Mary G. (1984). *Aztec City-States.* Ann Arbor: University of Michigan Museum of Anthropology Memoirs No. 18.
Jermann, Jerry V. and Robert C. Dunnell (1979). "Some Limitations of Isopleth Mapping in Archaeology." In *Computer Graphics in Archaeology*, S. Upham, ed. Tempe: Arizona State University, Anthropological Research Papers 15, 31–60.
Katz, S. H., M. L. Hediger, and L. A. Valleroy (1974). "Traditional Maize Processing Techniques in the New World." *Science* 184: 765–73.
Kellogg, Susan (1988). "Cognatic Kinship and Religion: Women in Aztec Society." In *Smoke and Mist: Mesoamerican Studies in Memory of Thelma D. Sullivan*, J. K. Josserand and K. Dakin, eds. Oxford: British Archaeological Reports International Series 402, 666–81.
Lewis, Oscar (1951). *Life in a Mexican Village: Tepoztlán Revisited.* Urbana: University of Illinois Press.
—— (1959). *Five Families.* New York: John Wiley & Sons.

250   E. M. Brumfiel

Litvak K., Jaime (1971). *Cihuatlán y Tepecoacuilco: Provincias Tributarias de México en el Siglo XVI*. México, D.F.: Universidad Nacional Autónoma de México, Instituto de Investigaciones Históricas.

Manrique C., Leonardo (1969). "The Otomi." In *Handbook of Middle American Indians*, vol. 8, R. Wauchope, ed. Austin: University of Texas Press, 602–37.

Mason, Roger D. (1980). Economic and Social Organization of an Aztec Provincial Center: Archaeological Research at Coatlan Viejo, Morelos, Mexico. Ph.D. dissertation, Anthropology Department, University of Texas.

McCafferty, Sharisse D. and Geoffrey G. McCafferty (1988). "Powerful Women and the Myth of Male Dominance in Aztec Society." *Archaeological Review from Cambridge* 7: 45–59.

—— (forthcoming). "Mexican Spinning and Weaving as Female Gender Identity." In *Textile Traditions of Mesoamerica and the Andes: An Anthology*, M. Schevill, J. C. Berlo, and N. Dwyer, eds. New York: Garland.

McGuire, Randall H., Joan Smith, and William G. Martin (1986). "Household Structures and the World-economy." *Review* 10: 75–98.

Mayer-Oakes, William J. (1959). "A Stratigraphic Excavation at El Risco, Mexico." *Proceedings of the American Philosophical Society* 103(3): 334–73.

Mendizábal, Miguel O. de (1947). "Evolución Económica y Social del Valle de Mezquital." In *Obras Completas*, vol. 6, 5–195. México, D.F.

Molíns Fábrega, N. (1954–5). "El Códice Mendocino y la Economía de Tenochtitlan." *Revista Mexicana de Estudios Antropológicos* 14: 303–37.

Motolinía (Benavente), Toribio de (1971). *Memoriales o Libro de las Cosas de la Nueva España y de los Naturales de Ella*. [1536–41] México, D.F.: Universidad Nacional Autónoma de México.

Nash, June (1976). "The Aztecs and the Ideology of Male Dominance." *Signs* 4: 349–62.

Parsons, Jeffrey R. (1976). "The Role of Chinampa Agriculture in the Food Supply of Aztec Tenochtitlan." In *Culture and Continuity*, C. Cleland, ed. New York: Academic Press, 233–62.

Parsons, Jeffrey R. and Mary H. Parsons (1990). *Maguey Utilization in Highland Central Mexico: An Archaeological Ethnography*. Ann Arbor: University of Michigan Museum of Anthropology, Anthropological Papers No. 82.

Parsons, Jeffrey R., Elizabeth M. Brumfiel, Mary H. Parsons, and David J. Wilson (1982). *Prehispanic Settlement Patterns in the Southern Valley of Mexico: The Chalco-Xochimilco Region*. Ann Arbor: University of Michigan Museum of Anthropology Memoirs No. 14.

Parsons, Mary H. (1972). "Spindle Whorls from the Teotihuacan Valley, Mexico." In *Miscellaneous Studies in Mexican Prehistory*, M. W. Spence, J. R. Parsons, and M. H. Parsons, eds. Ann Arbor: University of Michigan Museum of Anthropology, Anthropological Papers No. 45, 45–80.

Paso y Troncoso, Francisco del, ed. (1979). *Relaciones Geográficas de México* [1580]. México, D.F.: Editorial Cosmos.

Pérez Espinoza, José Genovevo (1985). "La Pesca en el Medio Lacustre y Chinampero de San Luis Tlaxialtemalco." In *La Cosecha del Agua en la*

Cuenca de México – La Pesca en el Medio Lacustre y Chinampero de San Luis Tlaxiatlemalco, T. Rojas and J. G. Pérez, eds. México, D.F.: Centro de Investigaciones y Estudios Superiores en Antropología Social, 113–29.
Rapp, Rayna (1978a): "Family and Class in Contemporary America: Notes Toward an Understanding of Ideology." *Science and Society* 42: 278–300.
—— (1978b). "The Search for Origins: Unraveling the Threads of Gender Hierarchy." *Critique of Anthropology* 3: 5–24.
Redfield, Margaret Park (1929). "Notes on the Cookery of Tepoztlan, Morelos." *Journal of American Folk-Lore* 42: 167–90.
Redfield, Robert (1930). *Tepoztlan: A Mexican Village*. Chicago: University of Chicago Press.
Reina, Ruben E. and Robert M. Hill, II (1978). *The Traditional Pottery of Guatemala*. Austin: University of Texas Press.
Rojas, José Luis de (1986). *México Tenochtitlan: Economía y Sociedad en el Siglo XVI*. México, D.F.: Fondo de Cultura Económica.
Sahagún, Bernardino de (1950–69). *Florentine Codex: General History of the Things of New Spain* [1577], 11 vols. A. Anderson and C. Dibble, tr. Santa Fe: School of American Research.
Sanders, William T., Jeffrey R. Parsons, and Robert S. Santley (1979). *The Basin of Mexico: Ecological Processes in the Evolution of a Civilization*. New York: Academic Press.
Silverblatt, Irene (1988). "Women in States." *Annual Review of Anthropology* 17: 427–60.
Smith, J., I. Wallerstein, and H. D. Evers, eds (1984). *Households in the World-Economy*. Beverly Hills: Sage.
Smith, Michael E. (1986). "The Role of Social Stratification in the Aztec Empire: A View from the Provinces." *American Anthropologist* 88: 70–91.
Smith, Michael E. and Kenneth G. Hirth (1988). "The Development of Prehispanic Cotton-spinning Technology in Western Morelos, Mexico," *Journal of Field Archaeology* 15: 349–58.
Soustelle, Jacques (1961). *Daily Life of the Aztecs*. P. O'Brien, tr. Stanford: Stanford University Press.
Sullivan, Thelma D. (1982). "Tlazolteotl-Ixcuina: The Great Spinner and Weaver." In *The Art and Iconography of Late Post-Classic Central Mexico*, E. H. Boone, ed. Washington: Dumbarton Oaks, 7–35.
Swanson, Eleanor C. (1979). "Household Task Allocation in a Rural Mexican Community." Ph.D. dissertation, Department of Anthropology, University of Connecticut.
Whetten, Nathan L. (1948). *Rural Mexico*. Chicago: University of Chicago Press.
Zorita, Alonso de (1963). *Life and Labor in Ancient Mexico* [1565]. B. Keen, tr. New Brunswick: Rutgers University Press.

Part IV

Gender and Food Systems

9

The Development of Horticulture in the Eastern Woodlands of North America: Women's Role

Patty Jo Watson and Mary C. Kennedy

Introduction

We begin with the words of some famous anthropologists:

The sound anthropological position is that certain sex-linked behaviors are biologically based, although subject to cultural modifications within limits. (Hoebel 1958: 391)

A limited number of sex-associated characteristics also appear to be transmitted at the genetic level, such as an apparent tendency shared with many other animals for dominance and passivity in the male and female, respectively . . . (Keesing 1966: 75)

The community recognizes that women must be accompanied by their babies wherever they go; hence they cannot hunt or fish as efficiently as the unencumbered males. Males are therefore free to be mobile and active while females have been accorded, by nature, a prior responsibility or obligation to rear additional members of the community in the only way this can be done. Hence the community assigns work involving more mobility to men and work involving less mobility to women. (Jacob and Stern 1952: 145–6)

Man, with his superior physical strength, can better undertake the more strenuous physical tasks, such as lumbering, mining, quarrying, land clearance, and housebuilding. Not handicapped, as is woman, by the physiological burdens of pregnancy and nursing, he can range farther afield to hunt, to fish, to herd, and to trade. Woman is at no disadvantage, however, in lighter tasks which can be performed in or near the home, e.g., the gathering of vegetable products, the fetching of water, the preparation of food, and the manufacture of clothing and utensils. All known human societies have developed specialization and cooperation between the sexes roughly along this biologically determined line of cleavage. (Murdock 1949: 7)

Up to about nine thousand years ago all human populations lived by hunting and most of them also by fishing, supplemented by the picking of berries, fruits and nuts, and the digging of roots and tubers. Perhaps the first division of labor between the sexes was that the male became the hunter and the female the food-gatherer. (Montagu 1969: 134)

Even in those societies where there are no professional or semi-professional artisans, all ordinary manufactures are delegated either to men or to women. Moreover, this sex division of labor is much the same wherever it occurs. Such universal patterns derive from universally present facts, such as the greater size and strength of the male, and his greater activity based on the differing roles of the two sexes in connection with the production and care of children. These factors unquestionably led to the earliest differentiation in food gathering activities. This must have begun at an extremely remote period. The males became the main providers of animal foods, since they were able to run down their prey and engage it in combat. The females being hampered throughout most of their adult lives by the presence either of infants *in utero* or in arms, were unable to engage in such active pursuits, but were able to collect vegetable foods and shell fish. . . . Thus to this day in the American family dinner the meat is placed in front of the father to be served and the vegetables in front of the mother. This is a folk memory of the days when the father collected the meat with his spear and the mother the vegetables with her digging stick. (Linton 1955: 70–1)

Thus, the sexual division of labor is neatly laid out, and simply and cogently explained. Men are strong, dominant protectors who hunt animals; women are weaker, passive, hampered by their reproductive responsibilities, and hence, consigned to plant gathering. Not only is that the case for every ethnographically observed society, but it is carried back to "extremely remote" periods. This received view could be schematized as:

men>hunt>animals>active
women>gather>plants>passive

All the introductory texts from which these excerpts were taken were written before the women's movement and the reorganization of contemporary American life that made women working outside the domestic sphere an inescapable reality.

Introductory texts are much more cautious these days. Conspicuously absent is the explicit male/active, female/passive dichotomy (e.g. Harris 1987: 127; Oswalt 1986: 104–5; Peoples and Bailey 1988: 254–60). Current texts acknowledge that in every known society there is a sexual division of labor; that men hunting and women gathering seems almost always to be the case, but that beyond this there is tremendous variation in which labors a particular society assigns to a particular sex. The received view today is that in foraging societies:

men>hunt>animals
women>gather>plants

For purposes of argument we accept this premise and attempt to formalize this very division of labor for a particular time, region, and cultural historical process: the origin and early development of plant cultivation and domestication in the Eastern Woodlands of North America. We draw upon three lines of evidence: archaeological data, ethnohistoric data, and general schemes of human social organization derived from ethnography.

Data Sources and Arguments of Relevance

Archaeological and archaeobotanical data

The time period relevant to the origin and early development of horticulture in the Eastern Woodlands is approximately 7000–2000 BP. Primary evidence for plant use during these five millennia comes from a variety of archaeological contexts, but only two basic categories: charred and uncharred plant remains. Charred plant remains are usually recovered by flotation-water separation systems; uncharred plants are recovered from dry caves and rockshelters; both categories are then analysed by paleoethnobotanists (Hastorf and Popper 1988; Pearsall 1989).

The evidence to date suggests three different episodes of domestication in the Eastern US (Smith 1987a; Watson 1989; Yarnell 1986). The first began about 7000 BP when a gourd-like cucurbit (*Cucurbita* sp.; perhaps *C. pepo*, perhaps *C. texana*, or even *C. foetidissima*) and bottle gourd (*Lagenaria siceraria*) begin to appear in archaeological deposits in the Eastern US. The second is from 3500 BP onward when domesticated forms of the weedy plants sumpweed, chenopod, and sunflower begin to appear. The third is the development of varieties of maize specific to the requirements of the Eastern US, a process that took place between 2000 and 1000 BP.

We are in the pioneer phase of knowledge expansion about prehistoric plant use. One characteristic of this pioneer phase is a scramble by interested scholars to synthesize the new data as they become accessible, not only in annotated inventories of the primary evidence (Yarnell 1977, 1983, 1986, forthcoming), but also in comparative discussions of regional developments (Asch and Asch 1985; Chapman and Shea 1981; Watson 1985, 1988, 1989), and in more general theoretical formulations (e.g. Chomko and Crawford 1978; Crites 1987; Lathrap 1987; Smith 1987a, 1987b). It seems desirable to launch an inquiry at yet another level: that of the women and men involved in the events and processes. While a great deal is being written about the evidence, it is, for the most part, gender-neutral writing; when actors are mentioned they are "people," or "humans," or "individuals". These accounts tend to be discussions of the archaeological evidence, the plant remains, rather than the people who manipulated the plants. We depart from that pattern here.

The ethnohistoric record

Although the archaeological record of plant use has only recently been sought, information about plant use by living peoples in the Eastern Woodlands has been available since the time of European entry in the sixteenth century. Thus, one source of data is historical or ethnohistorical such as that provided by Dye (1980), Hudson (1976), Le Page du Pratz (n.d.), Parker (1968), Swanton (1948), Will and Hyde (1917), Willoughby (1906), Wilson (1917), and Yarnell (1964). For example, in an often-quoted passage, Le Page du Pratz (n.d.: 156–7) describes the planting of *choupichoul* (Smith 1987c), an Eastern Woodlands cultigen being grown in Louisiana by the Natchez at the time of European entry into the Southeast: "I have seen the Natchez, and other indians, sow a sort of grain, which they called Choupichoul, on these dry sand-banks. This sand received no manner of culture; and the *women and children* covered the grain any how with their feet, without taking any great pains about it" (emphasis added). Throughout the ethnohistoric and ethnographic literature of the Eastern US are similar examples of women planting, reaping, collecting, and processing plants.

License to use the ethnographic and ethnohistorical information for archaeological inference would presumably be granted because it fulfills the criteria for the use of ethnographic analogy (the most comprehensive recent discussion is Wylie 1985, but see also Ascher 1961; Salmon 1982: 57–83; Watson, LeBlanc, and Redman 1971: 49–51, 1984: 259–63). That is, the information in question comes from the same or a very similar physical environment, and from people who are closely related physically and culturally. Therefore, the ethnographic/ethnohistoric information carries a certain degree of prior probability, of plausibility or likelihood, with respect to the archaeological materials. That does not mean, however, that it is to be accepted uncritically.

Social organization

There is another necessary source, and that is the more abstract and theoretical literature in anthropology about the organization and functioning of human groups at various levels of technological complexity. For present purposes we are content to evoke Fried (1967), Friedl (1975), Murdock and Provost (1973), Sahlins (1963, 1968), Service (1962, 1971), Steward (1948), and White (1959) and refer to them in general as the authority for some basic assumptions:

1 In small-scale, non food-producing, egalitarian societies, subsistence activities are divided on the basis of age and sex.
2 For biological reasons relating to gestation and lactation, adult women are primarily responsible for nourishing and socializing infants and small children, although various others can assist in these tasks.
3 For biological reasons relating to greater physical strength and hormone levels, adult men are charged with the primary responsibility for safeguarding the social units in which children are born and reared, and – in general – with tasks that require sudden bursts of energy, such as running after game.
4 Because of these biological constraints on men and women, groups tend to divide labor between the sexes so that women are responsible for activities that do not interfere with childcare and that can be performed near the habitation – cooking and "domestic activities" – as well as the collecting of stationary resources such as plants and firewood. Men are responsible for exploiting mobile resources, primarily the hunting of game, as well as for defense, and a variety of other such tasks.

Using these assumptions about the sexual division of labor, as well as evidence from the archaeological record and the ethnohistoric/ethnographic record, we depart from the usual gender-neutral perspective to discuss one of the most recent and most comprehensive theoretical treatments we know for the development of horticulture in the Eastern Woodlands: Bruce Smith's (1987a) paper, "The Independent Domestication of Indigenous Seed-Bearing Plants in Eastern North America."

The Domestication of Plants

Women and coevolution in the Eastern Woodlands: weedy plant domestication

Smith's interpretive formulation may be rendered schematically as follows: at about 8000 BP, the beginning of the Middle Archaic period, human populations in the Eastern Woodlands are thought to have been small, few, and dispersed rather widely across the landscape. Their subsistence systems – hunting-gathering-foraging with some emphasis on deer and several kinds of nuts, especially hickory and acorn – were further characterized by residential mobility, probably cycling through similar or the same series of locales, season after season, year after year. Occupation sites were small, although summer camps on river terraces or levees were probably considerably larger than winter residential units in the uplands.

Geological studies indicate significant changes in Mid-Holocene (8000–5000 BP) fluvial systems throughout the East, partly as a result of a long drying trend, the Hypsithermal. Rivers stabilized and aggraded so that previously ephemeral or rare features such as meanders and oxbow lakes, bars and shoals, sloughs and backwater lagoons became much more common and long-lasting than in the previous post-Pleistocene millennia. As a result of these changes, human subsistence-settlement patterns also changed. When slackwater habitats, shoals, etc. took shape as relatively permanent features, then the abundant flora (edible bulbs, rhizomes, shoots, seeds) and fauna (many different kinds of fish, amphibians, mollusks, and waterfowl) characterizing them became readily accessible on a predictable, seasonal, long-term basis. Human settlements – in the form of base camps occupied from late spring to summer and on through fall, and oriented to these resource points – increased in size and were permanently occupied for at least four to five months each year for hundreds of years. This process resulted in the first recognizable anthropogenic locales in the archaeological record of the Eastern US; i.e. these sites represent the first long-lasting impact on this physical environment produced by human activity. Archaic shell mounds and midden mounds are then the scene where the rest of the story unfolds: these "domestilocalities", as Smith calls them, are the crux of his formulation.

The mounds and middens are significant and long-lived disturbed areas, highly congenial to the weedy species ancestral to the earliest cultivated and domesticated food plants. Smith discusses a series of four important factors in the coevolutionary interplay between human and plant populations at the domestilocalities; sunlight, fertile soil, continually disturbed soil, and continual introduction of seeds. He also stresses that some of the selective pressures operating on the weedy plants colonizing such locales are congruent with the best interests of humans who harvest them for food, most significantly big seeds and thin seed coats.

Intense competition among pioneer species in these rich openings favors seeds that sprout quickly and grow quickly. These traits translate botanically into seeds with reduced dormancy (a thin seed coat is one good means of effecting reduced dormancy) and large endosperm (food reserves to sustain rapid, early spring growth), the two morphological characteristics enabling identification of the earliest domesticates: sumpweed and sunflower (bigger seeds than in wild populations) and *Chenopodium berlandieri* ssp. *jonesianum* (seeds with thinner seed coats than in wild *C. berlandieri*).

Finally, Smith outlines the main stages or steps in the general coevolutionary trajectory between ca.6500 and 3500 BP in numerous places in the Eastern Woodlands.

At about 6500 BP. In the first stage, domestilocalities are inhabited by humans and by a series of weedy, colonizing, or pioneering plant species for several months during each growing season. Natural selective pressures operate on the plants in the directions just noted to produce big seeds and thin seed coats.

In the second stage, humans tolerate the useful edible species, but ignore, or even occasionally remove the useless or harmful species.

In stage three, humans actively encourage the useful species (which have gradually become even more useful), and while systematically harvesting them also systematically remove competing non-useful plants. Thus, the incidental gardens of stage 2 become true managed gardens, the proceeds of which are stored to augment the winter and early spring diet.

In stage four, humans deliberately plant seeds of the useful species each year, carefully tending and caring for the resulting crops.

At about 3500 BP. In stage five, plants emerge that are clearly recognizable morphologically as domesticates.

The entire process is quite low-key, and there is no drastic alteration in the diet as a result of it, but there is an increase in dependable plant resources.

If we populate Smith's evolutionary stages with gendered human beings chosen to accord with the four operating assumptions for the division of labor already noted, and with the ethnographic record for the Eastern Woodlands, then we must conclude that the adult women are the chief protagonists in the horticultural drama of the domestilocalities. Although the entire human group contributes to the sunlight and soil fertility factors, it is the women who are primarily responsible for soil disturbance and continual introduction of seeds. Smith lists as examples of disturbance: the construction of houses, windbreaks, storage and refuse pits, drying racks, earth ovens, hearths. Most of these probably represent women's work as do the majority of other examples he mentions: primary and secondary disposal of plant and animal debris, and a "wide range of everyday processing and manufacturing activities."

As to the continual introduction of seeds, Smith notes harvesting plants for processing and consumption at the domestilocality. Seed loss during processing, storage, and consumption (plus defecation subsequent to consumption) continually introduce seeds to the fertile soil of the domestilocality. Once again – although everyone joins in consumption and defecation – it is the women who are responsible for processing, and for food preparation and storage.

Have we not then definitively identified woman the gatherer, harvester, and primary disturber of domestilocalities in the prehistoric Eastern Woodlands as woman the cultivator and domesticator? Yes, we have. But anyone persuaded by Smith's or similar coevolutionary constructions would doubtless respond "So what?" Our conclusion, with which they would probably readily agree, is at best anti-climactic because the coevolutionary formulation downplays stress, drive, intention, or innovation of any sort on the part of the people involved, in this case the women. The coevolutionary formulation highlights gradualness; the built-in mechanisms adduced carry plants and people smoothly and imperceptibly from hunting-gathering-foraging to systematic harvesting to at least part-time food production with little or no effort on anyone's part. The plants virtually domesticate themselves.

> While a number of the initial and ongoing selective pressures acting on these plants within such disturbed habitats were clearly related to human activities, these activities were unintentional and "automatic" rather than the result of predetermined and deliberate human action toward the plant species in question.
> . . . It is this simple step of planting harvested seeds, even on a very small scale, that if sustained over the long-term marks both the beginning of cultivation, and the onset of automatic selection within affected domestilocality plant populations for interrelated adaptation syndromes associated with domestication.
> . . . This continuing evolutionary process did not require any deliberate selection efforts on the part of Middle Holocene inhabitants of domestilocalities in the Eastern Woodlands. All that was needed was a sustained opportunistic exploitation and minimal encouragement of what were still rather unimportant plant food sources. (Smith 1987a: 32, 33, 34)

This is in keeping not only with the current scheme for division of labor women>gather> plants,

but also with the earlier (Keesing, Linton, et al.) scheme

women>gather>plants>passive.

Are we to be left with such a muted and down-beat ending to the Neolithic Revolution in the Eastern Woodlands?

Shaman the cultivator: gourd domestication

The domestication of the native cultigens described by Smith was apparently preceded by introduction of another type of domesticate, *Cucurbita* gourd and bottle gourd, in various parts of the Eastern US beginning about 7000 years ago. In an article entitled, "The Origins of Plant Domestication in the Eastern United States: Promoting the Individual in Archaeological Theory," Guy Prentice (1986) constructs a scenario for that earlier transformation.

Prentice first details the evidence for the tropical squash, *Cucurbita pepo*, in archaeological deposits dating from 7000–3500 BP, some of the earliest evidence for domesticated plants in Eastern North America. Investigators agree that *Cucurbita pepo* fruits would have been used primarily as containers, or perhaps as rattles, rather than food (Prentice 1986: 104). He then argues (ibid.: 106) that the species was probably introduced through some form of trade with the tropical areas in which it grows naturally. The sites at which the earliest evidence for *Cucurbita pepo* is found are those of Archaic period, hunting and gathering, band-level societies. He notes that authoritarian controls in such societies would have been weak, and that shamans and headmen were probably exercising the strongest control within these groups (ibid.: 107). Prentice presents information from studies indicating that change is not an automatic process in human societies, that certain conditions must be met before an innovation is accepted (ibid.: 108–11). An innovation will take hold if it is introduced by an individual of high status, a specialist, an ambitious person who is in contact with outsiders and who is oriented toward commerce rather than subsistence:

> By postulating a ritual use for cucurbits during the Archaic period, one is led to conclude that it would be the shaman who would be most likely to adopt cucurbit agriculture. He would be the one most interested in new religious paraphernalia. He would have the greatest knowledge of plants. He would have been in communication with other shamans and probably exchanging plants and plant lore. If gourds were introduced as magical rattles and ritualistic containers for serving stimulants and medicines, he would have gained a very impressive "medicine" in the eyes of his patients. In fact, the gourd itself may have provided the medicine. (Prentice 1986: 113)

Here is an instance in which at least one archaeologist is not arguing for

women>gather>plants.

Why not? Perhaps because this is a discussion of innovation, and

women>gather>plants>passive

– although it might lead to dinner – would not lead to *innovation*. Rather, this is a scenario for

man>trade>ceremony>active>innovation>cultivation>domestication.

Perhaps it really was like that (see Decker 1988 and Smith 1987a for alternative views on the development of *Cucurbita* cultivation in eastern North America), but we are leary of explanations that remove women from the one realm that is traditionally granted them, as soon as innovation or invention enters the picture.

Women and maize agriculture in the Eastern Woodlands: the creation of northern flint

Maize was the most important domesticate among the horticultural societies of North America at the time of European contact. Although there was enormous variety among the indigenous subsistence economies in the Eastern and Western United States, wherever crops were grown maize was central, often being literally deified (e.g. Cushing 1974; Hudson 1976; Munson 1973; Stevenson 1904; Swanton 1948). Yet, as the latest evidence makes clear (Chapman and Crites 1987; Conard et al. 1984; Doebly, Goodman, and Stuber 1986; Ford 1987; Yarnell 1986), maize is a rather late entrant into the Eastern Woodlands, probably introduced from the Southwest, and appearing about 1800 BP. The development of horticulture in the Southwest seems to have been very different from that in the East (Minnis 1985, in prep.; Wills 1988), and maize is much earlier there, apparently present by ca.4000 BP.

There is great unclarity in the literature about the exact definitions and time-space distributions of contemporary maize varieties, but there is some consensus that the earliest kinds known in the East (and grown together with sunflower, sumpweed, chenopod, maygrass, knotweed, etc.) are of a type with 10 to 12 rows of kernels, and called Chapalote, Tropical Flint, North American Pop, and/or Midwestern 12-row. These varieties were developed from the earliest Maize, which was originally created from wild populations occurring in Mesoamerica, Central America, or South America (or all three), but exactly where and how has been hotly debated for some 20 years (e.g. Galinat 1985b; Lathrap 1987).

Our concern here, however, is with the transition in the more northerly Eastern Woodlands from the early, higher row-number maize to a lower row-number variety variously known as Maiz de Ocho, Northern Flint, or Eastern 8-row maize, which appeared in the Northeast around AD 800–900, became quite standardized, and was the dominant agricultural crop of this region from approximately AD 1000 to historic times (Wagner 1983, 1987). There are at least three alternatives as to how this happened: (1) Eastern 8-row was created in the Eastern Woodlands from the Earlier Midwestern 12-row varieties; or (2) it, like the older form itself, was developed somewhere south of the Border and later diffused to the Eastern US; or (3) both (1) and (2) are too simple, and the origin of Northern Flint/Eastern 8-row involved more complicated combinations of both southerly (the Tropical Flint or Chapalote type) and northerly (the Northern Flint/Eastern 8-row type) maize varieties originating in several parts of northern, central, and southern America. Lathrap (1987) provides a comprehensive presentation of the second alternative (see also Upham et al. 1987), and Bruce Smith favors the third (Smith in prep.). Although there is now a very solid corpus of information on Fort Ancient maize (Wagner 1983, 1987), primary evidence about Middle Mississippian maize is only beginning to be available (Blake 1986; Fritz 1986; Scarry 1986), so it is not yet possible to assess definitively the relative merits of these three suggestions.

At the moment one can suggest, without contravening the scanty available evidence and in fact remaining congruent with it, that the original form of Northern Flint (Eastern 8-row) was developed from a Chapalote (Midwestern 12-row, Tropical Flint) type of maize at one or several places in the northerly portions of Eastern North America. The earliest date now known for Northern Flint is ca. AD 800–900 from one site in western Pennsylvania and two near the north shore of Lake Erie (Blake 1986; Blake and Cutler 1983; Stothers 1976). Northern Flint is present by AD 1000 in the cultural context called Fort Ancient located in the Ohio River drainage of southern Ohio and Indiana, northern Kentucky, and northern West Virginia (Wagner 1983, 1987). On the present evidence, robust forms of Northern Flint appear later or not at all as one moves west and south from Fort Ancient territory (Blake 1986; Fritz 1986; Johannessen 1984; Scarry 1986). Thus, we believe we are justified in accepting, at least for purposes of our argument here, that the Northern Flint variety of maize was developed indigenously in northeastern North America from an older, Chapalote form that came into the east 1800 or 1900 years ago.

We assume that the first Chapalote or Chapolote-like forms of this tropical cultigen to enter northern latitudes in the Eastern U.S. were not well suited to that physical environment, even if the plant diffused northward gradually from Mesoamerica. Day-length, annual temperature and moisture cycles, growing-season length, and substrate characteristics probably all differed significantly from those of the locales where Chapalote was initially grown. Hence, the Middle Woodland groups who planted and hoped to harvest this novel crop in the most northerly North American regions may have had more failures and near failures than successes. Lower row numbers on maize cobs are thought to be a botanical reflection of poor growing conditions such as short growing seasons, drought, or even unchecked competition from weeds (Blake and Cutler 1983: 83–4). Thus, it is possible that adverse climate was compounded by neglect in the development of Northern Flint.

We think it more likely, however, that cultivators in the northeasterly portions of North America actively encouraged, against environmental odds, the new starchy food source. Accepting the AD 800–900 dates from the Lake Erie and western Pennsylvania sites as the first establishing of Northern Flint, and noting the rapidity with which Northern Flint agriculture spread throughout the central Ohio River drainage (Fort Ancient) area immediately thereafter, we conclude that deliberate nurturing of maize in an inhospitable environment is a more plausible interpretation than is neglect in the development of this hardy variety.

Two points are implied from the above discussion: (1) maize acceptance and cultivation north of the Border was purposeful and deliberate; and (2) it was surely the women sunflower-sumpweed-chenopod gardeners in Middle and Late Woodland communities who worked (with varying success and interest) to acclimatize this imported species, by planting it deeper or shallower, earlier or later, in hills or furrows, and who crossed varieties to obtain or suppress specific traits. From ca.AD 1100–1200 to the time of European contact in the sixteenth century, Northern Flint was the main cultivated food of the hamlets, villages, towns, and chiefdoms that arose in the Ohio River Valley and the vast region north to the Great Lakes. To the west and south, in the Mississippi River and its tributary drainages, Northern Flint was also sometimes grown but in combination with other varieties having higher row-numbers (Blake 1986; Fritz 1986; Johannessen 1984; Scarry 1986; Smith in prep.) Thus Northern Flint, together with pumpkins, squashes, sunflowers, and a long list of other cultigens, planted, tended, harvested, and processed by the women agriculturalists (Hudson 1976; Parker 1968; Swanton 1948; Will and Hyde 1917; Willoughby 1906; Wilson 1917), supported many thousands of people each year for hundreds of years. The accomplishments of these women cultivators is even more impressive when one realizes that their creation, Northern Flint, is the basis (together with Southern Dent, a maize variety that entered the southeastern United States somewhat later) for all the modern varieties of hybrid "Corn Belt Dent" maize grown around the world today (Doebley et al. 1986; Galinat 1985a).

Conclusions

We close with a few further thoughts about the first women gardeners in the Late Archaic domestilocalities. Their contribution of domesticated sumpweed, sunflower, and chenopod (and possibly maygrass as well) to the diet and the archaeological record of initial Late Holocene human populations in the Eastern Woodlands may not have been so automatic a process with so insignificant a result as the coevolutionary formulation makes it out to be.

In the first place, the natural history, natural habitat and distribution, ecology, and genetic structure of most of the Late Archaic/Early Woodland cultigens and domesticates are not well understood. On closer inspection, it may turn out to be the case that some if not all the species initially domesticated would have required special, self-conscious, and deliberate treatment to convert them to garden crops, and to cause the very significant and progressive changes in seed size that at least two of them (sumpweed and sunflower) exhibit. Sunflower and maygrass were apparently being grown outside their natural ranges by 3000–2500 BP, and this must have been done purposefully.

Secondly, the best and most comprehensive dietary evidence for the early horticultural period comes from the long series of human paleofecal and flotation derived remains in Salts Cave and Mammoth Cave, west central Kentucky. The fecal evidence dates to 2800–2500 BP and is quite clear and consistent: over 60 per cent of the plant foods consumed were seeds of indigenous domesticates and cultigens: sunflower, sumpweed, and chenopod (Gardner 1987; Marquardt 1974; Stewart 1974; Watson and Yarnell 1986; Yarnell 1969, 1974, 1977, 1983, 1986, forthcoming). If maygrass, whose status is uncertain but which is here beyond its natural range, is added, then the total proportion of indigenous cultigens rises to well over two-thirds. This single and well-established datum for a period relatively early in the history of the indigenous domesticates might be taken to cast some doubt on the generalization that the addition of the domesticate species had only a slight dietary impact. The doubt is strengthened by corroborating evidence from Newt Kash (Jones 1936; Smith and Cowan 1987), Cloudsplitter (Cowan 1985), and Cold Oak (Gremillion 1988; Ison 1986; Ison and Gremillion 1989) shelters in eastern Kentucky (see also Smith 1987b).

A third matter to think about is the fact that – quite apart from all other considerations – the women plant collectors and gardeners of 3500–2500 BP were the first to devise and use techniques of tilling, harvesting, and processing the new domesticates. These same techniques must have been in use throughout the later periods, and were then applied to the production and processing of maize as well as the older cultigens. As Bruce Smith (1987a) points out, more than 60 years ago Ralph Linton described significant differences in the tools and techniques used for maize production and processing in Eastern North America vs. those of the Southwest and Mexico, and suggested that in the East maize "was adopted into a preexisting cultural pattern which had grown up around some other food or foods" (Linton 1924: 349).

The fourth and last point is somewhat more tenuous, but we think it is important to consider the implications of one issue unanimously demonstrated by all the relevant ethnographic and ethnohistorical literature: the extensive and intensive botanical and zoological knowledge possessed by people in hunting-gathering-foraging societies. Botanical knowledge is (and would have been in prehistory) greatest among the women who gather, collect, harvest, and process plant resources. Such knowledge goes far beyond foodstuffs to include plants and plant-parts useful for dyes and for cordage and textile manufacture, as well as a vast array of medicinal leaves, bark, roots, stems, and berries. The ethno-graphically-documented women who exploited these various plant resources knew exactly where and when to find the right plant for a specific purpose. Surely their prehistoric predecessors controlled a similar body of empirical information about their botanical environments, and were equally skilled at using it for their own purposes. Viewed against such a background, the image of unintentional and automatic plant domestication by Late Archaic women pales considerably.

We think that archaeologists operate under at least two different schemes for explaining gender and labor in prehistoric foraging groups. The first is based upon the assumption that women are seriously encumbered and disadvantaged by their reproductive responsibilities and that men are unencumbered by theirs. In this scheme, these physical limitations are combined or conflated with certain personality traits that are thought by some to apply universally to the sexes. This is the scheme of Linton, Montagu, Hoebel, Keesing, etc.; in it women cannot be responsible for culture change because they are not men and therefore they are not active:

men>hunt>animals>active
women>gather>plants>passive

The second scheme is based upon a universal sexual division of labor for hunter-gatherers derived from available ethnographic evidence, but does not suppose that any innate psychological characteristics or activity levels separate males and females:

men>hunt>animals
women>gather>plants

We do not know who domesticated plants in the prehistoric Eastern Woodlands, but faced with a choice between an explanation that relies on scheme number one and one that relies upon scheme number two, we prefer the alternative we have presented: based on available ethnographic evidence for the Eastern United States in particular and the sexual division of labor in general, women domesticated plants. We would like to think that they domesticated them on purpose because they were bored, or curious, or saw some economic advantage in it, that they acted consciously with the full powers of human intellect and that their actions were a significant contribution to culture change, to innovation, and to cultural elaboration. We prefer this explanation because it makes explicit a formulation that anyone who has ever studied anthropology has to some degree absorbed, i.e. that food plants in foraging societies are women's business. Neither Prentice nor Smith argues that women did *not* domesticate plants in prehistoric North America, yet Prentice does argue that a particular group of men were responsible for this major innovation and Smith argues that the innovation was not consciously achieved. It may be the case that shamans were responsible for the introduction of horticulture. It may be that the invention of horticulture was largely unintentional, or passive. But until there is convincing evidence for either of these hypotheses, we prefer to pursue a third alternative: prehistoric women were fully capable not only of conscious action, but also of innovation.

ACKNOWLEDGMENTS

We are grateful to Joan Gero and Meg Conkey for enabling us to contribute to this volume, and to Joan Gero for the extraordinary attention she gave to editing the initial version of this chapter. We also wish to thank David Browman, Leonard Blake, Julie Stein, as well as the participants in the original "Women and Production in Prehistory" conference for kindly reading and commenting upon earlier drafts of our paper. Although we alone are responsible for the final version, we benefited a great deal from the suggestions of these scholars.

REFERENCES

Asch, David L. and Nancy B. Asch (1985). "Prehistoric Plant Cultivation in West-Central Illinois." In *Prehistoric Food Production in North America*, Richard Ford, ed. Ann Arbor: University of Michigan Museum of Anthropology, Anthropological Papers No. 75, 149–204.

Ascher, Robert (1961). "Analogy in Archaeological Interpretation." *Southwestern Journal of Anthropology* 17: 317–25.

Blake, Leonard (1986). "Corn and Other Plants from Prehistory into History in the Eastern United States." In *The Protohistoric Period in the Mid-South: 1500–1700. Proceedings of the 1983 Mid-South Archaeological Conference*, D. Dye and R. Bristler, eds. Mississippi Department of Archives and History, Archaeological Report 18, 3–13.

Blake, Leonard and Hugh C. Cutler (1983). "Plant Remains from the Gnagey Site (36SO55)." Appendix II, in R. George, "The Gnagey Site and the Monongahela Occupation of the Somerset Plateau." *Pennsylvania Archaeologist* 53: 83–8.

Chapman, Jefferson and Gary Crites (1987). "Evidence for Early Maize (*Zea mays*) from the Icehouse Bottom Site, Tennessee." *American Antiquity* 52: 352–4.

Chapman, Jefferson and Andrea Brewer Shea (1981). "The Archaeological Record: Early Archaic to Contact in the Lower Little Tenneessee River Valley." *Tennessee Anthropologist* 6: 64–84.

Chomko, Stephen A. and Gary W. Crawford (1978). "Plant Husbandry in Prehistoric Eastern North America: New Evidence for its Development." *American Antiquity* 43: 405–8.

Conard, N., D. Asch, N. Asch, D. Elmore, H. Gove, M. Rubin, J. Brown, M. Wiant, K. Farnsworth, and T. Cook (1984). "Accelerator Radiocarbon Dating of Evidence of Prehistoric Horticulture in Illinois." *Nature* 308: 443–6.

Cowan, C. Wesley (1985). "From Foraging to Incipient Food-Production: Subsistence Change and Continuity on the Cumberland Plateau of Eastern Kentucky." Unpublished Ph.D. dissertation, University of Michigan.

Crites, Gary (1987). "Human–Plant Mutualism and Niche Expression in the Paleoethnobotanical Record: A Middle Woodland Example." *American Antiquity* 52: 725–40.

Cushing, Frank H. (1974). *Zuni Breadstuff*. New York: Museum of the American Indian Hey Foundation, Indian Notes and Monographs 8 (reprint edn).

Decker, Deena (1988). "Origin(s), Evolution, and Systematics of *Cucurbita pepo* (Cucurbitaceae)." *Economic Botany* 42: 4–15.

Doebley, J., M. Goodman, and C. Stuber (1986). "Exceptional Genetic Divergence of Northern Flint Corn." *American Journal of Botany* 73: 64–9.

Dye, David (1980). "Primary Forest Efficiency in the Western Middle Tennessee Valley." Ph.D. dissertation, Department of Anthropology, Washington University, St. Louis.

Ford, Richard I. (1987). "Dating Early Maize in the Eastern United States."

Paper read at the 10th Annual Conference of the Society of Ethnobiology, Gainesville, FL.

Fried, Morton H. (1967). *The Evolution of Political Society.* New York: Random House.

Friedl, Ernestine (1975). *Women and Men: an Anthropologist's View.* New York: Holt, Rinehart, and Winston. Reprinted 1984 by Waveland Press, Prospect Heights, IL.

Friedman, J. and M. J. Rowlands, eds (1977). *The Evolution of Social Systems.* London: Duckworth.

Fritz, Gayle (1986). "Prehistoric Ozark Agriculture: the University of Arkansas Rockshelter Collections." Ph.D. dissertation, Department of Anthroplogy, University of North Carolina, Chapel Hill.

Galinat, Walton C. (1985a). "Domestication and Diffusion of Maize." In *Prehistoric Food Production in North America*, Richard Ford, ed. Ann Arbor: University of Michigan Museum of Anthroplogy, Anthropological Papers No. 75, 245–78.

—— (1985). "The Missing Links between Teosinte and Maize: A Review." *Maydica* 30: 137–60.

Gardner, Paul S. (1987). "New Evidence Concerning the Chronology and Paleoethnobotany of Salts Cave, Kentucky." *American Antiquity* 52: 358–67.

Gremillion, Kristin J. (1988). "Preliminary Report on Terminal Archaic and Early Woodland Plant Remains from the Cold Oak Shelter, Lee County, Kentucky." Report submitted to Cecil R. Ison, USDA Forest Service Station, Stanton Ranger District, Stanton, Kentucky.

Harris, Marvin (1987). *Cultural Anthropology*, 2nd edn. New York: Harper & Row.

Hastorf, Christine and Virginia Popper, eds (1988). *Current Paleoethnobotany: Analytical Methods and Cultural Interpretations of Archaeological Plant Remains.* Chicago: University of Chicago Press.

Hoebel, E. Adamson (1958). *Man in the Primitive World: An Introduction to Anthropology.* New York: McGraw-Hill.

Hudson, Charles (1976). *The Southeastern Indians.* Knoxville: University of Tennessee Press.

Ison, Cecil R. (1986). "Recent Excavations at the Cold Oak Shelter, Daniel Boone National Forest, Kentucky." Paper presented at the Kentucky Heritage Council Annual Conference, Louisville.

Ison, Cecil R. and Kristin J. Gremillion (1989). "Terminal Archaic and Early Woodland Plant Utilization Along the Cumberland Plateau." Paper presented at the Society for American Archaeology Annual Meeting.

Jacobs, Melville and Bernhard Stern (1952). *General Anthropology.* New York: College Outline Series, Barnes and Noble. Reprinted 1964.

Johannessen, Sissel (1984). "Paleoethnobotany." In *American Bottom Archaeology*, C. Bareis and J. Porter, eds. Urbana and Chicago: University of Chicago Press, 197–214.

Jones, Volney (1936). "The Vegetal Remains of Newt Kash Hollow Shelter." In *Rock Shelters in Menifee County, Kentucky*, William Webb and W.

Funkhouser, eds. Lexington: University of Kentucky, Reports in Archaeology and Anthropology 3.

Keesing, Felix M. (1966). *Cultural Anthropology: The Science of Custom*. New York: Holt, Rinehart, and Winston.

Lathrap, Donald W. (1987). "The Introduction of Maize in Prehistoric Eastern North America: The View from Amazonia and the Santa Elena Peninsula." In *Emergent Horticultural Economies of the Eastern Woodlands*, William Keegan, ed. Carbondale: Center for Archaeological Investigations, Southern Illinois University, Occasional Paper No. 7, 345–71.

Le Page du Pratz, Antoine Simon (n.d.). *The History of Louisiana*. Pelican Press, Inc.

Linton, Ralph (1924). "The Significance of Certain Traits in North American Maize Culture." *American Anthropologist* 26: 345–9.

—— (1955). *The Tree of Culture*. New York: Alfred A. Knopf.

Marquardt, William H. (1974). "A Statistical Analysis of Constituents in Paleofecal Specimens from Mammoth Cave." In *Archaeology of the Mammoth Cave Area*, Patty Jo Watson, ed. New York: Academic Press, 193–202.

Minnis, Paul (1985). "Domesticating Plants and People in the Greater American Southwest." In *Prehistoric Food Production in North America*, Richard Ford, ed. Ann Arbor: Museum of Anthroplogy, University of Michigan, Anthropological Papers No. 75, 309–40.

—— (in prep.). "Earliest Plant Cultivation in Desert North America." In *Agricultural Origins in World Perspective*, Patty Jo Watson and C. W. Cowan, eds. MS chapter. For submission to Smithsonian Institution Press.

Montagu, Ashley (1969). *Man, His First Two Million Years: A Brief Introduction to Anthropology*. New York: Columbia University Press.

Munson, Patrick J. (1973). "The Origins and Antiquity of Maize-Beans-Squash Agriculture in Eastern North America: Some Linguistic Implications." In *Variation in Anthropology; Essays in Honor of John C. McGregor*, D. Lathrap and J. Douglas, eds. Urbana: Illinois Archaeological Survey, 107–35.

Murdock, George P. (1949). *Social Structure*. New York: The Free Press.

Murdock, George P. and Caterina Provost (1973). "Factors in the Division of Labor by Sex: A Cross-cultural Analysis." *Ethnology* 12: 203–25.

Oswalt, Wendell H. (1986). *Life Cycles and Lifeways: An Introduction to Cultural Anthropology*. Palo Alto, CA Mayfield Publishing.

Parker, Arthur C. (1968). "Iroquois Uses of Maize and Other Plant Foods." In *Parker on the Iroquois*, W. Fenton, ed. Syracuse: Syracuse University Press, 1–119.

Pearsall, Deborah (1989). *Paleoethnobotany: Reconstructing Interrelationships Between Humans and Plants from the Archaeological Record*. San Diego, CA: Academic Press.

Peoples, James and Garrick Bailey (1988). *Humanity: An Introduction to Cultural Anthropology*. St. Paul, MN: West Publishing.

Prentice, Guy (1986). "Origins of Plant Domestication in the Eastern United States: Promoting the Individual in Archaeological Theory." *Southeastern Archaeology* 5: 103–19.

Sahlins, Marshall (1963). "Poor Man, Rich Man, Big-Man, Chief: Political Types in Melanesia and Polynesia." *Comparative Studies in Society and History* 5: 285–303.

—— (1968). *Tribesmen.* Englewood Cliffs, NJ: Prentice-Hall.

Salmon, Merrilee (1982). *Philosophy and Archaeology.* New York: Academic Press.

Scarry, C. Margaret (1986). "Change in Plant Procurement and Production During the Emergence of the Moundville Chiefdom." Ph.D. dissertation, Department of Anthropology, University of Michigan, Ann Arbor.

Service, Elman (1962). *Primitive Social Organization.* New York: Random House.

—— (1971). *Primitive Social Organization,* 2nd edn. New York: Random House.

Smith, Bruce D. (1987a). "The Independent Domestication of the Indigenous Seed-Bearing Plants in Eastern North America." In *Emergent Horticultural Economies of the Eastern Woodlands,* William Keegan, ed. Carbondale: Center for Archaeological Investigations, Southern Illinois University, Occasional Paper No. 7, 3–47.

—— (1987b). "Hopewellian Farmers of Eastern North America." Paper presented at the 11th International Congress of Prehistoric and Protohistoric Science, Mainz, West Germany.

—— (1987c). "In Search of Choupichoul, the Mystical Grain of the Natchez." Keynote Address, 10th Annual Conference of the Society of Ethnobiology, Gainesville, Florida.

—— (in prep.). "Prehistoric Plant Husbandry in North America." In *Origins of Agriculture in World Perspective,* Patty Jo Watson and C. W. Cowan, eds. MS chapter. For submission to Smithsonian Institution Press.

Smith, Bruce D. and C. Wesley Cowan (1987). "The Age of Domesticated *Chenopodium* in Prehistoric North America: New Accelerator Dates from Eastern Kentucky." *American Antiquity* 52: 355–7.

Stevenson, Matilda G. (1904). *The Zuni Indians.* Washington: Annual Report of the Bureau of American Ethnology 1901–1902, vol. 23.

Steward, Julian (1948). *Patterns of Cultural Change.* Urbana: University of Illinois Press.

Stewart, Robert B. (1974). "Identification and Quantification of Components in Salts Cave Paleofeces, 1970–1972." In *Archaeology of the Mammoth Cave Area,* Patty Jo Watson, ed. New York: Academic Press, 41–8.

Stothers, David M. (1976). "The Princess Point Complex: A Regional Representative of the Early Late Woodland Horizon in the Great Lake Area." In *The Late Prehistory of the Lake Erie Drainage Basin,* David Brose, ed. Cleveland: Cleveland Museum of Natural History, 137–61.

Swanton, John R. (1948). *The Indians of the Southeastern United States.* Washington: Bureau of American Ethnology Bulletin 137. Reprinted 1979 by Smithsonian Institution Press.

Upham, S., R. S. MacNeish, W. C. Galinat, and C. M. Stevenson (1987). "Evidence Concerning the Origin of Maiz de Ocho." *American Anthropologist* 89: 410–19.

Wagner, Gail E. (1983). "Fort Ancient Subsistence: The Botanical Record." *West Virginia Archaeologist* 35: 27–39.

—— (1987). "Uses of Plants by Fort Ancient Indians." Ph.D. dissertation, Department of Anthropology, Washington University, St. Louis.

Watson, Patty Jo (1985). "The Impact of Early Horticulture in the Upland Drainages of the Midwest and Midsouth." In *Prehistoric Food Production in North America*. Richard Ford, ed. Ann Arbor: University of Michigan Museum of Anthropology, Anthropological Papers No. 75, 73–98.

—— (1988). "Prehistoric Gardening and Agriculture in the Midwest and Midsouth." In *Interpretation of Culture Change in the Eastern Woodlands During the Late Woodland Period*, R. Yerkes, ed. Columbus: Ohio State University, Department of Anthropology, Occasional Papers in Anthropology No. 3, 38–66.

—— (1989). "Early Plant Cultivation in the Eastern Woodlands of North America." In *Foraging and Farming: the Evolution of Plant Exploitation*, D. Harris and G. Hillman, eds. London: Allen and Hyman, 555–70.

Watson, Patty Jo and Richard A. Yarnell (1986). "Lost John's Last Meal." *Missouri Archaeologist* 47: 241–55.

Watson, Patty Jo, Steven A. LeBlanc, and Charles L. Redman (1971). *Explanation in Archaeology: An Explicitly Scientific Approach*. New York: Columbia University Press.

—— (1984). *Archaeological Explanation: The Scientific Method in Archaeology*. New York: Columbia University Press.

White, Leslie (1959). *The Evolution of Culture*. New York: McGraw-Hill.

Will, George F. and George E. Hyde (1917). *Corn Among the Indians of the Upper Missouri*. Lincoln: University of Nebraska Press.

Willoughby, Charles C. (1906). Houses and Gardens of the New England Indians. *American Anthropologist* 8: 115–32.

Wills, W. H. (1988). *Early Prehistoric Agriculture in the American Southwest*. Sante Fe, NM: School of American Research Press.

Wilson, Gilbert L. (1917). *Agriculture of the Hidatsa Indians, an Indian Interpretation*. University of Minnesota Studies in the Social Sciences 9. Reprints in Anthropology 5 (May 1977), J&L Reprint Co. Lincoln, NB.

Wylie, Alison (1985). "The Reaction Against Analogy." In *Advances in Archaeological Method and Theory*, vol. 8, Michael Schiffer, ed. Orlando, FL: Academic Press, 63–111.

Yarnell, Richard A. (1964). *Aboriginal Relationships Between Culture and Plant Life in the Upper Great Lakes Region*. Ann Arbor: University of Michigan, Museum of Anthropology, Anthropological Papers No. 23.

—— (1969). Contents of Human Paleofeces. In *The Prehistory of Salts Cave, Kentucky*, Patty Jo Watson, ed. Springfield: Illinois State Museum. Reports of Investigations No. 16, 41–54.

—— (1974). "Plant Food and Cultivation of the Salt Cavers." In *Archaeology of the Mammoth Cave Area*, Patty Jo Watson, ed. New York: Academic Press, 113–22.

—— (1977). "Native Plant Husbandry North of Mexico." In *Origins of Agriculture*, C. Reed, ed. The Hague: Mouton, 861–75.

—— (1983). "Prehistory of Plant Foods and Husbandry in North America." Paper presented at the Annual Meeting of the Society for American Archaeology, Pittsburgh.

—— (1986). "A Survey of Prehistoric Crop Plants in Eastern North America." *The Missouri Archaeologist* 47: 47–59.

—— (forthcoming). "Sunflower, Sumpweed, Small Grains, and Crops of Lesser Status." In *Handbook of North American Indians*, W. Sturtevant, ed. Washington, DC: Smithsonian Institution Press.

10

Gender, Shellfishing, and the Shell Mound Archaic

Cheryl P. Claassen

Shellfishing Engendered

Hundreds of ethnographic accounts describe women habitually, children usually, and men occasionally, shellfishing for food (see May 1982; Waselkov 1987). It is an activity through which women have made a significant contribution to the diets of hundreds of cultures, and provides an excellent starting point for a feminist perspective on culture. But in spite of the ethnographic evidence, in spite of the general assumption that women gather molluscs for food, and in spite of our commitment to recover as much information as we can about the past, we persistently de-gender and de-culture this activity in our studies of prehistoric shellfishing.

The common act of de-gendering shellfishing is accomplished either by ignoring gender ("people X gathered shellfish") or by avoiding mention of the activity itself ("people X subsisted on shellfish"). This is done for various reasons: (1) the gender of the gatherer (and/or the investigator's assumption of gender) is deemed unimportant to the study; (2) assumptions of gender seem unwarranted; and (3) the investigator believes that all (or both) genders of the society gathered shellfish. In all three cases, researchers seem to recognize no merit in pursuing more specific behavioral information about the organization of gender-related subsistence tasks.

To see how shellfishing is removed from its cultural context we need only examine the published explanations of why shellfishing intensified and declined at various places and times in prehistory. Brauner (1975: 26–9), for example, proposes that an environmentally induced decimation of the salmon population between 4000 and 3500 BP stimulated increased shellfishing in the Tucannan phase of the lower Snake River, and Lohse (1984: 288) uses the increasingly xeric conditions after 4000

BP to explain the lack of shell in sites on the upper Columbia River. The most commonly cited explanation for the intensification of shellfishing in the Eastern US is that the molluscan populations benefited from the climatic alteration of the Hypsithermal (Dye 1980: 150; Walthall 1980: 65). With more shellfish available, people would automatically use them as a food resource.

As generally depicted, scenarios of shellfishers deny gender, deny human choice, and recognize no consequences of adopted cultural behaviors – no seasonal scheduling conflicts, no weekly activity schedules to be arranged, no change in sex role assignments for specific tasks, no change in the symbolic meaning or status of particular food stuffs. Archaeologists struggling to explain the use or disuse of shellfish in a regional prehistory have failed to ask what their data imply about changes in the activities of women, children, or men, or about possible reorganization of the social units that collect and consume shellfish. As Bender (1985: 52) puts it, we have rejected "both specific history and principles of social structure in favor of an assumed ecological common denominator."

In spite of a widespread attitude in our profession that gender considerations are untestable (but see Spector, this volume), gender can be productively incorporated into our enterprise and indeed provides nothing short of a revitalization movement for archaeology, offering new vigor to research undertakings as it has in many other academic fields. Without a doubt, the gender of prehistoric actors impacts the archaeological record, and modern gender issues impact archaeologists and our inquiry; gender must be an issue for us all, and testibility cannot stand as the only criterion by which so fundamental a social phenomenon is admitted into archaeology. As I will show in this paper, our assumptions about the gender of shellfishers have implications for dietary reconstructions, optimal foraging models and interpretations of site function. Attention to gender will be shown here to provide alternative hypotheses for testing and will alert readers to biases that muddy the formulation of problems. I will begin by considering first women shellfishing and then men shellfishing. With shellfishing engendered I will approach the problem of the demise of the Shell Mound Archaic to illustrate how gender can revitalize research.

Women shellfishing

Women almost universally act as primary collectors of shellfish. It is at least in part the unacknowledged but widely recognized identification of women with shellfishing that is responsible for the common reputation of shellfish and molluscs as a low priority foodstuff in ethnohistoric and ethnographic accounts, including the Aleuts and most Pacific Northwest coast groups. (The opposite attitude can be found among other groups such as the Anbarra, however; see below.)

It is not surprising that male explorers and priests heard male whale hunters, kayakers, chiefs, warriors, hunters, and trading partners describe shellfish as inessential, a low ranking food, and/or untasty. While Aleuts have verbalized their own low opinions of shellfish, Laughlin (1974/5) has argued that the availability of intertidal resources, particularly shellfish, has provided food, autonomy, and a social contribution for elderly, young and infirm Aleuts. Moreover, Laughlin argues that the reliance on shellfish was responsible for the extreme longevity of both prehistoric and historic Aleuts. Ethnographically reported low rankings of this foodstuff may be fundamentally biased by relying on male accounts and would undoubtably be different if informants were aged women, children, or handicapped members of society! Different questions would also elicit different responses; shellfish might emerge with higher status if the question "what foods do you prefer?" were replaced with "what foods do you usually eat?" Typically women's and children's labor and products are underrated by both men and women in spite of their essential contribution to both social and physical needs.

Related to the low ranking that is accorded a molluscan diet is its in-appropriateness for banquets and ceremonial feasts. In at least one Polynesian culture, molluscs collected by women are deemed unsuitable for guests (Kirch and Dye 1979). Instead, a host will dive for a particular deep-dwelling bivalve species, whose meat is presented to the honored guest. A remarkably similar situation was recorded by Lund (1983: 350) for fish from the lower Ohio River:

> [Miles] maintained that the waters of the early Midwest were so full of game fish that only those caught with difficulty . . . were offered to guests, "because of the vanity of the master of the household, whose sportsman-ship was thus best exploited". Other species, such as bluegills, crappies, bullheads and perch, were for women and children to catch, "admitted to the table on ordinary occasions," and apologized for "if a guest was at the board."

Undoubtably some ethnographers recorded their own ideas about the suitability of molluscs as food. In Leviticus 11: 9–11, the Hebrews were told not to eat shellfish, and that attitude of avoidance passed into Christian lore. While the shell was prized, the meat was avoided as an abomination. Mary Douglas (1966: 54–72) says the Hebrew stricture stems from the abnormal mode of mollusc locomotion as water-dwellers, while Fischer et al. 1977 link taboo shellfish food to allergic reactions. Meehan (1982: 8) reminds us that Linnaeus and Cuvier considered molluscs horrible, naked, and gruesome. In fifteenth and sixteenth-century England, apprentices and those living in poor houses were fed mussels, thus imparting a social stigma to mussel consumption. In modern Wales, public opinion holds that only poor, mining valley folk eat cockles and mussels. I suspect that the nomen "mussel" for freshwater bivalves in the eastern United States resulted from the analogous sociological context of their use – by the poor and the uncouth – more than from any resemblance to the true marine mussels familiar to the English (there is little).

> To those imbued with the ethic of hard work dominant in European thought from the mid-nineteenth to the mid-twentieth century the spectacle of people scrabbling in sand and mud between the high and low tides to obtain their food . . . was not likely to lead to a high opinion of their cultural status [or of their foods from that zone]. (Meehan 1982: 8–9)

Thus, the contribution that women regularly make to subsistence diet is devalued, ignored, hidden from outsiders, and generally disparaged. A systematic study of recorder bias and food sociology could significantly alter the dietary rankings in ethnographic literature, but several critical issues already emerge by recognizing women's roles as lowly shellfishers.

While most shellfish species are lower in calories than other animal foods, it is in protein and essential minerals that many mollusc species rival other sources of meat for nutritional benefits (see table 10.1). In light of this fact, the assumptions underlying Ernestine Friedl's (1975) widely accepted discussion of male and female roles in hunting/gathering societies need to be reexamined.

Although Friedl mentions that women collect intertidal resources, in her subsequent discussion she refers to men obtaining protein and women contributing vegetable foods to the household diet. Women and children are dependent on men for protein.

> Women in their turn must receive meat from men when the hunt is successful if they and their children are to share in the benefits of a mixed protein-vegetable diet. . . . Those early foragers among whom protein was distributed to women and children had a better chance of survival . . . (Friedl 1975: 20)

This overly simplified view denies the active role of women and children in environments with molluscan resources, in the provisioning of their own and others' protein needs with meat as well as plant proteins. The average Anbarra woman gathered 100 g of flesh, 200 g of protein, and 800 Kcal for each kilometer walked and for every hour she

Table 10.1 Variation in nutrition between mollusc species and other foods per 100g.

Marine Molluscs	Kcal	Protein[a]	Fat[a]	Carbo	P/mg	Ca/mg	K/mg	Ref.[b]
Western Atlantic								
Argopecten gibbus (20)*		15.9–18.5%	0.11–0.31%		160–270	20–60		3
Aequipecten gibbus (4)		15.6–16.4g	0.50–0.70g					4
Aequipecten irradians (24)		13.4–17.0g	0.3–0.9g	1.4–1.9g				4
Buccinum undatum	91	18.50g	1.90g					1
Chiton marmoratus*		47.69%	6.20%					7
Cittarium pica*		65.15%	1.44g					7
Littorina littorea	74	15.30g	1.40g					1
Mya arenaria (20)		5.5–11.7g	0.4–2.6g		110–206	17–73		3
Mya arenaria (10)		9.7–15.6g	1.4–2.5g	1.7%				4
Mytilus edulis	89	17.20g	2.00g	2.9g				1
Mytilus sp.	87	14.40g	2.20g	3.3g				8
Nerita peloranta*	95	42.68%	6.20					7
Ostrea edulis		10.80g	0.90g					1
Placopecten magellanicus*	51	17.1–19.0%	0.02–0.3%		150–320	20–30		3
Purpura patula*		67.95%	1.11					7
Eastern Atlantic								
Buccinum undatum	91	18.50g	1.90g					1
Cardium edule	48	11.30g	0.30g	3.4g				1

Western Pacific

Batissa violacea*	105	48.90%				180	505	9
Pecten maximus		17.50g	0.10			163		9
Tapes hiantina*		77.00%					746	9
Telescopium telescopium		0.1				144	500	9

Eastern Pacific

Clinocardium nuttalli	79	13.50g	0.70g	4.7g				8
Haliotis sp.	98	18.70g	0.50g	3.4g				8
Haliotis kamtschatkana (4)		10.4–18.2g	0.3–0.7g					4
Mopalia muscosa	234	22.00g	16.30g	0				8
Ostrea lurida	82	9.60g	2.50g	5.4g				8
"Pacific oyster"	126	14.70g	3.10g	8.9g	213	118		1
Protothaca staminea	77	13.50g	1.00g	3.5g				8
Saxidomus nuttalli	79	13.00g	1.20g	4.1g				8
Tivela stultorum	74	11.20g	1.40g	4.0g		607		8

US freshwater molluscs

Actinonaias carinata	58	7.80g	0.70g	4.5g	520	320	26	10
Amblema costata*		8–9%						10
Megalonaias gigantea*		8–9%						13
Pleurocera canaliculatum	58	10.40g	1.20g	1.5g	108	1182	46	11
Proptera alata	77	9.50g	0.80g	7.8g	812	370	41	11
Viviparus georgianus	72	11.10g						12

Table 10.1 (cont.):

Marine Molluscs	Kcal	Protein[a]	Fat[a]	Carbo	P/mg	Ca/mg	K/mg	Ref.[b]
Miscellaneous molluscs								
Pecten spp. (7)		12.9–14.8g	0.09–0.43g			180–250	20–80	4
Venerupis semi decusata		12.2–13.6g	0.70–0.90g					4
Volegalea wardiana		0.1g				158	680	4
Other food								
Juglans nigra (walnut)	525	10.60g	5.0g	51.5g				1
Quercus agrifolia (acorn)	254	4.60g	9.8g	36.8g			175	8
Phaseolus vulgaris (bean)	272	22.10g	1.7g	45.0g				8
Pinus monophylla (pine)	481	7.80g	24.0g	58.4g	604			8
Zea mays	123	4.10g	22.8g	2.3g				1
Colinus virginianus (quail)	168	25.00g	6.8g	0g				10
Meleagris gallopavo (turkey)	218	20.10g	14.7g	0g				10
Meleagris gallopavo	171	28.00g	6.5g					
Odocoileus virgineanus	198	35.00g		6.4g				1
" (deer)	126	21.00g	4.0g	0g	249	10		10
Sylvilagus sp. (rabbit)	73	21.00g	5.0g	0g			385	8
"	135	21.00g	5.0g	0g				10
Sylvilagus floridanus	179	27.30g	7.7g					1
Genyonemus lineatus (croaker)	79	18.00g	0.80g	0g				8
Aplodinotus grunniens (drum)	121	17.30g	5.2g	0g			286	10

Ictalurus sp. (catfish)	103	17.60g	3.1g	0g	330	10
Mustelus vulgaris (shark)	91	19.70g	0.90g	1.1g		8
Notorynchus maculatus (shark)	189	15.30g	13.1g	2.5g		8
Phoca vitulina (seal)	143	26.00g				8
Cancer sapidus (crab)	82	11.9–19.2g	0.4–1.5g	0.5–2.0g		4

[a] I have specified grams or percent according to the referenced analysis.

[b] References:

1 Waselkov 1982: 101
3 Sidwell et al. 1973: 19
4 Sidwell et al. 1974: various
7 Goodwin 1979: 407
8 Erlandson 1988: 104
9 Meehan 1982: 143
10 Parmalee and Klippel 1974
11 Klippel and Morey 1985: 17
12 Cumbaa 1974: 52
13 Post 1982: 71

collected (personal observation). Although I agree with Friedl's premise that the giving and receiving of foodstuffs by men is one basis of higher male status in hunting/gathering societies, it is not as simple as men = protein and women = vegetable foods, or even men = meat protein and women = vegetable protein, which she suggests in several places.

That shellfish are frequently reported to be a low priority foodstuff and of little nutritional value has undoubtably biased models of prehistoric subsistence, and, in particular, has frustrated and challenged modeling attempts based on optimal foraging theory. Optimal foraging theory (OFT) has been applied by many archaeologists in studies of prehistoric hunter-gatherers (e.g. Winterhalder and Smith 1981).

Based on principles of evolutionary ecology, OFT assumes that individuals will engage in behaviors that lead to an increase in their reproductive fitness. It assumes that foragers will seek to maximize their foraging efficiency in terms of such variables as search time, pursuit time, and kilocaloric yields per kilocalorie of energy expended. Moreover, it employs a concept of "work" as it is experienced in a capitalistic society. In spite of the fact that archaeologists live in a social milieu where many kinds of work are practiced, the archaeological applications of OFT refer only to one sort of work: laborious, onerous work that is to be minimized in duration and frequency. "Work" takes one away from "home," is isolating, encourages competition with oneself and with others, and prevents one from doing "other things." Therefore, the work of foraging and gathering is to be undertaken with efficiency such that there is a cost minimization of calories and of time spent.

The applications of OFT to prehistoric shellfish subsistence (e.g. Lewis 1979; Neumann 1979; Perlman 1976; Yesner 1981) adopt these assumptions while at the same time illustrating an acceptance of the biased and devalued status of shellfishing discussed earlier. There are several reasons for the poor fit between shellfishing and OFT; specifically we can turn to Betty Meehan's (1982) portrayal of shellfishing by Anbarra women and children, a study that is strongly reconfirmed by my own recent ethnoarchaeological work in the Bahamas (see below). It should be of interest to optimal foraging modelers that the Anbarra women intentionally collected from beds where the shellfish were smaller and less plentiful than at neighboring beds (which they also harvested); that on 91 of 194 days (47 percent) that shellfish were gathered, only a single species was collected although dozens of other species that they eat were on the same beds; and that one species which is exposed twice daily nearly every day of the lunar cycle represented only 7 percent of all shellfish collected in the year of observation, being ignored in preference to species exposed on only some days of the lunar cycle (Meehan 1982). Thus, we see that among the

Anbarra, the activity of shellfishing is far from the OFT conception of efficient; some women even walked the round trip and collected nothing although their companions gathered for several hours.

Among other things, OFT was designed to measure the fitness of an individual's foraging behavior over a brief interval of time (Keene 1983; McCay 1981). As Keene and others point out, however, this emphasis on the individual forager may not be appropriate when studying humans. Social reproduction requires more than the reproduction of individuals and more than the feeding of animals. Again turning to the Anbarra, we see that shellfishing is a social event involving a dozen or more women and sometimes including as many as four generations. Children play nearby or collect their own shellfish supply; adult conversation is almost constant. The actual collecting permits women to be alone for short periods of time, and if she has left camp without her children she may be alone longer. She can also be "alone" with other adult women or "alone" with her children.

> For the duration of most shell gathering expeditions, provided it is not cold, a happy atmosphere prevails . . . These matri-oriented groups do not appear to compete with each other . . . They all work within talking distance of each other and conversation interspersed with laughing and joking continues throughout. (Meehan 1982: 86)

I made similar observations while watching and participating in shellfishing on San Salvador Island, Bahamas. In this mixed subsistence system that includes agriculture and purchased foodstuffs, shellfishing represents for women and their children recreation and family time. As play, it was pursued as we might describe work: there was a goal of filling a container, collecting was continuous, the necessary tools were transported to the rocks, all persons present participated in the activity, and there was task specialization by age. If enough molluscs were collected, a reward was the temporary thwarting of the cash economy.

Among the Anbarra, women particularly good at shellfishing or acquiring any other foraged food are given the same title and respect as men adept at hunting. Several women regularly enjoy group praise and status as good hunters because of their shellfishing.

I do not deny that some optimizing behavior may be going on among the Anbarra but it is not optimal *foraging* behavior if energy is the currency, as in most OFT applications. Not only would optimal foraging modelers have us consider all food getting activities to be work rather than play or pleasure, but they would also have us consider all activities that result in edibles to be subsistence activities. Perhaps we need to think in terms of subsistence, sociosubsistence, and ideo-subsistence activities, to paraphrase Binford (1962).

Women do most of the shellfishing in most societies when the shellfish
are used for food. Emphasizing gender in shellfishing raises several
interesting questions. In the interior Eastern US, shellfishing probably
entered the work agenda of prehistoric women between 8000 and 9000
years ago. How did women accommodate this activity in their work
schedules? Were innovations in subsistence and technology such as
shellfishing or horticulture (see Watson and Kennedy, this volume), or
pottery production (see Wright, this volume) simply added to women's
workload, so that the PaleoIndian woman had little and the Mississipian
woman much too much to do? Alternatively, do we imagine substitution
of tasks such that some activities are no longer performed in order to
accommodate new activities? Or were tasks reallocated, re-selected with
the advent of new activities? Do we imagine task specialization
developing, and if so at what scale? What were children doing before,
during and after shellfish were important in subsistence? Until we
inspect the division of labor more carefully, we have written into
prehistory a time management crisis for women, and an inventory of
activities tacitly assumed to have been "women's work" produces
superwomen, carefree children, and sportsmen.

Indeed, not all adult women in extended families among the Anbarra
or the Bahamians participate equally in shellfishing, and some families
consume less shellfish than others. Accommodation for differences in
proclivity and aptitude, then, made it possible for the prehistoric woman
to pursue some tasks and ignore others, rather than to perform all of
them. Regular shellfishers probably consumed more shellfish than other
women in the group. I consider implausible all attempts to reconstruct
population size and nutrition at shell midden sites since the intervening
calculations assume uniform collecting behavior and consumption for all
adults in the population. Here again, the engendering of prehistoric
subsistence provides a means to reassess normative models.

Men shellfishing

Waselkov (1987: 99) noted, in his comprehensive review of the
ethnographic literature on shellfishing, that "in no society did men
participate in [shellfishing] activities as often as women" although when
they did collect mussels or clams, "men make proportionally greater
contributions for the time they invest." In fishing societies, however,
there is an important place for shellfish as bait.

Archaeologists assume that shellfish collecting is solely for food and
done by women, although on San Salvador shellfishing was more often
observed and reported by men in conjunction with fishing activities.
Recognizing that molluscs are used as bait in significant numbers has a

profound impact on our dietary reconstructions, arguments about optimal foraging, site function and occupation, contemporaneity of debris, and even about gender assignments in shellfish gathering. Optimal foraging modelers often pair shellfish with other gathering activities performed by women such as plant collecting for time and effort estimates; dozens of archaeological reports have quantified nutritional yields for shell debris versus vertebrate debris while others have argued ranking issues and original diets. Assuming that shellfish are collected by women for food, archaeologists interpret shell middens either as base camps (when rich with artifacts) or as special activity areas (when poor in artifacts). They may instead represent men's special activity areas. The next section of this paper, inspecting hypotheses for the demise of the Shell Mound Archaic, will incorporate several of these observations.

The Demise of the Shell Mound Archaic

Earlier I argued that the inclusion of gender in research problems could revitalize our studies, a point I hope to demonstrate in returning to the issue of why Shell Mound Archaic peoples ceased shellfishing. This problem has only occasionally been raised and never dealt with adequately.

In the eastern United States, the Shell Mound Archaic is most apparent in the archaeological record 5500–3000 years ago. Shell accumulation appears to have begun 8000 years ago on the Tennessee and Duck rivers in northwestern Tennessee. The phenomenon spread southward along the Tennessee River into the Pickwick area which straddles the Alabama/Tennessee state line (11 mounds) and further upstream into the Wheeler Basin area (four mounds) by 4000 years ago (Morse 1967: 149). It also spread northward into central Kentucky along a series of rivers: on the Tennessee in Marshall County near its confluence with the Ohio, on the middle Cumberland River, on the Green River (36 shell middens and mounds), and on the Ohio, particularly around the fall line and sporadically upriver to the confluence with the Little Miami River. The West Virginia panhandle also contains some shell mounds (figure 10.1). Paralleling Rolingson (1967: 3), I do not include the Archaic period shell middens on the Savannah River, the St. Johns River (Florida), and the Georgia Coast, nor do I include the Riverton Culture on the Wabash River. The Shell Mound Archaic definition as used here requires three particular traits: the mounding of shells, the use of the mounded shell for burial, and no evidence of permanent housing.

Our knowledge of the Shell Mound Archaic lifeway consists

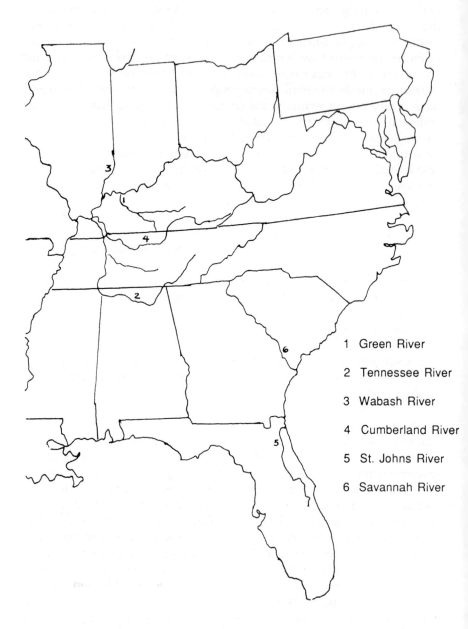

Figure 10.1 Locations mentioned in text.

1 Green River

2 Tennessee River

3 Wabash River

4 Cumberland River

5 St. Johns River

6 Savannah River

principally of subsistence data. Fauna found are plentiful molluscs, most still paired in the ground (see below), and some deer, fish, and turtle. The SMA people gave even greater attention to plant foods, especially hickory nuts (Marquardt 1985). In addition, thousands of stone and bone artifacts, thin clay floors, fire hearths, and pits have been recovered. No evidence of house structures have been found on the Tennessee or Green rivers. The sites in Kentucky have been interpreted variously as base camps, settlements, transient camps or hunting camps (Winters 1974), occupied either year round (Lewis and Lewis 1961) or seasonally (Claassen 1985; Marquardt 1985; Rolingson 1967).

A distinctive characteristic of sites in this culture is the use of shell for the burial of people and dogs, usually flexed, in round graves and without artifacts. More women than men were sprinkled with red ochre. A significant portion of the excavated ceremonial equipment – medicine bags, turtle shell rattles, and flutes – was found with women. No significant differences in health were noted between the sexes, and judging from skeletal studies, both women and men habitually performed certain common kinds of labor (Marquardt 1985). Entire populations were buried in these mounds, but at Indian Knoll (Green River) at least, "status positions marked by the inclusion of multiple artifact categories in a grave were open only to adult males and to children" (Rothschild 1979: 671). Technomic artifacts were found with adults but not with sub-adults. Fishhooks, among other objects, were found only with males. Webb and DeJarnette (1942: 311) claimed that the middens on the Tennessee in Alabama (Pickwick and Wheeler basins) had their closest counterpart in materials and sites on the Green River, sharing 23 of 69 traits.

After 4950 BP, the vigorous development of the Shell Mound Archaic in the falls of the Ohio region declined rapidly, and the area experienced a sharp drop in population density (Janzen 1977: 139). This decline predates that of the Green River sites at approximately 3500 BP. For unknown reasons, shell accumulation ceased at many of the more southerly sites, and dozens of shell mounds were capped by shell-free soil transported to them (Stein 1982). For example, artifact-rich midden without any shell caps the shell mounds of Indian Knoll, Carlston Annis, DeWeese (Green River), Eva, Big Sandy, McKelvey (Tennessee River), and Ervin (Duck River). The lack of terminal dates at most of these mounds prevents us from knowing whether the shell accumulation ended abruptly or gradually at sites in any one valley. Recent excavators of Carlston Annis posit an end of shell accumulation there 3000 years ago (Marquardt and Watson 1983). The Walker Site shell mound on the Tennessee River has a C14 date of 2915±80 BP (Dye 1980: 96) and Hofman (1986: 198) suggests that Eva shellfishers relocated to neighboring sites like Cherry. A simultaneous cessation of shellfishing is, of course, assumed by those who have speculated that environmental change was the precipitating cause.

Three common hypotheses for the cessation of musseling in the SMA are: (1) overexploitation of the mussel population by humans; (2) environmental change; and (3) human emigration, with occupants of these shell mounds moving outside the Green and lower Tennessee River areas. Attributing the decline to overexploitation, Winters (1974) suggested the Indian Knoll folks moved onto the Wabash, although this reconstruction demands further investigation given the differences in trait lists. Significantly, the three excavated Wabash River sites yielded no burials and plenty of house remains. Alternatively, people from Eva, Big Sandy, and the Green River could have moved into the Pickwick and Wheeler Basins and continued shellfishing. Just how much shellfishing occurred after the Late Archaic in these two basins is unclear.

While it is possible to clean out a mussel bed, it would be virtually impossible to denude an entire river of the mussel fauna through human predation, particularly relying only on seasonal exploitation. Given that mussel spat is transported by fish, recovery of the mussel population on any one bed should occur within the lifespan of even a short-lived Archaic person, if not more rapidly. If these shell mounds were indeed seasonal encampments it is hard to imagine why the groups did not relocate elsewhere on the river, or on neighboring rivers, to avail themselves of shellfish. Why no Archaic shell mounds occur on the lower Cumberland River, for instance, has been a major research problem for the Lower Cumberland Archaeological Project (Casey 1987; Nance 1987: 96).

The environmental changes used to explain both the advent and cessation of SMA shellfishing are associated with the Hypsithermal. From 9000 to 5000 years ago, peaking at 7000 BP, temperatures warmed an average of two to three degrees above today's. Summer rainfall diminished and the rate of water evaporation increased. Slow shallow rivers facilitated human collecting (e.g. Lewis and Lewis 1961: 9) and/or presented conditions more favorable to the establishment of molluscan communities than deep, rapid water (Ahler 1984: 546; Lewis and Lewis 1961: 20; Neusius 1982: 75; Styles 1985; Winters 1962: 2–5). Other authors have argued that Hypsithermal dessication of upland areas forced people to the banks of various rivers such as the St. Johns in Florida (Milanich and Fairbanks 1980: 146) and the Savannah (Anderson and Schuldenrein 1985: 709), two rivers arguably a part of the Shell Mound Archaic phenomenon.

By 4500 BP, however, the Hypsithermal had given way again to wetter climate. The absence of conditions that facilitated shellfishing

4000 years earlier is then offered as an explanation for the cessation of shell accumulation in mounds of the interior Eastern US. More rainfall raised river levels and increased the rate of water flow, hazardous to both humans and mussels. Increased moisture also enticed people away from rivers and into the uplands when looking for settlement locations.

The arguments for environmental change have convincingly identified an association between intensive shellfishing and the Hypsithermal, but I find this association insufficient to explain either the beginning or the end of the Shell Mound Archaic. While the climatic changes of the hypsithermal impacted the entire United States, the intensification of shellfishing occurred only on some rivers in the Eastern US and the phenomenon of mounding freshwater shells was even more localized, restricted to the St. Johns (not a SMA expression), the Duck, and the Harpeth, where gastropods were mounded, and the Ohio, the Tennessee, and the Green, where both bivalves and gastropods were mounded. It is precisely the fact that Archaic shell middens occur on so few rivers that suggests that neither environmental change, population pressure, optimal foraging strategies, nor overexploitation account for either the beginning or end of the Shell Mound Archaic.

Given the serious doubts that can be raised about each of the common hypotheses for the demise of the SMA, other hypotheses are needed. No new mound accumulations began during the Early Woodland in the Green River valley or in adjacent valleys; apparently no new use for shell developed; and a mass die-off is insufficient to explain why the Green River mound residents did not relocate. Although OFT could be employed in this problem with the aim of demonstrating that shellfishing had been maladaptive, I suspect that we need to be concerned with the organization of shellfishing, an issue not conducive to OFT (Keene 1983: 147). What then could account for the dramatic end of shellfishing 3000 years ago?

Interestingly, the hypotheses considered above all have the same ramification, namely that the activities of women and children are directly impacted by the cessation of shellfishing. Perhaps instead of a radical change in women's activities resulting from one of these hypotheticals, a change in women's labor allocation was the *cause* of the cessation of shell gathering. Perhaps a suitable explanation for this problem has eluded us because we have ignored gender and society as potential arenas of process and sources of hypotheses, and because the typical emphasis on environmental change has dulled our imaginations. I will now present several hypotheses that probe gender and related social ideologies of the Shell Mound Archaic culture.

The starchy seed hypothesis

The activities of women and children evidently changed with the cessation of the Shell Mound Archaic; if women and children were no longer harvesting mussels, what is it they were doing instead, and why? I have proposed elsewhere (Claassen 1985) that SMA shellfishers were drying molluscan flesh for consumption during winter and spring as well as consuming the flesh fresh at the time of processing. Theler (1985) makes a similar proposition for prehistoric Wisconsin Indians. In the course of testing the Carlston Annis Mound and removing a 25 × 25 cm column sample from the DeWeese Mound, both on the Green River, a high percentage of paired valves were encountered. The 35 units in the three meter long DeWeese column sample contained anywhere from 30 percent to 100 percent paired valves. Morse (1967) also commented on the high number of paired valves in the Robinson Mound. Perhaps masses of animals were dumped onto coals, steamed open, and the meats rapidly removed. Empty (but still connected) shells were then gathered up and dumped by the basket load into the same heap. The mass of accumulating shells then pressed the valves closed and held the shells *in situ*.

If freshwater mussels were being steamed open and dried for delayed consumption, then their absence in the Early Woodland diet of the inhabitants of the Shell Mound Archaic area takes on new significance. Before an easily gathered, highly storable resource would be dropped from the diet, people must have identified another storable foodstuff offering equal or higher dietary value, or, alternatively, the need for a storable winter/spring food had been obviated.

An activity that might have competed with shellfishing for a woman's time in late summer and fall when musseling is easiest due to low water, one that would have produced a comparable storable foodstuff, is the intensive harvest of one or more domesticated edible crops. Perhaps musseling stopped at the time that horticultural activities intensified in this area approximately 3000 years ago. Recent summations of data on domesticates in the Eastern Woodlands (e.g. Smith 1987) demonstrate starchy seed horticulture in this region at that time. Chenopodium and knotweed produce seeds in late summer and early fall, and maygrass seeds in the late spring/early summer. The oily seeds of marsh elder and sunflower are also available in late summer/autumn.

Confidence in this solution to the problem wanes, however, when one considers that nuts also ripen in fall and were collected during the SMA simultaneously with shellfish. Moreover, subsequent maize horticulturalists simultaneously gathered molluscs and farmed, activities that completely overlapped in labor requirements. Furthermore, not all adult women would be engaged in either seed gathering or shell gathering, so that both activities could be carried out in the same subsistence system.

Neumann (1979: 421) points out that the ever growing Woodland period population "required an influx of energy proportional to the growth of that population", an energy requirement "well above that provided by the mussels." He argues that the problem of securing more calories was solved by increasing the dependence on mast: "The mast network provided one thing which the mussels of the Archaic no longer could – a sheer abundance of calories" (Neumann 1979: 423). However, Neumann never suggests that the mast network alone could support this growing population. In fact, he argues that the mast network, plus fish, *mussels*, fowl, and other game were utilized during the Woodland, as indeed they were in areas north and south of the Green River.

Not only were nut harvesting and shellfishing carried on simultaneously, but shellfishing and agriculture were as well, at other times and in other places in the Eastern US, diminishing the strength of this explanation. Furthermore, the fact that more foodstuffs, not fewer foodstuffs, would be needed by the growing Early Woodland populations, also weighs against the idea of starchy seeds eliminating the need for shellfish flesh.

The fishing hypothesis

Perhaps it is to a change in men's activities rather than women's that we should look for a cultural cause for the cessation of musseling and shell mound building. The question becomes, what would have caused men in this region to stop shellfishing 3000 years ago? If the shell accumulated primarily as fish bait debris, what would have prompted them to stop collecting shellfish as bait? The possibilities are numerous, but in fact a change in the quantity of fish is not indicated by the Carlston Annis data (Patty Jo Watson, personal communication 1988). Perhaps baited fishing techniques (baskets, hook and line, and chuming) faded in importance around 3000 years ago while non-baited techniques (spearing, gill-nets, pound nets) increased in use. Species ratios might reveal such a change in fishing technology.

Prentice (1986) has proposed that cultigens first appeared in ceremonial contexts under the jurisdiction of men's organizations. The suite of activities involved in these rituals could have competed directly with late summer/fall musseling and fishing by men. Engendering the prehistoric shellfishers as male suggests many new research directions.

Change in social unit collecting and/or consuming shellfish

It is possible that the density of women and households accounts for the density of shell debris. Women in Middle or Late Archaic communities in the Ohio, Green, and Tennessee valleys, organized into large groups, created mounds of shell debris, while women and households in Early Woodland society, which was less socially complex, were highly dispersed over the landscape. With women dispersed, shell debris was dispersed. Shell is highly susceptible to diagenesis in freshwater contexts, and shell deposited in low densities most assuredly had dissolved by now. This hypothesis will require further research.

Ceremonialism using shells

There remains the possibility that the meat inside the shells was incidental to some use for the shell. An alternative motivation for SMA shellfishing would have been to erect burial mounds of shells which themselves had symbolic importance and ritual significance. These mounds, then, would constitute the earliest artifically created burial contexts in the Eastern US. Support for this proposition comes from the tremendous number of burials in the shell mounds of the Green River (Marquardt estimates a density of 1.2 burials per square meter – Patty-Jo Watson, personal communication 1988) as well as in other SMA shell middens.

In the Eastern US, the association of shell with human burials is at least 6,200 years old, for shell beads were found in a burial of this date at the Ervin site in Tennessee (Hofman 1986). Throughout the Archaic and in Middle Woodland times, marine shell ornaments were among the most numerous and most widely dispersed of all exotic goods, repeatedly found in the greatest numbers in graves. Marine shell objects were one of the few exotics traded through the Ohio River Valley in Late Woodland times (Ottesen 1979). Mississippian ceremonial use of shells is well known, from dippers for Black Drink to shrouds.

For the Maya, shell also had a complex symbolic role and had probably held these symbolic associations for many years prior to the Mayan florescence.

Shells, particularly conch shells, symbolized the earth, the underworld, and the realm of the dead . . . A representation of a shell added to the sun glyph converted it to a symbol for night. (Thompson 1950: 49).

On monuments, an inverted, conventionalized univalve shell represented south, associated with the death god and the underworld. (ibid.: 49, 85, 271)

Conventionalized Olivia shells, and bivalves, sometimes in combination with the representation of a hand, symbolized completion and possibly zero. (ibid.: 138) . . . The idea of completion may have been equivalent to death. (ibid.: 186). However, shells were also symbols of the moon goddess and procreation. (ibid.: 133–4) (Moholy-Nagy 1963: 71–2)

Curiously, at Tikal, Moholy-Nagy found that the contents of structure and monument caches, apparently ceremonial in origin, were most often paired bivalves (1963: 73).

Additional support for this hypothesis comes from the fact that shell mounds are only one type of Late Archaic site in the SMA region. Better candidates than the shell mounds can be found for base camps, but there are no better candidates for ceremonial centers. The characterization of mounds like the Eva site as a large village with year round occupation is strained by the data presented (Lewis and Lewis 1961); other mounds with high percentages of paired valves such as Carlston Annis, DeWeese, and Robinson very surely indicate little post-depositional disturbance. Hofman (1986) argues that these mounds served as seasonal aggregation points for a dispersed hunting-gathering population and, more specifically, were "a preferred burial location" (1986: 153). Most notably, "individuals active in reproductive and economic affairs of the aggregate social group" were buried in shell mounds, while younger and older individuals were more frequently found in non-shell sites (Hofman 1986: 182).

I propose that shellfish were gathered seasonally and ceremoniously and that many of the meats were ignored or were stored for winter use (accounting for the frequent paired valves). Shells in DeWeese, Indian Knoll and Carlston Annis mounds may even have been brought from elsewhere since Stein (1982) argues that the Green River was deep, sluggish, and muddy, yet the species are riffle/run inhabitants. It was the shell itself that was valued, to erect monuments and as a burial context for a specific subset of community members including many women who themselves may have been shellfishers, provisioners of storable protein, and shamans by virtue of an ideological system that associated shell with value, procreation and death.

While it is unlikely that horticulture prevented women from having the time to shellfish, I agree with Prentice (1986) that horticulture changed religious practices. Among other changes, I suspect that it lessened the symbolic relevance of shell. Prentice asserts that "the adoption of cucurbit gardening by eastern Archaic peoples was accompanied by the adoption of new mythological concepts, of new perceptions of proper human–plant relationships and probably new ideas regarding the life and death relationship" (1986: 115)." If the ritual items associated with many of the female skeletons at Indian Knoll signify them as shamans, then, following Prentice's logic, the shellfishers among them would be among the first individuals to adopt the new practices and would thus create powerful stimuli for social change. [Prentice (1986: 113), however, apparently sees the change to have been in the hands of men.] Like shells, gourds are a fertility symbol, and cucurbit symbolism may have been substituted for the prior symbolism of shells. Given that this change is ideological and consequently slow to occur, shell mounding was probably abandoned at different times in the region. The test implications for this hypothesis are many, although its ultimate disproof may be impossible.

Conclusion

This paper has explored some theoretical and methodological implications of the gender of shellfishers. The problem of the demise of the Shell Mound Archaic was examined, and I concluded that overexploitation, optimal foraging, population pressure and environmental change are dead-ends in solving this problem. Instead, I proposed a set of alternative hypotheses that take gender as a central issue and concluded with a new and compelling interpretation of the Shell Mound Archaic, one that recognizes the centrality of women in societies associated with shellfish. While other hypotheses about relocation outside the SMA area, about horticulture and about fishing, would explain the cessation of the shell mounding, the ceremonial center hypothesis renders understandable the origin, demise and localization of the SMA, while focusing on gender ideology as a critical variable in understanding prehistory.

While the variable "gender" has been central to this paper, nowhere has it been necessary to challenge the stereotypes about sex roles in the past. To do so might unleash many additional hypotheses. Nor is it necessary to test these assumptions about gender. In the hypothesis that shellfishing ceased because women's time was taken by horticulture, or shellfishing ceased because men no longer used baited fishing techniques, it is not the gender of the actor that is to be subjected to the scientific cycle but the propositions about horticulture and fishing. We would not derive test implications for the gender specified but for the activity specified.

The focus of the latter half of this paper might indicate to the reader that I believe the androcentric bias in archaeology can be eliminated by doing better science. This is not so; remedial work with the scientific method will not eliminate sexism in archaeology. The academic training we undergo rarely counters the sexism we have already absorbed, and usually reinforces it. Field projects frequently perpetuate sexism as do many job settings. The task of eliminating sexism may be unrealistic, but the rewards for chipping away at it will be realized immediately; perhaps the greatest harm our sexism does to our ability to interpret the past is to limit our imaginations.

ACKNOWLEDGMENTS

Thanks to Pat Watson for allowing me access to the DeWeese site in 1983 and to Julie Stein, Alison Wylie, Janet Levy, Patty Jo Watson, Alan May, and Bill Marquardt for helping me remove a column sample that summer and understand the project's work. Martha Rolingson read and commented on the initial version of this paper. Pat Watson in particular and the conference participants in general provided much support for the continuation of this exercise. Patrica Teltser dealt out some particularly testy comments about the testability of gender that sent me to Sandra Harding's writing and helped me focus some of the rewrite. The final rewrite benefited greatly from Joan Gero's and Meg Conkey's editing.

REFERENCES

Ahler, Steven (1984). "Archaic Settlement Strategies in the Modoc Locality." Ph.D. dissertation. Ann Arbor: University Microfilms.

Anderson, David and Joseph Schuldenrein (1985). "Prehistoric Human Ecology Along the Upper Savannah River, A Synthetic Overview." In *Prehistoric Human Ecology Along the Upper Savannah River: Excavations at the Rucker's Bottom, Abbeville and Bullard Site Groups*, assembled by David Anderson and Joseph Schuldenrein, vol. II: 695–722. Atlanta: National Park Service Archeological Services.

Bender, Barbara (1985). "Emergent Tribal Formations in the American Midcontinent." *American Antiquity* 50: 52–62.

Binford, Lewis (1962). "Archaeology as Anthropology." *American Antiquity* 28: 217–25.

Brauner, David (1975). *Archaeological Salvage of the Scorpion Knoll Site, 45As41*. Washington State University, Washington Research Center, Pullman: Washington Project Reports 23.

Casey, Joanna (1987). "Aboriginal and Modern Mussel Assemblages of the Lower Cumberland River." *Southeastern Archaeology* 6: 115–23.

Claassen, Cheryl (1985). "An Analytical Study of Shellfish from the DeWeese Mound, Kentucky." In *The Archaeology of the Middle Green River*, William Marquardt and Patty Jo Watson, eds. Kent State University Press; in press.

Cumbaa, Stephen (1976). "A Reconsideration of Freshwater Exploitation in the Florida Archaic." *Florida Anthropologist* 29: 49–59.

Douglas, Mary (1966). *Purity and Danger*. New York: Penguin Press.

Dye, David (1980). "Primary Forest Efficiency in the Western Middle Tennessee Valley." Ph.D. dissertation. University Microfilms International.

Erlandson, Jon (1988). "The Role of Shellfish in Prehistoric Economies: A Protein Perspective." *American Antiquity* 53: 102–9.

Fischer, John, Ann Fischer, and Frank Mahony (1977). "Totemism and

Allergy." In *Culture, Disease, and Healing*, David Landy, ed. New York: Macmillan, 154–9.

Friedl, Ernestine (1975). *Women and Men: An Anthropological Perspective.* New York: Holt, Rinehart, and Winston.

Goodwin, R. C. (1979). "The Prehistoric Cultural Ecology of St. Kitts, West Indies: A Case Study In Island Archaeology." Ph.D. Dissertation, Ann Arbor: University Microfilms.

Hofman, Jack (1986). "Hunter-Gatherer Mortuary Variability: Toward an Explanatory Model." Ph.D. Dissertation, University of Tennessee.

Janzen, Donald (1977). "An Examination of Late Archaic Development in the Falls of the Ohio River Area." In *For the Directory: Research Essays in Honor of James B. Griffin*, Charles Cleland, ed. Ann Arbor: University of Michigan Museum of Anthropology, Anthropology Papers 61, 123–43.

Keene, Arthur (1983). "Biology, Behavior, and Borrowing: A Critical Examination of Optimal Foraging Theory in Archaeology." In *Archaeological Hammers and Theories*, James A. Moore and Arthur Keene, eds. New York: Academic Press, 137–56.

Kirch, Patrick and T. S. Dye (1979). "Ethno-archaeology and the Development of Polynesian Fishing Strategies." *The Journal of Polynesian Society* 88: 53–76.

Klippel, W. and D. Morey (1986). "Contextual and Nutritional Analysis of Freshwater Gastropods from Middle Archaic Deposits at the Hays Site, Middle Tennessee." *American Antiquity* 51: 799–813.

Laughlin, William (1975). "Holocene History of Nikolski Bay, Alaska, and Aleut Evolution." *Folk* 16, 17: 95–115.

Lewis, Robert Barry (1979). "Hunter-Gatherer Foraging: Some Theoretical Explorations and Archaeological Tests." Ph.D. Dissertation, University of Illinois at Urbana-Champagne.

Lewis, Thomas and Madeline Lewis (1961). *Eva.* Knoxville: University of Tennessee Press.

Lohse, E. S. (1984). *Archaeological Investigations at Site 45-OK-11, Chief Joseph Dam Project, Washington.* University of Washington: Office of Public Archaeology Institute for Environmental Studies.

Lund, Jens (1983). "Fishing as a Folk Occupation in the Lower Ohio Valley (1982)." Ph.D. dissertation, Ann Arbor: University Microfilms International.

McCay, Bonnie (1981). "Optimal Foragers or Political Actors? Ecological Analyses of a New Jersey Fishery." *American Ethnologist* 8: 356–82.

Marquardt, William (1985). "Complexity and Scale in the Study of Fisher-Gatherer-Hunters: An Example from the Eastern United States." In *Prehistoric Hunter-Gatherers: The Emergence of Cultural Complexity*, T. Douglas Price and James Brown, eds. Orlando: Academic Press, 59–89.

Marquardt, William and Patty Jo Watson (1983). "The Shell Mound Archaic of Western Kentucky." In *Archaic Hunters and Gatherers in the American Midwest*, James Brown and J. Phillips, eds. Orlando: Academic Press, 323–39.

May, Jack Alan (1982). "Midden Formation Modeling Using Ethnographic and Archaeological Data: A Trend Surface Analysis of Midden Deposits at the

Carlston Annis Site." Ph.D. Dissertation. Ann Arbor: University Microfilms.

Meehan, Betty (1982). *Shell Bed to Shell Midden.* Canberra: Australian Institute of Aboriginal Studies.

Milanich, Jerald and Charles Fairbanks (1980). *Florida Archaeology.* Orlando: Academic Press.

Moholy-Nagy, Hattula (1963). "Shells and Other Marine Material from Tikal." In *Estudios de Cultura Maya,* vol. 3: 64–83.

Morse, Dan (1967). "The Robinson Site and Shell Mound Archaic Culture in the Middle South." Ph.D. dissertation, University of Michigan.

Nance, Jack (1987). "Research into the Prehistory of the Lower Tennessee-Cumberland-Ohio Region." *Southeastern Archaeology* 6: 93–9.

Neumann, Thomas (1979). "Culture, Energy, and Subsistence: A Model for Prehistoric Subsistence." Ph.D. dissertation, Ann Arbor: University Microfilms.

Neusius, Sarah (1982). "Early Middle Archaic Subsistence Strategies: Changes in Faunal Exploitation at the Koster Site." Ph.D. dissertation, Ann Arbor: University Microfilms.

Ottesen, Ann (1979). "A Preliminary Study of the Acquisition of Exotic Raw Materials by Late Woodland and Mississippian Groups." Ph.D. dissertation, Ann Arbor: University Microfilms.

Parmalee, Paul and Walter Klippel (1974). "Freshwater Mussels as a Prehistoric Food Resource." *American Antiquity* 39: 421–34.

Perlman, Stephen (1976). "Optimum Diet Models and Prehistoric Hunter-Gatherers: A Test on Martha's Vineyard." Ph.D. dissertation, Ann Abor: University Microfilms.

Post, Alan (1982). "Evaluation of Freshwater Mussels (Megalonaias gigantea) as a New Protein Source." Unpublished Ph.D. dissertation, Ann Arbor: University Microfilms.

Prentice, Guy (1986). "Origins of Plant Domestication in the Eastern United States: Promoting the Individual in Archaeological Theory." *Southeastern Archaeology* 5: 103–19.

Rolingson, Martha (1967). "Temporal Perspective on the Archaic Cultures in the Middle South." Ph.D. dissertation, University of Michigan.

Rothschild, Nan (1979). "Mortuary Behavior and Social Organization at Indian Knoll and Dickinson Mounds." *American Antiquity* 44: 658–75.

Sidwell, V. D., J. Bonnett, and E. Zook (1973). "Chemical and Nutritive Values of Several Fresh and Canned Finfish, Crustaceans and Molluscs, Part I: Proximate Composition, Calcium, and Phosphorus." *Marine Fisheries Review* 35(12): 16–19.

Sidwell, Valerie, P. R. Foncannon, N. Moore, and J. H. Bonnet (1974). "Composition of the Edible Portion of Raw (Fresh or Frozen) Crustaceans, Finfish, and Molluscs. I. Protein, Fat, Moisture, Ash, Carbohydrate, Energy Value, and Cholesterol. *Marine Fisheries Review* 36(3): 21–35.

Smith, Bruce (1987). "Hopewellian Farmers of Eastern North America." Paper read at the Mainz Congress.

Speck, Frank (1946). *Catawba Hunting, Trapping, and Fishing.* Museum of the University of Pennsylvania Philadelphia Anthropological Society, joint publication No. 2.

300   C. P. Claassen

Stein, Julia (1982). "Geologic Analysis of the Green River Shell Middens." *Southeastern Archaeology* 1: 22–39.
Styles, Bonnie (1985). *Aquatic Exploitation: Paleoecological and Cultural Change.* Evanston: Northwestern University Archaeology Program.
Theler, James (1985). *Woodland Tradition Economic Strategies.* Iowa: Office of the State Archaeologist, Report 17.
Thompson, J. E. S. (1950). *Maya Hieroglyphic Writing.* Washington: Carnegie Institute of Washington, Publication 589.
Voorhies, Barbara (1976). "Chantuto People: An Archaic Period Society of the Chiapas Littoral, Mexico." *New World Archaeological Foundation*, Paper 41.
Walthall, John (1980). *Prehistoric Indians of the Southeast.* University, AL: University of Alabama Press.
Waselkov, G. (1982). "Shellfish Gathering and Shell Midden Archaeology." Unpublished Ph.D. Dissertation, Ann Arbor: University Microfilms.
—— (1987). "Shellfish Gathering and Shell Midden Archaeology." In *Advances in Archaeological Method and Theory*, vol. 10, Michael B. Schiffer, ed. New York: Academic Press, 93–210.
Webb, William and David DeJarnette (1942). *An Archaeological Survey of Pickwick Basin in the Adjacent Portions of Alabama, Mississippi, and Tennessee.* Washington: Bureau of American Ethnology, Bulletin 129.
Winterhalder, Bruce and Eric Smith, (eds) (1981). *Hunter-Gatherer Foraging Strategies.* Chicago: University of Chicago Press.
Winters, Howard (1969). *The Riverton Culture.* Illinois State Museum, Reports of Investigations 13. Springfield.
—— (1974). Introduction to the New Edition. In *Indian Knoll*, W. Webb. Knoxville: University of Tennessee Press.
Yesner, David (1981). "Archaeological Applications of Optimal Foraging Theory: Harvest Strategies of Aleut Hunter-Gatherers." In *Hunter-Gatherer Foraging Strategies*, Bruce Winterhalder and Eric Smith, eds. Chicago: University of Chicago Press, 148–70.

11

Pounding Acorn: Women's Production as Social and Economic Focus

Thomas L. Jackson

Introduction

"Woman the Gatherer" has been adopted as a banner title for studies that emphasize the crucial role played by women in subsistence procurement and food production (e.g. Dahlberg 1981; Slocum 1975). Much of what has been written in archaeology about women's productivity derives from historical and ethnographical studies. Making the necessary theoretical and methodological extrapolations from such investigations for analyses of prehistoric material is a precarious task, as are attempts to shift gender attribution from specific artifacts to production roles (e.g. Conkey and Spector 1984: 11–12; Spector 1982). One effective approach to the study of an engendered past is through the use of carefully constructed analogies which link historical and prehistoric data.

In this paper I discuss women's production related to the procurement and processing of certain basic subsistence resources. I present a case study employing historical, ethnographic, and archaeological data from which I argue that, among those historic and late prehistoric Indian cultures of the western Sierra Nevada of California, women's food procurement and production activities were fundamental in structuring subsistence and settlement systems and other inter- and intra-community social and economic relations.

The geographical area of interest is the western slope of the southern Sierra Nevada of California, in the area of the upper San Joaquin and Kings rivers (figure 11.1). Historically this area was occupied by Western Mono (also known as Monache), Southern Sierra Miwok, and Yokuts groups (Gayton 1948; Gifford 1932; Kroeber 1925, 1959; Merriam 1904, 1930, 1966–7; Spier 1978a and b). Among these groups the procurement and processing of acorns by women was of major dietary and economic

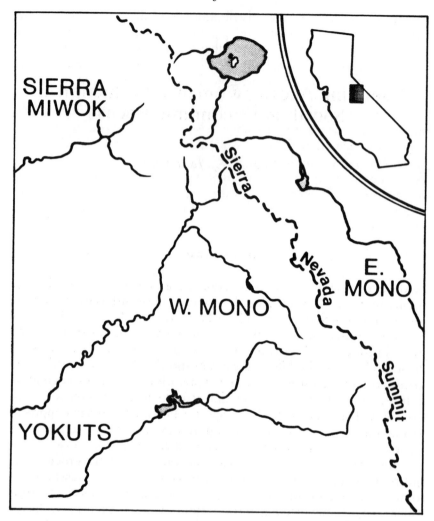

Figure 11.1 Location of the study area in the southern Sierra Nevada, California.

importance. The engendered nature of this production in Western Mono society is the focus of this study.

The processing of acorns into food products was accomplished exclusively by women, using bedrock milling and acorn storage facilities constructed and maintained by women. The distribution of these milling and storage facilities on the archaeological landscape constitutes a map of the logistical strategies employed by women engaged in subsistence production. Likewise, the distribution of milling facilities within archaeologically defined sites reveals an intra-site spatial organization which suggests that women's production was spatially segregated in some settlements (e.g. large winter villages) but spatially integrated in small summer camps where men would be expected to be frequently absent on hunting or trading treks.

With the innovation of fixed food processing facilities on the landscape women were probably less mobile than their ancestors. Production focused at these fixed locations would have complemented reproduction and childrearing. When we consider that the fixed acorn processing facilities on the landscape were apparently owned by the women who made them, we can then address issues of how women's property was maintained and distributed in Western Mono society and we can begin to interpret the material cultural record of these relations of property.

Many archaeological (and broader anthropological) implications are raised by this discussion. One purpose of this study is to demonstrate the considerable value of conjoining a theoretical perspective that engenders the past with an empirical data base in contemporary archaeology.

Balanophagy or Acorn Processing

Procurement and preparation of acorns

Historic Indian populations in California were dependent on acorns to supply a major portion of their dietary needs. Acorn food products remain important to many California Indians, and some Indian women still process acorns using traditional methods, including pulverizing acorns in bedrock mortars. Many ethnographic accounts describe acorn gathering and processing (what Gifford 1936 called "balanophagy"), and some anthropologists have suggested that the role of acorns in California societies was similar to that of cultigens in horticultural or agricultural cultures (e.g. Baumhoff 1978; Bean and Lawton 1973; Meighan 1959). Although acorn collecting was supplemented by the gathering of a tremendous variety of other plant resources, acorns were extremely important because of their abundance and storability. Despite the large number of accounts which acknowledge the importance of acorns in the native diet, detailed descriptions of aspects of procurement and processing strategies are lacking.

Ethnographies of southern Sierra Indian cultures consistently remark on the dietary importance of acorns, and ethnographic reports agree that acorn collecting involved all competent family members, male and female, and adult and child. During the period that acorns ripen, it was essential that a maximum labor effort be mounted since they are also quickly removed at that time by birds and arboreal mammals. As the seeds become more mature they are prone to insect damage, and acorns which fall to the ground are very quickly consumed by mammals, especially deer and bear (Barrett 1980; Griffin 1980; Koenig 1980; Verner 1980).

The logistics of acorn harvesting in the southern Sierra Nevada are complex: different oak species produce acorns in either one- or two-year cycles; various groves of trees produce greater or lesser mast yields; acorns on oaks at different altitudes ripen at different times; and acorns from some species (especially black oak, *Quercus kelloggii*) are preferred by Indians over other species for their flavor and oil and gluten content (Baumhoff 1963; Gifford 1932: 17). Harvesting strategies must evaluate all these factors as well as the logistics of transporting collected acorns to winter villages and storage facilities.

Among the Western Mono (the behavior among Yokuts or Miwok groups is noted where different), the role played by men in acorn foods processing was restricted to the harvesting stage. All other production was carried out by women. Acorn collecting commenced at higher altitudes in the mountains where most Mono family groups spent the summer months. The principal oak species there is black oak, and this was the preferred acorn. These usually begin ripening in late September and harvest may continue through October. Collected acorns were placed in burden baskets and taken to the lower elevation winter base camp in relays, apparently by women (Gayton 1948: 222; cf. Theodoratus et al. 1982: 10).

We know from archaeological observation that a granary, or granaries, would often be constructed near bedrock mortars. Presumably these upland storage facilities were used only when it was decided that enough acorns had been stored in the lower altitude settlement since upper elevation granaries would not be accessible during most winter months due to deep snow and extreme cold.

Acorn processing is a very time-consuming endeavor, performed exclusively by women.[1] The acorns had to be dried and then shelled (although green acorns may be "peeled" for more immediate use). A thin, papery "skin" covers the acorn meat and had be removed before pulverizing. Modern Mono women use a paring knife to remove this "skin", but they report that in earlier times an obsidian flake was used (Blount, personal communication). The shelled and skinned acorns were then ready for pounding.

Acorn pulverizing was accomplished using a bedrock mortar and pestle. (Yokuts and Miwok groups also employed portable bowl mortars of stone and wood for pulverizing acorns, but Mono deny the use of these.) Initial pounding to a coarse flour took place in a "starter" mortar which usually did not exceed 5.5 cm in depth (McCarthy 1987; McCarthy et al. 1985). From time to time the meal was removed from the mortar and sifted, using a basketry tray specifically designed for the purpose. Too large particles were returned to the mortar for further pulverizing.

The coarse flour was reduced to a finer consistency in a "finishing" mortar. The depth of these mortars ranges from 5.5 to 9.5 cm (McCarthy 1987; McCarthy et al. 1985). Bits of acorn and flour which scatter from the mortar during preparation were swept up using a brush made of soaproot (*Chlorogalum pomeridianum*). Flour was removed from the mortar holes by hand and with the use of a brush. Thus, the tool kit for preparing acorn flour consisted of a set of baskets and basketry trays, one or more soaproot brushes, and mortars and pestles.

There are very few descriptions of the amount of acorn flour that can be produced in a given period of time. Goldschmidt (1974: 52–3) reported for the Hupa that 2.7 kg of dry, shelled acorns could be reduced to flour in about 180 minutes. Gayton (1948: 178) recounts for Chukchansi Yokuts: "Nearly a whole day was spent at this work [making acorn flour], producing a quantity sufficient to last an average family two or three days."

To remove tannic acid the acorn flour is leached. The flour is placed in a shallow leaching basin and either cold or hot water poured gently and repeatedly over the meal until the tannic acid has been removed, a process requiring several hours. Cold water is preferred for leaching as it conserves the oil content of the meal, but hot or warm water is used when women are impatient. The volume of water necessary for leaching is considerable and probably was a consideration in the preferential location of settlements (and hence archaeological sites) near dependable water supplies.

After leaching, the meal is removed from the basin and prepared as a variety of soups, gruels, mushes, and breads. Gathering of wood for cooking was apparently a task for men and boys, but actual preparation of the food was accomplished by women. Cooking acorn preparations requires considerable fuel which generates a large amount of ash and charcoal. Soils with high ash and carbon content are generally referred to as "midden" by regional archaeologists and are taken to represent activity areas related to the preparation of acorn foods. Midden soils at archaeological sites almost invariably occur in direct association with bedrock mortars.

Acorns were consumed year-round. Family groups carried acorns and acorn flour with them when they traveled. Acorns were transported during trans-Sierran expeditions to be pulverized at camp sites along the

way, and acorns were traded to Eastern Mono. Acorns were also traded
to neighboring groups who might have experienced food shortages.

Bedrock food processing features and implements

Bedrock food processing features consist of mortars and "slicks"
fabricated in outcroppings of bedrock or on free-standing boulders.
While the term "bedrock" is not strictly correct in all cases, it provides
an appropriate connotation of immobility.

Ethnographic records and Indian consultants indicate that mortars are
principally used for the pulverization of seeds and other fruit and
vegetable materials, but also for meat, pigments, and clay used for
making pottery.[2] It should be emphasized, however, that acorn flour
preparation was the single predominant activity for which bedrock
mortars were employed, and meat and pigments were more frequently
ground in small portable mortars (Gayton 1948; Gifford 1932). Mortars

Figure 11.2 Northfork Mono woman Mollie Cheepo pounding manzanita
(*Arctostapholos*) berries in a bedrock mortar using a cobble pestle. Photograph
made ca.1918 by E. W. Gifford and originally published in Gifford (1932).
(Photograph courtesy of Lowie Museum of Anthroplogy, The University of
California at Berkeley)

Figure 11.3 Northfork Mono women pounding acorn and sifting acorn meal. The women are seated under a brush sun arbor with additional brush placed around the perimeter as a windbreak. The woman at right has just delivered the pestle into a mortar containing acorns. Note the collar of meal that has developed around the mouth of the mortar. The woman at left is using a basketry tray to sift acorn meal. Photograph made ca.1918 by E. W. Gifford. (Photograph courtesy of the Lowie Museum of Anthropology, The University of California at Berkeley)

used for processing small hard seeds usually exceed the maximum depth of "finishing" mortars for acorn pounding, and may be as much as 25 cm deep (cf. McCarthy 1987).

The Western Mono functional classification of mortar types as "starter", "finishing" and "seed" mortars, has been verified by ethnographers taking Indian women to archaeological sites and asking them to describe the use of various mortars. Consultants are very consistent in their typological assignments, which are based primarily on mortar dimensions. More importantly, Indian consultants relate that mortars were manufactured by women to desired dimensions (Blount, personal communication; McCarthy 1987; McCarthy et al. 1985).

Archaeological studies indicate that the number of individual bedrock mortars at archaeologically defined "sites" in this area of the southern Sierra Nevada ranges from one to about 200. It is difficult to suggest an average number of mortars per site because the number of mortars varies according to site type and environmental setting. Also, there are cognitive and methodical problems with the way archaeologists define a "site". But it is reasonable to say that most archaeologically defined sites with bedrock mortars have approximately six to eight mortars. Sites with outcrops containing more than 60 mortars are rare and may represent places at which large numbers of people aggregated for special occasions.

Bedrock mortars were excavated into solid granite in virtually all cases in this study area, and prehistorically this was accomplished without metal tools. Ethnographic information indicates that women made bedrock mortars. Thus, the creation of bedrock mortar features represents an enormous investment of women's labor.

"Slicks" associated with bedrock mortars are often interpreted by archaeologists to be the functional equivalent of millingstones or "metates", a flat stone milling surface on which seeds are ground using a handstone or "mano". There are technical reasons to disagree with this interpretation, and contemporary Indian women consultants say that slicks were areas on the bedrock where soft seeds, berries, and other such plant foods were pulped or lightly crushed, using a handstone (Blount, personal communication),implying that no hard grinding was involved.

Pulverization of plant material in mortars is achieved using a pestle. Pestles are usually unshaped stream cobbles, roughly triangular in plan and usually weighing four to six kilograms. Some pestles are shaped by pecking and abrading, but these are not common in the Sierra Nevada. The diameter and length of the pestle is appropriate to the diameter and depth of the mortar. It is not uncommon to find a bedrock mortar feature with a number of pestles left adjacent to, or in, the mortar holes on the outcrop.

Granaries

Several types of granaries were constructed and maintained by women to store acorns. Granaries were placed either on raised free-standing platforms, in trees, or on stone foundations built on open, sloping granite bedrock outcrops or boulders. The latter are recognizable archaeologically. Granaries were used only for acorns; other kinds of seeds and foodstuffs were stored differently. Dried, unshelled acorns were poured into the storage bin as it was constructed (Gayton 1948: 216–17; Gifford 1932: 20–1). Shelled acorns for more immediate use were kept in baskets in the family dwelling. Shelling acorns apparently was a regular nightly chore undertaken by women and children.

The geographical distribution of rock granary foundations reveals much about the logistics of acorn storage. As one might expect, granary foundations are situated near lower elevation village sites and represent stockpiles tapped during the winter when the upper altitude regions were covered in snow and (presumably) uninhabited. However, granary

The Maun-a-sou-ron Comes Back

Figure 11.4 Mrs Julia Charley (Dunlap Mono) standing by acorn granaries ("maun-a-sou-ron") constructed on circular rock foundations. December 1936. (Photograph courtesy of the *Fresno Bee* newspaper)

foundations are also found at higher elevations, and in settings that apparently are not close to large settlements, suggesting that they may have been erected in areas where the acorn crop was bountiful. Such caches could serve as an emergency food supply if winter has prolonged and food ran short in the winter villages, and they could provide a "fresh" supply of acorns for people in the high country in the spring and summer, until the fall harvest.

The storability of acorns is an important factor. Gayton (1948: 187) reports that Chuckchansi Yokuts families maintained granaries with a supply of acorns to last up to two years, and such granaries were the personal property of women. Modern informants report storing acorns for as much as four years. The significance of storage *vis-à-vis* social complexity in gatherer-hunter societies has been examined by Testart (1982) and Woodburn (1980, 1982) but neither has evaluated the implications of storage as engendered production and accumulation of surplus.

Acorn Processing in Ethnohistory and in the Archaeological Record

Acorn milling in the history of the southern Sierra Nevada

The record of acorn exploitation in prehistoric central California has
been described best by Schulz (1981; see also Basgall 1987), and there is
no need here to repeat his relevant arguments regarding subsistence
implications of mano/metate (hard seed grinding) and mortar/pestle
(acorn pounding) tool kits. The critical factors in acorn processing are an
efficient pulverizing technology and an effective method for leaching out
the toxic tannic acid which renders most acorn varieties unpalatable. The
apparently rapid growth of prehistoric populations in much of California
after ca.AD 500 may be related to improvements in these two areas of
acorn processing.

In the southern Sierra Nevada and foothills, the earlier milling slab/
handstone tool kit was succeeded by bedrock mortar and pestle as the
dominant processing technology. The timing of this succession, however, is
uncertain. Bedrock mortar facilities are difficult to date because they are
not integral to stratigraphic cultural deposits, a dating problem similar to
that for pictographs and petroglyphs. Suggested ages for the innovation
of bedrock mortar features in the southern Sierra Nevada and foothills
range between 1,650 and 450 years ago (McGuire and Garfinkle 1980;
Moratto 1984: 317; Wren 1976: 53). I believe bedrock mortars became
the dominant processing technology by ca.1,000 years ago, but the
mortar technology did not altogether replace the milling slab/handstone
tool kit (Jackson and Dietz 1984: 210).

The Western Mono are relatively recent settlers on the west slope of
the Sierra Nevada. Their immigration is apparently related to the broader
"Numic spread" in the Great Basin (Bettinger and Baumhoff 1982;
Fowler 1972; Lamb 1958). Kroeber (1925, 1959) and Lamb (1958)
suggest that the linguistic divergence of Eastern and Western Mono
occurred no more than 500 years ago, and the ancestors of Western
Mono on the western Sierra slope, either ancestral Yokuts of Miwok,
most likely introduced bedrock mortars into the southern Sierra Nevada
region.[3] Economic interaction spanning several thousand years between
western and eastern Sierran cultures is documented archaeologically,
especially for obsidian exchange (Hall 1983). It is probable that Mono
knowledge of acorn processing using bedrock milling features was
acquired in the context of this economic history.

Archaeological interpretations of bedrock mortars are not well
developed, and it previously has not been considered that Indians (much
less Indian *women*) intentionally made bedrock mortars. Lacking the

ethnographic classification of mortar types discussed above, archaeologists have concluded that mortars become deeper with use, and that when they became too deep they were abandoned (after Barrett and Gifford 1933; Gifford 1932; cf. Bennyhoff 1956 and Moratto 1972). This deduction ignores the fact that the impact of the pestle in the mortar is largely, if not entirely, mitigated by the meal packed in the bottom of the mortar hole. Acknowledging that Indian women deliberately manufactured mortars also explains the non-random, tri-modal depth distribution which parallels the typology offered by contemporary Mono women (Jackson 1985; McCarthy et al. 1985).

Spatial distribution of bedrock milling features

Bedrock mortars are among the most frequently recorded archaeological features in the Sierra Nevada. A great deal of data about their distribution and, more specifically, about the attributes of mortar distributions within sites has been collected. Regrettably these data have not been extensively analyzed.

I have suggested elsewhere (Jackson 1984, 1985; Jackson and Dietz 1984) that we can distinguish at least two sorts of sites with bedrock mortars: one type representing habitation by relatively small populations for relatively brief periods, and another with significantly more complex occupational deposits that might relate to the presence of larger populations for longer periods of time, or redundant periodic occupation at a given location. I have referred to these latter sites as "K-sites" (Jackson 1984, 1985). K-sites are distinguished by the presence of "midden" soils, high densities of lithic debitage and artifacts, and bedrock mortar features with a minimum of 14 mortars.[4]

Sites with bedrock mortars are ubiquitous in the Sierra Nevada. Sites with large numbers of mortars are less common, and a study of the distribution of these K-sites reveals interesting patterns for which several "rules" may be noted:

1 K-sites are located a maximum of ca.3,000 meters from their nearest K-site neighbor (this does not mean that all K-sites are 3,000 meters apart).
2 K-site geographical spacings are quite regular, but vary geometrically.
3 Within 1,000 meters of K-sites, an average minimum of three other smaller sites, with between one and six bedrock mortars, occur.
4 K-sites are located no more than 200 meters from a reliable water source.
5 Distance between K-site neighbors appears to be a function of subsistence resource density (e.g. oak population).

Figure 11.5 illustrates the spacing of known K-sites in a middle altitude (ca. 2,100 meters) environment in the southern Sierra Nevada. The known K-sites are spaced approximately 3,000 meters apart. I attribute this relatively wide spacing to the fact that the location is in the upper altitudes of black oak distribution, and oaks in this area are irregularly clustered with large areas of open granite exposures.

A few miles to the west, at a slightly lower elevation approximating the median altitude for black oak distribution and with a greater abundance of oaks, K-sites are spaced regularly approximately 2,000 meters apart. At still lower altitudes, where winter settlements were situated, archaeologically defined K-sites cluster, but these clusters of K-sites are regularly spaced nevertheless. This observation of a regular spacing of K-sites is congruent with models of evolutionary economic development which predict the intensification of subsistence procurement strategies, including the relatively systematic (logistical) "mapping onto" the physical environment (*sensu* Binford 1980).

Of greater relevance to the issue at hand, these food processing sites represent the creation by women of *fixed production facilities* on the landscape which are related directly to the organization of women's labor and production. Regular spacing of camp sites would be of no particular advantage for men in their principal endeavor of hunting larger game animals (e.g. deer), a pursuit usually undertaken by individuals. However, there does appear to be a coincidence between the locations of K-sites and proximity to spring and fall migratory routes of deer (figure 11.5).

It is not known if K-sites were occupied contemporaneously or successively in a given season, or periodically in a given year depending upon resource yields. Regardless, the spacing of K-sites reflects women's decisions about appropriate distances relating to the performance of production activities. The regular spacing of K-sites suggests that the facilities were situated to accommodate systematic annual movements across the landscape to collect and process, primarily, the acorn resource. As a number of other studies have demonstrated, collectors operate within certain distance constraints relative to some base camp. When resources are diminished within a socially and economically defined range, the group moves to a new base (Binford 1980; Lee 1969).

Cognitive transformations: concepts of place

With the development of bedrock mortar facilities there must also have occurred a transformation in the way people perceived the landscape they inhabited. Mobile groups, transporting the tools necessary for subsistence, certainly would have viewed the land differently than

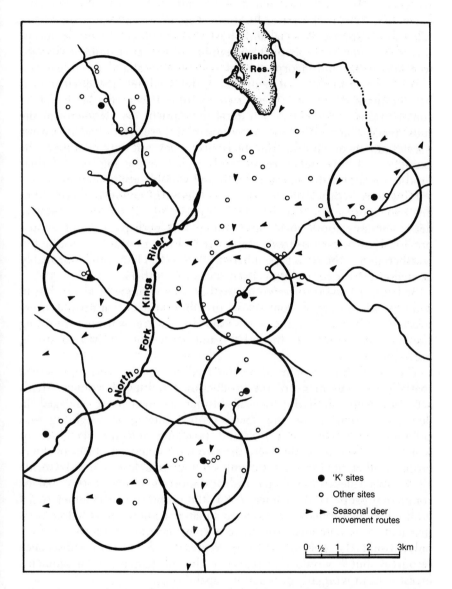

Figure 11.5 Distribution of "K-sites". Sites are consistently spaced at ca.3,000 meter intervals. Circles around K-sites have a radius of 1,500 meters. Arrows trace radio monitored seasonal deer movement routes through the area.

groups who relate to fixed production facilities at specific places. As Ardener (1981: 12) has stated "behavior and space are mutually dependent." Bedrock mortar locations were established by women as a calculated response to social and physical environmental considerations. But at the same time, people's perceptions of that environment changed to acknowledge and incorporate these technological and social features.

With the innovation of bedrock mortar facilities, the environment became marked with features that symbolized women's labor. These constructions represented a capital investment by women in the subsistence system. With the development of these mortar facilities came a series of new decisions about the environment, not only relating to the extraction of subsistence resources but also to the logistics of their production and distribution as foods and storable accumulations.

How were bedrock mortar locations selected? Obviously there had to be an exposure of suitable rock, generating a set of qualitative determinations about rock outcroppings that perhaps had not existed previously. Rock exposures suitable for bedrock mortars cannot be too weathered, nor the rock type inherently too soft. Hence, there probably existed criteria for selecting certain rocks over others.

Bedrock mortar features are invariably near a source of water, but in addition we can argue from spatial distribution data that settings were selected to offer pleasant views and to receive warming morning sunlight, but which, on the other hand, were not exposed to strong prevailing winds.

The establishment of fixed mortar facilities on the landscape served spatially to focus many of the production activities of women. Men's activities were similarly focused insofar as men were engaged in defensive activities for the social group. Inter-group fighting was common in native California, and poaching and the slaughter of women's collecting parties were the two most common causes of inter-group conflict cited in the California ethnographic literature (McCorkle 1978). Regardless of whether bedrock mortars were the personal or communal property of women versus the property of the larger social group, they nevertheless represented a material adjunct to resource areas that had to be defended from take-over by neighbouring groups. Not only would the loss of territory represent the loss of subsistence resources, but it would also represent the substantial loss of women's investment in women's production capability.

The arrangement of mortar features on the landscape, then, is basically the result of decisions by the women who made and used these facilities. These choices are mapped for archaeologists in the spatial patterning of sites with bedrock mortar features. Encoded in this map are elements of western Sierra culture that define appropriate spatial, social, and symbolic ordering of women and women's production. Issues relating to gender and space have been discussed most cogently by Moore (1988), and her insights can be brought to bear very effectively in this kind of study, especially regarding intra-site spatial organization.

Intra-site spatial organization

The study of intra-site distributions of bedrock mortar features is scarcely developed. An example illustrates one avenue for investigation in which the spatial organization of women's production is manifest in the distribution of mortar features within archaeologically defined sites. Figure 11.6 is a sketch map of an archaeological site at Chawanakee Flats in Fresno County, California. Chawanakee Flats was occupied by Mono Indian people, some apparently living in traditional house structures until the influenza epidemic of 1917–18 (Jackson 1979). Note in the figure the spatial relationship between the bedrock mortar areas, midden, and house pits. In almost all cases where house pits are preserved, they occur in midden areas with mortar features close by. But notice also the relative isolation of two mortar areas approximately 50 meters from the central midden and house areas, suggesting a discrete women's space.

The spatial isolation of some bedrock mortars is a common feature of large, low elevation sites in the southern Sierra Nevada. Such isolation is not common at upper elevation sites where, in contrast with the lower elevation winter sites, we would anticipate that men did not spend a great deal of time on site.

Bedrock mortar features often are found distributed over several boulders or rock outcrops, some with one or a few mortars, others with many. Modern Indian women suggest that the spatial relationships among mortars of different types on an outcrop indicates whether acorn pounding was done by several women or by single individuals. Indian women say that processing chores often were shared, with some women making the initial coarse meal (in "starter" mortars) and others preparing the finished flour (in "finishing" mortars), accounting for the observed clustering of mortars of one type on some part of a rock exposure.

It is not unusual to find outcrops with no more than a single, or perhaps two or three, mortar cups. These may be located at some distance from the central site area, or well away from another outcrop which has a large number of mortars on it. This perhaps would suggest a processing area for an individual woman. Sometimes only a single type of mortar occurs; sometimes a starter and a finishing mortar. Mono women say the preferred distance between a starter mortar and finishing mortar for a woman working alone was approximately 20 cm (Blount, personal communication; cf. McCarthy et al. 1985).

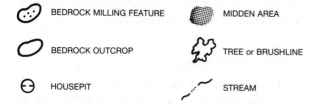

BEDROCK MILLING FEATURE   MIDDEN AREA

BEDROCK OUTCROP   TREE or BRUSHLINE

HOUSEPIT   STREAM

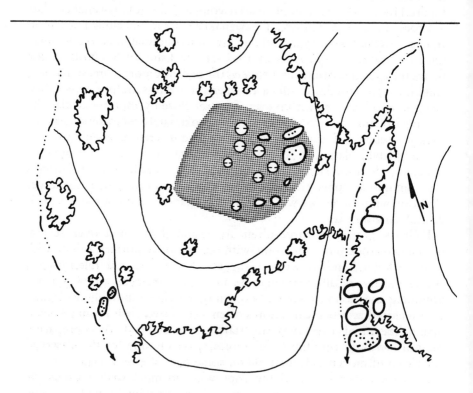

Figure 11.6 Sketch map of an archaeological site at Chawanakee Flats. Note the distribution of bedrock milling features. Some features are located immediately adjacent the main habitation area in proximity to house remains. Other milling features are located ca.50 meters away from the central midden area in a more isolated setting.

It is interesting to note the artifact content of midden soils found associated with bedrock milling facilities. Middens invariably have a relatively high density of artifacts and other occupational debris. Midden soils contain both archaeologically and ethnographically male- and female-assigned tools, including projectile points and edge modified flake tools (but see Gero, this volume), pestles, handstones, etc. In some sense middens suggest a spatial integration of female/male activities. Ethnographic accounts indicate that the men's sweathouse was located away from the main living and daily activity areas, perhaps thereby balancing the living arrangement between the exclusively female work area and the exclusively male sweathouse, with the midden area as a social interaction area.

Bedrock mortar facilities would have certainly served as communication centers. Although mortar stations were used exclusively by women, information about women's activities as well as men's activities was exchanged at these places. Information that was "input" at the household level was distributed at the community level at the food processing station, and vice versa: news of the latest expedition over the Sierra to visit relatives on the east side also informed of pine nut abundance, the time of scheduled ceremonies, the deaths or births of friends and relatives, etc.

Production and reproduction

The relationship between *production* and *reproduction* is a concern for studies of women in prehistory. As Dahlberg (1981: 20–4) has discussed, perceptions of women's roles must address perceived constraints relating to childbearing and rearing. Women's obligations to children are perceived to restrict their activities to the "domestic sphere" (Rosaldo 1974: 23) and reduce their participation in the greater "public sphere". The relationship between child maintenance and subsistence activities is also debated (e.g. Brown 1970; Lee 1981; Sacks 1979). But acorn food production and reproductive biology are perhaps more compatible than a highly mobile foraging subsistence strategy.

Bedrock mortar facilities generally offer a good vantage from which to observe the activities of children. Women working together would have an opportunity to discuss children's development and exchange philosophies of childrearing and socialization. Pounding acorns is a time-consuming task, but it also affords time for female–child interaction. Unlike more mobile gatherers, people engaged in an acorn subsistence economy have considerable time on site, more like village horticulturalists or agriculturalists than stereotypical nomadic gatherer-hunter groups.

The shift to an acorn-based subsistence economy very likely resulted in a substantial reduction in gatherer mobility, or certainly necessary mobility. The abundance and storability of acorns meant that with a month of intensive labor a family or community could accumulate a storable surplus of food that would last for at least a year. The gathering of plant foods to supplement acorns, and to add zest and variety to the diet, became a chore free from the pressing demands of a subsistence mode where long-term storage of food was not an option. Recall the statement by the Yokuts woman that a day spent pounding acorn provided meal for two or three days for the average family. This suggests that a day spent processing is a day not gathering. Thus, mobility is reduced one day in three or one day in two, a reduction in mobility of 33–50 percent.

One indication of the effects of an acorn-based economy on reproduction may be the apparently rapid growth of the Western Mono population once it became established in the western Sierra Nevada. I have suggested a population growth rate of about 1.0 percent for the Mono during the 500 or so years of their residence in the western Sierra (Jackson and Dietz 1984: 196–7). This growth rate is comparable to that (1.07 percent) proposed by Koyama (1978) for populations in the Middle Jomon Period in Japan, for example. In any event, reported population densities in the western Sierra are double or triple those of Mono and Shoshonean people in the eastern Sierra and the western Great Basin (cf. Baumhoff 1963).

Social relations of property and production

With the innovation of bedrock mortars and the incorporation of these facilities into the material culture of women's labor, there must have arisen the question of how these facilities would be treated as property, especially as regards domestic property held during a woman's lifetime, property transferred with marriage and inheritance. Obviously, bedrock mortars are not like beads, baskets, or other portable personal property which might stay with the woman should she change her domicile. Thus some accommodation of property rights must have been necessary when the fixed bedrock mortar facilities were incorporated into the society's material culture.

Gifford (1932: 32–3) cites an informant's comment for the Northfork Mono: "Most men lived with their wives' folks all the time. That was the rule." He goes on to state, "The Northfork Mono family was strongly maternal, for in addition to husband, wife, and children the wife's relatives rather than the husband's often formed the balance of the household." This strong maternal relationship extended to food gathering and processing where it is reported that women would gather seeds from their mother's plots and process them at their mother's bedrock mortar facility. Women also would claim certain trees and seed plots by marking them. Disputes arising over claims were adjudicated by the village headman (Gayton 1948).

The pattern of post-nuptial matrilocal residence is one response where significant property, that is, bedrock mortar features, must remain fixed and where rights to that property remain with the woman. However, this apparently is not the case among other Sierran groups. Patrilocal, patrilineal residence and inheritance rules are strongly expressed among the Miwok, with the implication that a woman who left to reside with her husband and his kin either must have recreated mortar facilities for her own use or shared the facilities of her husband's kin. This difference between the more recently arrived Mono accommodation to fixed property versus the Yokuts and Miwok response is most interesting.

As mentioned earlier, Mono and Yokuts women may also have laid claim to granaries and their contents. Given the arguments of, for example, Testart (1982) and Woodburn (1980, 1982) about the significance of storage for the development of social complexity among gatherer-hunters, the implication that storable surplus was controlled by women, but possibly manipulated for inter-group exchange by men, is a fascinating perspective on the relations of production that structure the entire social organization.

Since California ethnographies make it clear that men dominated inter-group exchange, it may be suggested that such roles would have been possible only after men had successfully negotiated for access to food surplus. Although the process and context of such negotiations are not documented for California and western Great Basin cultures, a comparable situation may be described by Hamilton (1980) for Aboriginal groups in the Western Desert of Australia. Hamilton describes a case "in which the ability of men to control sectors of women's labour, and to appropriate their product, is the essential basis on which the elaboration of male secret ceremonial (and therefore political) life depends" (1980: 5). Another parallel between the California and Australian cases is the use of fixed milling facilities on the landscape by women in both cultures.

Conclusions

One goal of a feminist archaeology is to rewrite history in a way that gives full credit to the role played by women in the evolution of human societies (cf. Chevillard and Leconte 1986; Leibowitz 1986; Tanner and Zihlman 1976; Zihlman 1978, 1981). Demonstrating the androcentric bias in archaeology is easily accomplished (e.g. Conkey and Spector 1984) but remedying the situation is not. One approach is to rethink archaeology with the assumption that gender is a fundamental element of culture, and that gender is expressed in the archaeological record. The irony of the previous two sentences is that American archaeologists are generally trained as anthropologists, and supposedly are taught that women's roles in cultures throughout the world are both different from, and complementary to, men's role. In other words, most archaeologists probably have some *knowledge* of a theoretical concept of gender relations. Why then do archaeologists not *acknowledge* gender in studying prehistoric cultures?

As Gero discusses in her paper in this volume, archaeologists often focus their attention on artifact assemblages and technologies that are presumed to be associated with male activities, including retouched lithic artifacts. A comparison of the "hunter-gatherer" literature dealing with flaked stone tools versus ground stone tools (e.g. mortars, pestles, milling slabs and handstones) would reflect this disproportionate emphasis. The lack of study of bedrock mortars in the Sierra Nevada seem part of this general trend. One hypothesis accounting for this behavior among archaeologists is that milling and other similar plant food processing equipment is presumed to be associated with women's labor and, corresponding with a general devaluation of women's work, this presumption then suffices as adequate interpretation.

The neglect of women's roles and the cultural significance of women's productivity is carried into the formulation of cultural/temporal schemes in the California and Great Basin regions (and elsewhere). The prehistoric periods defined in these schemes invariably emphasize changes in flaked stone technology as indicative of social transformations. For example, the technological shift from throwing stick and dart to bow and arrow is credited with far-reaching effects in the cultural system. By contrast, the shift from milling slab/handstone to bedrock mortar/pestle food processing technology is barely acknowledged as anything more than a simple historical development or a necessary response to environmental change (cf. Chartkoff and Chartkoff 1984; Moratto 1984), and hardly recognized as an "invention" at all.

The organization of women's production was a fundamental structuring element in Western Mono culture, and doubtless in other historic and prehistoric Indian cultures as well. Western Mono women created fixed food processing facilities which represented direct investments in long-term productivity. The introduction of these cultural features onto the landscape probably changed the way the landscape was perceived and altered the way in which the environment was exploited. Women controlled the means and the products of their labor, yet it seems that, at least in part, these products were negotiated into the hands of men who controlled inter-group exchange, a situation perhaps directly comparable to that described for Australian Aborigines by Hamilton (1980).

In this case study I have attempted to demonstrate not only that gender relations are expressed in the archaeological record, but also that once the idea of such fundamental structural relationships is credited, we are launched on a new course in the exploration of prehistoric human social relations. By juxtaposing an ethnographic record which is demonstrably androcentric against an archaeological data base which is reexamined from a feminist perspective, it can be suggested that much of the theoretical basis for the study of gatherer-hunters will require reconsideration. By including gender as a part of these future studies we gain a more sapient perspective on humankind in the past, a perspective that derives from, and informs upon, our present-day efforts at shedding the androcentrism of our own (post-Modern?) culture.

NOTES

1 The male berdache participated in women's food gathering and processing activities, including the pounding of acorns in bedrock mortars (Gayton 1948: e.g. 236, 274).
2 The only reference to the Western Mono use of bedrock mortars for the preparation of clay relates to the Patwisha (Gayton 1929: 245). The Wukchumni Yokuts (Gayton 1929: 245) and Tübatulabal (Voegelin 1938: 30–3) also pounded clay in mortars but it is expressly stated for all these groups that the mortars were no longer used for food processing. This is in keeping with other reports of food gathering and processing implements being kept impeccably clean.
3 Eastern and Western Mono differ at the dialect or super-dialect level.
4 Very few confirmed K-sites have as few as 14 bedrock mortars; most have at least 20.

REFERENCES

Ardener, S. (1981). "Ground Rules and Social Maps for Women: An Introduction." In *Women and Space*, S. Ardener, ed. London: Croom Helm, 11–34.
Barrett, Reginald H. (1980). "Mammals of California Oak Habitats – Management Implications." In *Proceedings of the Symposium on the Ecology, Management, and Utilization of California Oaks*. Berkeley: United States Department of Agriculture, Forest Service, Pacific Southwest Forest and Range Experiment Station, General Technical Report PSW-44, 275–91.

Barrett, S. A. and E. W. Gifford (1933). "Miwok Material Culture." *Bulletin of the Public Museum of the City of Milwaukee* 2(4): 117–376.

Basgall, Mark E. (1987). "Resource Intensification among Hunter-Gatherers: Acorn Economies in Prehistoric California." *Research in Economic Anthropology* 9: 21–52.

Baumhoff, Martin A. (1963). "Ecological Determinants of Aboriginal California Populations." *University of California Publications in American Archaeology and Ethnology* 49(2): 155–236.

—— (1978). "Environmental Background." In *Handbook of North American Indians*, vol. 8. Washington: Smithsonian Institution, 16–24.

Bean, L. J. and H. W. Lawton (1973). "Some Explanations for the Rise of Cultural Complexity in Native California with Comments on Proto-Agriculture and Agriculture." In *Patterns of Indian Burning in California: Ecology and Ethno-history*, H. Lewis. Ramona, CA: Ballena Press Anthropological Papers 1, v–xlvii.

Bennyhoff, J. A. (1956). "An Appraisal of the Archaeological Resources of Yosemite National Park." *University of California Archaeological Survey Reports* 34: 1–71.

Bettinger, Robert L. and Martin A. Baumhoff (1982). "The Numic Spread: Great Basin Cultures in Competition." *American Antiquity* 47: 485–503.

Binford, Lewis R. (1980). "Willow Smoke and Dogs' Tails: Hunter-Gatherer Settlement Systems and Archaeological Site Formation." *American Antiquity* 45: 4–20.

Brown, Judith K. (1970). "A Note on the Division of Labor by Sex." *American Anthropologist* 72: 1073–8.

Chartkoff, Joseph L. and Kerry Kona Chartkoff (1984). *The Archaeology of California*. Stanford: Stanford University Press.

Chevillard, Nicole and Sebastien Leconte (1986). "The Dawn of Lineage Societies: The Origins of Women's Oppression." In *Women's Work, Men's Property: The Origins of Gender and Class*, S. Coontz and P. Henderson, eds. London: Verso, 76–107.

Conkey, Margaret W. and Janet D. Spector (1984). "Archaeology and the Study of Gender." In *Advances in Archaeological Method and Theory*, vol. 7, M. B. Schiffer, ed. New York: Academic Press, 1–38.

Dahlberg, Frances (1981). *Woman the Gatherer*. New Haven: Yale University Press.

Fowler, Catherine S. (1972). "Some Ecological Clues to Proto-Numic Home-lands." *Desert Research Institute Publications in the Social Sciences* 8: 105–22. Reno.

Gayton, A. H. (1929). "Yokuts and Western Mono Pottery-making." *University of California Publications in American Archaeology and Ethnology* 24(3): 239–51.

—— (1948). "Yokuts and Western Mono Ethnography." Berkeley: University of California Anthropological Records 10.

Gifford, E. W. (1932). "Northfork Mono." "*University of California Publications in American Archaeology and Ethnology* 31(2): 15–65.

—— (1936). "California Balanophagy." In *Essays in Anthropology Presented to*

A. L. Kroeber, 87–98. Reprinted 1971 in *The California Indians: A Source Book*, R. F. Heizer and M. A. Whipple, eds. Berkeley: University of California Press, 301–5.

Goldschmidt, Walter (1974). "Subsistence Activities among the Hupa." In *Indian Land Use and Occupancy in California*, vol. 1, R. Beals, ed. New York: Garland Publishing Company, 52–5.

Griffin, James R. (1980). "Animal Damage to Valley Oak Acorns and Seedlings, Carmel Valley, California." In *Proceedings of the Symposium on the Ecology, Management, and Utilization of California Oaks*. Berkeley: United States Department of Agriculture, Forest Service, Pacific Southwest Forest and Range Experiment Station, General Technical Report PSW-44, 242–5.

Hall, Matthew Clyde (1983). "Late Holocene Hunter-Gatherers and Volcanism in the Long Valley–Mono Craters Region: Prehistoric Culture Change in the Eastern Sierra Nevada." Ph.D. dissertation, Department of Anthropology, University of California at Riverside.

Hamilton, Annette (1980). "Dual Social Systems: Technology, Labour and Women's Secret Rites in the Eastern Western Desert of Australia." *Oceania* 51: 4–19.

Jackson, Thomas L. (1979). "Report of the Chawanakee Flats Archaeological Survey." Report submitted to the Sierra National Forest, Supervisor's Office, Fresno, CA.

—— (1984). "Predictive Model of Prehistoric Settlement Patterning in the Southern Sierra Nevada." In *Cultural Resources Overview of the Southern Sierra Nevada*, prepared by Theodoratus Cultural Research, Inc. and Archaeological Consulting and Research Services, Inc. Fresno, CA.: USDA, Sierra National Forest, 174–203.

—— (1985). "Prehistoric Settlement Patterning in the Southern Sierra Nevada, California." Paper read at the 19th Annual Meeting of the Society for California Archaeology, San Diego.

Jackson, Thomas L. and Stephen A. Dietz (1984). *Archaeological Data Recovery Excavations at CA-FRE-798 and CA-FRE-805, Siphon Substation 33kV Distribution Line and Balsam Meadow Hydroelectric Project*. Rosemead: Southern California Edison Company.

Koenig, Walter D. (1980). "Acorn Storage by Acorn Woodpeckers in an Oak Woodland: An Energetics Analysis." In *Proceedings of the Symposium on the Ecology, Management, and Utilization of California Oaks*. Berkeley: United States Department of Agriculture, Forest Service, Pacific Southwest Forest and Range Experiment Station, General Technical Report PSW-44, 265–9.

Koyama, S. (1978). "Jomon Subsistence and Population." *Senri Ethnological Studies* 2: 1–65.

Kroeber, A. L. (1925). *Handbook of the Indians of California*. Bureau of American Ethnology Bulletin 78.

—— (1959). "Ethnographic Interpretations: Recent Ethnic Spreads." *University of California Publications in American Archaeology and Ethnology* 47(3): 259–81.

Lamb, Sidney M. (1958). "Linguistic Prehistory in the Great Basin." *International Journal of American Linguistics* 24: 95–100.

Lee, Richard B. (1969). "!Kung Bushman Subsistence: An Input-output Analysis." In *Contributions to Anthropology: Ecological Essays*, D. Damas, ed. Ottawa: National Museums of Canada Bulletin 230, 73–94.

—— (1981). "Politics, Sexual and Nonsexual, in an Egalitarian Society: The !Kung San." In *Social Inequality: Comparative and Developmental Approaches*, G. D. Berreman, ed. New York: Academic Press, 83–102.

Leibowitz, Lila (1986). "In the Beginning . . .: The Origins of the Sexual Division of Labour and the Development of the First Human Societies." In *Women's Work, Men's Property: The Origins of Gender and Class*, S. Coontz and P. Henderson, eds. London: Verso, 43–75.

McCarthy, Helen (1987). "The Bedrock Milling Station at CA-FRE-341." In *Prehistoric and Ethnoarchaeological Investigations at CA-FRE-341, Big Creek Expansion project, Powerhouse 3, Fresno County, California*, T. Jackson and H. McCarthy. Rosemead: Southern California Edison Company, 36–48.

McCarthy, Helen et al. (1985). *Cultural Resources of the Crane Valley Hydroelectric Project Area*, vol. I. San Francisco: Pacific Gas and Electric Company.

McCorkle, T. (1978). "Intergroup Conflict." In *Handbook of North American Indians*, vol. 8. Washington: Smithsonian Institution, 694–700.

McGuire, Kelly R. and Alan P. Garfinkel (1980). *Archaeological Investigations in the Southern Sierra Nevada: The Bear Mountain Segment of the Pacific Crest Trail*. Bakersfield, CA: United States Department of the Interior, Bureau of Land Management.

Meighan, C. W. (1959). "California Cultures and the Concept of an Archaic Stage." *American Antiquity* 24(3): 289–318.

Merriam, C. Hart (1904). "Distribution of Indian Tribes in the Southern Sierra and Adjacent parts of the San Joaquin Valley, California." *Science* 19(494): 912–17.

—— (1930). "The Em-tim-bitch, A Shoshonean Tribe." *American Anthropologist* 32(3): 280–93.

—— (1966–7). *Ethnographic Notes on California Indian Tribes*. Berkeley: University of California Archaeological Survey Reports 68.

Moore, Henrietta L. (1988). *Space, Text and Gender: An Anthropological Study of the Marakwet of Kenya*. Cambridge: Cambridge University Press.

Moratto, Michael J. (1972). "A Study of Prehistory in the Southern Sierra Nevada Foothills, California." Ph.D. dissertation, Department of Anthropology, University of Oregon.

—— ed. (1984). *California Archaeology*. Orlando: Academic Press.

Rosaldo, M. (1974). "Women, Culture and Society: A Theoretical Overview." In *Women, Culture and Society*, M. Rosaldo and L. Lamphere, eds. Stanford: Stanford University Press, 17–42.

Sacks, Karen (1979). *Sisters and Wives: The Past and Future of Sexual Equality*. Westport, CT: Greenwood Press.

Schulz, Peter D. (1981). "Osteoarchaeology and Subsistence Change in Prehistoric Central California." Ph.D. dissertation, Department of Anthropology, University of California at Davis.

Slocum, Sally (1975). "Woman the Gatherer: Male Bias in Anthropology." In

Toward an Anthropology of Women, R. Reiter, ed. New York: Monthly Review Press, 36–50.

Spector, Janet D. (1982). "Male/Female Task Differentiation among the Hidatza: Toward the Development of an Archaeological Approach to the Study of Gender." In *The Hidden Half: Studies of Native Plains Women*, P. Albers and B. Medicine, eds. Washington: University Press of America, 77–99.

Spier, R. F. G. (1978a). "Monache." In *Handbook of North American Indians*, vol. 8. Washington: Smithsonian Institution, 426–36.

—— (1978b). "Foothill Yokuts." In *Handbook of North American Indians*, vol. 8. Washington: Smithsonian Institution, 471–84.

Tanner, Nancy and Adrienne Zihlman (1976). "Women in Evolution, Part I: Innovation and Selection in Human Origins." *Signs* 1(3): 104–19.

Testart, A. (1982). "The Significance of Food Storage among Hunter-Gatherers: Residence Patterns, Populations Densities, and Social Inequalities." *Current Anthropology* 23: 523–37.

Theodoratus, Dorothea J., Clinton M. Blount, and Clark L. Taylor (1982). "An Ethnographic Survey of the proposed Dinkey Creek Hydroelectric Project." Fresno, CA: Kings River Conservation District.

Verner, Jared (1980). "Birds of California Oak Habitats – Management Implications." In *Proceedings of the Symposium on the Ecology, Management, and Utilization of California Oaks*. Berkeley: United States Department of Agriculture, Forest Service, Pacific Southwest Forest and Range Experiment Station, General Technical Report PSW-44, 246–64.

Voegelin, Erminie W. (1938). *Tübatulabal Ethnography*. Berkeley: University of California Anthropological Records 2(1).

Woodburn, J. (1980). "Hunters and Gatherers Today and a Reconstruction of the Past." In *Soviet and Western Anthropology*, E. Gellner, ed. London: Duckworth, 95–117.

—— (1982). "Egalitarian Societies." *Man* (n.s.) 17: 431–51.

Wren, Donald G. (1976). "Two High Sierra Sites: FRE-534 and FRE-535." Report to Pacific Gas and Electric Company, San Francisco.

Zihlman, Adrienne L. (1978). "Women in Evolution, Part II: Subsistence and Social Organization in Early Hominids." *Signs* 4(1): 4–20.

—— (1981). "Women as Shapers in the Human Adaptation." In *Woman the Gatherer*, F. Dahlberg, ed. New Haven: Yale University Press, 75–102.

Part V

Images of Gender

12

Whose Art Was Found at Lepenski Vir? Gender Relations and Power in Archaeology

Russell G. Handsman

Illiterate. Denied vision. Excluded, excluded,
excluded from council, ritual, activity, learning,
language when there was neither biological
nor economic reason to be excluded.

Tillie Olsen, Silences (1978)

Introduction

Whenever I look at my shelves of books, searching for something
(anything) about women in prehistory, I am reminded of Virginia
Woolf's notes about the emptiness of her shelves, the formidable
difficulties faced by women writing in the past. How that act – even
thinking about it – would have been contained, controlled, and
marginalized. "Let me imagine," she says, "since facts are so hard to
come by, what would have happened had Shakespeare had a wonderfully
gifted sister, called Judith, let us say" (Woolf 1929: 48). The continuing
absence of prehistoric women from our shelves reflects relations of
writing and production which determine and enforce our silences now,
inhibit both the desire and ability to empower an imagination, and
discipline us to ignore women, or to render their works and power
invisible. All of this would be familiar to Virginia Woolf.

Silences (Olsen 1978) here means censorship of self as well as by
others: struggling to find time and space to read and write; the
devaluation of emerging work through patriarchal judgements and the
demand for a unified theoretical canon (Schiffer 1988); being coerced to
excavate, think, and write factually "like a scientist" (like a man). Such
silences pervade the discipline, making it no different from the society
outside. Its works – our narrative writings and how we work –

contribute to, preserve, and legitimize relations of exploitation, inequality, and domination within archaeology and everywhere outside it.

Some argue that, because archaeology is archaeology, or because it is a science (or a neutral search for factual truths, as Washburn 1987 believes), it has no color, no class, no sex. True, but archaeologists do,[1] and with these facts we also have, no matter how unacknowledged, evidences of discrimination against women (Gero 1985; Kramer and Stark 1988) and interpretive biases that are sexist (Conkey and Spector 1984). The writing which follows positions itself within the grid defined by the omnipresent and infinite relations between power and knowledge. Such a positioning is always oppositional because the same acknowledgement of the hidden facts and evidences carries with it a responsibility that can neither be dismissed nor avoided:

> The creative act is not pure. History evidences it. Ideology demands it. The writer loses Eden, writes to be read, and comes to realize that he is answerable. The writer is *held responsible*, and the verbal phrase is ominously accurate; for the writer not only had laid upon him responsibility for various interpretations of the consequences of his work, he is "held" before he begins by the claims of different moralities asserted upon him: artistic, linguistic, ideological, national, political, religious. He learns that the creative act was not pure even while being formed in his brain. (Gordimer 1985: 137)

This language is exact and uncompromising, leaving no room for work that seeks to conceal and preserve the inequalities present in contemporary societies. Instead, Nadine Gordimer demands an awareness and a recognition: we are responsible as writers, more specifically here as archaeologists, to criticize normal discourse and its politics of (mis)representation, to multiply and enrich (pre)history, to listen to lived memories and oral traditions as authentic representations, and to make visible what is unseen by interfering in our discipline and the society outside (Eagleton 1986, Said 1985). And in taking responsibility against the present, we will have to give away that part of us that imagines writing and other creative acts always to be male. This essential gesture is a way to begin.

Lepenski Vir

Sculptures at an exhibition

It was a colorful, beautifully designed printed poster that compelled me to visit "The Art of Lepenski Vir" at the Southampton City Art Gallery

in England in 1986. Planned to coincide with the World Archaeological
Congress, the installation consisted of two small, dramatically lighted
rooms filled with 91 pieces of monumental sculpture, carved altars, and
instruments of ritual and magic, recovered during intensive excavations
of a stratified series of prehistoric settlements situated along the Danube
River in northeastern Yugoslavia (figure 12.1). Eight habitation levels are
recognized in Lepenski Vir's complex deposits, representing a long
history of the construction and reconstruction of trapezoidal "houses"
with floors of hardened limestone plaster, some of which were burnished
with red and white pigments. Inside the houses' entranceways, carefully
built stone-lined hearths, together with associated altars (sometimes
carved) and spherical boulders (sometimes carved), were often the focus
for inhumations or the reburial of selected skeletal parts, especially those
associated with the head (Tringham 1971: 43, 53–6).

Figure 12.1 An elevation drawing for a museum exhibition, "The Art of
Lepenski Vir."

The exhibit's purposes, stated explicitly, were to share evidence of the
"great unifying force of art and culture", "to provide a precedent for the
museum's contemporary art", and "to enable each of us to learn
something of the highly developed art, culture, and civilization of the

exceptionally interesting region of Yugoslavia."[2] The political content and the sociopolitical consequences of these statements are almost satirical. Yet in them and throughout this exhibit, two other political questions are well hidden and unvoiced. Why is this art now; why was it art then? It must be art now because it is arranged that way, because the dramatic presentation of actual objects is physically removed from any consideration of archaeological or social context (summarized elsewhere in a separate gallery), and because some of the names transform artifacts into art ("pestles" are called sceptres, for example) or else employ an artistic code: Black Obelisk I and Black Obelisk II are the names given to two sculpted forms. It is also art now because this sample of 91 artifacts represents conscious choices made by the exhibition organizer to enhance and enrich our sense that aesthetics was a domain in the late Mesolithic along the Danube River in the sixth millennium BC.

It was art then because it is art now and because there is no other conceptual category or social process in archaeologists' imaginations that might be used to explore why a coherent, yet diverse system of symbolic representations and meanings was created and reconstructed in that place over hundreds of years. Calling these objects art – "art at the very beginning of a long history of artistic endeavor and civilizational achievements" – displaying them as art, and describing them with a vocabulary from art, really does make them art. But this process of categorization also makes sense to us because it expresses the tacit, agreed-upon assumption that aesthetic achievement and the competence to identify it are universally shared and timeless. We can almost hear the docents as they guide their groups, talking in hushed voices, through the art of Lepenski Vir:

> Art is art; you know it when you see it. These "sculpted representations of the human form", visual expressions of "workmanship and artistic worth", are thousands of years old. Archaeologists think they are statements about religious beliefs that linked the people of Lepenski Vir to their ancestors and to the lands and rivers from which their ancestors came. So these people long ago created a religious and mythical art that reminded them of their place in the universe. We can still sense the power of their creative acts; their art speaks to us across the millennia.[3]

We find this art powerful and evocative; its beauty, form, dignity, and style communicate to us about prehistoric artists, their lives, and their work. But what is really being said; *whose art was this?* This question is not voiced in the exhibit; nevertheless it is one that is answered – *Males' Art*. The men of Lepenski Vir, we are told, were not ordinary hunter-gatherers but creative artists, philosophers, and leaders who, as they "radically transformed a traditional way of life", created patriarchal culture and art. These were the men who were the "first in Europe to establish complex economic and social relations", as well as "the first to develop a specific architecture and to model monumental sculptures from gigantic boulders" (Srejović and Babovic 1986).

[Same as it ever was:]
One had the impression that the building of a house at Lepenski Vir was preceded by a ritual ceremony, and that the system of measuring the foundations was a secret rite into which an exceptionally small number of persons was initiated, perhaps only one enlightened member of the community. On the strength of the shapes and proportions revealed in the construction it may be concluded that this "architect magician" made use of definite measures for the drawing of all lines, that he knew how to divide these lines in half, that he knew how to determine levels on a three-point system, to draw curves and establish the focus of the inscribed circle within the triangle. (Srejović 1972: 79)

[My suspicion: Women evidently weren't mathematicians in prehistory.]

In the formality and mathematics of the planning and construction of their dwellings, the male architects of Lepenski Vir (figure 12.2), we are told, both anticipated Plato and reenacted the way "in which the universe was constructed in times immemorial" (Srejović and Babovic 1986: 4). These are the same men whose power and authority, positions and creative abilities, and art and aesthetic perspectives are represented by the names given to some of the prehistoric sculpture on display: Adam, the Sorcerer, the Barbarian, the First Father, the Old Chief, the Founder of the Tribe.

Where are the women?

They are not invisible; rather, they are present as the Lady of Lepenski Vir, the Mermaid, the First Mother, and a Vulva. That is, women are "discovered" in all the most familiar social, mythical, and sexual places, and their roles, archaeological presence, and cultural positions are, restricted to these places. By seeing and talking about women in this way the exhibit says that prehistoric art can be about women but it cannot empower them, nor can it be made by them. Thus one sees here more "proof" that women's work, spheres, and roles have always been different and separate from those of men. This categorization of the women of Lepenski Vir expresses and legitimizes the modern ideology of gender difference. There is much more.

As the exhibit presumes that the men of Lepenski Vir were the artists, and that women were one of the objects of their art, so it also expresses the idea that a prehistoric art about women will always be about their reproductive, procreative function. In this by now familiar and oppressive story, women are doubly encompassed by the customary male gaze that limits their purposive roles to birth and childrearing and sees their sexuality only as an expression of the means to guarantee the survival of the group. Through this gaze, representational art as it is both made and interpreted is used to control women and empower men.

Lepenski Vir, as popular text, scientific monograph, exhibit, and prehistoric art, represents one series of closely-linked moments defined by the union within archaeology among power, knowledge, and gender inequality. Archaeological work and writing are not simply passive expressions or representations of the ongoing hierarchical relations between men and women. Instead our discourse is productive and protective of such inequalities inside and outside the discipline. Rather than declaring our innocence, we need to confront and explore the oppressive relations between knowledge and social power (Foucault 1978, 1980; Said 1986), to see how our discourse contributes to the control, marginalization, and silencing of women. As we undertake these

Figure 12.2 The male architect of Lepenski Vir at work. Beginning about 7000 years ago, twenty or so houses – some call them religious shrines – were built at Lepenski Vir during each major period of use. Although varying in size, their plans were remarkably consistent; evidently an exact mathematical ratio was used to calculate the length and curvature of the walls. This coordinated building effort and standardized design were probably the work of a single individual, thought by archaeologists to be the head man, an old chief, "the Founder of the Tribe".

critical explorations, we will be seeking to open up new understandings of women in prehistory while we deconstruct the ideology of gender difference.

Working against the ideology of gender difference means interrogating the scientific and social construction, as well as the political effects, of the wrongheaded idea that gender is a matter of bipolar, essential, exclusive categories, one male and the other female. This ideology of difference obscures and deflects our vision, so gender relations are not seen as matters of hierarchy, domination, resistance, and control (MacKinnon 1987a; Scott 1988a). The continuing realness of asymmetry, inequality, and standardization (as in the acceptance of the male perspective as the norm in science; see Harding 1986) in the relations between the sexes is concealed beneath the illusion that gender consists of fixed and timeless oppositions given by some god, reflected in myth, or inscribed in nature and biology. To see gender as differences is to accept as natural, inevitable, and universal the constant facts that males have power while women have to struggle to get it:

> Inequality comes first; differences come after. Inequality is substantive and identifies a disparity; difference is abstract and falsely symmetrical. If this is so, a discourse of gender differences serves as ideology to neutralize, rationalize, and cover disparities of power, even as it appears to criticize them. Difference is the velvet glove on the iron fist of domination. (MacKinnon 1987a: 8)

The presumption that men were the artists and architects of Lepenski Vir, and that women were their subjects, is only one specific representation of the ideology of gender difference. As the ideology is expressed here, it also structures how some archaeologists see society, culture, the relations between men and women, and the meaning of art in a prehistoric settlement. This story's particular plot and themes are repeated constantly throughout archaeological practice, as well as social discourse, whenever we encounter "obvious" (and thus unavoidable) symbolic or realistic representations of women (figure 12.3).

[Fragments of the Same/Old/Story:]

Although the bands may be widely scattered most of the year, they need each other and come together on special occasions to arrange marriages outside the extended family and to conduct initiation ceremonies. If this life-style held for the Cro-Magnon, the Venus figurines found over large areas were probably passed from tribe to tribe, relay fashion. . . . the same pattern probably accounts for the distribution of furs, pelts, amber, shells and special flint blades throughout the central Russian plain. (Pfeiffer 1986: 82)

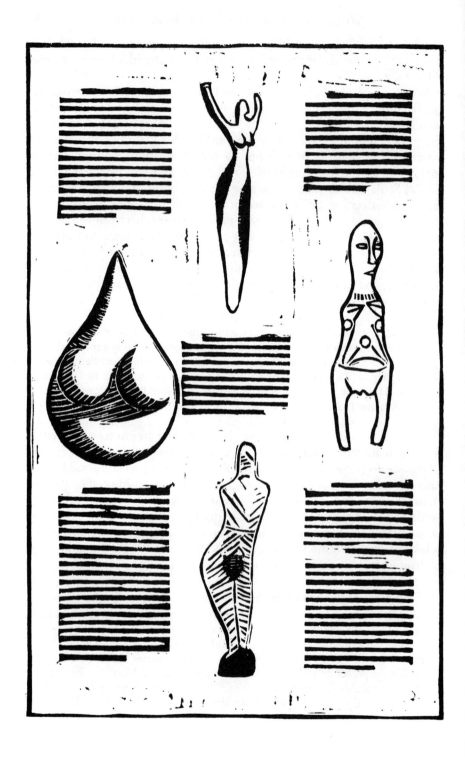

[My suspicion: The trade in women is like the trade in other goods so women and their reproductive potential are just other commodities to be bought, sold, or exchanged in yet another strategy for survival (see Gamble 1982).]

You cannot ignore the male role in heredity. It is men who make invasions, kill the defenders, seize their property, take the women as wives or concubines. (Milford Wolpoff, quoted in Putman 1988: 463)

The astonishing unity of Neolithic art is based on a very real community of religious belief. The mainspring of these beliefs is to be found in the almost universal cult of the Mother Goddess, the incarnation of fertility. (Entry for "Neolithic art" in the *Praeger Encyclopedia of Art*, vol. 4 Praeger Publishers 1971: 1456)

As for the role of women in Old European society, there are a number of indicators that women could and undoubtedly did hold high status. The number and quality of female figurines from the Old European Neolithic seem to indicate this. There may have even been matrilineal inheritance. However, none of these observations warrant the extreme interpretation that the society was "dominated" by the mother. . . . Women sometimes have inferior status, and sometimes they have equal status to that of men. But on the whole it appears that men hold the critical reins of power in traditional societies, that is, physical and armed force. And males generally appear unwilling to relinquish these or to assume inferior status. (Hayden 1986: 26)

Reading what everyone says about Venus figurines, Neolithic statuary, Cro-Magnon art, and mythologies of female power (see Campbell 1988: 66–73), and noticing what has been appropriated and used outside archaeology (Lippard 1983: 40–75), forces an understanding of how pervasive, persistent, and common the ideology, its literary expressions (Kaplan 1986), and archaeological representations have become. Gender difference is everywhere in archaeology and in archaeological studies of prehistoric art. The archaeological legitimation of gender difference, through the domain of prehistoric art, is likewise everywhere in society.

The ideology of gender difference is given a scientific basis through archaeological theory, analysis, and writing, thereby transforming a socially constructed inequality into a scientific matter of fact. However the problem is even deeper and more acute. As archaeologists situate and scientize gender differences throughout prehistory, we provide a time

Figure 12.3 An imaginary page from an encyclopedia of art. Female figurines are common in texts about archaeology and art history. Usually this art is said to symbolize fertility, womanhood, and reproduction. However, by seeing these figures as representations of widespread matriarchal societies in the past, women today are providing themselves with an enduring history and mythology.

depth or chronological frame for the ideology, making it seem a priori, as a constant and universal fact of life. Our writing creates and sustains an unending series of precedents and analogues for an idea that accepts and rationalizes contemporary sexual discrimination as society's logical recognition of the natural, timeless, and prehistoric differences between women and men (Scott 1988a). In everyday conversations, the routines of the workplace, in the statistics which continue to reveal that there is not equality in the academy, and in the inability of the legal system to see gender as domination and exploitation (MacKinnon 1987b), the ideology of difference is both pervasive and perpetuated. Because archaeologists contribute, participate, and write, we are responsible. In making this admission, a challenge is posed to those committed to building an archaeology of women and production over the next decade: *how will that project theorize gender and women's power?*

An archaeology of women and production in prehistory can mean more than reversing the androcentric flow of interpretation or enriching our knowledge of the range of women's experiences through a more empirical documentation of their work and contributions (Barrett 1986; Fox-Genovese 1982; Silverblatt 1988). Neither of these goals is trivial, nor have they become, at least in archaeology, part of the normal scientific routine. Yet either of these analytical strategies implicitly necessitates the idea of gender as a fixed, essential, and separate category. In contrast, *archaeologies of gender relations* will constantly deconstruct, rather than objectify, the ideology of gender difference (Harris and Young 1981; Scott 1988b).

> I am thinking all the time about power; the simplicity of the force and the complexity of the authority that make male supremacy a specific politics, and the changing shades of complicity, its feminine face. (MacKinnon 1987a: 3)

The key to working against the exclusions and silences which render women invisible in the past is to realize – do we dare imagine – that gender (not adaptation, complexity, or subsistence) is actually the pivotal domain and terrain where histories of social and productive relations were made, resisted, and challenged in the past. As gender is intertwined throughout alliance, exchange, and kinship; the organization of labor and the production of surplus; the specialization of work and the ordering of space; and the social reproduction of communities – in short, throughout everyday life, its representations, and transformations – then gender is embedded within and surrounds culture, society, and politics. Not to be theorized as either categories or differences, gender must be explored as relational histories of inequality, power, ideology and control, and resistance and counter-discourse (Connell 1987; Handsman 1988; Harris and Young 1981; Hodder 1984; McDonough and Harrison 1978; Moore 1986; Welbourn 1984). Seen this way, gender becomes central to the emergence and future of a postprocessual archaeology (Hodder 1985), to the desire to learn more about humankind, to the rereading of what happened in prehistory. Gender relations are the key to overturning the normal narrative accounts about the women of Lepenski Vir, as well as to seeing their lives and struggles in new ways.

So who made the art of Lepenski Vir: women or men?

Posed this way, the question misdirects our analytical attention (as well as our interpretive intentions) towards a search for clear, consistent, and patterned evidence of activities differentiated by sex. However in the assemblages from the late Mesolithic levels at Lepenski Vir (Srejović 1972) and other nearby and associated sites in the Danube Gorge, including Vlasac (Prinz 1987; Srejović and Letica 1978), such linkages are obviously neither categorical nor redundant. Indeed the clarity of sex linkages which sometimes can be identified, often at one analytical scale, is blurred or even contradicted by other associated sets of contextual data.

For example, the strong association between the ritual placement of men's skulls and their commemoration by boulders (carved and uncarved) within some of the stone sanctuaries in Lepenski Vir Ic is matched by the fractional burial of men's skulls in carefully constructed graves or stone-lined boxes in Vlasac II. In neither "settlement" are women, or their skulls, similarly treated. Likewise, some associational sets from inhumations at Vlasac indicate that red ochre was sprinkled differentially across some women (their pelvic regions) and some men (placed on their arms and legs, but not their pelvises). Yet some children and at least two women here were stained in their entirety, evidence which renders ambiguous the other, more overt signs of sexual differentiation (figure 12.4). In the same way, the absence of any explicit patterns of sexual inequality or separations in the distribution of grave goods (in fact such goods were encountered only rarely at both Lepenski Vir and Vlasac), and the fact that women were sometimes buried with men, or that women's body parts were sometimes piled with men's, suggests that gender was not a matter of explicit, standardized, or normative categories in this Mesolithic social world.

What can be read from this record of the past? Variously one might see an egalitarian society or primitive communism where men and women were equally powerful and their works equally valued, or one might discover female divinity and a mythical matriarchy (see Gimbutas 1974).

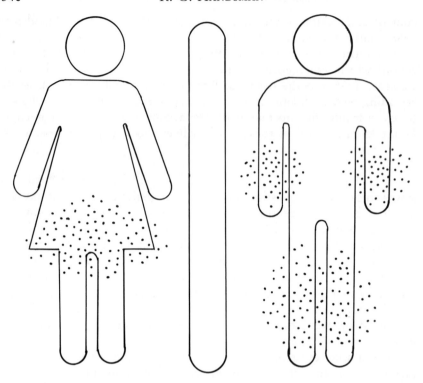

Figure 12.4 How red ochre was sprinkled across some women and some men at Vlasac. Women and men are treated differently in some Mesolithic burials from the Iron Gates Gorge. Men's skulls, not women's, are often placed in stone-lined pits; dissimilar parts of women's and men's bodies are painted with ochre at Vlasac. Elsewhere however, women and men are buried together or their bones are intermingled, blurring explicit gender differences. This suggests that Mesolithic gender relations are variable and could be about equality, inequality, independence, and control.

Or one could simply ignore these data, asserting that the men of Lepenski Vir were the artists, architects, and leaders, the ones who "chose the head man", the same ones who "must have played the most important role, both in society and in the family" (Srejović 1972: 136).

All of these conflicting interpretations have been written and read. Each ignores the clear signs of the simultaneous presence of hierarchy yet equality; the asymmetry of men over women yet the expression of women's power and independence; and the changing meanings of women and their sexuality, men and their heads, and both women and men and the architectural spaces they built for life and death. In our inability to recognize and account for the presence and meanings of these contradictory signs, we both ignore the realness of the archaeological record and trivialize the complexity of the relations between women and men, women and women, and men and men in prehistory. And in these actions which render the past and the women who lived then invisible, we deny ourselves – and everyone else – the opportunity to conceptualize, and even make, gender something different from what it is today.

The women and men who inhabited both sides of the Iron Gates Gorge, along a 145 kilometer stretch of the Danube River, lived and worked in definite social relations which were not static or petrified. To see these relations as an unchanging and seamless Mesolithic culture, patriarchal or not, is both to ignore and render invisible the extraordinary amount of contextual variability present. Despite the limitations imposed by the published presentations of the data, it is possible to imagine other narrative histories of what might have happened. Through such accounts, normal archaeological science and its misrepresentations of women and their power everywhere can be challenged.

Towards "True Stories" from the Archaeology of Lepenski Vir

For almost ten centuries (6000–5000 BC), Mesolithic hunter-gatherers in the Gorge inhabited a series of permanent and perhaps seasonal settlements (Prinz 1987: 22–46, table 12), using the lands and resources available from the river and immediately adjacent habitats. The groups in these settlements evidently were lineage-based, tied by mutual relations of alliance, exchange, and obligation into a cohesive and social whole. This whole was comprised of two parts, reflected in the dual organization of spaces and settlements seen throughout the stratigraphic sequences of Lepenski Vir I and Vlasac (Srejović 1972: 45–79; Srejović and Letica 1978). At the wider level of a cultural geography, their world exhibited another duality in the opposition between the near and immediate environments of the river – its terraces and the adjacent cliffs and talus slopes, the source of fish, birds, boar, and deer (red and roe) inside the Gorge – and the mountains, plains, and forest steppes outside (figure 12.5), where wild ox (aurochs) were hunted and Neolithic villagers lived (Bökonyi 1972; Prinz 1987; Tringham 1971: 53–7; Whittle 1985: 114–31).

Cross-cutting the mutual relations embedded in this kin-based system were differences inherent in the structural contradictions and asymmetries in power between age sets (elders and not), sexes, families or households, and lineage-segments (Kahn 1981; Meillassoux 1978). These contradictions were real in that their basis was the communal appropriation, control, and allocation of surplus labor (Saitta 1988). For example, communal relations of production are implicated in the organization of labor

Figure 12.5 The sacred space of Lepenski Vir. Like many of the Mesolithic sites within the Iron Gates Gorge, Lepenski Vir is situated on an older river terrace. The Danube and its immediately adjacent habitats (talus slopes, cliff tops, canyon mouths) were an important part of this social world. In the loess plains and forest steppes beyond the valley, some Mesolithic hunter-gatherers visited early agricultural villages. There they traded smoked fish for monochrome pots which were brought back to their settlements in the gorge.

required for net fishing and the possible use of fish weirs, the quarrying and transport of stone slabs used in the construction of hearths from sources more than 100 kilometers away (Srejović 1972: 130), and in the construction and constant renewal of the "houses" and limestone floors at Lepenski Vir.

In these activities, and in some of the more routine subsistence and processing tasks, communal production required organizing technical or sexual divisions of labor, controlling emerging forms of redistribution, and limiting access to specific raw materials, critical resource locations (traditional fishing places), and important social rituals. The web of everyday life in this Mesolithic society was woven as much from relations of power, inequality, and hierarchy as it was from principles of kinship, underproduction, and communalism. The conceptual distinction between this Marxian view of communal relations and a romanticized model of egalitarian, non-class, gender-blind societies is critical to imagining specific women's histories in the past. By realizing that communal relations must have involved differentials of power and control – and thus the creation of authoritative discourses as well as challenges to them – we admit the possibility of differences and struggles between people living in the same society. This means that gender and other relations were not necessarily egalitarian in prehistory despite our efforts to represent them as such.

Even if surplus labor is appropriated and allocated collectively, that is, by individuals who are themselves included in the social body, communal relations of production will always involve tension, struggle, and resistance. These social processes will be enacted at the level of individuals, groups, or classes, any of which may encompass the specific interests of some women or some men or both (Saitta 1988: 154–5). Because of these dynamics, history and ideology were constants in the Gorge. As the women and men of Lepenski Vir both made and struggled against their own society and one another, they created a rich, varied, and complex material culture to represent the plurality of their lives, their perspectives, and actions.

In part the abundant signs of diverse and often opposing sets of archaeological associations reflect this plurality and conflict: *as different people expressed their lives differently, so they were* (Hodder 1982). Too, the constancy of the contradictions embedded in this society are evidenced in the construction and use of formalized features which emphasized the integrity, solidarity, and unity of both the group and its lineages. The redundancy in the trapezoidal geometry of houses; the organization of the overall settlement into two sections, each associated with a house turned slightly on its axis (nos 36 and 58); and the construction of a somewhat larger, centrally located structure (no. 54a), all during the initial phase Ia of Lepenski Vir (Srejović 1972: 50–6, 62–4), reflected and actively created an integrative *ideology of community*.

The enactment of periodic rituals also contributed to this ideology as is evidenced in the explicitly delineated and constructed stone-lined graves and circular stone "boxes" used respectively for inhumations and fractional reburials at Vlasac (Srejović and Letica 1978: 148–50). In the early settlements of Lepenski Vir Ia and Ib, this ritualization was also expressed in symbolic spaces (figure 12.6) defined by stone-lined rectangular hearths, thresholds formed from large stone slabs, and the careful placement of egg-shaped or spherical boulders (Srejović 1972: 52–3, figure 8). As the people built their houses and these spaces, shared them momentarily with their dead during periods of ritual celebration (rites of passage?), and then returned again and again to renew both the spaces and their connections to the dead, they reaffirmed their relations with their lineages as well as confirmed their commitment to the community.

The true loci of everyday life and work were the "villages" and seasonal settlements occupied by the Mesolithic people of the Gorge.[4] In the archaeological records of Vlasac, Icoana, Schela Cladovei, and other related sites (Prinz 1987: 44, 239–40; Srejović and Letica 1978: 157), we should be able, through comparative and contextual studies of house floors, to isolate evidence of disparities or inequalities between individuals,

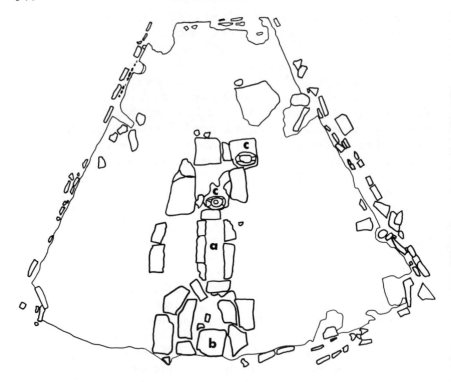

Figure 12.6 Interior floor plan for a shrine at Lepenski Vir (redrawn after Srejović 1972: 52). Within the fronts of many of the shrines, a symbolic space was carefully defined by a stone-lined, recessed "hearth" (a), a stone threshold (b), and one or more spherical boulders (c), called altars or sculptures. The remarkable consistency among the shrines in the site's early phases (Ia, Ib) suggests these features were a locus for rituals undertaken to integrate a community differentiated by age, gender, lineage, and inequality.

households, or groups of households within each lineage's space. Here in life, unlike the representations in death, specific raw materials and the products of surplus production were differentially appropriated and distributed. From within Lepenski Vir's sacred space and its houses, the contradictions and inequalities of everyday life and work could be resolved, made to appear acceptable, or perhaps be hidden from view.

At yet another level, the archaeological records of the Gorge show the emergence of an increasing separation and inequality between the lineages themselves. This is clearly represented in the ongoing conscious manipulation, reconstruction, and ritual use of the sacred architecture and symbolic spaces at Lepenski Vir. Its most explicit, and least

ambiguous, expression is preserved in the somewhat later settlement plan
of phase Ic. There are three lines of evidence:

1   The initial plan of the sacred settlement, reflective of the mutual and
    complementary relations between the lineages, as well as the ideology
    of community, is blurred. The once central position and integrative
    function of House 54a is diminished through the construction of two
    new large structures (nos 37, 27b) which emphasize lineages over the
    community (figure 12.7). The central house is "deliberately slighted",
    and its surrounding spaces become "disorganized" (Srejović 1972:
    68).
2   The relative uniformity in house size seen throughout the early
    phases is replaced in Lepenski Vir Ic by a bimodal construction of
    either "exceptionally large buildings or quite small ones" (Srejović
    1972: 68). Again the ideology of community is subverted through an
    architecture which stresses simultaneously the importance of lineage

Lepenski Vir Ic

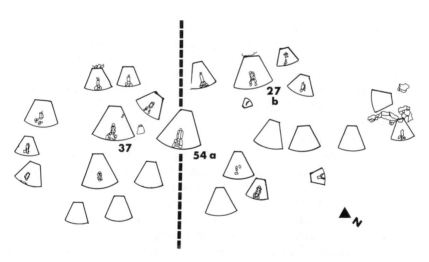

Figure 12.7 Settlement plan from Lepenski Vir Ic (redrawn after Srejović 1969:
70). As alliance relations among the lineages within the Gorge became reordered,
the once cohesive community plan was altered to express separation and
inequality. Two new large houses (37, 27b) were built, each serving as a center
for ritual now focused on creating and maintaining solidarity and alliance within
each lineage (divided by the axis). Monumental stone heads, carved to express an
emerging ideology of ancestral clans, were placed within the old and new shrines
primarily in the south section of Lepenski Vir.

over community as well as the supposed equality of all people in each lineage.

3   The most explicit expression of the valuation of a specific lineage over the social whole is represented in the carving of monumental stone heads (figure 12.8) and their deliberate placement within the symbolic and ritual triad of hearths–burials–thresholds situated inside the stone sanctuaries. In Lepenski Vir Ic the distribution of these heads, associated carved stone altars, and the ritual spaces containing them, was neither random nor symmetrical. An inspection of maps (Srejović 1969: figures 14, 15) and tables (Srejović 1972: 115–16) suggests that the southern "half" of the settlement now contains more of these artifact classes as well as more of the elaborately constructed ritual spaces.[5]

In these archaeological patterns can be seen evidences and representations of ongoing yet discontinuous histories of social transformations in which an earlier Mesolithic cultural order, interlineage relations of equality and alliance, and an ideology of community began to be deconstructed. Initial signs of such histories can be seen in Lepenski Vir Ib; their obviousness and clarity become more marked in the architectural activities and behavioral patterns encoded in the Ic level. But what actually happened in this society; why did some Mesolithic men and women begin to build their world anew, while others questioned and resisted the legitimacy of their actions and positions?

The history of the emerging separations and inequalities between the lineages is in part embedded within the structural contradictions and asymmetries in power characteristic of the appropriation of surplus labor in communal relations of production. The acquisition of specific raw materials (stone slabs used to construct sacred features) and the production of some subsistence products (ox bone, some of the red and roe deer seasonally), both from areas outside the Gorge, could be undertaken and controlled by specific subgroups formed primarily from the membership of one of the lineages. A complementary specialization of labor and production, focused on the Gorge itself (fish, lithic sources, and the limestone used for house floors), would be the domain of the second lineage division. Although the core membership of these subgroups would be recruited largely from one lineage or the other, additional individuals become involved as their age, abilities, or marital relations change during the course of their lives.

Such an extended communal division of labor – also a social division of work and geographic space – requires specific processes for redistributing the subsistence products and ritual values produced. Through their exchange, the solidarity, mutual dependence, and integration

Figure 12.8 The monumental heads of Lepenski Vir. Pecked and ground from large sandstone boulders obtained from outcrops ten kilometers away, these heads represented the living and dead leaders of the dominant lineage in the Gorge. As such, this political art legitimated individuals even as their positions and power were being challenged.

of the lineages is affirmed (Saitta 1988). However, these same relations of specialized production and exchange simultaneously imply social structures of control, authority, and hierarchy. By overseeing the appropriation and allocation of necessary subsistence values, by possessing a new and different sacred knowledge concerned with specific resources and their uses (such as the conscious manipulation of specific seed plants – see Prinz 1987: 75–82), and by controlling access to raw materials of sacred importance, some people, either as individuals or as members of lineage subgroups or classes, would emerge in positions of authority and power.

The extended communal division of labor is also implicated in processes of social fragmentation and lineage reconstruction. Those people responsible for producing social values outside the Gorge would come in contact with members of other Mesolithic and Neolithic societies, creating opportunities for broadening the scale of alliance and exchange networks. As the frequency and intensity of such contacts increased, the traditional relations within and between the Gorge's lineages would be disrupted (see Friedman's 1975 model). Lines of descent within lineages would be broken as some subgroups linked themselves with other lineage segments encountered in the wider social landscape beyond the Gorge. In this way, the traditional social order, characterized by symmetry and complementarity, would open to include relations of asymmetry, power, and hierarchy. The locus of these newly-emerging relations would be situated in two different yet connected spheres: individuals or small subgroups (or segments) rising to power within each lineage and one lineage rising to power within the society as a whole.

The archaeological evidences for these "true stories" are represented by the three patterns of rising inequality preserved in the settlement record of Lepenski Vir Ic. The submergence of the architecture of an ideology of community and the expression of an asymmetry between the lineages seen there are a frozen cross-section of this history. Within this changing social context, the carving of monumental heads to represent important powerful living individuals as well as the ancestors of the now dominant lineage, becomes a visually compelling materialization of an *ideology of ancestral clan.*

Instead of stressing horizontal links and community integration, this ideology celebrates the separations and inequalities between the lineages. The dominant lineage, whose members buried their dead in the south section of the site during phase Ic, emphasized their new alliances outside the Gorge by including rare sherds of Neolithic pottery in their "graves" or sanctuaries (Srejović 1972: 134–35, Tringham 1971: 56). The heads themselves symbolized the vertical links (the lines of descent) which connected the living leaders of the dominant lineage to their ancestors who were also seen as the mythical forebears of the entire community. The partial shift, from social relations seen horizontally to a clan ideology represented vertically, was expressed through the deliberate placement of the stone heads within the traditional ritual spaces inside the sanctuaries at Lepenski Vir. The heads (and their vertical axes) stood above and disturbed the two-dimensional horizontal plane created by the association of hearths–burials–stone thresholds (figure 12.9). Also, the association between these carved, mythical, and somewhat unreal stone heads and the burial of actual skulls – almost exclusively of men – inside the sanctuaries, established substantive links between remote, unknown ancestors and remembered individuals. In the same way, the burial of children beneath some floors, a practice that appears in the Ic settlement, stressed lineage membership and clan descent above community (Srejović 1972: 119).

By incorporating an obvious, intrusive, and explicit material culture into a long-standing sacred settlement and the ritual spaces present there, the leaders of the new and dominant lineage created a purposive connection between their lives, positions, and authority, the dead, and the traditional order that was continuing. Through such links they legitimized themselves and their actions, as others challenged their roles and resisted the inequalities emerging within the social order.

The women of Lepenski Vir

Where are their actions, their perspectives in this story? How can we see them in this material record? We need a contextual approach to the archaeological histories of these Mesolithic sites which assumes that women were much more than passive participants in these histories, which searches out evidence of their resistances as well as their acceptance. That we should be able to find women resisting – any resistance at all – is neither surprising nor unbelievable. The processes involved were not participated in by everyone acting identically, nor did what happen affect everyone's life and position in the same way. The histories themselves certainly were neither lineal nor progressive to the people in the Gorge. There are more than enough discontinuities and interruptions in the record to tell us that there was as much resistance and denial of change as adaptation.

Even though the ideologies of community and ancestral clans actively contained and controlled both individual and shared actions of criticism and challenge – by ritualizing solidarity or legitimizing emerging inequality – no ideology is ever an entirely dominating, seamless text. When represented and embedded in everyday life, ideologies do limit the

diversity of meanings and alternative interpretations and thus restrain resistance. However it is always possible for people to confront and oppose the authoritative discourse of an ideology. Some have the reflexive and critical ability to argue against and resist inequality and transformation, even as others work to produce material and behavioral representations and rationalizations to support them (Moore 1986).

In the theoretical separation between ideology and practice, between a cultural representation of space and the historical realities of living in and reconstructing space (Bourdieu 1977), we will always find women, their voices, and their actions. Not as an autonomous category or inevitable difference, women will be here in a rich multiplicity of roles, social relations, resistances, and responsibilities. They created specific and changing connections to the representations, ideologies, and histories of society, production, and politics made within the Gorge. The women of Lepenski Vir were neither invisible nor powerless; they were sometimes respected elders, at other times recognized voices in support of traditionalism. Also, in their often changing and conflicting roles as wives, sisters, mothers, and laborers, these women empowered themselves, and expressed their resistance in words and actions and perhaps through art. Their artistic representation and power were also controlled, muted, and appropriated by others.

The plurality of women's lived experiences and histories in the Gorge is reflected in the multiple and often contradictory archaeological evidence that can be used as clues for framing further research. For example, the associations between elderly men and women, as well as the absence of any differential treatment of them in the earlier inhumations at Vlasac (Srejović and Letica 1978: 148, 156), represents a respect for the position, knowledge, and authority of elders of both sexes in life and death. Similarly, some of the early secondary reburials seen in Lepenski Vir Ib, consisting of piles of men's and women's bones (Srejović 1972: 118–19), express the deference and care accorded elders.

As the alliance relations integrating the lineages were fragmented and as inequalities intensified within and between the lineages, the locus, specificity of position, and relative authority of women and men elders were redefined. But these changes occurred differentially within the contextual politics of each lineage. The position of the elders in the ascending lineage became gendered and more limited; as the control over surplus labor and its values shifted to younger males, who were the new headmen of the lineage, women elders and their knowledge were devalued. Male elders' roles too were marginalized, they became

Figure 12.9 Stone heads in a shrine at Lepenski Vir. Beginning in phase Ic, lineage leaders placed carved heads within long-used ritual spaces. Their deliberate actions established links between themselves and an older, more traditional ideology of community.

primarily guardians of ritual knowledge, continuing to perform burial rites inside the sanctuaries of Lepenski Vir Ic.

In the second group, the more traditional and subordinate lineage, elders, both women and men, maintained their positions and power within a wide range of social, economic, and ritual domains. They continued to be authoritative and respected, participating in the reorganization and transformation of the communal relations of labor and production in this section of the Gorge's society. Archaeological signs of these contrasts and changes are probably preserved in the record of Lepenski Vir, although not immediately obvious. If this is one of the "true stories", then we should be able to isolate contrastive rituals of death associated with elders in the different parts of settlement Ic. In the southern area, used primarily by the now dominant lineage, elder men are rarely buried with any obvious care and respect and never with elder women. This pattern is very different from that present in the northern section, the locus of use for those allied with the traditionalists. Here the early association between older women and men in death continues throughout the remaining life of the settlement, in strata Id, Ie, and II.[6]

The social and ritual continuity in the northern section is remarkable, since there are abundant signs elsewhere of endemic change in patterns of use, spatial organization, and ideology. Beginning in phase Id and continuing for some three centuries (Quitta 1972), the formality of architectural treatment and the consistency in the symbolic construction and ritual use of the sanctuaries diminishes (Srejović 1972: 69–77). By phase Ie, the earlier disparity seen in the elaboration and intensity of burials shifts from the southern to northern section where the long-established tradition of sacredness continues (figure 12.10). Meanwhile, the southern half is under-used, suggesting that the now dominant lineage no longer needs to construct links between their ideology of clan and the sacred place of Lepenski Vir.

Even in Lepenski Vir II, one sees evidence that some people in the Gorge continued to maintain their links to one another, their lineage, and the sacred place. Yet the links now expressed are more a matter of a cultural overlay of "confused, overburdened, and detailed references to the past" (Srejović 1972: 75–6), than an intense participation in a formal, well understood and enacted ritual. The geometry and internal organization of the houses becomes less rigid, as does the construction of the ritual hearths. The limestone floors are no longer prepared, and the raw materials used in the houses come primarily from within the Gorge (Srejović 1972: 73–7). The one constancy in this changing material and social record is the use of carved stone heads, mostly in the newly rebuilt central house XLIV (figure 12.11). Systematically excavated and removed from sanctuaries in the Id and earlier settlements by the last Mesolithic

Lepenski Vir Ie

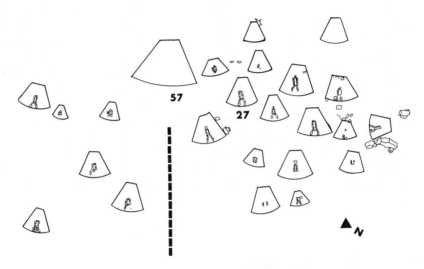

57

27

N

Figure 12.10 Settlement plan from Lepenski Vir Ie (redrawn after Srejović 1969: 75). South of the axis marking the division between lineages, many of the shrines are abandoned during the late period. Evidently this lineage's dead are now buried elsewhere, perhaps in newly created sacred spaces shared with lineage segments from the agricultural villages outside the Gorge. Meanwhile the ritual use in the northern section of the site intensifies as others, participating in an enduring tradition, continue to bring their dead here.

occupants of Lepenski Vir, these sculptures are used to remember another world and society. Now those earlier times live only in the memories of the old women and men who come to Lepenski Vir with their children and grandchildren to bury the dead, remember how life once was, and talk about what should be done when they die.

There is another way to approach the archaeological histories of the women of Lepenski Vir: by wondering about the transformation of their labor, their roles in and contributions to the social reproduction of both society and lineages, and their creation of discrete social spaces and symbolic expressions through which they empowered themselves and actively voiced resistance. How did the women of Lepenski Vir value themselves within the social structures and communal relations they confronted? How were women and their values stereotyped; how was their art appropriated by others?

One effect of the growing separations and inequalities between the Gorge's lineages was the disruption and fragmentation of the communal relations of production and extended division of labor which formerly bound and integrated the lineages and their subgroups. Divisions of labor and the relations of exchange through which diverse values (subsistence and ritual) were distributed became more localized and restricted. It was as though there were now two exchange and alliance networks: one focused on the dominant lineage and its widening relations outside the Gorge and the other situated more narrowly within the lineage subgroups inside the Gorge. These networks overlapped only partially, so each lineage had to produce a greater abundance and diversity of subsistence and ritual values than before. In order to do this, each group's labor was intensified and specialized predominantly along gender lines. Work, living spaces, and relations of production were formerly embedded in lineage and community; now they were separated into women's spheres and men's spheres, women's work and men's work, women's spaces and those of men.

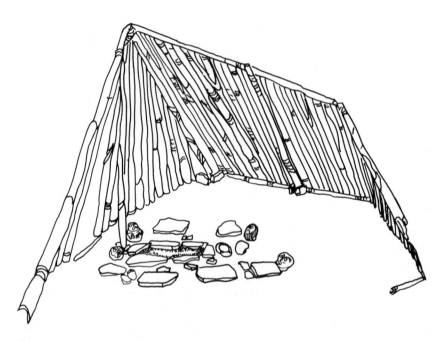

Figure 12.11 House XLIV from Lepenski Vir II (redrawn from Srejović 1972: 76). Positioned similarly to earlier large shrines, the central structure was a focus for activity in the latest Mesolithic settlement. By now much of the former meaning and ordering of ritual space at the site was forsaken. Instead a few stone heads were removed from earlier deposits and placed together in House XLIV. The sacred space created was used by some of the last hunter-gatherers in the Gorge, perhaps in memory of their ancestors and their traditions.

The labor products of the women of Lepenski Vir, what they produced for household use and communal redistribution, had always been important to the social reproduction of the Gorge's community. As women's labor intensified and their roles in producing specific critical resources became almost exclusively their domain, the appropriation of their labor values became significant in men's efforts to dominate women and in women's efforts to resist and empower themselves. These struggles were situationally defined within each lineage or household and were enacted by women, individually and collectively.

Material signs of the gendering of work and surplus labor and of the increasingly critical importance of women and their positions should be apparent in the archaeological records from Vlasac and other settlement sites inside the Gorge. Unlike Lepenski Vir in the later phases, these sites represent much of the entire range of everyday life and social histories; their patterns of spatial and architectural organization and the contextual associations within them of diverse artifact assemblages need to be reanalyzed. Encoded there will be evidence of an emerging elaboration of the domestic spaces and features within and immediately adjacent to houses. Probably reflected in changes in the location and segregation of specific activities, in the construction of new and unique features inside houses, and in the ritualization of common routines of food processing and sharing (Hodder 1982, 1984), this elaboration is an explicit and conscious representation of *an ideology of separate spheres*. Through this ideology, women, their work, and their roles were made more obvious and visible as the social value of their labor products increased.

In the later phases of the settlement of Vlasac, the elaboration of the domestic context apparently is voiced in the increased production, and subsequent placement inside houses, of painted, small, spherical or egg-shaped boulders; engraved, non-utilitarian objects of bone and antler; and decorated utilitarian tools (Prinz 1987: 97–100, Srejović and Letica 1978: 153–4, 156–8). The contrastive associations between specific raw materials and tool categories may also be expressive of an increasingly elaborate gender separation. For example, utilitarian tools used for processing fish and in domestic activities focused on the house were made predominantly of bone and boar's tusk, while tools made of antler (hoes, mattocks, axes, hammers) were used outside the settlement (Srejović and Letica 1978: 151). The gender links between women, bone, and boar's tusks and men and antler is also apparent at Lepenski Vir, where many of the male burials (both fractional and secondary piles) were accompanied by antlers and sometimes the whole skulls of deer (Srejović 1972: 120).

The material representation of the gendering of labor and space and of an ideology of separate spheres reflects the growing reality that women, their independent status, and their power now have a more substantial base in their production and control over critical resources and values. Simultaneously, the new facts of women's power within each lineage means that these spaces and relations of production become contested terrain where the women and men of the Gorge struggled over the appropriation and allocation of subsistence and ritual values, the emergence of an elite of younger males, and the separation and growing inequalities between the lineages.

These almost invisible histories of resistance – histories of women working against the grain – are controlled and marginalized, rendered ambiguous and thus neutralized, through acts of appropriation which help to maintain and legitimize the ongoing histories of social re-construction and differentiation. For example, the critiques and challenges of women affiliated with the dominant lineage, in part embedded in conflicts over the appropriation of their surplus labor, are negated after death. The independence of some women is subverted by the stereo-typical stressing of their pelvic regions with ochre (at Vlasac), by mixing their bones with those of men inside sanctuaries (Lepenski Vir), and by incorporating their bones into the foundations of the sanctuaries. Through such acts, the independence of these women and their challenges to authority and hierarchy could be marginalized by incorporating their voices into the ideology of clan and by restricting their roles to biological reproduction. *Same as it ever was.*

[Susquehannock Indian women and Blue Rock Valenced pots:]

As the 17th century began, European states and the representatives of their merchant economies moved into the homelands of the Susquehannock Indians, in southern Lancaster County, Pennsylvania. During the next quarter-century, the customary communal and kin-based relations of production became gendered as some native men shifted their labor to the production of commodities needed for trade with the white colonists. The position and power of Susquehannock women intensified, in part because of their control over the production, allocation, and redistribution of critical agricultural surpluses. Through their power and independence, some women spoke out and challenged the ongoing emergence of a patriarchal elite of Susquehannock "kings".

Susquehannock women expressed their resistance through the produc-tion of a distinctive pottery, Blue Rock Valenced. Unlike the contempor-aneous and dominant style which symbolized clans, clan leaders, and the hierarchal position of kings, the decorative motifs of this ware stressed the solidarity, integration, and alliances between lineages, lineage segments, and all of the Susquehannock people.

However, the clarity of this materialized resistance, and thus the strength of women's voices, was subverted by the production of yet another pottery in which the unique motifs of valenced pots were surrounded by references to clan and clan leaders. Thus the non-ambiguity of women's messages and ideas was blurred, their political content was appropriated, and their struggle for the future of the Susquehannocks was contained. (Handsman 1989)

[Same as it ever was.]

Communal resistance to the transformation of society and production apparently was also expressed in the Gorge through the intensified production of a second art, seen primarily in monumental decorated boulders (referred to as ornamental sculpture in the Lepenski Vir report) and in smaller engraved or sculpted objects and tools (so-called applied art) found at Lepenski Vir and Vlasac. In contrast to the monumental sculpted heads, this art's characteristic features of intricate arabesques, coils and spirals, and concentric, "wavy" meanders refer to nature, to the Danube and its unceasing flow, and to the fish (and their scales) taken from the river (figures 12.12 and 12.13). In this art the traditional social order and communal relations of life within the Gorge are stressed, while resistance to emerging inequalities, the dominance of one lineage over the other, and the construction of wider alliance and exchange networks beyond the Gorge is voiced.

Figure 12.12 Stylistic motifs carved on boulders and altars from the Mesolithic shrines of Lepenski Vir. These representations refer to the riverine environments and fishing economies traditional to the Gorge. At first this art expressed an ideology of community; later these motifs became symbols of some women's independence and their power to challenge an emerging elite.

The more monumental representations of this resistance are seen primarily in the later phases of Lepenski Vir (Srejović 1972: 102–12, figure 27); however, a parallel representation was produced and used simultaneously in living settlements such as Vlasac. Associated here with the elaboration of domestic contexts and the ideology of separate spaces, this art "for the Gorge-community-tradition" was made and used in everyday life by some women in both lineages. As such its representations

Figure 12.13 Pecked and ground "sceptre" from Lepenski Vir. The incised wavy lines, chevrons, and arabesques, similar to those seen on altars, refer to the Danube River. The fish living there were an important food resource as well as a focus for communal labor and exchange.

of the river and fish refer to the source and resources upon which women's power and independence were founded.

Thus it is predictable that these symbols of resistance, in part an expression of women challenging the authority of elite males and their dominant discourse, would also be appropriated. In the sanctuaries of Lepenski Vir, beginning in phase Ic and continuing into phase II, one sees a few sculpted heads on which are also carved the meandering furrows of waves and scales (figure 12.14). These hybrid or syncretic forms are the ultimate expression of an involuted ideology of clan. In them we see represented an unbroken, continuous line joining the clan, its leaders, and their heads to the river, its fish, and the mythical ancestors of all the women and men who lived and died in the Gorge. Through this art style, the men of the dominant lineage – by now a patriarchal clan – rendered ambiguous the claims and criticisms of women, thereby silencing them and hiding their histories. More than six thousand years later, this head is excavated, named the "Naiad", and presented as an artistic expression of "the birth out of water of the first living beings, the first parents of men and, perhaps, of the entire living world" (Srejović and Babovic 1986: 9). The Mesolithic men of Lepenski Vir could have written these words; instead they carved them in their ongoing effort to empower themselves and control others.

Will Archaeological Histories of Gender Relations be Feminist?

When we look at the art of Lepenski Vir in a gallery, archaeological text, or museum catalogue, what is represented, and what do we see? Men's art, women's art, an art for all time? We are seeing social expressions of domination and resistance, evidence of how art may be used representationally to control as well as to empower. But we also see "a way of seeing" (Berger 1977), a male gaze which, even as it makes women its interpretive object, renders their perspectives and histories invisible. The men of Lepenski Vir used this gaze as they attempted to control women and appropriate their power. Contemporary archaeologists also use it, consciously or not, often achieving the same political effects.

In the art of Lepenski Vir, gendered histories of power and resistance were expressed by the people who made and lived those histories. When we look at their sculpted heads, the lives of these Mesolithic women and men are forgotten, while ours are foregrounded. Nevertheless, what was once there can still be seen. Feminist archaeologists do not discover another past simply by looking where no one else has. Instead, they look differently at what has always been there, seeking to understand how people lived and worked in definite and changing social spaces and relations. This makes some of them no different apparently from other postprocessualists in archaeology (Hodder 1985, 1986).

Still this work, as it is now emerging, is distinct. There is a puzzling, overlapping, and interrupted style in the narrations some feminist

Figure 12.14 The Naiad. Excavated from one of the later shrines, this syncretic sculpture combines features seen on monumental heads with the arabesques and meanders characteristic of altars. Some artists legitimated a patriarchy by representing its leaders as the mythical ancestors – half fish, half human – of all of the Mesolithic inhabitants of the Iron Gates Gorge.

archaeologists write because they are consciously looking simultaneously at the present and the past. This is in order to trace and make obvious the connections between archaeological theorizing, the sexual politics embedded within the discipline and the academy outside, and the continuing inequalities between women and men in science and society. Here it is argued that archaeological ideas, taken-for-granteds, or interpretive stories – related aspects of a single discourse – misrepresent the power and authenticity of women's histories. By assuming that prehistoric art is unquestionably made by men, thereby situating women in nature and outside society and production, archaeologists contribute to the ongoing legitimation of an ideology of gender difference. It is this very same ideology which underlies and rationalizes the inequalities faced by women today.

To counter this ideology, feminist archaeologists are building theory to conceptualize gender as historically constructed relations of power, inequality and resistance, identity, and appropriation. Seen this way, gender is never a matter of fixed, universal categories – one female, the other not. Instead gender is relational in both society and space; gender relations are actively constructed and negotiated to reflect, intersect, or even repudiate the interests of a specific class, age set, clan, or race (Mohanty 1988). Gender relations and their histories thus become a critical axis in understanding power, inequality, and social differentiation in any society, past and present.

By shifting the interpretive, and thus political, focus to gender relations, we learn to examine hierarchy instead of equality, domination instead of difference, and resistance instead of acceptance. Gender as relations seen historically is the key to understanding who made which art and why in the Gorge, and to exploring the culturally specific connections between material expression and social reproduction throughout prehistory. Gender is also the key to realizing that women, their labor, and the values of what they produced were central to communal relations in all prehistoric societies as well as constructive of the conflicts and struggles within them. Thus gender is not a way to find an original matriarchy or to trace its gradual and inevitable loss to the emergence of complex states or capitalism. Instead feminist archaeologists reject these narrations of closure (Elshtain 1986) because they homogenize sexes, define gender domination as a problem only of capitalism, and make women and their struggles – women's histories – invisible in prehistory.

The male gaze makes us see the art of Lepenski Vir as something it was not. Learning to view that art differently makes us see gender in a way that will challenge the lives we lead and the work we do. It may also make us wonder about any art, or any representation we choose to call art (Handsman 1987). Who is being controlled, who is being empowered, how is the art being made or interpreted as an instrument and hierarchal relation of power? The histories of disparate Susquehannock women, struggling against patriarchal domination and control in the seventeenth century, are not exactly identical to those of the Mesolithic women of the Gorge. But the strategies of resistance used, their material expression through artistic styles, and the appropriation of this language as a means of control, define a commonness, a shared history, between these women. Gender becomes an interpretive and critical bridge between societies separated widely in time, space, and normal discourse.

We need systematic collaborative projects to compile archaeological histories of gender relations throughout prehistory and history. We also need to study how archaeological discourse, inside and outside the discipline, has become another technology of control, empowering men and some women, while disenfranchising many women. If we are willing to tolerate and support such feminist projects, then we must be willing to be critical of ourselves and the ongoing, often ignored inequities in the discipline. We must also be willing to nurture, support, and listen to work which challenges and overturns normal archaeological discourse, which asks us to imagine women in prehistory the way that Virginia Woolf dared us to remember Shakespeare's sister: not because she existed as fact, but because she was silenced.

If we are not willing to work against such silences, then there is no reason to insist that there is equality and freedom in archaeology and the societies which preserve it. Enough is enough.

ACKNOWLEDGMENTS

Meg Conkey and Joan Gero kindly invited me to participate in the 1987 conference "Women and Production in Prehistory." They have been interested and supportive critics and patient editors. Martin Wobst and Ruth Tringham shared their knowledge of Eastern European prehistory as well as their libraries. My thanks to George Nicholas, Adine Storer, Elena Filios, and Christine Hoepfner for what they did, and to Danny Miller and Barbara Bender who demanded I tell them about what happened in the Gorge. Through his talent and creativity, Gordon Whitbeck produced an art which both challenged and extended my ideas and writing; he always does. This essay is for all those people with whom I lived and worked while at The Wedge in admiration of their commitment, courage and contributions. It is also for those I live with still, the two from whom I have learned so much.

NOTES

1 This insight I owe to Lucy Lippard whose essays on women's art (1976) inspired me to wonder how the discipline will react to, and attempt to devalue, the work of feminist archaeologists.

2 These observations and quotes were collected during several visits to see "The Art of Lepenski Vir" at the Southampton City Art Gallery in early September 1986.

3 I imagined what the tour guide would say by reading the exhibition brochure available at the gallery as well as the published catalogue which accompanied the installation (see Srejović and Babovic 1986).

4 S. Bökonyi (1972) suggests, with others, that the houses of Lepenski Vir "were not true houses but shrines", implying that the people's villages were elsewhere in the Gorge.

5 The asymmetry between the site's southern and northern halves in the Ic settlement is clearly depicted in the spatial plan reproduced in the original monograph, published in Serbo-Croat (Srejović 1969: figures 14 and 15).

6 For example in house 21 (stratum Id), the extended burial of a male elder (in his sixties) included the skull of an old woman. The man's skull, in the subfloor grave, was marked above ground by a carved boulder decorated with meanders and arabesques (Srejović 1972: 90, 120).

REFERENCES

Barrett, Michèle (1986). "Feminism and the Definition of Cultural Politics." Excerpts reprinted in Feminist Literary Theory. A Reader, M. Eagleton, ed. Oxford: Basil Blackwell, 160–3.

Berger, John et al. (1977). Ways of Seeing. London: British Broadcasting Corporation and Penguin Books.

Bökonyi, S. (1972). "The Vertebrate Fauna." In Europe's First Monumental Sculpture. New Discoveries at Lepenski Vir, D. Srejović. New York: Thames & Hudson, 186–9.

Bourdieu, Pierre (1977). Outline of a Theory of Practice. Cambridge: Cambridge University Press.

Campbell, Joseph (1988). Historical Atlas of World Mythology. Vol. I, The Way of the Animal Powers. Part 1, Mythologies of the Primitive Hunters and Gatherers. New York: Harper & Row.

Conkey, Margaret W. and Janet D. Spector (1984). "Archaeology and the Study of Gender." In Advances in Archaeological Method and Theory, 7, M. Schiffer, ed. New York: Academic Press, 1–38.

Connell, R. W. (1987). Gender and Power. Society, the Person and Sexual Politics. Stanford: Stanford University Press.

Eagleton, Terry (1986). "Marxism and the Past." Salmagundi 68–9: 271–90.

Elshtain, Jean B. (1986). "The New Feminist Scholarship." *Salmagundi* 70–1: 3–26.

Foucault, Michel (1978). *A History of Sexuality*. Vol. I, *An Introduction*. New York: Vintage Books of Random House.

—— (1980). *Power/Knowledge. Selected Interviews and Other Writings, 1972–1977*, C. Gordon, ed. New York: Pantheon Books.

Fox-Genovese, Elizabeth (1982). "Placing Women's History in History." *New Left Review* 133: 5–29.

Friedman, Jonathan (1975). "Tribes, States, and Transformations." In *Marxist Analyses and Social Anthropology*, M. Bloch, ed. New York: John Wiley & Sons, 161–202.

Gamble, Clive (1982). "Interaction and Alliance in Paleolithic Society." *Man* 17: 92–107.

Gero, Joan M. (1985). "Socio-Politics and the Woman-at-Home Ideology." *American Antiquity* 50(2): 342–50.

Gimbutas, Marija (1974). *The Gods and Goddesses of Old Europe, 7000 to 3500 B.C. Myths, Legends, and Cult Images*. Berkeley: University of California Press.

Gordimer, Nadine (1985). "The Essential Gesture: Writers and Responsibility." *Granta* 15: 135–51.

Handsman, Russell G. (1987). "Stop Making Sense: Toward an Anti-Catalogue of Woodsplint Basketry." In *A Key into the Language of Woodsplint Baskets*, A. McMullen and R. G. Handsman, eds. Washington, CT: American Indian Archaeological Institute, 144–64.

—— (1988). "Algonkian Women Resist Colonialism." *Artifacts* 16(3–4): 29–31. Washington, CT: American Indian Archaeological Institute.

—— (1989). "Native Women and the Susquehannock 'Kings': An Archaeological Story about Colonialism." Paper presented in a session "Archaeology and Politics", first Joint Archaeological Congress, Baltimore.

Harding, Sandra (1986). *The Science Question in Feminism*. Ithaca: Cornell University Press.

Harris, Olivia and Kate Young (1981). "Engendered Structures: Some Problems in the Analysis of Reproduction." In *The Anthropology of Pre-Capitalist Societies*, J. S. Kahn and J. R. Llobera, eds. London: Macmillan, 109–47.

Hayden, Brian (1986). "Old Europe: Sacred Matriarchy or Complementary Opposition?" In *Archaeology and Fertility Cult in the Ancient Mediterranean*, A. Bonanno, ed. Amsterdam: B. R. Gruner, 17–30.

Hodder, Ian (1982). *Symbols in Action. Ethnoarchaeological Studies of Material Culture*. Cambridge: Cambridge University Press.

—— (1984). "Burials, Houses, Women and Men in the European Neolithic." In *Ideology, Power, and Prehistory*, D. Miller and C. Tilley, eds. Cambridge: Cambridge University Press, 51–68.

—— (1985). "Postprocessual Archaeology." *Advances in Archaeological Method and Theory* 8 M. Schiffer, ed. New York: Academic Press, 1–26.

—— (1986). *Reading the Past. Current Approaches to Interpretation in Archaeology*. Cambridge: Cambridge University Press.

Kahn, Joel S. (1981). "Marxist Anthropology and Segmentary Societies: A

Review of the Literature." In *The Anthropology of Pre-Capitalist Societies*, J. S. Kahn and J. R. Llobera, eds. London: Macmillan, 57–88.

Kaplan, Cora (1986). *Sea Changes. Essays on Culture and Feminism*. London: Verso.

Kramer, Carol and Miriam Stark (1988). "The Status of Women in Archeology." *Anthropology Newsletter* 29(9): 1, 11–12.

Lippard, Lucy R. (1976). *From the Center. Feminist Essays on Women's Art*. New York: E. P. Dutton.

—— (1983). *Overlay. Contemporary Art and the Art of Prehistory*. New York: Pantheon Books.

McDonough, Roisin and Rachel Harrison (1978). "Patriarchy and the Relations of Production." In *Feminism and Materialism. Women and Modes of Production*. A. Kuhn and A. Wolpe, eds. London: Routledge & Kegan Paul, 11–41.

MacKinnon, Catharine A. (1987a). "The Art of the Impossible." In *Feminism Unmodified. Discourses on Life and Law*, C. A. MacKinnon. Cambridge: Harvard University Press, 1–17.

—— (1987b). "Difference and Dominance: On Sex Discrimination." In *Feminism Unmodified. Discourses on Life and Law*, C. A. MacKinnon. Cambridge: Harvard University Press, 32–45.

Meillassoux, Claude (1978). " 'The Economy' in Agricultural Self-Sustaining Societies: A Preliminary Analysis." In *Relations of Production. Marxist Approaches to Economic Anthropology*, D. Seddon, ed. Totawa, NJ: Frank Cass, 127–57.

Mohanty, Chandra (1988). "Under Western Eyes: Feminist Scholarship and Colonial Discourses." *Feminist Review* 30: 61–88.

Moore, Henrietta L. (1986). *Space, Text and Gender. An Anthropological Study of the Marakwet of Kenya*. Cambridge: Cambridge University Press.

Olsen, Tillie (1978). *Silences*. New York: Dell.

Pfeiffer, John E. (1986). "Cro-Magnon Hunters Were Really Us, Working out Strategies for Survival." *Smithsonian* 17(7): 74–85.

Prinz, Beth (1987). *Mesolithic Adaptations on the Lower Danube. Vlasac and the Iron Gates Gorge*. Oxford: BAR International Series 330.

Putman, John J. (1988). "The Search for Modern Humans." *National Geographic* 174(4): 438–77.

Quitta, H. (1972). "The Dating of Radio-Carbon Samples." In *Europe's First Monumental Sculpture. New Discoveries at Lepenski Vir*, D. Srejović. New York: Thames & Hudson, 205–10.

Said, Edward W. (1985). "Opponents, Audiences, Constituencies and Community." In *Postmodern Culture*, H. Foster, ed. London: Pluto Press, 135–59.

—— (1986). "Foucault and the Imagination of Power." In *Foucault: A Critical Reader*, D. C. Hoy, ed. Oxford: Basil Blackwell, 149–55.

Saitta, Dean J. (1988). "Marxism, Prehistory, and Primitive Communism." *Rethinking Marxism* 1(4): 145–68.

Schiffer, Michael B. (1988). "The Structure of Archaeological Theory." *American Antiquity* 53(3): 461–85.

Scott, Joan W. (1988a). "Deconstructing Equality-versus-Difference: Or, The Uses of Poststructuralist Theory for Feminism." *Feminist Studies* 14(1): 33–50.

—— (1988b). "Gender: A Useful Category of Historical Analysis." In *Gender and the Politics of History*, J. W. Scott. New York: Columbia University Press, 28–50.

Silverblatt, Irene (1988). "Women in States." *Annual Review of Anthropology* 17: 427–60.

Srejović, Dragoslav (1969). *Lepenski Vir*. Beograd: Srpska knjizevna zadruga.

—— (1972). *Europe's First Monumental Sculpture: New Discoveries at Lepenski Vir*. New York: Thames & Hudson.

Srejović, Dragoslav and Ljubinka Babovic (1986). *The Art of Lepenski Vir*. Catalogue published to accompany the exhibition at the Southampton City Art Gallery. National Museum of Belgrade and the Directorate of Leisure, Tourism and Amenities, Yugoslavia.

Srejović, Dragoslav and Zagorka Letica (1978). "Vlasac. A Mesolithic Settlement in the Iron Gates." Summary report in English. *Monographs of the Serbian Academy of Sciences and Arts* 512: 145–63.

Tringham, Ruth (1971). *Hunters, Fishers and Farmers of Eastern Europe, 6000–3000 B.C.* London: Hutchinson.

Washburn, Wilcomb E. (1987). "A Critical View of Critical Archaeology." *Current Anthropology* 28(4): 544–45.

Welbourn, Alice (1984). "Endo ceramics and Power Strategies." In *Ideology, Power and Prehistory*, D. Miller and C. Tilley, eds. Cambridge: Cambridge University Press, 17–24.

Whittle, Alasdair (1985). *Neolithic Europe: A Survey*. Cambridge: Cambridge University Press.

Woolf, Virginia (1929). *A Room of One's Own*. New York: Harcourt Brace Jovanovich.

13

Women in a Men's World: Images of Sumerian Women

Susan Pollock

To be born a woman has been to be born, within an allotted and confined space, into the keeping of men.

John Berger, *Ways of Seeing* (1972)

In a recent paper on women in ancient Mesopotamian art, Irene Winter begins by posing the question, "why so few?" (Winter 1987: 189). This query could also be extended to the domain of women in Mesopotamian literature. The relative invisibility of women in art and literature is striking, but we find that the picture is far more complex as we explore other domains and investigate the nuances of the representational evidence, as Winter, among others, has shown. Women are portrayed in inconsistent and contradictory ways in different representational media. At the very least, this raises questions about the ideologies of representation and their correspondence to what women "really" did. Representations may also offer important insights into changing relations of gender and power. In this paper I explore some of the ambiguities in representations of women in the historical context of early Sumerian and Akkadian civilization. I examine three forms of representations: written texts, burials, and the iconography of cylinder seals.

The Setting

The heartland of Sumerian civilization was southern Mesopotamia, a region also known as Sumer and Akkad. This area included, more or less, the land between the channels of the Tigris and Euphrates Rivers, from the area where they enter the alluvial plain in the north (near modern Baghdad) to the ancient head of the (Persian/Arabian) Gulf in the south

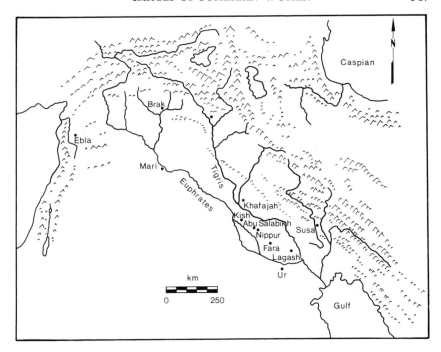

Figure 13.1 Map of Mesopotamia, with major Early Dynastic and Akkadian Period sites indicated.

(figure 13.1). "Classic" early Sumerian civilization refers to a period toward the middle of the third millennium BC (conventionally dated to ca.2600–2350 BC), known archaeologically as Early Dynastic (ED) III. A trend toward urbanization that had begun more than a millennium earlier took the form at this time of a constellation of city-states. Each city-state included one, or sometimes a few, large urban communities, surrounded by an agricultural hinterland under their immediate control. The relative power of these city-states waxed and waned, with no single city-state ever achieving a lasting political or economic dominance over the whole area. Inter-state relations were marked by chronic warfare and shifting allegiances, as well as by a strong degree of economic inter-dependence and a shared social and cultural history. The economy was based on plant cultivation, herding, and fishing, the products of which were exchanged locally and in an extensive trade network that provided Mesopotamia with a wide variety of raw materials that it lacked, including stones, metals, and woods.

ED III was followed by the Akkadian or Sargonic period, when, for the first time as far as we know, much of Mesopotamia was united under a single political rule. This achievement is credited to a man named Sargon, who ruled from Akkad, a region in the northern part of southern Mesopotamia. Sargon and his successors managed to maintain some degree of political unity for approximately a century. Although they instituted a change in the (written) language of administration from Sumerian to Akkadian, this linguistic change was probably not closely – or simply – equated with ethnic identity.

The late ED and Sargonic periods are sometimes classified as "early historic", a reference to the existence of written records. The earliest known evidence of writing in Mesopotamia comes from the Late Uruk period, during the last few centuries of the fourth millennium BC. However, it is not until the later Early Dynastic period that we have, at present, a fairly large, diverse, and comprehensible corpus of excavated texts, albeit still tantalizingly fragmentary and laconic in many respects. Much of the written material is in the form of specially prepared clay tablets, inscribed in the cuneiform script that was used to write both Sumerian and Akkadian. There are also inscriptions in stone, on such objects as stelae and cylinder seals.

Representations of Women

Representations cannot be simply equated with "reality" or the "objective conditions of existence". But representations are integral to experience of the world, structuring conceptions of the world and positions and actions in that world (cf. Berger 1972). In this sense, it is not possible to adequately conceptualize relations of power without also considering prestige, or socially recognized and valued positions and actions.

Women in literary compositions

Among the written texts pertaining to the early Sumerian and Sargonic periods are those that have been termed "literary". The texts grouped under this rubric include "myths", "epic tales", "hymns", and accounts of events such as victories in battle. One of the dangers in using these texts is that many of the presumed early examples are known only or mainly from later "copies", raising questions about how "true" they are to their ostensibly original versions. For the moment, however, let us consider the literary texts that are purported to refer to the Early Dynastic and Sargonic periods.

A striking impression of these compositions is how seldom and how few (human) women are mentioned. [*The texts do not always specify – in terms that we understand – whether a particular individual is female or male; rather, scholars have attributed gender on the basis of their understanding of personal names. How much may we be using this ambiguity to substantiate our own preconceptions?*] Those women who do figure in these texts are depicted in auxiliary, nurturing roles, often acting to further the aims and positions of men (Winter 1987: 189). Most of the protagonists of these compositions are political rulers or "heroes" of some sort, and they are almost invariably men.

We do, however, read in texts that have been characterized as "economic" that women occasionally held political offices of some importance, usually as queens. Not all wives of kings seem to have been given this title (Hallo 1957: 30; Moorey 1977: 27–8), which may be related to contexts in which it was or was not appropriate to specify a title. Certain queens are said to have had control over land and the administration of economic activities on sizable estates (Foster 1987; Hallo 1976; Kramer 1976; Lambert 1987; Michalowski 1981). Although the "authenticity" of the Sumerian King List as a document of Mesopotamian dynasties and rulers must be questioned (Michalowski 1983), an intriguing twist comes from a mention in the King List (Jacobsen 1939) of a *king* (literally, "big man") of the city of Kish who was a woman. A second possible female king of Kish is identified by Shaffer (1983). These instances throw the connection between political dominance and "maleness" into sharp relief. Titles aside, some women seem to have had significant, *recognized* political and economic power, but the number of such women who were written about was few in comparison to the number of men in such positions.

A significant domain in which women regularly held official positions was the temple hierarchy, although they were usually appointed to these positions by men (Lambert 1987: 125). Three different ranks of priestesses are documented for the ED period (Asher-Greve 1985: 157–8). The daughters and sisters of rulers were often made high priestesses and in that role were forbidden to bear children (see Shaffer 1983). One particularly renowned example was Enheduanna, daughter of Sargon. She was installed by her father as high priestess (*en*-priestess) of the moon god, Nanna, at Ur – and perhaps also of the sky god, An, at Uruk (Hallo and van Dijk 1968: 8). Enheduanna's placement at Ur, and possibly Uruk, can be interpreted as a deliberate political ploy by Sargon to further establish his control in the southern cities, to ensure their allegiance to the empire in much the way that a dynastic marriage might do (Hallo and van Dijk 1968: 7–9; Moorey 1977: 38; Winter 1987: 200–1). Indeed, in Mesopotamian understanding, the high priestess was in some sense married to the god she served (Sollberger and Kupper 1971: 100; Weadcock 1975: 101).

An even more powerful interpretation of Enheduanna's position comes from a reading of Mesopotamian history proposed by Nissen (1988). He has suggested that there was a long history of tension between centralizing political aims – usually associated with "secular" political leaders – and local, decentralizing ones. In these terms, Sargon's ambitions fall squarely on the side of centralizing political power. But Sargon also attempted to consolidate and legitimate this position by placing his daughter in a traditional female domain through which he could hope to both pacify and control the local powers that opposed him. If positions in local temple hierarchies had indeed been the principal positions of political and economic power open to women of individual city polities, the Sargonic dynasty's "coup" in imposing a centralized political organization might also represent an undercutting not just of local power but of women's power.

Whatever Sargon's motives, Enheduanna does not appear to us as simply a pawn. She is credited with the composition of at least three literary works. One of these, "The Exaltation of Inanna" (Hallo and van Dijk 1968), is a powerful political statement couched in religious terms. According to this composition, she has been driven out of her priestly office at Ur (and Uruk as well?), probably in the context of a political rebellion against Sargon (ibid.: 58–9). She complains that Nanna, the god she serves in Ur, has not helped her in her plight. She appeals to Inanna, a goddess closely associated with the Sargonic dynasty, to restore her to her position, which Inanna does. We could read this text to mean that Enheduanna, through her actions, was furthering her father's political ambitions. But at the same time, she seeks to be restored to what she deems to be her rightful position of authority.

After banishment from Ur, Enheduanna seeks recourse from Nanna, who responds by giving her a dagger and a sword, saying that they become her. This has been interpreted by Hallo and van Dijk (1968: 59) as a suggestion that she immolate herself. A more intriguing reading is that the dagger and sword symbolize male political power, something that is considered inappropriate for a woman. Such a symbolic association can be suggested on the basis of both iconographic and burial evidence (e.g. Pollock 1983: 253; Watkins 1983). In this interpretation, Enheduanna can be seen as assuming male powers and male roles, and taking on the symbolic trappings of those powers and roles.

Enheduanna looms large in any picture of ancient Mesopotamian women, in part because of the quantity of inscriptional material we have by and about her. Yet with all her stature and presence, she represents one among relatively few women who held important political or economic roles, as recorded in written documents. For many elite women, as for Enheduanna, the primary route to political and economic power seems to have been through the domain of priestesshood and associated ritual offices. For men, there was a range of "secular" positions to which they might aspire, most notably that of *lugal* or king. They also could hold priestly roles within the temple organization, including that of high priest in cities where the patron deity was a goddess.

If elite women, as portrayed in written documents, occupied a limited number of official positions of power compared to men, the same is not true of female deities. Many cities' patron deities were goddesses (Lambert 1987: 128), and goddesses figure prominently in literary compositions where they play active and even dominant roles. While the attributes and prerogatives of Mesopotamian deities change through time and according to context (Jacobsen 1976), nevertheless each deity had a certain range of characteristics. In many cases, goddesses controlled domains that would seem to have been inappropriate for human females, for example the goddess Inanna's association with warfare. There does not seem to have been any simple equation between the human and divine worlds.

Thus far, I have avoided the sticky question of the audience that the texts addressed. Yet audience is critical in the sense that the understanding of any text or representation can be conceived as a product of both its context of production and the context of its reading (Berger 1972; Moore 1986). In a society in which most people were non-literate – including many members of the elite, officials, even kings – who read or otherwise used written texts? Texts were written by scribes, usually men, who must have read them as well as written them down. In the case of economic texts, scribes presumably had responsibility for both the recording and retrieval of information. Literary texts are more problematic. For the Old Babylonian period, Michalowski (1987) has suggested that literary texts may have been an integral part of the school curriculum, used in an "in-house" indoctrination of scribes who learned to write by copying texts. Perhaps it was also the possession of these mysterious sources of knowledge – in a medium that was very durable and hence permanent – that was key, rather than the ability of the possessor to decipher the contents. Such an interpretation fits best in the cases of inscriptions that accompany pictorial representations, as on stelae or seals, where the picture tells the story for all to read (cf. Winter 1985).

Women at work: economic texts

The documents that are generally categorized as "economic" are those that detail accounts of transactions, such as the distribution of rations to workers or the receipt of shipments of goods. Texts of this sort comprise the bulk of the written material that we have from the mid-third millennium.

These accounts indicate that women formed a sizable, if not predominant, portion of the labor force at least of large "households" (including "private" estates, "palaces", and "temples") (Gelb 1976: 200). They were involved in a diverse range of tasks that included textile production, cooking, agricultural work, herding, midwifery (Asher-Greve 1987; Zagarell 1986). Men are said to have performed agricultural tasks, herding, canal maintenance, scribal functions, merchant activities, craft manufacturing (e.g. smiths, carpenters) (Zagarell 1986). Women routinely received smaller rations in return for their work than men; girls got less than boys at least some of the time (Gelb 1965: 232–5). From these accounts, we get a picture of women as actively involved in the economic structure of daily life. As queens and perhaps as *en*-priestesses (Weadcock 1975: 103) women may also have managed the operation of estates.

Women are also mentioned in legal texts that document the sale and purchase of land. Although these transactions were much more commonly carried out and authorized by men (Asher-Greve 1985; Diakonov 1969; Gelb 1969), women are attested as sellers and witnesses.

Women in death: Royal Cemetery of Ur burials

Burials are representations too. Burials incorporate stereotypes and ideologies: the appropriate ways to treat a deceased person ("funerary ritual"), the appropriate ways to express gender (and other) roles and categories. Yet this medium of expression and representation may be very different from that of images in texts.

In my examination of burials as representations, I focus on the Royal Cemetery of Ur during the first part of ED III – ED IIIA – when Ur enjoyed a period of political and economic ascendancy. This choice of a "case study" around which to base discussion is influenced by my own familiarity with the Royal Cemetery (see Pollock 1983) and the wealth of material offered by the cemetery.

The Royal Cemetery was discovered and so named by Sir Leonard Woolley who, in the 1920s and 1930s, conducted excavations at Ur (Woolley 1934). The cemetery includes more than 2,000 graves dug into rubbish heaps in what was probably the central part of the site, in proximity to the main temple area dedicated to the moon god, Nanna. This area was used as a graveyard continuously for at least 500 years, beginning around 2600 BC, although many people during these centuries must have been buried elsewhere, probably in other cemeteries or within their houses. Approximately 153 graves, containing the burials of 482 individuals, can be attributed to ED IIIA (Pollock 1985). The cemetery received its designation "royal" from 16 of the graves, all of which date to ED IIIA. While dissimilar from each other in many respects, these 16 graves stand out from the others in that they have chambers built of stone and/or brick; they include simultaneous burials of up to 75 individuals; and the richest of them includes a wealth of material unparalleled in the other graves. In two of these tombs, cylinder seals were found bearing inscriptions that include the term *lugal* (king). On this basis, as well as the presence of human sacrifice which he thought to be the prerogative of kings, Woolley argued that all 16 of these tombs were the graves of royalty, accompanied by retainers who were sacrificed at the time of the principal occupant's death. Although the ascription of royalty can be disputed on a number of grounds (Moorey 1977), the name, and often the assumption, has remained with us.

Woolley's excavation, recording, and publishing of the Royal Cemetery is commendable in many respects, given archaeological field standards at the time. Nevertheless, there are many areas in which the evidence is sadly lacking. In particular, very few of the skeletons were examined by a trained specialist, so direct information on sex and age[1] is minimal. However, it is possible to detect gender divisions among some of the burials.

For high status burials, gender divisions seem quite clear (Moorey 1977: 34–7; Pollock 1983: 153–6). These divisions are based primarily on non-overlapping sets of objects accompanying the burials. One category, presumably associated with females, includes those objects referred to by Woolley as hair ribbons, wreath headdresses, "combs", double lunate earrings and dog-collar necklaces. The second or male category consists of axes, daggers or knives, whetstones, "brims" (headdresses – see below), and toilet instruments. That these two distinct sets of objects can be ascribed to females and males is suggested by several lines of evidence. First, those few Royal Cemetery bodies that were sexed by a trained observer were associated with their sex-ascribed objects. Secondly, at the Kish A cemetery, which dates to the latter part of the ED III period and is thus immediately subsequent to the Royal Cemetery burials that we are considering, some of these types of objects were also found. Many of the Kish skeletons were examined by physical anthropologists (Buxton and Rice 1931; Field 1947; Rathburn 1975), and again the physical evidence supports the gender-based attributions. Finally, contemporary iconography shows some of these objects in association with men and women.

All of the female objects can be categorized as jewelry, in our sense of that word (Figures 13.2 and 13.3). Hair ribbons are narrow strips of gold

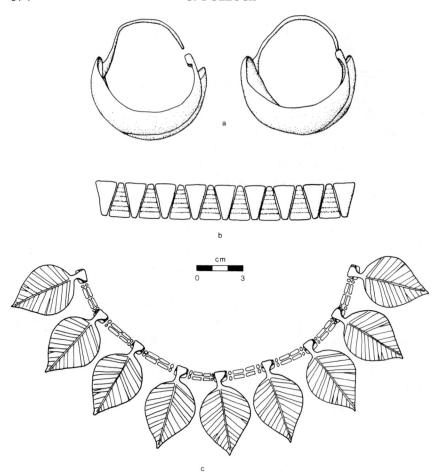

Figure 13.2 Female-associated artifacts from ED IIIA Ur: (a) pair of gold double lunate earrings (Grave 1237); (b) "dog collar" of lapis and gold triangular beads (schematic); (c) gold leaf wreath, on double string of lapis and carnelian beads (schematic).

or silver found wrapped around the head. Wreath headdresses were also worn around the head in such a way that they dangled over the forehead. There are several variations of these headdresses but all consist of multiple rows of lapis and carnelian beads from which are suspended gold or silver pendants in the form of leaves, rings, or discs. "Combs" are also a form of ornamentation worn on the head. They are gold or silver with a thin stem that could be pushed into the hair, broadening out to a thin flat sheet of metal with inlaid rosettes on spikes on their ends.

cm

0   3

Figure 13.3 Female-associated artifact from ED IIIA Ur: silver "comb" with rosettes inlaid with lapis, carnelian and shell (schematic).

"Double lunate" earrings, just one variety of earrings found in the cemetery, are gold, formed of two large, hollow, crescent-shaped lobes side by side. Finally, the items that Woolley so graphically called "dog collars" are choker-style necklaces of triangular gold and lapis elements.

In the male-associated category (figure 13.4), axes are generally of cast copper/bronze – although silver and gold examples occur – socketed and hafted on a wooden handle. Usually, it would seem, they were carried over the shoulder. Daggers or knives include short-bladed pieces, usually copper/bronze but also of silver or gold, with elongated knob-like or crescent-shaped pommels. These were usually worn at the belt, held in rush-work sheaths. Whetstones are small, carefully shaped stones, pierced at one end for suspension, and worn at the belt. "Brims" consist of several large beads of stone and/or metal, on either end of which are gold or silver link chains. They were worn around the forehead and secured behind the head. The so-called "toilet instruments" include a small metal case which contains several tools including tweezers, a tiny cosmetic applicator, and a stiletto. They are usually found at the waist, presumably hung from a belt.

There are broad differences between the kinds of objects found with high status females and males. High status females were marked as such, at burial, by the types and quantities of jewelry that they wore. In a sense, they (and these objects) were on display. Males were also on display. They, too, wore the accompanying objects, but some of these objects symbolized a more active stance. Whether or not the actual artifacts in the graves, the axes and daggers and the whetstones to sharpen them, were used as tools, they remain symbols of things to be wielded, in battle, in defense of flocks, or in other active causes.

Both high status females and males were marked, made "visible" in death. But many lower status people were not clearly differentiated by gender, or at least not in ways that I have yet been able to recognize or that are preserved archaeologically. Possibly, however, gender may be more clearly or more often marked for "non-elite" males than females. There are numerous burials in which the deceased person carries an axe or a dagger, and may also be provided with at most a few pots, some beads, a copper pin, some shells containing cosmetics. These people are marked as male by their axe or dagger, but their overall burial equipment is not rich or elaborate (Pollock 1983: figure 8, 252–3; *contra* Watkins 1983). For females, on the other hand, there does not seem to be anything comparable: elite women were visible in death, "non-elite" women were not. This pattern also seems to hold for the people buried in the A cemetery at Kish. On the whole, the Kish burials were much less rich than those in the Royal Cemetery (Mackay 1925; Moorey 1978). Even so, it is possible to isolate a number of markers of maleness (here

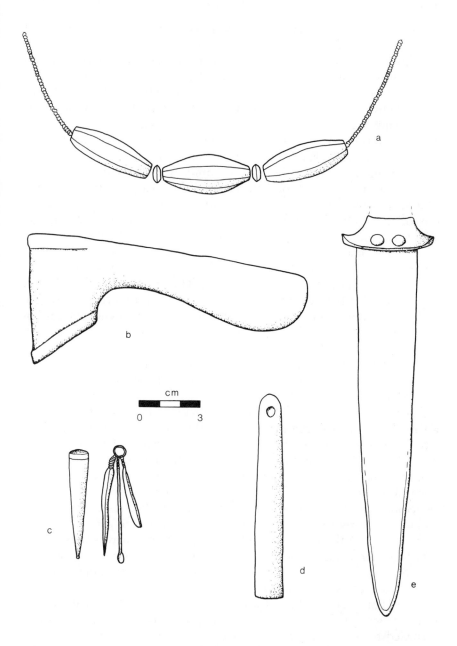

Figure 13.4 Male-associated artifacts from ED IIIA Ur: (a) brîm of gold, lapis and carnelian beads, and gold chains (Grave 1312); (b) copper/bronze axe (Grave 1136); (c) copper/bronze reticule and toilet instruments (schematic); (d) whetstone (Grave 389); (3) copper/bronze dagger (Grave 1618).

supported by physical anthropological examinations of biological sex), whereas there are few clear-cut markers of femaleness.

Within the Royal Cemetery, the Royal Tombs are distinctive from a variety of standpoints, regardless of whether they should be attributed to royalty. They are characterized by the presence of multiple burials of up to 75 individuals who were all apparently interred simultaneously to accompany the deceased. Clearly, this "human sacrifice" was in part a display of the deceased person's rights or power over the lives of occupants of the Royal Tombs and of their retinues.

Unfortunately, all of the Royal Tombs were looted in antiquity, causing varying amounts of disturbance and damage in different tombs. Not surprisingly, the main occupant of the tombs was a prime target; one of the results is that we often have very little remaining evidence about that person. In only four cases can we identify the sex of the tomb's principal occupant with any real degree of confidence. Of these, one is certainly female (RT 800)[2] and another probably so (RT 1054), and two are male (RT 1618 and 1648). The two females had 24 and approximately[3] 14 attendants respectively, the males approximately four each. In every tomb where the genders of the attendants can be ascertained, there are both males and females, although the proportions vary widely. Overall, females seem to predominate. The evidence suggests that both females and males received tomb burial as principals, implying that some individuals of both sexes had rights over the lives of subordinates, also of both sexes.

For the vast majority of the Royal Cemetery ED IIIA burials, there is a strict division between male and female markers; an individual may have objects from the female category or the male but not both. She or he may have one or more gender-neutral items in addition to or instead of female or male objects. In contrast to this majority pattern are seven high status burials with both female and male items. Two of the seven skeletons were sexed: one is female and one male. In five of these burials, including the two just mentioned, the objects of one gender category were placed on the body, in the "usual" position, whereas those of the other gender category were separate from the body, sometimes all together in a pile. However, in the remaining two burials, objects of *both* gender categories were placed on the body of the deceased individual.

We might interpret the objects found separate from the body as gifts from participants in the funeral, indicating a degree of honor and prestige accorded to the deceased but without implying that the individual had rights to or use of these symbols – and their accompanying prestige and power – during her/his life. In a similar vein, these items might have been intended for use by the deceased as offerings in the underworld (Moorey 1977: 29). In a text that has been entitled "The Death of Ur-Nammu and

His Descent to the Netherworld" (Kramer 1967), we read of the gifts that Ur-Nammu, a king of Ur around 2100 BC, gave to each of the famous occupants of the Netherworld when he died and descended to the world of the dead. All Mesopotamian accounts of the Netherworld portray it as a dreary, dismal place; a mortal's hope of even minor respite seems to have lain in currying favor with the powers that be through lavish gifts. These interpretations are not entirely satisfying, however, especially for the two burials in which objects from both gender categories were found *on* the dead person's body. Here perhaps we can begin to talk about some cross-cutting of gender roles, with women pushing at some of the traditional boundaries,[4] especially those that may have usually denied them access to political roles. [*No, I cannot be **sure** that these are not men pushing at **their** boundaries!*]

Women in iconography

From representations of women in words and burials, we can turn to representations in images. Cylinder seals comprise the most numerous class of materials from the mid-third millennium to incorporate images. Seals were used to authorize or witness transactions. Rolling a seal across a piece of wet clay left an impression of the design cut into it. In addition to the impressions, or sealings, that could be created with a seal, possession of the seal itself seems to have been important. If the positions in which seals were placed in graves can be any guide, they were often worn attached to a pin that probably held a garment at the shoulder (Collon 1987: 110; Pollock 1983: 184), a position that would seem to be inconvenient for use of the seal to produce an impression. Rather, it may be the display of the seal itself that was important in such instances (see also Rathje 1977: 26).

Seals cannot automatically be assumed to imply ownership or even personal authorization; some seem to have been associated with offices rather than with particular individuals who occupied those offices (Collon 1987: 15–16; Nissen 1977, 1988: 77–8). There is, however, a gradual shift toward more individualization of seals. During the time span from the beginning of the third millennium through the Sargonic period, cylinder seals become more and more common in burials, and an increasing proportion of them bear inscriptions that name a particular person (Collon 1987: 105; Nissen 1977; Pollock 1983: 224–5, 266).

Most ED III cylinder seals can be divided into the category of "banquet" or "contest" seals on the basis of their iconography (Collon 1987). Generally, a seal contains a scene or scenes of only one type, but some have one horizontal register depicting a banquet and a second one with a contest. Banquest scenes portray one or more seated figures holding a cup in one hand or sitting before a large jar provided with straws. The drinkers are waited on by attendants, sometimes shown bringing in or standing before heaps of food. Musicians and dancers may also be present. Stated succinctly, in banquet scenes participants sit and attendants wait on them. The seated drinkers may be women or men, as indicated by their hair and clothing styles. In the set of banquet seals from ED IIIA burials in the Royal Cemetery, there are 22 examples of scenes (registers) with both men and women drinkers, eleven with men only and four with women only.

Contest seals depict a scene of struggling figures, the theme of which seems to be the attack of domesticated animals by wild ones and, usually, the defense of the flocks by humans or half humans. These are invariably male. In contrast to banquest scenes, contest scenes are filled with movement and action.

Both banquet and contest scenes are "ritualized" portrayals. Both are linked to important themes in Sumerian society and culture: feasting on the one hand, and the ceaseless struggle between domestic/tamed and wild/untamed on the other. Both kinds of scenes are also found in media other than seals, such as "votive" plaques and inlaid scenes on wooden boxes, musical instruments, and game boards.

Among the ED IIIA Royal Cemetery burials, males and females seem to be equally likely to have a seal. However, seals with banquet scenes show a strong association with females (16 with females, five with males ((of which two have one contest and one banquet register)), and eight with burials of unmarked gender), and contest scenes with males (ten with males, two with females ((both with a second register containing a banquet scene)), and 12 with people of unmarked gender). In the Kish A cemetery, there is also a strong association between males and seals bearing contest scenes; very few banquet seals occur in the cemetery and none with burials of identifiable gender (see Mackay 1925, 1929; Moorey 1978). At the site of Khafajah, the six graves that have published illustrations of contest seals all have "male items"; there are no published illustrations of banquet seals from the graves (Delougaz et al. 1967; Frankfort 1955).

Despite the marked difference in iconography, an approximately equal proportion of females and males buried in the Royal Cemetery have seals. But what does "having" a seal mean? Does it imply that women and men had equal opportunities to *use* seals and thus the responsibility and authority that went with their use? To answer this, we must distinguish possession of the object (the seal) from its use in authorization (the sealing). From rubbish heaps into which the Royal Cemetery graves were dug come a collection of sealings (Legrain 1936). Those from "seal impression strata and 1 and 2" are approximately contemporary with the Royal Cemetery burials that we are considering. There is only one illustrated impression of a banquet seal from these strata, but 26 impressions of contest seals. Although this is a single and limited sample, it is suggestive of a limited use of banquet seals for sealing. For women, seals may have been more a form of jewelry than a means of authorizing or witnessing economic transactions.

Inscriptions are relatively uncommon on ED III seals. When they are present, they name an individual; sometimes they also specify a family relationship, and sometimes they indicate the individual's title or occupation. Of the 29 Royal Cemetery banquet seals, only five contain inscriptions. Three of these give only a name, but one specifies the person as a *nin*, lady of high rank or queen, and another as priestess. Seven of 23 contest seals from the Royal Cemetery contain inscriptions, including one that mentions the title "scribe" and two that term the person "king".

It would seem, then, that the motifs on seals found with females and males, based on occurrences in burials and limited inscriptional evidence on the seals themselves, are markedly different. Females usually have seals that portray both women and men in what is probably a ritually important act but one that involves little action (cf. Asher-Greve 1985: 168). In contrast, males' seals with contest motifs depict only males, engaged in active struggle. An intriguing implication is that males frequently participate in rituals with females, but there are other (ritual) domains that are exclusively the purview of males.

In contrast to the limited number of themes and very conventionalized representations on ED III seals,[5] earlier cylinder seals, especially those of Late Uruk and Jemdet Nasr date, are much more diverse. They include numerous images of women engaged in a wide range of productive activities, such as weaving, harvesting, pottery making, dairying, animal husbandry, as well as a range of ritual activities (Asher-Greve 1985: 48–54). Some scholars have suggested that these seals may have belonged to "public" or large "private" institutions, perhaps those in which women performed these labors (Collon 1987: 15–16; Nissen 1988: 77–8; cf. Asher-Greve 1985: 58–60). Certainly the types of productive activities shown on Late Uruk seals are very much in line with those that women are reported doing in ED III economic texts. This perhaps represents a trend toward making the labor of women (and men . . .) in "economic" activities less visible. The seal evidence can also be "read" in somewhat different terms, to indicate a more general movement away from the portrayal of mundane, productive tasks toward an emphasis on ritual scenes (undoubtedly with strong political undertones). In the process of making this transition, women come to be shown less frequently and to be relegated to less active poses. Men, on the other hand, remain active, albeit in different ways.

Iconography depicting women and men is not confirmed to cylinder seals; "votive" plaques, statues, stelae, and inlay on boxes, musical instruments and game boards all incorporate such representations. Without reviewing these in detail, the late ED and Akkadian examples seem to follow a pattern similar to that on seals in which women are shown in static, usually ritual and/or auxiliary poses (Asher-Greve 1987: 27, 1985: 168). Interestingly, statues include large numbers of representations of women. These statues are usually associated with buildings interpreted as temples and portray individuals in stationary standing or seated poses. At the sites of Khafajah and Asmar where many such statues were found, women constitute slightly less than half of the statues of identifiable gender (see Frankfort 1939). However, within each site, it is only in the Sin Temple (Khafajah), dedicated to the god of the mooh, that there are more statues of women than men.

In contrast to women, representations of men portray them doing things, including dairying, soldiering, bearing burdens, making music. In these representations women are participants in fewer domains than men and fewer than women in earlier (i.e. Late Uruk/Jemdet Nasr) seal depictions.

Might this imply that we are seeing women (and men) through the eyes of men, rather than women's portrayals of themselves? We do not know who made these images, but they do suggest a "man's view" of gender roles – even if women actually made some of them (cf. Moore 1986).

Conclusion

New streets had been opened, automobiles brought in, mansions built, roads constructed, newspapers published, clubs organized – Ilhéus was transformed. But the ways men think and feel evolve more slowly. Thus it has always been, in every society. (Amado 1978: 2)

Of possible conclusions there are many, variable in their tenor and timbre. In a tentative key, I might emphasize such points as the problems of identifying females and males from textual references, the difficulties of working with unsexed burials. On a moore soothing note, I could point to those women who made a name for themselves, quite literally, in the Sumerian and Sargonic world. And then there is the more discordant theme, of women with limited opportunities, women whose scope for action and for recognition was being restricted, but whose voices can still be heard, if we listen.

I began this paper by pointing to the minimal and contradictory representations of women in Sumerian art and literature. I suggest that one reason for this may lie in the prevailing male-dominated discourse of mid-third millennium Sumerian society. This discourse, as it was translated into representations, glorified action, specifically action in the domain of *political*/"heroic" struggles. It was precisely in this domain that women were denied recognized roles *as women* (the female "king" of Kish is a dramatic case in point), leaving little place for them in such representational fields. Another major theme of Early Dynastic representations is ritual attendance, and it is there that we find many of the portrayals of women – in statuary, plaques, banquet seals, and in burials within the Royal Tombs. On a more general note, feminist anthropologists are increasingly drawing our attention to the multiple and contradictory powers and manipulations of gender relations as well as individuals' actions within a social context (see especially Silverblatt 1988).

The representations I have discussed include women of distinctly different social classes. There is every reason to think that women (and men) of different classes experienced the world in significantly different ways – we should not aim to investigate some monolithic entity called "women's status".

Many low status, perhaps "semi-free" women and men worked for large households, engaged in a diverse range of specialized productive activities. Many Early Dynastic and Akkadian economic texts touch at least peripherally on this organization of labor, but pictorial images of this segment of economic life, especially on cylinder seals, became less common over time. Texts represent these activities but were much less accessible to most people than images, serving as they did specific bureaucratic accounting purposes.

Women were able to attain positions of high status and power mainly through ritual rather than "secular" political domains. Both ritual and political domains held a potential for some degree of economic power and control. To the extent that centralized political interests were gaining power at the expense of locally based ritual/religious interests, I would argue that we may also speak of an erosion of women's power in the higher social echelons. The undercutting of women's sources of power seems to be a common strategy and product of the formation of states, although neither the form nor the degree of women's subjugation is uniform from case to case (Silverblatt 1988). There are indications, in the Royal Cemetery burials and in the works of Enheduanna, that some women may have gained access to male domains of political power, perhaps as their traditional opportunities were being denied to them. That they were granted some of the symbolic trappings of male positions implies some degree of social recognition of their aspirations and achievements, but whether for their achievements *as women* or not is more difficult to say (cf. Moore 1986: 115).

I have suggested that women of intermediate social ranks may have been more "invisible", at least in death, than men. Those who were visible, most notably some of the attendants in the Royal Tombs, may have been so in part as displays of the power of their superiors (some of whom were women).

Overall, fewer women than men attained *recognized, represented* positions of political and economic power. When they did, their possibilities were often circumscribed. The domains in which women could act and aspire to power and prestige were more limited than those open to men. Nevertheless, we must not assume from this that Sumerian women were "invisible" or passively accepted their socially given roles. To the contrary, they strove to achieve some measure of esteem and prestige within the world of male voices and values in which they found themselves.

ACKNOWLEDGMENTS

My thanks to the conference participants, who offered helpful comments on this work and contributed to a memorable experience. I would also like to thank the following people who read and commented on one or more versions of this paper: Jane Collins, Caroline Steele, Henry Wright, Lon Bulgrin, Randall McGuire, Roger Moorey, Piotr Michalowski, Ann Stahl, and Irene Winter.

NOTES

1 It seems that the vast majority of the individuals buried in the Royal Cemetery were adults. Woolley noted those bodies that he thought were children or infants; while his assignments are unlikely to have been entirely accurate, he was probably a careful enough observer to recognize juveniles.
2 All grave numbers refer to Wooley's (1934) published numbering system.
3 The approximation is due to the fact that the bodies were often badly disturbed and fragmentary. In these cases, the number given should be regarded as a minimum figure.
4 I would like to thank Jane Collins who suggested this interpretation to me.
5 In the Akkadian period, contest scenes on seals continue. Banquet scenes begin to be replaced by "presentation" scenes portraying a highly ritualized scene of introduction of a mortal to a deity (Collon 1987: 32).

REFERENCES

Amado, Jorge (1978). *Gabriela, Clove and Cinnamon.* New York: Avon.
Asher-Greve, Julia (1985). *Frauen in altsumerischer Zeit.* Malibu: Undena.
—— (1987). The Oldest Female Oneiromancer. In *La Femme dans le Proche-Orient antique,* Jean-Marie Durand, ed. Paris: Éditions Recherches sur les Civilisations, 27–32.
Berger, John (1972). *Ways of Seeing.* England: BBC and Penguin.
Buxton, L. H. D. and D. T. Rice (1931). "Report on the Human Remains found at Kish." *Journal of the Royal Anthropological Institute of Great Britain and Ireland* 61: 57–112.
Collon, Dominique (1987). *First Impressions. Cylinder Seals in the Ancient Near East.* London: British Museum Publications.
Delougaz, Pinhas, Harold Hill, and Seton Lloyd (1967). *Private Houses and Graves in the Diyala Region.* Chicago: University of Chicago Press.
Diakonov, I. M. (1969). "The Rise of the Despotic State in Ancient Mesopotamia." In *Ancient Mesopotamia: Socio-Economic History,* I. M. Diakonov, ed. Moscow: Nauka Publishing House, 173–203.
Field, Henry (1947). "Human Remains from Kish, Iraq." Washington: American Documentation Institute, Microfilm No. 2345.
Foster, Benjamin (1987). "Notes on Women in Sargonic Society." In *La Femme dans le Proche-Orient Antique.* Jean-Marie Durand, ed. Paris: Éditions Recherches sur les Civilisations, 53–61.
Frankfort, Henri (1939). *Sculpture of the Third Millennium B.C. from Tell Asmar and Khafajah.* Chicago: University of Chicago Press.
—— (1955). *Stratified Seals from the Diyala Region.* Chicago: University of Chicago Press.
Gelb, I. J. (1965). "The Ancient Mesopotamian Ration System." *Journal of Near Eastern Studies* 24: 230–43.
—— (1969). "On the Alleged Temple and State Economies in Ancient Mesopotamia." In *Estratto da Studi in Onore di Edoardo Volterra* 6: Chicago: University of Chicago Press, 137–54.
—— (1976). "Quantitative Evaluation of Slavery and Serfdom." In *Kramer Anniversary Volume,* Barry Eichler et al., eds. Neukirchen-Vluyn: Neukirchener Verlag, 195–207.
Hallo, W. W. (1957). *Early Mesopotamian Royal Titles.* New Haven: Yale University Press.
—— (1976). "Women of Sumer." In *The Legacy of Sumer,* Denise Schmandt-Besserat, ed. Malibu: Undena, 23–40.
Hallo, W. W. and J. J. A. van Dijk (1968). *The Exaltation of Inanna.* New Haven: Yale University Press.
Jacobsen, Thorkild (1939). *The Sumerian King List.* Chicago: University of Chicago Press.
—— (1976). *The Treasures of Darkness.* New Haven: Yale University Press.
Kramer, Samuel N. (1967). The Death of Ur-Nammu and his Descent to the Netherworld. *Journal of Cuneiform Studies* 21: 104–22.

—— (1976). "Poets and Psalmists: Goddesses and Theologians. Literacy, Religious, and Anthropological Aspects of the Legacy of Sumer." In *The Legacy of Sumer*, Denise Schmandt-Besserat, ed. Malibu: Undena, 3–21.

Lambert, W. G. (1987). "Goddesses in the Pantheon: A Reflection of Women in Society?" In *La Femme dans le Proche-Orient antique*. Jean-Marie Durand, ed. Paris: Éditions Recherches sur les Civilisations, 125–30.

Legrain, Leon (1936). *Ur Excavations*. Vol. III, *Archaic Seal-Impressions*. London: The British Museum.

Mackay, Ernest (1925). *Report on the Excavation of the "A" Cemetery at Kish, Mesopotamia. Part I*. Chicago: Field Museum of Natural History Anthropology Memoirs 1(1).

—— (1929). *A Sumerian Palace and the "A" Cemetery at Kish, Mesopotamia. Part II*. Chicago: Field Museum of Natural History Anthropology Memoirs 1(2).

Michalowski, Piotr (1981). "Tudanapsum, Naram-Sin and Nippur." *Revue d'Assyriologie* 75: 173–6.

—— (1983). "History as Charter: Some Observations on the Sumerian King List." *Journal of the Amerian Oriental Society* 103: 237–48.

—— (1987). "Charisma and Control: On Continuity and Change in Early Mesopotamian Bureaucratic Systems." In *The Organization of Power: Aspects of Bureaucracy in the Ancient Near East*, McGuire Gibson and Robert Biggs, eds. Chicago: Oriental Institute, 55–68.

Moore, Henrietta (1986). *Space, Text and Gender. An Anthropological Study of the Marakwet of Kenya*. Cambridge: Cambridge University Press.

Moorey, P. R. S. (1977). "What Do We Know about the People Buried in the Royal Cemetery?" *Expedition* 20(1): 24–40.

—— (1978). *Kish Excavations 1923–1933*. Oxford: Clarendon Press.

Nissen, Hans (1977). "Aspects of the Development of Early Cylinder Seals." In *Seals and Sealing in the Ancient Near East*, McGuire Gibson and Robert Biggs, eds. Malibu: Undena, 15–23.

—— (1988). *The Early History of the Ancient Near East 9000–2000 B.C.* Chicago: University of Chicago Press.

Pollock, Susan (1983). "The Symbolism of Prestige: An Archaeological Example from the Royal Cemetery of Ur." Ph.D. dissertation, University of Michigan.

—— (1985). Chronology of the Royal Cemetery of Ur. *Iraq* 47: 129–58.

Rathbun, Ted (1975). *A Study of the Physical Characteristics of the Ancient Inhabitants of Kish, Iraq*. Coconut Grove, Miami: Field Research Projects.

Rathje, William (1977). "New Tricks for Old Seals: A Progress Report." In *Seals and Sealing in the Ancient Near East*. McGuire Gibson and Robert Biggs, eds. Malibu: Undena, 25–32.

Shaffer, Aaron (1983). "Gilgamesh, The Cedar Forest and Mesopotamian History." *Journal of the American Oriental Society* 103: 307–13.

Silverblatt, Irene (1988). "Women in States." *Annual Review of Anthropology* 17: 427–60.

Sollberger, Edmond and Jean-Robert Kupper (1971). *Inscriptions royales sumériennes et akkadiennes*. Paris: Les Éditions du Cerf.

Watkins, Trevor (1983). Sumerian Weapons, Warfare and Warriors. *Sumer* 39: 100–2.

Weadcock, Penelope (1975). "The *Giparu* at Ur." *Iraq* 37: 101–28.

Winter, Irene (1985). "After the Battle is Over: The Stele of the Vultures and the Beginning of Historical Narrative in the Art of the Ancient Near East." In *Pictorial Narrative in Antiquity and the Middle Ages*, Herbert Kessler and Marrianna Simpson, eds. Washington: National Gallery of Art, 11–32.

—— (1987). "Women in Public: The Disk of Enheduanna, The Beginning of the Office of En-Priestess, and the Weight of Visual Evidence." In *La Femme dans le Proche-Orient antique*, Jean-Marie Durand, ed. Paris: Éditions Recherches sur les Civilisations, 189–201.

Woolley, Sir C. Leonard (1934). *Ur Excavations.* Vol. II, *The Royal Cemetery.* London: The British Museum.

Zagarell, Allen (1986). "Trade, Women, Class and Society in Ancient Western Asia." *Current Anthropology* 27: 415–30.

14

What This Awl Means: Toward a Feminist Archaeology

Janet D. Spector

Introduction

I have been trying to delineate the parameters of an explicitly feminist archaeology since the early 1970s when scholars in socio-cultural anthropology and other fields began new theoretical, historical, and cross-cultural research on gender. This has been a complex task given the continuing evolution of feminist scholarship over the past two decades.

During this time we have increasingly laid bare the full ramifications of the fact that, until very recently, the production and distribution of western, academic knowledge has been dominated almost exclusively by white, western, middle-class men socialized in cultures that systematically discriminate on the basis of gender, race, and class. Early feminist studies documented bias in the treatment of women both as students and workers within academic professions and as subjects of scholarly inquiry.

Critics working across the disciplines demonstrated that the perceptions and experiences of women were too often ignored, trivialized, peripheralized, or stereotyped. Studies about "man" claiming to be gender-inclusive were shown to be gender-specific in that researchers focused disproportionate attention on the experiences, accomplishments, and social lives of men as if they represented all members of a given group (Minnich 1982).

Archaeology has been no exception. Feminist critiques of this field revealed pervasive androcentric bias (Conkey and Spector 1984, Gero 1985, Spector and Whelan 1989). In addition to presenting "man" as the measure, archaeologists all too often project culturally specific, contemporary notions about the roles, positions, activities, and capabilities of men and women onto the groups they study. Such projections implicitly suggest that gender arrangements have been static and unvarying regardless of temporal or cultural contexts.

My first response to this exposure of androcentrism was to try to develop a strategy for studying gender archaeologically. The key questions for me were: precisely how and what can we learn about men and women based on archaeological traces of their activity patterns, social relations and beliefs? What are the material dimensions of gender systems? Which of these might enter and be preserved in the archaeological record? Can contemporary researchers recognize and interpret such indications of gender given the historical and cultural distance between us and the people we study?

Developing methods to study gender archaeologically seemed an essential prerequisite for the systematic revision or replacement of androcentric treatments of the past. By the late 1970s, drawing on feminist scholarship about gender along with approaches in ethnohistory and ethnoarchaeology, I proposed a "task differentiation" framework for the archaeological study of gender (Conkey and Spector 1984: 24–7; Spector 1983). Then, in 1980, I initiated a research project about nineteenth-century Eastern Dakota people living at the Little Rapids site in Minnesota which promised to yield archaeological and related documentary information suitable for actually testing the potential of the task differentiation approach.

As work on this project progressed I again returned to the core issue in feminist criticism: the ramifications of excluding groups from the production and distribution of knowledge. That interest was refueled in 1985 when, for the first time in my 20-year career of research in the Great Lakes region, I began an active collaboration with Indian people on a field project. This experience stimulated me to think more deeply about what it might mean to *do* a more inclusive feminist archaeology. The initial feminist critique exposed androcentrism, argued for the importance of including women both as researchers and as subjects of study, and demonstrated the significance of gender as an analytical category. More recent feminist criticism addresses issues of difference and diversity among women (e.g. by race, class, age) and cautions against universalistic notions of generic "women" and the privileging of experiences and perspectives of white, western women (see Moore 1988: 186–98).

I began to think more concretely about the ramifications of including Indian people in the production of archaeological knowledge about their histories and cultures. How will this affect the ways we set our research agendas, organize field projects, treat archaeological materials? How would their inclusion shape the ways we generate, express and present our understandings of the past or the audiences we write for? In other words, how would an inclusive feminist approach transform the character of archaeological practice beyond incorporating gender as a significant and legitimate area of study?

As these issues captured more of my attention and interest, I began to re-orient my thinking about Little Rapids and the way I wanted to portray the people whose cultural landscapes were unearthed at "Inyan ceyake atonwan" (Village at the Rapids), as the site is known in the Dakota language. Through the task differentiation framework I had learned a great deal about nineteenth-century Dakota gender arrangements. The challenge then became to find a way to write about what life was like for the people at Little Rapids. I wanted to keep my focus on women and gender but I also wanted to respond to my increasing awareness about the problematical portrayal of Indians in archaeology, problems I believe are aggravated by conventional norms of writing archaeology.

In this paper I discuss the evolution of my thinking about feminist archaeology as I shifted my attention from methdological issues to a concern with the presentation of archaeological knowledge. The interpretive narrative "What this Awl Means" presented later in this essay, was inspired by a small, inscribed antler awl handle we found in a midden at Little Rapids in 1980. I am certain that this one tool conveyed a great deal of information about the accomplishments of the woman who used it to her nineteenth-century Dakota contemporaries. It became an important material symbol to me as well, long after her death, leading me to unexpected insights about aspects of Dakota gender arrangements and about the depth and the transforming nature of the feminist critique of academic scholarship.

The Task Differentiation Approach to an Archaeology of Gender

When I initiated work at Little Rapids in 1980, I hoped to use the site material and related written records to test the task differentiation approach I'd developed in the mid 1970s to study gender archaeologically (Conkey and Spector 1984, Spector 1983). In designing that approach, I tried to take into account some of the complexities of gender revealed in then current feminist anthropology and the complexities of the archaeological record. Both considerations seemed essential for generating new methods for an archaeology of gender which avoids simplistic projections of present notions about gender into the past.

I thought that the best way to proceed was to examine relationships between material and non-material aspects of gender in known or documented cases where we could learn about gender specific tasks, behaviors, and beliefs *and* their material/spatial dimensions. I emphasized task patterns assuming that these would have definable material dimensions and that the linkages between activities, spaces, and materials would influence the character of archaeological sites of any given group.

Working with a team of graduate and undergraduate research assistants to explore such correlations, I analyzed several different Indian groups as described in selected historical and ethnographic sources. For each group we examined women's and men's activity patterns on a task by task basis focusing on: the social composition of task groups, the frequency, duration, and season of task performance, the environmental and community (or site) location of various tasks, and the artifacts, structures, and facilities associated with each task.

We highlighted those particular dimensions of task performance because they seemed to be most directly related to the formation of archaeological sites. In combination they would determine or significantly influence the frequency, variations and spatial distributions of materials, facilities, and/or structures at sites. A multi-dimensional approach also underscores the complexity and potential variability of gendered divisions of labor challenging simplistic and often androcentric notions about activities like hunting, gathering, foraging, farming, and child-rearing. Too often archaeologists treat these as single, indivisible entities rather than multi-task activities which could be organized in varied ways.

I hoped that with sufficient study we would be able to see relationships between people's task differentiation systems described in the written records and their sites. If so, with comparative studies, I thought we could eventually isolate some material regularities or patterns about different types of task systems which then could be identified archaeologically. This would place us in a better methodological position to study gender for undocumented groups living in more remote time periods.

I was encouraged by the results of our initial studies. Though the written records for the groups we examined often were partial and androcentric, the framework did illuminate and help organize detailed, empirical information about men's and women's activity patterns. This enabled us to compare their technical knowledge and skills, mobility patterns, use of resources, equipment, materials and space, and the general tempo of their lives. The volume of data generated through the task differentiation framework helps undermine androcentric stereotypes about "the" sexual division of labor and its consequences.

The approach also reinforces a point made by many feminist scholars but not yet incorporated into archaeology: in order to adequately understand processes like culture change, contact, or conflict we have to engender our analyses. Men and women may experience any of these areas differently, depending at least in part on the character of their task differentiation system.

What I could not do in my initial studies was examine which aspects of a given task system might be expressed archaeologically and which parts would be essentially inaccessible. For that I needed some site specific data and the Little Rapids site seemed appropriate. By 1986, after completing four seasons of fieldwork and six years of archival research, I had assembled a large sample of archaeological and documentary materials of known cultural affiliation and time period. The evidence shows that the portion of Little Rapids we sampled was occupied during the summer months in the 1840s by a community of Wahpeton people, members of one of the seven Dakota "council fires" or divisions.

In 1987 I began to write up the results of my Eastern Dakota task differentiation investigations using Little Rapids as a case study. Although both the ethnohistoric and archaeological records were partial and fragmentary, I had enough information to organize and analyze within the specifications of the task framework.

I started with two sets of data: the Little Rapids site information mapped, sorted, identified, and counted, and the documentary evidence about Eastern Dakota task patterns and other features of their gender system. I had organized the documentary material into a series of tables with titles like: "Gender-Specific Task Inventory: Women/Men"; "Task Seasonality"; "Task Materials: Women/Men"; "Men's and Women's Material Inventory". Though most written accounts were authored by Euro-American men, I also had eyewitness accounts from several women and the books of Dr Charles Eastman, a Wahpeton man who described his childhood experiences in the mid 1800s (Eastman 1971).

The sources were consistent and often quite detailed in their descriptions of the activity patterns of Eastern Dakota men and women, although authors certainly differed in their attitudes about the Dakota system of dividing labor and especially about the volume of work performed by women compared to men (Eastman 1971; Eastman 1853; Pond 1986; Riggs 1893; Schoolcraft 1851–4). Philander Prescott, who was married to a Dakota woman, described their division of labor like this:

> The men hunt a little in summer, go to war, kill an enemy, dance, lounge, sleep, and smoke. The women do everything – nurse, chop wood, and carry it on their backs from a half to a whole mile; hoe the ground for planting, plant, hoe the corn, gather wild fruit, carry the lodge, and in winter cut and carry the poles to pitch it with; clear off the snow, etc., etc.; and the men often sit and look on. (Prescott 1852: 188).

Early chroniclers repeatedly and in varying tones of approval or disapproval described the strength and "industry" of Dakota women. Given the task system described in historical records, it is likely that most of the materials we recovered at Little Rapids were manufactured, produced and/or used by women. With the exception of actually killing deer, birds, and muskrat – which the men did – women were responsible for most other resource procurement and processing tasks. They planted and tended the corn, made, repaired, and decorated clothing and most artifacts, built and repaired household equipment, structures and facilities. Men quarried catlinite that was used for pipes and other objects, and only men were explicitly associated with the guns, traps, and iron rat spears procured through the fur trade. But the vast majority of goods and equipment made and/or used by the Dakota, regardless of the source of origin (locally produced or acquired through the fur trade), were associated with women. The Little Rapids assemblage undoubtedly reflects this.

At Little Rapids we had recovered evidence of numerous resource procurement, processing and storage activities, signs of manufacturing clothes, tools, ornaments, and ammunition, and some evidence of rituals and housing. By organizing documentary information about men's and women's activity patterns within the specifications of the task differentiation framework, we could link specific elements of the archaeological assemblage to Wahpeton men and women.

Yet as I continued to work with this approach to the Little Rapids materials, at the same time reflecting about my experiences working with descendants of people who had lived at Little Rapids, I became increasingly dissatisfied with the task framework. It had "worked" to organize documentary and archaeological information about gender in an orderly way. But it also inhibited my ability to express what I'd learned through a variety of sources about the Wahpeton men, women, and children who had lived at Little Rapids during a particularly disruptive period of their history when American colonial expansion was rapidly accelerating in Minnesota.

Like other archaeological taxonomic schemes, the task differentiation framework generates distanced, generic, and lifeless descriptions. Working with Dakota people had heightened my awareness of the problematic portrayals of Indian people in archaeological literature. Like earlier nineteenth-century documents, contemporary site reports and monographs typically reinforce Eurocentric stereotypes and images. While the task differentiation framework draws attention to gender it does not alter the way we present knowledge of the past. I wanted to become more attentive to the explicit and implicit images I conveyed in my writing about the Wahpeton people at Little Rapids. I abandoned my

case study of task differentiation and began to experiment with a new
way of presenting the archaeological and ethnohistoric knowledge I had
acquired.

Toward a More Inclusive Feminist Archaeology

After publishing some of the results of the first three field seasons of
work at the site (Spector 1985), I realized it was critical for me to involve
Dakota people in the project, particularly in light of my feminist
criticisms of archaeology. What had become clear to me by then was that
the same general problem that afflicted archaeology with respect to
women also applied to the situation of Indian people (see Martin 1987,
McNickle 1972, Trigger 1980). Their exclusion from the production of
academic knowledge about Indian histories and cultures resulted in the
same types of distortions and stereotyping as the exclusion of women
had in terms of understanding gender historically and cross-culturally.
In a fundamental sense, given the role of scholarship in the acculturation
process, these exclusions and distortions perpetuate both sexism and
racism.

As I started planning in the 1986 field season at Little Rapids, I
actively enlisted Dakota participation in the project so that their visions,
voices, and perspectives could be incorporated. Fortunately, I met Dr
Chris Cavender, an educator and scholar of Dakota history and culture.
As it turned out, Chris is related to Mazomani, a Dakota leader who
lived at Little Rapids during the early to middle nineteenth century,
through his mother, Elsie Cavender. She had been raised by Isabel
Roberts, Mazo okiye win, the daughter of Mazomani and Ha-za win.
This family connection to the site clearly prompted Chris Cavender's
willingness to work with me.

We were able to secure funding for an interdisciplinary, team-taught
field program at Little Rapids including myself, Chris, and his aunt,
Carolynn Schommer, a Dakota language instructor at the University of
Minnesota (as well as Professor Ed Cushing, an ecologist, and Professor
Sara Evans, an historian). The field experience that summer was
immeasurably enriched and transformed by the participation of Dakota
people. Through Chris and Carrie, we met other Dakota people and
learned about new sources of information about their history and
culture. These experiences and relationships profoundly influenced my
appreciation for and understanding of the Eastern Dakota and my
decisions about how I wanted to present their past as I wrote about Little
Rapids.

After that field experience I became particularly self-conscious about the ways I had learned to write about Indian people, their material culture, and their sites. Though the task differentiation framework had deepened my understanding of gender and how it might be investigated archaeologically, it did not provide an appropriate structure or format for presenting what I'd learned about Dakota men and women.

As a way to engage differently with the material, I turned my attention to a small antler awl handle we'd found at Little Rapids in 1980 (figure 14.1). I had been drawn to this small, delicate handle since the day we found it buried 20 cm beneath the ground surface along with deposits of ash, broken and lost artifacts, and the remains of plants and animals. Someone had inscribed it with a series of small dots, several still showing signs of red pigment, incised a series of lines on it, and drilled five holes through it. I wondered why they treated the handle that way and was curious about how it got deposited in the midden, imagining that its owner would have missed it.

I learned how much this one tool might have meant in the context of nineteenth-century Dakota culture when a student working on the project, Sarah Oliver, brought me Royal Hassrick's *The Sioux: Life and Customs of a Warrior Society* (1964). This text provided the key for deciphering the meaning of the inscriptions on the handle.

Hassrick's book is about the nineteenth-century Lakota, a group linguistically and culturally related to the Eastern Dakota. Citing a Lakota woman named Blue Whirlwind as the source for much of his information about women he wrote:

> In the same way that men kept war records, so did women keep count of their accomplishments. Ambition to excel was real among females. Accomplishments were recorded by means of dots incised along the handles of the polished elkhorn scraping tools. The dots on one side were black, on the other red. Each black dot represented a tanned robe; each red dot represented ten hides or one tipi. When a woman had completed one hundred robes or ten tipis, she was privileged to placed an incised circle at the base of the handle of her scraper. (Hassrick 1964: 42)

Hassrick implies that awls were also important material symbols of women's skills and values. He was told that in the nineteenth century when a girl experienced her first menses

> ... she notified her mother, who took her to a separate wigwam or small tipi. Isolated there for four days, the mother would ceremoniously teach her the art of quill embroidery and moccasin-making. As one old person expressed it, "Even though she has learned quilling before, the girl must quill continuously for four days. If she does this she will be good with the awl; if she does not, she will never be industrious." (Hassrick 1964: 41–2)

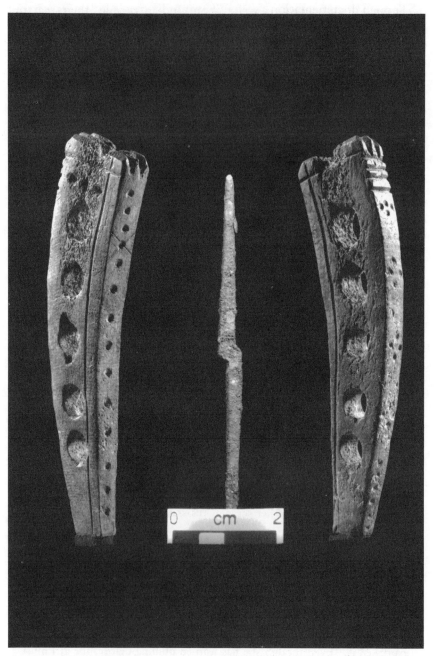

Figure 14.1 A metal tip and two views of the inscribed awl handle from the Little Rapids site. (Photo by Diane Stölen).

Though documentation about Wahpeton women's hideworking tools was not so detailed, I was able to confirm that they were also inscribed to record accomplishments. The practice is briefly mentioned in *Ehanna Woyakapi* a history of the Sisseton-Wahpeton Tribe written by members of that community in South Dakota. In describing elkhorn and wooden handled scrapers, the authors report that "it was a custom to make marks on the handle to show the number of hides and tipis completed" (Black Thunder et al. 1975: 106).

Very soon after learning all of this I abandoned the task analysis and wrote the narrative below, based on the archaeology at Little Rapids, documentary and oral accounts, my relationships with Mazomani's family, information from the Dakota–English dictionary, and my general impressions from having worked for four summers at the same place that the Wahpeton people had their planting village 150 years earlier. This narrative is not meant to stand alone as an interpretation of life at Little Rapids. Rather, it will be the centerpiece of a book containing descriptions, photographs, and interpretations of site materials, reproductions of Seth Eastman's sketches and paintings (Eastman 1853), and a series of essays. The essays will elaborate and annotate elements in the awl narrative, providing the basis for my inferences or discuss other aspects of Dakota life represented at Little Rapids. Other essays will expand on this discussion of feminist archaeology.

The point of presenting the narrative here is to provide a concrete example of a new way of writing archaeology. It conveys a very different sense of the Little Rapids community and the nineteenth-century historical context than is possible employing more conventional ways of writing.

What This Awl Means

A TIME OF LOSS ONE SUMMER DAY AT LITTLE RAPIDS

The women and children from Inyan cetake atowan (Little Rapids) had been working at the sugar camps since the Moon of Sore Eyes (March), while at the same time, most of the men had been far from the village trapping muskrat. The members of the 12 households that formed the community were glad to be reunited in their bark lodges in the Moon for Planting (May) despite the hard work they now anticipated as they began to replenish their stores of food and other supplies used over the winter months.

One day some of the people brought their finished furs and sugar over to the lodge of the trader Faribault, who lived among them a few months each year with his Dakota wife Pelagee, to exchange for glass beads, silver ornaments, tin kettles, and the iron knives, axes, hatchets, and awls they used for most of their summer tasks. They could tell Faribault was uneasy as he told them the news he'd just heard: that one of the "praying-men" named Riggs planned to visit them soon.

Faribault admired Mazomani (Iron Walker), one of the most prominent men of the community. He knew he was an important leader of the Medicine Dance among the Wahpeton and he knew that Mazomani had already announced a Dance to be held just at the time Riggs was to arrive. Faribault also knew that the missionaries were contemptuous of the Medicine Lodge and found the practices associated with it both imposing and absurd. In hopes of preventing an inevitable conflict between Riggs and Mazomani if the Dance were held as scheduled, he suggested a delay in the Medicine Dance which the elders, after some discussion and deliberation, agreed to.

Riggs didn't stay long at Little Rapids. Speaking Dakota as well as he could despite his failure to understand Dakota ways, he asked to speak to the "chief men". Mazomani and several others came forward curious to see what he wanted. They were surprised at how little he knew when he asked to establish a mission there. First, Riggs offered to teach the men how to plow as if they would ever consider such an idea, or as if the women would willingly give up their cornfields. They found his ideas about proper men's and women's work amusing and his suggestion of injuring the earth by cutting it with a plow incomprehensible. Then Riggs unknowingly insulted them further by suggesting that he could replace Mazomani as the spiritual leader of the community. They told Riggs to leave, and after only a half day, he and his party left to continue up the Minnesota River looking for another station for their mission, never really understanding why they refused his offers. The next day, Mazomani announced that the Medicine Dance would be held during the Month the Corn was Gathered (August) and the community resumed their summer work without further intrusions by such outsiders.

Ha-za win (Blueberry Woman) and Mazomani were proud of their daughter, Mazo okiye win (One who talks to Iron). One day after visiting Faribault, they brought her a new iron awl tip and some glass beads. Even though she was still young (unmarried), she had already established a reputation among the people at Inyan cetake atonwan for hard work, creativity, and excellence through her skills in quill and bead work.

Her mothers and grandmothers taught her to keep careful record of her accomplishments, so whenever she finished quilling or beading a skin bag or pair of moccasins, she remembered to impress a small dot on the fine antler awl handle Ha-za win had made for her when she first went to dwell alone ("isnati", i.e. at the time of her first menses). When Mazo okiye win completed more laborious work like sewing and decorating buckskin dresses or leggings, she created diamond-shaped clusters of four small dots, one to the north, one south, one east, and one west, a pattern she designed to represent the powers of the four directions which guided her life in so many ways. She liked to expose the handle of this small tool as she carried it in its beaded carrying case so others could see that she was doing her best to ensure the well being of their community.

When she engraved the dots into her awl she carefully marked each with pigment she made by boiling the tops of sumac plants with a small root found in the ground near the village. Red, she knew, was a color associated with women and their life forces. Everyone in her own and other Dakota communities knew the significance of that color: it represented the east where the sun rose giving all knowledge, wisdom, and understanding. It was the appropriate color to symbolize her aspirations toward these highly valued qualities.

One hot day in the Month the Moon Corn is Gathered (August), just after Mazomani had led people in the Medicine Dance near the burial place of her ancestors, Mazo Okiye win gathered together all of the work she'd completed since they had returned to Inyan cetake atonwan after the spring hunt and sugar season. Now, after several months back at their planting village, the women were getting ready to harvest the corn, much of which they would dry and store in the large bark barrels kept underground in storage areas near their lodges for winter use when fresh vegetables were not available. They had already finished making new clothes, bags, moccasins, and tools in anticipation of the fall deer hunt.

Mazo okiye win eagerly anticipated the quilling contest and feast which had been announced by a woman of a neighboring household to honor a family member who'd just been initiated into the Medicine Lodge. She knew she'd produced more beaded and quilled articles than most of the young women her age and she looked forward to bringing recognition to her parents and grandparents.

The lodge where the contest was held grew hot during the day as the women spread out their articles for others to admire. They stayed inside for shade to avoid the intense heat and sun, but as an impending thunderstorm grew closer, the lodge grew stifling. One of the elders asked Mazo okiye win to bring more water for the women in the lodge. She ran down the slope to the spring near the slough, glad to be out of the heat of the lodge and close to the cool water. She thought of taking a quick swim but the thunder grew closer and soon it started to rain, lightly at first, and then, as it did so often on those hot summer days, the rain fell in great sheets across the village.

She started uphill carrying her "miniapahtapi" (skin bottles for water) carefully and with practiced skill, but near the quilling contest lodge, she slipped on the wet and worn footpath where water had pooled in the driving rain. As she struggled to regain her footing and balance without dropping the water, the leather strap holding her awl in its case broke and the small awl dropped into the grass outside the lodge entrance.

She didn't miss it until the next day because as she entered the lodge with the water, the host of the contest took her hand and escorted her to the center of the crowd. When the host had counted each woman's work, distributing sticks for each piece, Mazo okiye win had accumulated more sticks in front of her work than all but three other women. With them, she was taken to the place of honor in the lodge and as the feast began, these four were given food first to honor them. Later, the results of this contest were recorded with marks representing the women's names and their works on the hides lining the walls of the lodge for all to see. Ha-za win and Mazomani were pleased.

The heavy rainstorm had scattered debris all over the village so the day after the quilling contest and the Medicine Dance, people were called together to clean up their community. They used old hides and baskets to carry loads of fallen branches, wet ash and charcoal from fires, and the remains of the feasts held the previous day to the dump on top of the crest overlooking the slough. Mazo okiye win's awl handle was swept up and carried off with the other garbage from the quilling contest lodge without anyone noticing. It was quickly buried as one basketload after another was emptied into the dump where it rested until it was found 140 years later.

Mazo okiye win and Ha-za win were saddened by the loss of this awl handle. They knew it was nearly worn out and both realized it was more a girl's tool than a woman's. Still, its finely incised dots and engraved lines showed how well Mazo okiye win had learned adult tasks, and she took as much pleasure in displaying it as her mother did watching others admire it. Mazo okiye win intended to keep this awl even though, following Dakota practice, she had

already drilled five holes through the handle, symbolically killing it
to mark an important transition in her life. She was now a woman
ready to establish her own household, no longer a child of her
mother's lodge. It was time to put aside her girl-tools.

Both mother and daughter knew that the awl handle was an
object of the past, not of the future. But when the handle was lost,
it saddened them more deeply than they could explain. One
evening as they stored the last of the harvested corn they laughed
together remembering the "prayer-man" Riggs and his ideas about
men planting corn. Then for some reason each thought of the antler
awl handle and they shared their sadness about its loss. They
realized that the feeling of loss they experienced wasn't simply
about the small tool. Instead, they discovered each shared a
pervasive sense of loss about the past and, even more, they felt
troubling premonitions about the future.

Some Other Archaeological Stories about Awls

The discovery of the awl and its meaning allowed me to experiment with
a new way of writing archaeology. It gave me a context and vantage
point to describe and interpret aspects of Dakota culture and gender in a
format I found far more compatible with my archaeological and feminist
interests and commitments than any of the usual archaeological modes of
writing. Let me illustrate this by showing how I would have described
awls from Little Rapids using conventional writing formats in Great
Lakes archaeology.

Both Lyle Stone (1974) and Ronald Mason (1986) discovered and
described awls and awl handles like those at Little Rapids at historic sites
in Michigan and Wisconsin. Had I followed their style, I would have
classified and discussed awls along with other, presumably related,
artifact types under a heading like "Household Context of Utilization –
Maintenance and Repair" (Stone 1974: 155–62). My description of the
metal awls' tips might read something like this:

> A total of 4 metal awls were found during excavations at Little Rapids. The
> description of awls is based on four attributes: (1) means of attachment of
> awl to handle, (2) cross-section shape, (3) size as defined by the dimension
> of length, and (4) material of manufacture. Two levels of taxonomic
> distinction are based on two of the above attributes: (1) Type which is
> distinguished by different materials, and (2) Variety which is distinguished
> by means of attachment.

402 J. D. SPECTOR

TYPES

Type 1: Iron
Variety a: Offset Attachment
Figure A–3 specimens (see photo); dimensions:
Length average ——; standard deviation ——

and so on until all the metal awls had been described and illustrated. Then, in a section called "Discussion", I might quote Stone directly and report that:

> Although awls have been reported from several other sites . . . this limited evidence does not permit cross-dating. The . . . quantity and . . . spatial distribution of awls indicate that they were commonly used . . . throughout the period of site occupation . . . trade-good lists indicate that awls were an important trade item with the Indians (Stone 1974: 159).

Stone does not discuss the bone or antler awl handles shown in a photograph, though like the metal tips they too vary in size, shape and form (Stone 1974: 156). Mason does allude to awl handles but only obliquely. In one chapter of his Rock Island report he shows photographs of some metal awls, including one hafted in a bone handle. The awl tips are presented in tables entitled: "European Trade Goods and Aboriginal Artifacts Made from Trade Materials" (e.g. Mason 1986: 60–1). He discusses neither the awls nor the handle in the text, although in a paragraph next to the photo he remarks: "It appears that bone and antler tool making survived longer in the native repertoire than pottery making and common flint knapping" (ibid.: 53).

These formats channel our attention as reader in specific ways but without acknowledgement from the authors. Messages pervade the text and authored stories are buried there despite the neutral, value-free, objective-sounding language. Unlike my narrative, which I intentionally crafted to reveal things I have found important and interesting about life at Little Rapids, Stone and Mason have conveyed stories about their sites which are not entirely conscious.

For example, a dominant theme in their presentations is that the European-produced metal awl tips are more significant than the Indian-produced handles. This story is built into their classifications, table titles, and general emphasis. It is then reinforced as the authors reiterate the significance of metal awl tips as markers of European influence on Indians and the disintegration of native culture in their discussions. I imagine Dakota (and undoubtedly other Indian) women would have found such stories amusing, irritating, or perhaps just wrong, particularly those who inscribed their bone or antler handles as a means to visually and publicly express their accomplishments.

Different plot elements are contained in Stone's classification scheme which states that awls functioned exclusively in the context of maintenance and repair, specifically within the household or domestic sphere. In the first place, awls here are classified with tools that (merely) maintain or repair other useful and completed objects and are differentiated, presumably, from primary tools essential in the production of new items. An implied ranking places "maintenance and repair" tools below "productive" tools that are needed to make things. Secondly, awls are placed in the context of the domestic sphere. Indeed, we today live in a culture where the domestic/public dichotomy is real, both socially and spatially. Political and economic life is often divided into two differentially valued parts, and the parts are gendered. The domestic sphere is seen as female and less important than the male-dominated public domain. Stone's classification system with its implied public/domestic split distorts the cultural reality of many Indian groups and uncritically imposes it on them through an artifact classification scheme. This leads us away from rather than toward any insights about the meaning or use of awl tips or handles in their original cultural context. Projecting the dichotomy back in time reveals as much or more about our own gender ideology and divisions as it does about groups in the past, a familiar androcentric theme in archaeology.

The awl descriptions communicate other unacknowledged messages. There are no people and no activities in these narratives. There is no sense of people making, trading for, displaying, or working with awls. The awls are without specific context, without associations, without meaning except in so far as they mark time or measure the influence of whites on Indians. Though the writing style is entirely depersonalized and object-centred, it is not without feeling, regardless of the intentions of the authors. The awl descriptions are dull, tedious, boring, hard to grasp. Do readers absorb these same feelings and transfer them to the people who once made or used these tools?

Some Conclusions

I developed the task differentiation framework in response to the feminist criticism of archaeology which documented pervasive andro-centrism in conventional portrayals of the past. Through it, I hoped to study aspects of gender archaeologically, so that we might revise prevailing theories which perpetuate and reinforce western ideologies about women and gender arrangements. While the framework does succeed in drawing attention to the significance of gender in its material dimensions, it does not alter the way we present our insights and

404 J. D. Spector

interpretations, an issue which increasingly captured my attention after working collaboratively with Dakota people.

That experience made me acutely aware of the ramifications of Indian exclusion from archaeology. As I tried to write about Little Rapids using the task differentiation framework, I found Wahpeton people and their history subordinated by the taxonomic device.

The contrast between the awl narrative and more conventional ways of writing about this class of artifacts reinforced and clarified my ideas about what it means to do more inclusive feminist archaeology. Including Dakota people in the project certainly deepened my knowledge and appreciation of their culture and their recent history. I also came to understand their resentment toward archaeologists and our rendering of Indian Culture.

In the awl narrative I attempted to present aspects of Wahpeton life as I'd come to understand them – particularly aspects of women's lives as materially expressed and enacted. It provided a way to write accessibly and empathetically about Wahpeton people during a particularly turbulent period of their history, hopefully capturing some essences or images of how people under very different conditions from our own may have thought about and confronted certain fundamental changes.

As with most ethnographies (see Rosaldo 1987) the dominant forms of writing archaeology produce problematic representations. Androcentric archaeology imposes culturally specific and often demeaning stereotypes of women onto women living in other times and places, reinforcing discrimination on the basis of gender. In a similar way, archaeological presentations of Indian histories and cultures reinforces their continued oppression. An inclusive feminist archaeology will emphasize gender as a centrally important category of cultural and historical analysis while at the same time addressing issues of difference and diversity. Ultimately, this approach will challenge all phases of archaeological practice from research design, funding, and fieldwork to publication.

My thinking and writing have been enormously enriched by discussions with graduate students and colleagues. The Wedge conference was an extraordinary and illuminating experience. I am grateful to Meg Conkey and Joan Gero for organizing it. I was encouraged and helped by the lively discussion which followed my presentation to the University of Minnesota "History and Society Workshop". In particular, Susan Cahn's insightful comments about feminist dimensions of the narrative helped crystallize my thinking.

I have had stimulating and ongoing discussions about the Little Rapids project and about the awl narrative with Randy Withrow, Diane Stolen, Sharon

Doherty, and Beth Scott who each read and commented on early versions of this paper. They have been a great source of energy and inspiration.

Black feminist scholars like Barbara Smith and Bell Hooks have had a strong influence on the development of more inclusive feminist approaches and studies in recent years.

My thinking about the socio-politics of academic writing and representations of "others" was galvanized by Renato Rosaldo when he presented his powerful paper, "Where Objectivity Lies: The Rhetoric of Anthropology" at the University of Minnesota in the Spring of 1987.

Finally, I wish to thank Susan Geiger for her skillful editing, her insights, her prodding and her confidence.

REFERENCES

Black Thunder, Elijah et al. (1975). *Ehanna Woyakapi, History and Culture of the Sisseton-Wahpeton Sioux Tribe of South Dakota*. Sisseton: Sisseton-Wahpeton Sioux Tribe.

Conkey, Margaret and Janet D. Spector (1984). "Archaeology and the Study of Gender." *Advances in Archaeological Method and Theory*, vol. 7, M. Schiffer, ed. New York: Academic Press, 1–38.

Eastman, Charles (1971). *Indian Boyhood*. New York: Dover Publications. Originally published 1902.

Eastman, Mary (1853). *The American Aboriginal Portofolio*, illustrated by Seth Eastman. Philadelphia: Lippincott, Grambo.

Gero, Joan (1985). "Socio-Politics and the Woman-at-Home Ideology." *American Antiquity* 50(2): 342–50.

Hassrick, Royal (1964). *The Sioux: Life and Customs of a Warrior Society*. Norman: University of Oklahoma Press.

Martin, Calvin, ed. (1987). *The American Indian and the Problems of History*. New York: Oxford University Press.

Mason, Ronald (1986). *Rock Island: Historical Indian Archaeology in the Northern Lake Michigan Basin*. Kent: Kent State University Press.

McNickle, D'arcy (1972). "American Indians Who Never Were." In *American Indian Reader*, Jeannette Henry, ed. San Francisco: The Indian Historian Press.

Moore, Henrietta (1988). *Feminism and Anthropology*. Minneapolis: University of Minnesota Press.

Minnich, Elizabeth (1982). "A Devastating Conceptual Error: How Can We *Not* be Feminist Scholars?" *Change Magazine*, April: 7–9.

Pond, Samuel W. (1986). *The Dakotas or Sioux as They Were in 1834*. St. Paul: Minnesota Historical Society Press. Originally published 1908.

Prescott, Philander (1852). "Contributions to the History, Customs, and Opinions of the Dacota Tribe." In Schoolcraft 1851–4: 168–99.

Riggs, Stephen Return (1893). *Dakota Grammar, Texts, and Ethnography*. Washington Government Printing Office.

Rosaldo, Renato (1986). "Where Objectivity Lies: The Rhetoric of Anthropology." Paper presented at the University of Minnesota.

Schoolcraft, Henry R. (1851–4). *Information Respecting the History, Condition and Prospects of the Indian Tribes of the United States*, Part II. Philadelphia: Lippincott, Grambo.

Spector, Janet D. (1983). "Male/Female Task Differentiation Among the Hidatsa: Toward the Development of an Archaeological Approach to the Study of Gender." In *The Hidden Half: Studies of Plains Indian Women*, Patricia Albers and Beatrice Medicine, eds. Washington: University Press of America, 77–99.

—— (1985). "Ethnoarchaeology and Little Rapids: A New Approach to 19th Century Eastern Dakota Sites." In *Archaeology, Ecology and Ethnohistory of the Prairie-Forest Border Zone of Minnesota and Manitoba*, Janet Spector and Elden Johnson, eds. Lincoln, NB: J&L Reprints in Anthropology 31, 167–203.

Spector, Janet D. and Mary K. Whelan (1989). "Incorporating Gender into Archaeology Courses." In *Gender and Anthropology: Critical Reviews for Research and Teaching*, Sandra Morgen, ed. Washington: American Anthropological Association, 65–94.

Stone, Lyle M. (1974). *Fort Michilimackinac, 1715–1781: An Archaeological Perspective on the Revolutionary Frontier*. East Lansing: Michigan State University Anthropological Series 2, in cooperation with Mackinac Island State Park Commission.

Trigger, Bruce (1980). Archaeology and the Image of the American Indian. *American Antiquity* 45: 662–76.

Epilogue

Henrietta L. Moore

As this volume makes clear, there could be no single narrative which would encompass all our understandings of women and production in prehistory. I hesitate, therefore, as I begin to write the epilogue I have been requested to produce. Any summing up or note of closure seems very inappropriate both to the spirit of this volume and to the more general task in hand. One of the successes of the feminist critique in the social sciences is that we can no longer write about women as an unproblematic and self-evident category in the world. As soon as feminists began to focus on women, to make their activities visible, and to take them seriously as subjects for research, the very object of their concern slipped away from them and they found themselves considering not women, but the whole theoretical and conceptual basis of the social sciences. Feminist scholarship is not in any straightfoward way simply about women, and neither is this volume.

Doing a feminist archaeology, engendering the archaeological record and archaeological practice, is not a matter of identifying women or their activities in the archaeological record. A feminist archaeology involves recognizing and theorizing the ways in which gender is a structuring principle in the archaeological record. It further involves acknowledging and analyzing the ways in which archaeological practice, including writing, produces and reproduces gender difference. The shift from women to gender is, of course, a fundamental one, and its proper recognition is essential for comprehending the potential impact and scope of the feminist critique within archaeology. One of the most valuable contributions of the articles in this volume is that they begin to demonstrate the ways in which a feminist archaeology will have far-reaching consequences for the development of theory and practice in the discipline as a whole (see chapter 1 for further elaboration of this point). One example of such a consequence – amply illustrated in this volume –

407

is the rethinking of the causal and temporal relationships between human cultural behavior and its material expression in the archaeological record which are usually implied in archaeological theorizing. This process of revaluation or rethinking can be described most easily as the death of the reflectionist paradigm. The archaeological record no longer simply reflects human behavior, activities, and institutions. There is, therefore, no argument about the extent to which it is or is not a distorted reflection of human behavior. Instead, there is a concern with the way gender difference produces and is produced and reproduced by the archaeological record. Feminist archaeology is by no means alone in bringing about such a revaluation. The death of the reflectionist paradigm has been advocated, if not entirely executed, by marxist and critical archaeology, but there is a sense in which the apparent reversal in causal and temporal sequences between behavior and record implied by a feminist archaeology is a more fundamental one. This can be best demonstrated by reference to some of the arguments put forward in the volume about the sexual division of labor.

Gender and the Division of Labor

One very dominant idea in the social sciences in recent decades has been that the sexual division of labor in society reflects or mirrors the biological and social differences between women and men. In many instances, this has led to arguments about the "naturalness" or inevitability of the sexual division of labor. In such arguments, a clear-cut temporal or causal sequence is implied, where gender comes first and the sexual division of labor and the organization of work come second. This temporal sequence is implicit even in the work of feminist scholars who make a strong distinction between biological sex and socially constructed gender. In other words, this form of argument is not just a feature of more essentialist readings of the relations between women and men. However, several articles in this volume make the opposite point. They argue that the division of labor creates gender difference and not the other way around. In more precise and theoretically rigorous terms, we can say that the divisions of labor and the forms of cooperation which existed in early human societies were the context in which gender emerged.

This point is a fundamental one and it has been raised by feminist scholars in a number of disciplines. It is a mistake, however, to assume that it is simply an argument which refers to the emergence or "origins" of gender, and that, as such, it is only a problem for prehistorians. Feminist scholars in sociology and social anthropology have demonstrated that even in societies where gender clearly exists, we have to understand the discourses, institutions, and practices concerned with the sexual division of labor as one domain or set of domains in which and through which gender differences are produced and reproduced – there are, of course, many other domains equally involved in this process. Features of social life such as the structure of employment and the organization of domestic activities are never a straightforward reflection of biologically or socially constructed differences betwen women and men. Instead, they are the arenas through which and in which gender difference is produced and reproduced.

There are a number of very important theoretical consesquences for archaeology which follow from this starting point. One is that gender should not be understood and analyzed as a pair of fixed categories, but rather as a set of historical relations. A second, and related, point is that gender is not a separate entity or domain which can be included or exluded in the analysis of social phenomena, but rather it is a set of processes and relations which are enmeshed in all aspects of everyday life. Gender differences are cross-cut by age, status, and class differences. They are used as symbolic markers for other forms of difference, and, in consequence, domains of social life apparently quite remote from relations between the sexes become highly gendered, and, in turn, the specific understandings of gender in the particular social context under consideration are shot through with the differences produced and reproduced in those domains of social action. Changes in gender relations are thus one of the primary determinants of human social and cultural behavior; as important, and sometimes more important, than such things as adaptation, mode of livelihood, level of complexity, exchange systems, etc. Once the pivotal role of gender relations is acknowledged then it becomes possible to ask new questions.

Gender and the Generation of Hypotheses

A number of authors in this volume comment on the fact that engendering the archaeological record provides a new source of hypotheses. Gender empowers the imagination. These new hypotheses are of very different kinds. For example, Jackson discusses the way hunter-gatherer women actually controlled storable surplus in a situation where milling was not a private/household activity, but something which transformed the nature of the landscape. Claassen proposes that instead of seeing the activities of women and children as affected by the cessation of fishing in the Shell Mound Archaic, we consider the possibility that a radical change in women's labor allocation was the cause of the cessation of shell-gathering. Many archaeological theories, as Wylie points out, imply that social relations are dependent on and adapt to larger-scale processes (climate, technology, subsistence) which they cannot control or determine. This leads to a particular view of temporal and causal processes, and many of the new hypotheses generated by acknowledging the pivotal role of gender relations explicitly challenge this view.

Some of the new hypotheses generated by a feminist archaeology rest on the necessity of rethinking western assumptions about gender, including how western ideas of gender influence a further set of assumptions concerning the individual, production, and work. A number of authors in this collection highlight the ways in which archaeology habitually uses concepts of work and the organization of labor which are based on capitalist society and which utilize western notions of individualism. This is of particular importance when considering the relationship between gender and technology because of the tendency to assign certain tasks to specific genders, to underestimate women's labor, and to assume that production activities were carried out by individuals rather than by groups of people (possibly consisting of women, men, and children). It is quite clear that contemporary western notions of gender severely bias the way in which we reconstruct the history of technology and its impact on social relations. Making women visible in archaeology does far more than merely add women to the picture of the past, it transforms the picture itself.

Gender and the Inscription of Difference

However, feminist archaeology, like critical and social archaeology, makes the very important point that archaeology itself cannot be seen as merely a reflection of the past. Archaeological accounts do not simply depict or reflect past worlds and happenings. They are always interested accounts, and, in the case of gender, they are overinterested accounts. There are a number of ways, therefore, in which a feminist archaeology is more about degendering the past than engendering it.

The ideology of gender difference – western ideologies of gender difference – are everywhere present in archaeology, and, as Conkey and Handsman point out, the result is that the archaeological legitimation of gender difference is everywhere in society – at least, in those societies which read archaeology books. Archaeology has served western culture well. It has produced an origin myth of incomparable richness and sophistication. The conventions of archaeological practice and the extant genres of archaeological writing draw us into this myth. It is, for many, a seductive place. The past, like the present, is heavily gendered.

A feminist archaeology has much to contend with. It must both engender and degender the archaeological record. It must theorize and analyze the social and productive relations and matrices in which gender emerged without falling prey to the origin myth of western culture. It must demonstrate the ways in which gender relations are historical relations, both in the past and in the present. It must force a rethinking of temporal and causal relationships in archaeological theory and reexamine the assumptions on which the discipline rests. It must question the role and purpose of a feminist archaeology in the contemporary world. This volume demonstrates quite clearly that the process is well under way.

Index

women (*cont.*):
  as shellfisher78, 277, 279, 285–6
  as subject32–4, 37, 50
  as tool maker78, 163, 168–9, 171, 175,
    185
  as weaver224, 226, 232, 236, 244
women's
  activities39, 77–8, 96, 113, 132, 138,
    144, 163, 168, 170, 172, 185, 195,
    198, 200–1, 210, 224, 255, 258–9,
    262, 279, 285, 291–2, 304, 317, 381,
    392–3
  contribution to diet267, 276, 279
  labor102, 150, 173, 202, 214, 226

production78, 224, 226, 243, 246, 301,
    314
  roles78, 81, 132, 171–2, 245, 317
  work19, 172, 243, 245, 286
women's movement, contributions of32,
    256
workshops210–13
written texts368–9, 371

Xaltocan, Mexico227, 232–5, 241
Xico, Mexico227, 232–5, 241

Yugoslavia103, 331